D1052175

ANCIENT
MYTH IN
MODERN
POETRY

ANCIENT
MYTH IN
MODERN
POETRY

LILLIAN FEDER

PRINCETON, NEW JERSEY
PRINCETON UNIVERSITY PRESS

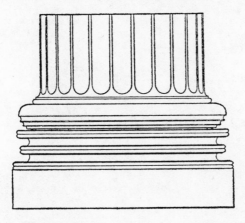

Copyright © 1971 by Princeton University Press
Published by Princeton University Press, Princeton, New Jersey
In the United Kingdom: Princeton University Press, Guildford, Surrey
ALL RIGHTS RESERVED

LCC 70–154994
ISBN 0–691–01336–5 (paperback edn.)
ISBN 0–691–06207–2 (hardcover edn.)

Pages 90–121, "Ezra Pound: The Voice from Hades," first appeared
in the *Michigan Quarterly Review*, X, 3 (Summer 1971)

This book has been composed in Linotype Granjon
Printed in the United States of America
by Princeton University Press

Second hardcover printing, with corrections, 1973
First PRINCETON PAPERBACK printing, 1977

For Rudolph Wittenberg

PREFACE

THE aim of this book is twofold: to develop a definition of myth as a continuous and evolving mode of expression, and to indicate how classical myth functions in modern English and American poetry as an aesthetic device which reaches into the deepest layers of personal, religious, social, and political life. I believe that such an approach elucidates the nature of myth as a key to unconscious mental processes and, at the same time, reveals some of the essential themes, symbols, and techniques of twentieth-century poetry.

In this study I focus on the work of four major poets—William Butler Yeats, Ezra Pound, T. S. Eliot, and W. H. Auden—and analyze their adaptation and use of ancient Greek and Roman myth as a creative instrument. I have chosen these writers not only because they are generally acknowledged as the best known and the most influential poets of their time, but also because each, though a deeply independent voice, incorporates feelings and attitudes toward art and society characteristic of the first half of this century. In the second section of the last chapter, through a brief study of many other poets, I have indicated the broad application of the theory of myth presented in Chapter I and developed in the main body of the book.

All the poets discussed in this book express their response to the special problems of modern life: the threat to or loss of faith, the mechanization of society and the consequent dehumanization of man, the contest of the self with a world that seems to deny the integrity of the individual consciousness. Furthermore, the use of myth as symbol and metaphor and the ritual effects so frequent in their poetry reflect stylistic tendencies of the period.

Because of the extreme importance of the psychoanalytic background of modern approaches to myth, I have dealt with this subject in a separate chapter. Obviously, neither in this chapter nor in the briefer introductory sections on Frazer in Chapter IV, and on Vico and Spengler in Chapter V, do I attempt to do more than indicate the particular significance of this cultural background to the study of myth. Since many readers of modern poetry are acquainted with the writings of Freud, Jung, Frazer, Vico, and Spengler, I considered it necessary to make clear my own position on their relation to the role of myth, not only in modern poetry but in modern thought as well.

The separation of myth into its functions in relation to the unconscious mind, to ritual practice, and to history aims chiefly at enlarging the critical perspective of this study through different emphases. That is why I have sometimes dealt with the same poem in more than one chapter. In modern poetry, of course, all of these functions are fused, as they were when myth had an active role in ancient society. My hope is that the close analyses of its separate functions will enable the reader to experience the effect of myth in modern poetry as a total emotional, intellectual, and aesthetic one, and will indicate that its distortions and disclosures originate in the same source.

ACKNOWLEDGMENTS

I SHOULD like to express my gratitude to the American Association of University Women for granting me a Missouri State Fellowship, which made possible a year's leave for some of the early work on this book. Throughout my research, I was assisted by the librarians at Columbia University, the New York Public Library, and Queens College of the City University of New York, particularly Mrs. Frieda Baroway and Mrs. Mimi Pechansky, who were extremely helpful in locating materials not easily available. I wish also to thank Dr. Nathaniel H. Siegel, Dean of the Faculty of Queens College, for granting me financial aid for the preparation of the index. I am most grateful to Miss R. Miriam Brokaw, Associate Director and Editor in Chief of Princeton University Press, for her continuing interest in this book. For their encouragement and practical assistance over a period of years, I am indebted to many other people, especially to my brother, Irving Leonard Feder, who has consistently been a most sensitive critic and a most reliable friend; to my colleagues at Queens College, Professors Konrad Gries and Bernard S. Solomon of the Department of Classical and Oriental Languages, and Professors Leslie Epstein, Malcolm Goldstein, and Myron Matlaw of the English Department; and to Professor S. F. Johnson of the English Department of Columbia University. My greatest debt is recorded in the dedication.

I am grateful to the following for permission to quote from copyrighted materials:

M. B. Yeats, Macmillan and Co. (London), and The Macmillan Company (New York), for excerpts from William Butler Yeats, *Per Amica Silentia Lunae*, Copyright 1918; *A Vision*, Copyright 1938 by The Macmillan Company; *The Collected Poems of W. B. Yeats*, Copyright 1903, 1906, 1907, 1912, 1916, 1918, 1919, 1924, 1928,

1931, 1933, 1934, 1935, 1940, 1944, 1945, 1946, 1950, 1956 by The Macmillan Company; Copyright 1940 by Georgie Yeats; *Essays and Introductions*, Copyright 1961 by Mrs. W. B. Yeats; *The Letters of W. B. Yeats*, Copyright 1953, 1954 by Anne Butler Yeats.

Excerpts from Ezra Pound, *Personae*, Copyright 1926, by permission of New Directions Publishing Corporation, and from *Collected Shorter Poems of Ezra Pound*, by permission of Faber and Faber, Ltd.; excerpts from Ezra Pound, *The Literary Essays*, Copyright 1918, all rights reserved, by permission of New Directions Publishing Corporation and Faber and Faber, Ltd.; excerpts from Ezra Pound, *The Cantos*, Copyright 1934, 1937, 1940, 1948, © 1956, © 1959, © 1968 by Ezra Pound, by permission of New Directions Publishing Corporation and Faber and Faber, Ltd.; excerpts from Ezra Pound, *Guide to Kulchur*, Copyright © 1970 by Ezra Pound, all rights reserved, by permission of New Directions Publishing Corporation and Peter Owen, Ltd.; excerpts from *The Selected Letters of Ezra Pound (1907-1941)* edited by D. D. Paige, Copyright 1950 by Ezra Pound, by permission of New Directions Publishing Corporation and Faber and Faber, Ltd.

Excerpts from Robert Duncan, *Roots and Branches*, Copyright 1964 by Robert Duncan, by permission of New Directions Publishing Corporation.

Excerpts from the poetry of T. S. Eliot are from his volume *Collected Poems 1909-1962* and are reprinted by permission of Harcourt Brace Jovanovich, Inc.; Copyright 1936, by Harcourt Brace, Inc.; Copyright © 1943, 1963, 1964, by T. S. Eliot, and by permission of Faber and Faber, Ltd.

Quotations from the various works of W. H. Auden are protected by copyright and have been reprinted by permission of Random House Inc. and Faber and Faber, Ltd. I am grateful also to W. H. Auden for permission to quote from "Moon Landing," and to W. H. Auden and Chester Kallman for permission to quote from *The Bassarids, Opera Seria with Intermezzo in One Act*.

Excerpts from *Brother to Dragons* by Robert Penn Warren, Copyright 1953 by Robert Penn Warren, reprinted by permission of Random House, Inc. and the William Morris Agency, Copyright © 1953 by Robert Penn Warren.

Excerpts from *Selected Poems* by John Crowe Ransom, Copyright 1924, 1969 by Alfred A. Knopf, Inc. and renewed 1952 by John Crowe Ransom, reprinted by permission of the publisher and Laurence Pollinger, Ltd. Excerpts from John Crowe Ransom, *God Without Thunder* reprinted by permission of Harcourt Brace Jovanovich.

Kathleen Raine, "The Transit of the Gods," from *The Collected Poems of Kathleen Raine*, Copyright © 1956 by Kathleen Raine (Hamish Hamilton, London).

Excerpts from H.D., "Demeter," reprinted by permission of Norman Holmes Pearson, owner of the copyright.

Grateful acknowledgment is made to Sigmund Freud Copyrights Ltd., The Institute of Psycho-Analysis, and The Hogarth Press Ltd., for permission to quote from the *Standard Edition of the Complete Psychological Works of Sigmund Freud*, revised and edited by James Strachey; to Basic Books, Inc., Publishers, New York, for permission to quote from *The Collected Papers of Sigmund Freud*, five vols., ed. Ernest Jones, M.D., 1959; to Basic Books, Inc. and George Allen & Unwin Ltd. for permission to quote from *The Interpretation of Dreams*, by Sigmund Freud, trans. and ed. by James Strachey, 1955; to W. W. Norton & Company, Inc. for permission to quote from the following works of Sigmund Freud: *Civilization and its Discontents*, trans. from the German and ed. by James Strachey; Copyright © 1961 by James Strachey; *New Introductory Lectures on Psychoanalysis*, trans. and ed. by James Strachey, Copyright 1933 by Sigmund Freud, Copyright renewed 1961 by W.J.H. Sprott, Copyright © 1965, 1964, by James Strachey; *The Psychopathology of Everyday Life*, trans. from the German by Alan Tyson, ed. with an introduction and additional notes by James Strachey, editorial matter Copyright © 1965, 1960, by James Strachey; translation Copyright © 1960 by Alan Tyson, and to Ernest Benn for permission to quote from *The Psychopathology of Everyday Life*.

ACKNOWLEDGMENTS

Excerpts from Robert Graves, *Collected Poems*, reprinted by permission of Collins-Knowlton-Wing, Inc., and Robert Graves; Copyright 1961 by Robert Graves. Excerpts from Robert Graves, *The White Goddess* (Vintage Books: New York, 1959), Copyright 1948 by Robert Graves, reprinted by permission of Farrar, Straus & Giroux and Robert Graves.

Excerpts from Edwin Muir, *Collected Poems*, and Conrad Aiken, *Collected Poems*, reprinted by permission of Oxford University Press. Excerpts from Edwin Muir, *An Autobiography*, reprinted by permission of the author's literary estate and The Hogarth Press.

Excerpts from George Barker, *Collected Poems 1930 to 1965*, Copyright © 1957, 1962, and 1965 by George Granville Barker, reprinted by permission of October House, Inc., and Faber and Faber, Ltd.

Excerpts from Robert Lowell, "The Mills of the Kavanaughs," in *Lord Weary's Castle and The Mills of the Kavanaughs* reprinted by permission of Harcourt Brace Jovanovich and Faber and Faber, Ltd. Reprinted by permission of Farrar, Straus & Giroux, Inc. excerpts from "Near the Ocean" by Robert Lowell, Copyright © 1963, 1965, 1966, 1967 by Robert Lowell, and from *Notebook* by Robert Lowell, Copyright © 1967, 1968, 1969, 1970 by Robert Lowell. Also by permission of Faber and Faber, Ltd.

Excerpts from *Poems* by Allen Tate reprinted by permission of Charles Scribner's Sons.

Excerpts from *Kaddish and Other Poems* by Allen Ginsberg, Copyright © 1961, reprinted by permission of City Lights Books.

Excerpts from "Getting There" in *Ariel* by Sylvia Plath, Copyright © 1963 by Ted Hughes. By permission of Harper and Row, Publishers, Inc.

Excerpts from W. S. Merwin, "Proteus," in *The Dancing Bears*, Copyright © 1954 by Yale University Press, reprinted by permission of Yale University Press and W. S. Merwin. Excerpts from W. S. Merwin, "The Gods," in *The Lice*, and "The Judgment of Paris," in *The Carrier of Ladders*, reprinted by permission of Atheneum Publishers and W. S. Merwin.

CONTENTS

CONTENTS

ANCIENT
MYTH IN
MODERN
POETRY

I

A DEFINITION OF MYTH

IT is often impossible to discover any relationship between the commentaries on myth—definitions, attacks on, and defenses of its use—which have appeared so frequently in the last few decades and the myths used extensively in twentieth-century literature: in the poetry written by W. H. Auden in the forties or by Auden today, in poems by Robert Lowell or Edwin Muir, or by any of the great number of contemporary poets who employ myth. Readers of anthropological studies of myth are told by one authority that the myths encountered in literature, ancient and modern, are really not myths at all, since they have no proved ritual connection;[1] or they are helped by another to understand "why we are inclined to think of myths both as systems of abstract relations and as objects of aesthetic contemplation."[2] One expert on myth deplores "the tragic existence" of twentieth-century man because he is "the result of the process of desacralization" and has lost the religious basis of the myths he cannot forsake,[3] and another warns us against the contemporary "mythomania," which he regards as a reactionary retreat from history, "the powerhouse of change."[4]

In the confusion of disputes over its definition, exaggerations of its values, and warnings of its dangers, one fact about myth is clear: it survives because it functions in the present, revealing a remark-

[1] E. O. James, *Myth and Ritual in the Ancient Near East* (London, 1958), pp. 302-303.

[2] Claude Lévi-Strauss, *The Savage Mind* (Chicago, 1966), p. 25.

[3] Mircea Eliade, *The Sacred and the Profane*, trans. from the French by Willard Trask (New York, 1959), pp. 203-204.

[4] Philip Rahv, "The Myth and the Powerhouse," in *Myth and Literature,* ed. John B. Vickery (Lincoln, Nebraska, 1966), 109-18.

able capacity to evolve and adapt to the intellectual and aesthetic requirements of the twentieth century. Critical controversy over myth and the diversity of poetic experimentation in its use reflect the vitality of myth as a means of expressing a variety of contemporary approaches to the inherited past, to time, history, and the yearning for order and meaning in a skeptical age.

The interest in myth, and with it the difficulties in limiting and defining the field, have been increased in the twentieth century by the contributions of the comparatively new sciences of anthropology and psychology. The special concerns of the anthropologist, the psychoanalyst, and the literary critic have led to disputes among the various branches investigating the field and among specialists in the same area, often terminating in an uneasy insistence on definitions applicable only to the needs and findings of a particular science or the point of view of a particular poet or scholar. But such compromises are never really satisfactory. Myth has had a significant role in human society from its beginnings as primitive religious narrative to its recent adaptation as an aid in the exploration of the unconscious mind. It has functioned for centuries in all the arts. Any valid study or use of the term myth must include the knowledge that all branches of investigation provide.

Though several fruitful contributions to an understanding of the nature of myth have appeared in the last two or three decades,[5] the

[5] The number of books and articles on the subject of myth which have appeared in the last twenty-five years is vast. Among these some of the most helpful and most interesting are: several volumes by Ernst Cassirer, *Essay on Man* (New Haven, 1944); *Language and Myth*, trans. from the German by Susanne Langer (New York, 1946); *The Myth of the State* (New Haven, 1946); *The Philosophy of Symbolic Forms*, trans. from the German by Ralph Manheim (New Haven, 1955); also, Susanne K. Langer, *Philosophy in a New Key*, 3rd ed. (Cambridge, Mass., 1967); Michael Grant, *Myths of the Greeks and Romans* (London, 1962); Herbert Weisinger, *The Agony and the Triumph, Papers on the Use and Abuse of Myth* (East Lansing, Michigan, 1964); Northrop Frye, *Anatomy of Criticism* (Princeton, 1957); *Fables of Identity, Studies in Poetic Mythology* (New York, 1963); Joseph Fontenrose, *The Ritual Theory of Myth* (Berkeley and Los Angeles, 1966); G. S. Kirk, *Myth, Its Meaning and Functions in Ancient and Other Cultures* (Berkeley and Los Angeles, 1970); and the following collections: *Myth, A Symposium*, ed. Thomas A. Sebeok (Bloomington, Indiana, 1955); *Myth*

definitions for the most part are either so narrow or so general[6] that they are not really applicable to the great body of literature in which allusions are made to the collections of tales generally regarded as ancient Greek and Roman myths, or in which these myths serve as basic subject matter, themes, and symbols.

Too often the issue is confused rather than elucidated by the criterion of ritual. Most scholars today would agree that in ancient societies there was an essential relationship between myth and ritual practice: myth clarified the prescribed action of rites, and rites enacted mythical narrative in stylized dramatic form. It is probably fair to say, however, that most readers seeking a definition applicable to the myths they encounter in literature, music, painting, and sculpture are weary of being informed that myth can be identified as *mythos*, the spoken element accompanying the *dromenon*, "that which is done," the rite performed, a proposition which, in some instances, may elucidate the role of myth in art or society, but in

---

and Mythmaking, ed. Henry A. Murray (New York, 1960); *Myth and Literature*, ed. John B. Vickery; *Myth and Law among the Indo-Europeans*, ed. Jaan Puhvel (Berkeley and Los Angeles, 1970).

[6] Northrop Frye's *Anatomy of Criticism*, while an important contribution to critical thought, is more effective in some of its particular analyses than in its general approach to the subject of myth. "Archetypal criticism," which Frye recommends, approaches all literature as mythical: "In literary criticism myth means ultimately *mythos*, a structural organizing principle of literary form" (p. 341). Though Frye's *Anatomy* does develop this thesis convincingly, the definition is itself too comprehensive, too inclusive, to elucidate the large body of literature in which actual myths are used and adapted. Moreover, Frye's conception of the "four *mythoi* . . . comedy, romance, tragedy, and irony," which he sees as "four aspects of a central unifying myth" (p. 192), is purely arbitrary in relation to myth and not very helpful in relation to literature. For several interesting essays on Frye's relevance to contemporary criticism, see *Northrop Frye in Modern Criticism, Selected Papers from the English Institute*, ed. Murray Krieger (New York, 1966). Richard Volney Chase in *Quest for Myth* (Baton Rouge, 1949) is as general as Frye and less profound. He says that "myth is literature" (p. vi) and proceeds to treat it as such. In an essay published a year later, Chase modifies his definition to some extent; here he says that "if myth is literature, it is also a certain kind of literature, namely, that kind in which the characters and events are instinct with a superhuman or quasi-transcendent force, or brilliance, and have about them an aura of unusual and portentous significance" ("Myth Revisited," *Partisan Review*, XVII [1950], 888).

far too many others seems questionable or irrelevant. In any case, though a discussion of origins and early functions cannot be omitted in any valid consideration of myth, it is certainly insufficient as a definition of a form that has flourished for thousands of years.

In attempting to define myth, literary critics usually make no distinction between pre-literary myth and myth as it is interpreted, allegorized, or actually transformed in ancient literature. Most anthropologists and scholars of the history of religion, on the other hand, consider evidence of ritual origin a criterion for identifying "true" myth and regard all other ancient tales as literary myth, legend, saga, or folktale. Bronislaw Malinowski, one of the first to insist that myth can be understood only as it functions in primitive society, was influential in discrediting as myth the literary developments of mythical narrative. To him these are "merely" stories, "without the context of a living faith." His definition of myth as "a narrative resurrection of a primeval reality, told in satisfaction of deep religious wants, moral cravings, social submissions, assertions, even practical requirements" has won wide acceptance as a description of myth as a vital element in primitive society.[7]

E. O. James, obviously influenced by Malinowski, also regards myth primarily as a form of religious and social expression. He summarizes his objections to the popular conception of myth as follows:

> True myth . . . is not a product of imagination in the sense of speculative thought or philosophizings about the origins of phenomena in the form of an aetiological tale invented to explain objects and events that arouse attention. It is not idealized history or allegorized philosophy, ethics or theology; still less is it an idle story told for intellectual amusement or for popular entertainment according to prescribed custom; or a day-dream to be interpreted by the symbols of psychoanalytical exegesis. All these may retain elements of the myth, but the myth itself is distinct from the fantasy, poetry, philosophy and psychology

[7] "Myth in Primitive Psychology" in *Magic, Science, and Religion, and Other Essays* (Boston, 1948), pp. 78-79.

6

with which it has become associated in its ramifications, developments and degenerations, and their interpretations.

James considers the stories about the Olympian gods, the great heroes, and monstrous creatures of ancient poetry and drama "types of traditional lore," literature rather than myth.[8]

While no one could object to the exclusion from the realm of myth of "idealized history," "allegorized philosophy," or any of the other categories James mentions, it does not necessarily follow that all myth which survives in ancient literature can be similarly excluded. Like Malinowski, James limits the appearance of "true" myth to primitive society, where, he says, precarious natural, social, and economic conditions are likely to promote its creation and growth.

In times of great tension, primitive man, according to James, seeks the help of supernatural agencies. Furthermore, "around crucial events such as the creation of the world, the loss of immortality, the destiny of man, the sequence of the seasons, and the struggle between good and evil, a sacred narrative has taken shape to bring them into direct relation with the existing physical, cultural, social, ethical and religious conditions and organization." The sacred narrative or myth is a means of maintaining "order both in nature and in society" and preserving conventional attitudes and patterns of behavior. These narratives are accompanied by sacred rites, which re-enact "the seasonal drama" or creation itself.[9]

I have quoted and summarized James's discussion of myth in primitive society because it is the most lucid and convincing description I have encountered in recent literature on the subject. My only objection—and it is a strong one—is that he would limit "true" myth to the function he so ably reconstructs in portraying the needs and desires of primitive man. It would perhaps be convenient to consider myth under two categories: "true" myth or sacred narrative, defined by its function—since James never actually defines the form—and "literary" myth, i.e., the stories of the ancient Greek and

[8] *Myth and Ritual in the Ancient Near East*, pp. 279-81.
[9] *ibid.*, pp. 282-92.

7

Roman gods and heroes, which Frazer, Malinowski, James, and others regard either as folktales or traditional lore. But in the face of the actual mythical stories these rigid categories will not stand.

Mythical thinking is individual as well as endemic. One cannot consider the evidence that man in ancient and primitive societies reacts in a particular way to intense internal and external pressures without recognizing the possibility that this reaction reflects a way of thinking peculiar not only to those living in a primitive environment but to all human beings. If whole societies throughout the ancient Near East engaged in ritual acts to the accompaniment of mythical narrative, then surely mythical thinking—which is in essence an attempt to control one's feelings and environment by non-rational means, e.g., magic, gods, spells, stories, or other devices, except practical or scientific ones, which the human imagination may devise—is an individual response channeled by ancient societies into communal religious expression. There is no doubt that as scientific and technological development increases, the obvious need for mythical thinking decreases. But human thought and behavior are usually not explicable by simple ratios.

Even Malinowski admits that primitive men—in this case the Melanesians—tend the soil and plant and harvest their crops with great skill, "guided by a clear knowledge of weather and seasons, plants and pests, soil and tubers," while "mixed with all their activities there is to be found magic, a series of rites performed every year over the gardens in rigorous sequence and order."[10] The same apparently contradictory activity was no doubt carried on by all ancient and primitive peoples; rational behavior provided the means of survival, but was too limited in its scope and accomplishment to provide assurance that it alone would be effective.

As societies develop technologically, mythical thinking and myth itself do not disappear; they emerge in more subtle forms, one of which is literature. The gods and heroes as they appear in Homer or Sophocles may not have been believed in or worshiped as literally as those of Paleolithic times, but they are not merely the delightful characters of stories told for sheer amusement. Often they retain

[10] *Magic, Science, and Religion*, p. 11.

obvious remnants of a ritual connection; sometimes, when they appear in legend or saga, their reaction to the events in which they participate suggests a mythical source. These gods and heroes may not be concerned with success in hunting, the problems of food supply, or the death of the year, but they do express a response to the terrible and perennial limitations of man—physical weakness, old age, and death, and perhaps more painful even than any of these, the fact that, though from the first day of his life to the last man seeks in some way to apprehend reality, he is continually confronted by the limitations of his own vision as he faces the unknown and, to a large extent, the unknowable in the universe, his fellow men, and himself. Legend, folktale, and myth are already fused in the *Iliad*, in which the legend or "heroic saga" of the Trojan War is inseparable from the rites performed in honor of the gods and the myths concerning the heroes' relation to them; man's practical concern with self-preservation in warfare is inseparable from the mythical expression of his search for knowledge of the nature of mortality. Myth does not attempt to explain these limitations or to interpret these experiences; it expresses an emotional and often unconscious response to them and an effort to control and direct fears which even the most effective practical means cannot allay and yearnings which they will not satisfy.

The wide acceptance of myth as an expression of unconscious drives and wishes originates in Freud's interpretation and use of myth as a guide to the human psyche, his discovery of the connection between myth and dream, and his effort "to transform *metaphysics* into *metapsychology*."[11] In the exploits of the gods and heroes of ancient Greek and Latin literature Freud saw expressions of instinctual drives and unconscious conflict. Myth provided him with a clue to the psychic history of the human species. Freud's approach to myth as it appears in literature, and the various theories and systems that stem from the Freudian view—supportive or opposing

[11] *The Psychopathology of Everyday Life, The Standard Edition of the Complete Psychological Works of Sigmund Freud,* trans. from the German under the general editorship of James Strachey in collaboration with Anna Freud (London, 1953-66), VI, 259. All references to Freud's works will be to this edition, hereafter referred to as SE.

—have influenced assumption, discussion, and use of myth to such an extent that it is impossible for the twentieth-century reader to draw a neat line between myth as social or psychological vehicle and myth as poetic symbol or metaphor.

Freud's speculation on the relationship between phylogenetic and individual development suggests another basis for the persistence of myth in human society long after it has ceased to function in any organized ritual activity. In an essay "The 'Uncanny,'" first published in *Imago* in 1919, he comments on the traces within the human unconscious of a mode of thinking that reflects earlier civilizations:

> It seems as if each one of us has been through a phase of individual development corresponding to this animistic stage in primitive men, that none of us has passed through it without preserving certain residues and traces of it which are still capable of manifesting themselves, and that everything which now strikes us as "uncanny" fulfills the condition of touching those residues of animistic mental activity within us and bringing them to expression.[12]

In examining mythical narrative as it functions both in ancient and in most recent poetry, we see that not only vestiges of animistic thinking but other manifestations of early phylogenetic development can be found in myth; it was and is, moreover, both a personal and social vehicle of thought and feeling, deeply united and expressed in symbolic form.

A definition of myth must thus include the characteristics operative in primitive religion and society as well as those which enable myth to evolve and adapt to the aesthetic and rational approaches of art and science. My own definition is as follows: Myth is a narrative structure of two basic areas of unconscious experience which are, of course, related. First, it expresses instinctual drives and the repressed wishes, fears, and conflicts that they motivate. These appear in the themes of myth. Second, myth also conveys the remnants within the individual consciousness of the early stage of phylogenetic

[12] SE XVII, 240-41. See also *Moses and Monotheism*, SE XXIII, 93-102.

development in which myths were created. This characteristic is evident mainly in its plots. Myth is a story involving human limitation and superhuman strivings and accomplishments which suggests through action—usually of a ritual, ceremonial, or compulsive nature—man's attempt to express and thus control his own anxiety about those features of his physiological and psychological make-up and his external environment which he cannot comprehend, accept, or master. The characters of myth may be gods, men, or monstrous creatures with the qualities of both, but even in myths dealing exclusively with immortals, the narrative material, the portrayal of conflict and sorrow, and the resolution or revelation are all reflections of human concerns.

The themes of myth express man's fear of and awe at the mysterious cycle of the death and rebirth of the year and his involvement in the mystery of his own birth, nature, and death. The mythical representations of such themes, moreover, indicate man's attempt to *do* something about the mysteries which continually remind him of his helplessness and at the same time challenge him with endless possibilities of control through his own imagination and action. This sense of control may spring from participation in ritual, which expresses anxiety through prescribed acts or assigns power to magic objects and words, or from the insight gleaned from the stark narrative of myth.

The plots of myth are inextricably connected with its themes; for purposes of definition, however, it is helpful to regard the action of myth as its plot. This always reflects man's persistent desire for extraordinary power, vision, and control. No man has ever behaved in the manner of a hero of myth, yet every man can readily identify with him as he undergoes danger and accomplishes heroic exploits, as he dares to face the world of the dead and the horror of his own acts of incest or infanticide. We identify with the hero of myth not only because he acts out our unconscious wishes and fears but also because in so doing he performs a continual rite of service for the rest of mankind: he asks our essential questions and he answers them. The mythical hero's whole career is devoted to action which raises questions about and indicates possible answers to those issues we usually avoid: death, our relation to time, destiny, freedom of will. For these answers he pays a price most men do not have the strength or courage to pay. The mythical figure's conflicts and actions are usually related to some social problem or issue, yet, as a result of behavior that offends his society, or because of some deep suffering, he often becomes an outcast. His endurance of pain, his violation of the most sacred ties to parents, wife, or children, are the metaphorical expression of man's efforts to understand and come to terms with his own nature and the conditions of human life.

Ancient Greek and Roman myths as they occur in literature vary in motif or plot, but all of them are concerned with the universal preoccupations of man in the early stages of civilization: the creation of the world and of man himself; the birth of gods and heroes, and their contests, victories, and defeats; the productivity of the earth; death, and resurrection. Structurally, moreover, they have certain common features: a ritual, ceremonial, or compulsive act, expressing deep emotional experience in a stylized form; an identification of personal anxiety or helplessness with a social problem; and an expression of a struggle to control and command both the external environment and the inner self.

Michael Grant points out that the connection between Greek myth and religious practice was generally accepted "when myths were regarded as an essential element in the philosophy of religion, representing the alleged creed or dogma of paganism." However, when scholars recognized that Greek religion was not based on dogma, myths were erroneously regarded as having artistic rather than religious functions. Grant concludes that though there is no doubt that Greek myths had no connection with dogma, the myths "are profoundly illustrative of Greek religion."[13] Even in their most sophisticated literary forms these myths often provide a clue to the ancient Greek's conception of the gods; they describe his prayers,

---

[13] *Myths of the Greeks and Romans*, p. 155. See also S. H. Hooke, ed., *Myth and Ritual* (London, 1933). Hooke suggests that "in the myths of Greece . . . there is a clue, a connecting thread which leads back to this ancient myth and ritual pattern." He cites the Minotaur and Perseus myths as examples which "involve an underlying pattern of human sacrifice, and take us back to a stage in which myth and ritual were united" (pp. 2-6).

sacrifices, and attempts to regulate and control his destiny through ritual.

One of the Greek myths in which it is possible to see obvious remains of religious ritual is that of Demeter and her daughter Persephone. Demeter was worshipped in the Mediterranean area long before the arrival of the Achaeans. Most scholars believe that as an earth goddess and a goddess of corn Demeter was celebrated, along with Persephone, the corn maiden, in seasonal rites which gave assurance that, after the harvest, the earth would burgeon again and that spring, like Persephone, would emerge after the long months of winter. A different point of view is held by Martin P. Nilsson, who is of the opinion that Demeter was specifically the corn mother rather than an earth goddess, and that the myth regarding the descent of Persephone into the earth for one third of the year originated in a festival connected with the storing of corn in subterranean silos from June to October. The "*anodos*, the ascent of the Corn Maiden," thus represents the bringing-up of the seed corn for sowing in the fall.[14]

Whether her origin may be traced to fertility rites or to those connected with restoration of the seed corn, the myth of Demeter recorded in *Homeric Hymn* II and in later literature contains evidence of Demeter's function as an agricultural deity and as the founder of the Eleusinian mysteries, through which she gave renewed life to the earth and immortality to man.

In the first section of the *Homeric Hymn* the author describes Demeter as a bereft mother whose daughter has been snatched from her. At first Demeter does not even know who has taken Persephone, for no one will tell her what has happened. Unable to eat or rest, she wanders about, seeking some news of her child. At this stage she seems more human being than goddess in her aloneness and her despair. Moreover, after learning from Helios that Hades has kidnapped Persephone, she avoids Olympus and the other gods, and, disguising her form, wanders, apparently a tormented woman, among the cities and fields of men.

---

[14] *Greek Popular Religion* (New York, 1940), p. 52.

In Eleusis, the daughters of Celeus pity Demeter, believing her
story that she is an old woman who has fled her captors. Only in
the secret arts she practices in caring for Demophoön is the goddess
manifest until the moment when she declares (l. 268), "I am Demeter," orders that a temple be built to honor her, and offers to teach
her rites, the Eleusinian mysteries. Even after this revelation of her
immortality, moreover, Demeter continues to grieve as a bereft
mother. The double quality of Demeter as the deprived woman and
the all powerful goddess is best exemplified in lines 302-307, in which
Demeter is described as "wasting" with anguish over the loss of her
child and laying waste the earth in her anger and despair. Throughout the rest of the hymn she retains this ambivalent nature: she is
the mother who finally accepts with joy the compromise by which
she will have her child for two-thirds of the year, and the all-power-
ful goddess who, once she is satisfied by this arrangement with
Hades, makes the earth fruitful again and establishes the rites of
Eleusis. The bereft mother Demeter, whose child has been taken
into the world of the dead, also bestows immortality through her
mysteries. Thus, the mythical story expresses man's yearning to
control the mysteries of barrenness and death. In the end, death is
known and regulated. It has been limited by the secret power of
its apparent victim.

Of course, the myth of Demeter and Persephone cannot be separated from the rites of Eleusis, which incorporated an enactment
of their story. The mysteries had two parts: the public rites and the
secret rites, held in the Telestrion, the temple of Demeter at Eleusis.[15] George Mylonas believes that these secret rites were held both
in the Telestrion and in the surrounding area, "around the very
landmarks supposed to have been consecrated by the actual experience and presence of Demeter." The oath of secrecy to which initiates were sworn was effective in preventing the disclosure of the
details of the second part of the ceremonies. Nonetheless, scholars
have been able to arrive at some idea of what the rites were like.
According to Mylonas, "there can be little doubt that part of the

[15] George Mylonas, *Eleusis and the Eleusinian Mysteries* (Princeton, 1961),
pp. 226-28.

dromena at least was a sacred pageant, the presentation of the story of Demeter and Persephone." He goes on to speculate: "Perhaps the initiates went about searching for Persephone, sorrowing for her disappearance, hopeful of news of her, gladdened by the promise of her discovery, finally elated by her return and her reunion with her Mother."[16]

In reenacting the story the initiates participated not only in the suffering of the mother and the daughter, but also in their power to recover from loss and sorrow. In the abduction of Persephone and the grief of Demeter they acted out their despair at human limitations; in the restoration to life of the daughter and the control of Demeter over the fertility of the earth they participated in superhuman power.

The enactment of the conquest of helplessness and fear through understanding and control, so explicitly dramatized in the story of Demeter's search for Persephone, is inherent in all ritual, though the progression is not always so openly expressed. Ritual is an expression through prescribed acts of the wish or need to exert power either forbidden or unattainable in ordinary life. Furthermore, the action prescribed by ritual is always symbolic, for the conquest, though ostensibly directed outward toward the gods, or death, or nature, is actually directed inward toward the participant's own wishes and fears. In this sense ritual results in both failure and success. The initiate somehow knows that he will never quite control the seasons, the gods, or death, for these are after all terms naming the conditions of life, but in a deeper sense he is victorious, for he has not only exhibited his hidden and perhaps forbidden wishes regarding such mysteries, he has also revealed and learned something about himself, and in so doing has defined and controlled a chaos within.

Through practical behavior, by cultivating the land, planting, and harvesting, man exerts a measure of control over a small section of the vast universe he can hardly hope to comprehend, and through this control he manages to survive physically. In somewhat the same

[16] *ibid.*, p. 262.

way, through a ritual act he attempts to put in order an inner universe equally mysterious, his physiological and psychological nature. Through repeated and prescribed acts he manages to achieve equanimity in the face of inevitable ignorance, sickness, and death.

Implicit in ritual is a search for reassurance, an answer to some "overwhelming question."[17] Through the ritual dance, sacrifice, or drama, the initiate symbolically provides an answer to the questions "Does my life have meaning?", "Do my aspirations to power or immortality have any basis in reality?" He is always answered in the affirmative, as in the ritual he identifies with the god or hero he has created to define the conditions of life.

Allusions to or metaphorical use of the myth of Demeter and Persephone in the most diverse types of poems indicate how a myth can recall its ritual connections with or without direct reference to actual ceremonies or rites. Sometimes one can sense the rite beneath the allusion as together they construct a metaphor. Poets from Hesiod (in the *Theogony*) and the author of the *Homeric Hymns* to such nineteenth-century poets as Keats, Tennyson, and Meredith, and many twentieth-century poets—Robert Graves, Ezra Pound, H.D., William Rose Benét, Edgar Lee Masters, Kathleen Raine, Robert Lowell, and others—have used this myth with varying degrees of effectiveness.

Though the subject of this book is twentieth-century poetry, it will be interesting to glance for a moment at an earlier use of the myth to see how ritual associations, developed so fully in contemporary use of myth, are suggested and exploited by Keats before the problem of the connection of myth and ritual had become so crucial in scholarship and criticism. In the "Ode on Melancholy" Keats uses Persephone, or Proserpine as he calls her, to suggest that true melancholy implies worship, a kind of religious devotion. Though he urges the initiate

> Nor suffer thy pale forehead to be kiss'd
> By nightshade, ruby grape of Proserpine,

[17] See Chapter IV, below, in which T. S. Eliot's "The Love Song of J. Alfred Prufrock" is analyzed in connection with this discussion of ritual.

this prohibition leads him to develop his conception of "sorrow's mysteries" or rites, to be truly celebrated only in the "very temple of Delight." Keats introduces Proserpine only to reject the response to melancholy which her name evokes, for she is associated with the perennial recurrence of death. Her permanence as a symbol is unsuited to his own concept of melancholy, which dwells with the ephemeral, the beautiful but fleeting rose or lady. The "mysteries" or rites that Keats recalls in connection with Proserpine, the prototype for ritual mourning, however, provide a traditional base for the new goddess he wishes to worship, Melancholy, who has her "shrine" in the "very temple of Delight" and who demands her own complicated rituals. Thus, Keats dethrones Persephone, only to renew the efficacy of her "mysteries," over which he gives a new goddess sovereignty.

Here the rituals associated with Persephone are essential to the development of the entire poem and are clearly and explicitly stated; in other poems, however, they may be absent, denied, or only suggested. In Robert Graves's "Escape,"[18] a rather lighthearted treatment of a grim episode in World War I, he deals with a false report of his death in battle. With mild irony he relates his experience in Hades, from which "Dear Lady Proserpine . . . stooping over [him] for Henna's sake," sent him back to life. The experience is told entirely in mythical terms—Lethe, Cerberus, demons, and heroes create an atmosphere of the traditional underworld. Graves's irony, however, seems to provide his escape from the world of the dead. The poet simply will not take it or its rituals seriously. Thus, he loosens the hold of death by rejecting the traditional approach to Persephone, Cerberus, and the shades of the underworld. Proserpine is a dear lady; Cerberus is drugged with an army biscuit. Only after he has escaped from death can the poet turn from his ironic manner to exclaim earnestly, "O Life, O Sun!"

In H.D.'s "Demeter"[19] myth and ritual are inextricably and directly connected. In the first stanza the goddess describes a ritual and sacrifice in her honor:

[18] *Poems (1914-26)* (London, 1927), pp. 58-59.
[19] *Collected Poems of H.D.* (New York, 1925), pp. 161-66.

Men, fires, feasts,
steps of temple, fore-stone, lintel,
step of white altar, fire and after-fire
slaughter before,
fragment of burnt meat,
deep mystery, grapple of mind to reach
the tense thought,

. . .

and ends the terse summary with the word "useless." These rites are useless because those who perform them do not understand the goddess they profess to worship. They do not recognize the fact that her power is greater than that of beautiful Aphrodite, Apollo, or Athene. In an explicit delineation of her double character Demeter declares herself "greatest and least." H.D. intensifies Demeter's ritual connections by bringing in Dionysus, who was celebrated along with Demeter in the Eleusinian mysteries, and even distorts the myth to serve her purpose, assigning to Demeter rather than to Zeus credit for saving Dionysus when Semele was consumed before his birth. Demeter regards Dionysus as "the child of my heart and spirit." Her love for this child and for her true child, Persephone, has taught Demeter all the secrets of productivity, death, and rebirth. Her fingers "are wrought of iron / to wrest from earth / secrets." The goddess implies that her knowledge is deeper and her power greater than men can comprehend in their "useless" rituals, for she is nature itself, whom man, for all his statues and sacrifices, will never really know or conquer.[20]

One of the most subtle and effective uses of the Persephone myth and its ritual associations occurs in a poem by Kathleen Raine, "The Transit of the Gods":[21]

[20] See Thomas Burnett Swann, *The Classical World of H.D.* (Lincoln, Nebraska, 1962). Though I cannot agree with Swann that "for twenty-five hundred years" before the appearance of H.D.'s "Demeter," "poems about Demeter had simply told a story about the goddess and her daughter" (p. 44), his analysis of the poem and his discussion of its background are of some value.

[21] *Collected Poems* (New York, 1956), p. 83.

Strange that the self's continuum should outlast
The Virgin, Aphrodite, and the Mourning Mother,
All loves and griefs, successive deities
That hold their kingdom in the human breast.

Abandoned by the gods, woman with an aging body
That half remembers the Annunciation
The passion and the travail and the grief
That wore the mask of my humanity,

I marvel at the soul's indifference.
For in her theatre the play is done,
The tears are shed; the actors, the immortals
In their ceaseless manifestation, elsewhere gone,

And I who have been Virgin and Aphrodite,
The mourning Isis and the queen of corn
Wait for the last mummer, dread Persephone
To dance my dust at last into the tomb.

Though the poet recognizes the gods as projections of her "loves
and griefs," she also sees them as real presences. Nor are love and
grief as goddesses inhabiting the human breast mere personifica-
tions; to experience love as Aphrodite and grief as the Mourning
Mother is to project oneself into a mythical framework, to take on
in fantasy the goddesses' capacities and their beauty. Now, abandoned by her own powers of imagination. conscious of age and
death, the poet perceives her past experience as self-dramatization.
Her roles as Virgin, Aphrodite, Isis, and Demeter are finished. Yet
even death is to be experienced through a myth. It is Persephone
whom she awaits, and Persephone will come performing a rite, "the
last mummer, . . . / To dance my dust at last into the tomb." Thus,
the poet denies her own statement, "the play is done," for, awaiting
Persephone, she does not perceive herself merely as a "woman with
an aging body," but as a character in another myth, an initiate in
a last ritual. If Aphrodite and Isis have superhuman power over life,
has not Persephone such power over death?

The poet goes easily from realistic to mythical thinking, suggesting their strange union in the human mind. She observes "the transit of the gods" as she observes the "self's continuum," and at the end she has control over both. The victory implicit in the last sad line is that of a mind which understands the attraction of mythical thinking yet recognizes its tragic limitations.

In Robert Lowell's "The Mills of the Kavanaughs"[22] the figure of Persephone is used even more forcefully to suggest the contradictory feelings and drives that can exist at one time in the human mind—particularly the ever-present conflict between a desire for fulfillment in love and a compulsive adherence to its opposite, death. Out of this basic struggle emerges the daily evidence of man's experience of mortality and his longing for omnipotence. The figure of Persephone, which contains this ambivalence, is Lowell's chief symbol.

The scene of the poem is, for the most part, the garden of the Kavanaugh estate, where Anne Kavanaugh sits, playing solitaire; at the end of the poem she rises and rows her boat down the stream. Actually, the events of the poem take place in the mind of Anne, where past and present merge in her associations and daydreams about her childhood, her marriage to Harry Kavanaugh, his madness, and death.

The myth of Persephone dominates the entire poem. The goddess is present as a statue in the garden, but she is more strikingly present internalized in the mind of Anne Kavanaugh. Lowell first mentions the statue of Persephone in an introductory note, in which he describes her as "the goddess who became a queen by becoming queen of the dead." The identification with Anne, inheritor of the estate of the Kavanaughs, who sits in the garden near the grave of her husband and plays solitaire, with the Douay Bible, which she calls Sol, as her imaginary opponent, is immediately apparent.

Anne's thoughts range over actual events of the past, her own response to them and fantasies built on them, and the game she is playing in the present—but only as it provides material for fantasies

[22] (1951) reprinted in *Lord Weary's Castle and the Mills of the Kavanaughs* (New York, 1961), pp. 75-94.

of the future possibility of victory over time and death. The three periods of time are united in her daydreams[23] through the figure and myth of Persephone. In all the important events of her life—her first meeting with Harry Kavanaugh, when she, one of thirteen children of a poverty-stricken family, was picking flowers on the great Kanavaugh estate, her adoption by the Kavanaughs, her marriage to Harry, her difficulties in their relationship—she sees herself as doomed and powerful, a goddess of the underworld, rather than as a weak and narcissistic woman. Her myth, employed to disguise the hideous reality of weakness, madness, death, and extinction, like her dreams, finally betrays her, revealing an underworld within of rage and despair.

Anne's associations lead her back to a night during which a dream she had precipitated her husband's attempt to murder her. In the dream she first sees herself "stalking" in her "moccasins / Below the mill-fall," like one of the Abnaki Indians, a tribe almost extinct; in this role she reveals her identification with the weak and the dying. Then the dream discloses her contempt for and fear of her husband and her desire for an idealized lover, a boy—really a creature of her narcissistic fantasy with whom she can cheat the despised Harry. Her husband, jealous of this phantom lover, attempts to strangle her. Though he fails, he becomes for her, as she faints, the king of the dead. In a typical reversal, Anne converts the pathetic madman into the ugly but powerful Pluto—as always, to feed her vanity and her compulsive need to avoid her feelings of guilt and failure.

As she resists her husband's attack, Anne cries out, "Harry, we're not accountable for dreams." Lowell's point, of course, is that we are accountable both for the dreams that reveal our unconscious wishes for godlike power and the daydreams into which our frustrated wishes and pride are projected. Thus, no one who has dreamed or daydreamed dares to condemn Anne Kavanaugh. Her flaw of pride, her childish and selfish vanity are the petty expressions of the

---

[23] See Chapter II, below, for commentary on Freud's analysis of the way in which fantasy unites past, present, and future time.

great war between love and death in her heart, symbolized in her identification with the goddess Persephone.

The allusions to Persephone are as varied in tone as are the associations of Anne Kavanaugh. Anne identifies with the goddess in a dignified ritual expressing her majesty and power:

> This was Avernus. There, about this time,
> Demeter's daughter first reviewed the dead—
> Most doomed and pompous, . . .

even as she herself engages in a ritual card-game in a last pathetic effort to arrest the drive toward death in her own being and in the society represented by the family of the Kavanaughs. She has named the Douay Bible Sol and, employing it as her "dummy," she competes with two traditional powers, pagan and Christian: the sungod and the Catholic Church. During this contest for control over inevitable decay, she records the score on a "life / Insurance calendar." Since this is an imaginary opponent, she is, of course, engaged in a ritual contest with herself, between the light and darkness within her. Desiring her antagonist's power, " '*Sol*,' she whispers, laughing, '*Sol*, / If you will help me, I will win the world.' " All her daydreams and recollections reflect this effort until, near the end of the poem, she gives up the card-game and "wakes."

Her last act is a ritual one: accompanied by the spirit of her husband, she rows her boat to Avernus. She has stacked her cards and left her contest with Sol, and now she begins to accept the reality of death. In the last stanza she thinks of Persephone as a young virgin: "She gave herself because her blood was warm—" then she adds, "And for no other reason, Love, I gave / Whatever brought me gladness to the grave." The long descent into herself and the last ritual to the dead have released Anne from her mythical role, and she faces the limits of love, joy, and life.

The poems discussed thus far all contain clear references to a traditional myth whose ritual elements, if not stated, are certainly easy to trace. But neither myth nor ritual is always so open in its appearance. Myth has a way of surviving even when its ritual associations are lost or even when it becomes part of legend or folktale. Unlike myths, legends deal with events in the lives of historical figures; however distorted the events may be and whatever marvelous and heroic qualities may be attributed to the participants, there is in legends some connection with fact. Folktales or fairy tales, on the other hand, have neither the religious nor social basis of myths, nor an origin in history; they are stories expressing significant psychological experience in the form of stylized and patterned behavior, and their purpose is entertainment. Yet, as Susanne Langer points out, the material of myth and fairy tale is the same: "No wonder psychologists have discovered that it [myth] is the same material as that of fairy tale; that both have symbols for father and son, maiden and wife and mother, possession and passion, birth and death. The difference is in the two respective *uses* of that material: the one, primarily for supplying vicarious experience, the other essentially for understanding actual experience."[24]

In ancient Greek and Latin literature myth is fused with legend and folktale or fairy tale. In the *Iliad* and the *Odyssey* the legends of the Trojan War and the bizarre folktales of the wandering Odysseus are enriched and broadened by the myths to which they are inextricably attached.

The mythical cause of the Trojan War is the abduction of Helen, who, though chiefly known as the most beautiful woman of the Greek world, was no doubt a pre-Hellenic agricultural goddess long before she became a heroine of epic. This mythical origin, moreover, persists in literature in spite of all the individual qualities she assumes as a woman in epic and drama. Her strange, ambivalent relationship with Paris and the other Trojans in the *Iliad* and her tie of hatred with Aphrodite suggest rituals older than those of heroic warfare over abduction. Furthermore, Richmond Lattimore, in discussing the "Pattern of the Lost One" in Greek tragedy, reveals Helen's resemblance to Persephone, another hint—this time in drama—of her origins as a figure in agricultural ritual: "Helen, the housewife and mother, enacts death and the maiden; like Persephone, she was snatched away while gathering flowers in the

[24] *Philosophy in a New Key*, p. 177.

23

meadow; and the lyric chorus sings the *fabula sacra* of Demeter's desolution and anger over the loss of her daughter."[25]

Achilles also, though almost a prototype of legendary courage and skill in battle, is equally exemplary as a mythical figure. Rhys Carpenter considers the qualities that suggest his mythical origin:

> Achilles' own name is obscure, but may derive from water and rivers, so that his stock epithet of "swift-running" may belong to him by natural right. As for his father Peleus, many moderns agree with Homer in connecting his name with the mountain Pelion, thus still further confirming him as an elemental evocation. Then the swift-running river, with a mountain for father and the sea for mother, may originally have been some sort of local hero or divinity of northern Greece, elected (for some unrecapturable reason) to become the central figure of some story, and, as such, decked out with the trappings and accouterments of folk tale.

Though Carpenter admits the possibility of error in the origins of Achilles suggested above, the character is certainly a mythical one: "Whatever his ultimate origin, Achilles must derive from a different realm from the severely practical Menelaos, the garrulous old politician Nestor, or for that matter almost all the other leading figures of the Achaean expeditionary force."[26]

It seems incredible that anyone reading the story of Achilles' adventures should need external evidence of his origin in myth. In his compulsive choice of a short, glorious life over a long inglorious one, Achilles acts out a mythical pattern. If he cannot live forever, as do the gods, he will still exert that inverse control over his mortality so characteristic of mythical figures. By shortness of life, by death itself, he assures his immortality. His excessive violence, almost to the point of madness, especially in his battle with the river, has the same patterned, compulsive, and mythical quality. On the

---

[25] *Story Patterns in Greek Tragedy* (Ann Arbor, Michigan, 1965), p. 53. Lattimore refers to Euripides' *Helen*, ll. 241-51 and ll. 1301-68.

[26] *Folk Tale, Fiction and Saga in the Homeric Epics* (Berkeley and Los Angeles, 1958), p. 73.

battlefield he is a dark and raging force. From this descent into a kind of ritual madness, he emerges finally to light; having murdered and sacrificed with ritual ceremony and cruelty, he becomes human again in his compassionate treatment of Priam.

Mythical thinking pervades and transforms the whole legend of the Trojan War. Battles are won not because of the superiority of weapons or manpower, but because of the will of the gods. Offending a prophet, misinterpreting a dream, omitting a sacrifice—all will bring untold destruction.

Myth persists in ancient Greek and Latin literature in its fusion with legend and folktale, its conversion to drama, its adaptation to history, and its distortions in naturalistic epistles and stories. Mythical characters like Oedipus exist side by side with naturalistic ones like Creon. Helen may contain qualities of an original agricultural goddess, but she is depicted in drama as a rather conventional, cold-hearted beauty.

In drawing on the great body of gods, heroes, and monsters, and on the collection of their difficulties, sorrows, and victories recorded in ancient literature, poets from the Middle Ages to the present have rarely been troubled by the distinction between myth, legend, and folktale. Mythical and legendary stories have served as allegory, allusion, and metaphor, sometimes as intrinsic expression, and at other times as elaborate and pretentious decoration. In literary criticism the distinction among them is significant because it helps to elucidate the function of particular allusions or metaphors. In studying myth in twentieth-century poetry, moreover, the distinction between myth, legend, and folktale has a special importance, for poets of our time, influenced by comparative mythology, archeology, anthropology, and psychology, have approached myth differently from their predecessors. Allegory and mythological decoration are rare in serious twentieth-century poetry. There have been, on the other hand, a conscious recognition and an exploitation of the ritual elements in myth and also a general awareness of the psychological implications of mythical tales. Furthermore, poets have consciously attempted to revive myth as a literary device.

When, in dealing with the work of Joyce and Yeats, both Eliot and

Auden discussed the importance of the "mythical method," they could have been describing their own point of view as poets. Writing about Joyce's *Ulysses* in 1921, Eliot says:

> In using the myth, in manipulating a continuous parallel between contemporaneity and antiquity, Mr. Joyce is pursuing a method which others must pursue after him. . . . It is simply a way of controlling, of ordering, of giving a shape and a significance to the immense panorama of futility and anarchy which is contemporary history. It is a method already adumbrated by Mr. Yeats, and of the need for which I believe Mr. Yeats to have been the first contemporary to be conscious. It is a method for which the horoscope is auspicious. Psychology (such as it is, and whether our reaction to it be comic or serious), ethnology, and *The Golden Bough* have concurred to make possible what was impossible only a few years ago. Instead of narrative method, we may now use the mythical method. It is, I seriously believe, a step toward making the modern world possible for art.[27]

Eliot views myth as antithetical to narrative, for he considers it in its most essential form a way of exerting control, establishing order, when man feels threatened by anarchy. Modern man's fears may spring from causes far different from those of his ancestors in the ancient past, but the symptoms are similar, and the method Eliot suggests that artists employ as a weapon against the threat of anarchy has its roots in ancient ritual.

In an essay on Yeats first published in 1948, Auden takes a similar position in respect to myth and the poet's need for a mythical framework in "a society in which men are no longer supported by tradition without being aware of it, and in which, therefore, every individual who wishes to bring order and coherence into the stream of sensations, emotions, and ideas entering his consciousness, from without and within, is forced to do deliberately for himself what in previous ages had been done for him by family, custom, church, and state, namely the choice of the principles and presuppositions in

[27] T. S. Eliot, "Ulysses, Order, and Myth," *The Dial*, LXXV (1923), 483.

terms of which he can make sense of his experience." Auden believes that "any poet today, even if he deny the importance of dogma to life, can see how useful myths are to poetry—how much, for instance, they helped Yeats to make his private experiences public and his vision of public events personal."[28]

Obviously related to this position is Auden's view that poetry is a "verbal rite," an idea he has dealt with in prose and developed in his own poetry. It is impossible to understand Auden's poetry without recognizing his attempt to create in his own work a ritual in which modern man may participate.

The revival of myth in the present time indicates, of course, that in his desire for order, for belief in some standard beyond his individual reaction, man turns back to traditional symbols, which evoke an emotional, if not a spiritual, sense of permanence, recurrence, and stability. This, however, is too simple an explanation to account for the reversion to myth in the present. The interest in myth in the twentieth century is complicated by the fact that it is considered both truth and falsehood by some of the very poets who employ it.

This problem is not peculiar to the twentieth century. It is well known that the truth of myth was challenged by ancient Greek Sophists, Stoics, and Epicureans. The Sophists and Stoics regarded myths as allegories capable of revealing qualities of external nature and man; the Epicureans attacked myths as deceptions, though the beautiful invocation to Venus at the beginning of the *De Rerum Natura* indicates that Lucretius felt free to employ myth as a means of symbolic expression.

Twentieth-century American and European poets have a more ambivalent attitude. The very poets who consider myth a vehicle for the expression of truth are also aware of the validity of the popular use of the word to mean a falsehood or an avoidance of reality. In "Apprehensions"[29] Robert Duncan, exploring his past, tells of his grandfather, "the tired old man," and then remarks:

[28] W. H. Auden, "Yeats as an Example," *The Kenyon Critics*, ed. John Crowe Ransom (New York, 1951), 111.
[29] *Roots and Branches* (New York, 1964), p. 37.

          but this is myth
   That Freud says lies in our blood, Dragon-wise
   To darken our intelligence.

The myth which "darkens" also reveals, suggests Duncan, if "we remember it all."

One of the most curious and most interesting qualities of myth is that it is both false and true at the same time. Myths, of course, express man's deepest self-deceptions—his creation of gods in his own image, his attribution to himself, or to a creature formed to mirror his marvelous fantasies, of powers of control beyond those of any human being ever born. Yet only in these fantastic forms can man reveal certain of his fears, his desires, and his tentative apprehension of the real world and of his own nature. What he discloses about himself in myth can be expressed in no other way, for the expository language of rational thought cannot contain it.

Like the lying tales of Odysseus, myth sometimes reveals more about the teller than does a factual description of his real experience. The difficulty is that to understand the truth that myth contains one must always be aware that myth is in some respects a deception. Of course, one could say that all story, or indeed all art, uncovers truth through indirection and fantasy, and thus, in a sense, deceives; but this similarity is only a surface one. Myth is not art, though it is used in all the arts; it promises more; its methods and functions are different. Myth is a form of expression which reveals a process of thought and feeling—man's awareness of and response to the universe, his fellow men, and his separate being. It is a projection in concrete and dramatic form of fears and desires undiscoverable and inexpressible in any other way. As it opens up the boundless reaches of man's vision, it defines the limits of individual life.

It is a mistake to interpret all imaginative literature as mythical or to define myth as literature. It is equally misleading to regard the appearance of myth in literature or art as unauthentic or of secondary importance.[30] The real vitality of myth in the twentieth

---

[30] It is surprising to read in a work by so astute an authority on myth as Theodor Gaster the statement, "Moreover, the impulse which inspires myth

century lies in its role in literature and the other arts, a most contro-versial one.

Perhaps the best known of many attacks on the current "mytho-mania" is Philip Rahv's essay "The Myth and the Powerhouse," which first appeared in 1953. Rahv argues convincingly that the present "cultic interest in myth" is actually a withdrawal from the challenge of historical change and development "which destroys custom and tradition in producing the future." He objects to the type of literary approach to myth which invests it "with all sorts of intriguing suggestions of holiness and sacramental significance." There is no question that Rahv's attack on such cultism and preten-tious mysticism in certain modern approaches to myth is salutary. Literary critics, moreover, are by no means the only offenders in this facile game. One could add to Rahv's list the many abuses of myth by pseudo-philosophical and pseudo-psychological mythomaniacs. But Rahv's essay, while valuable as an exposure of the misuse of myth, is also onesided and in some respects misleading. His state-ment that the "appeal" of myth "lies precisely in its archaism"[31] is an oversimplification, referable only to those who seek in Jungian archetypes a substitute for established religion or, like Mircea Eliade, romanticize archaic man's periodic return through myth to what took place *in illo tempore* in order to "renew the world," regretting that this *regressus ad originem* is unavailable to modern Western man.[32] This is certainly one of the ways in which myth is adapted and often distorted in our time. Those who seek to revitalize ancient myth in the twentieth century by reading into it mystical, philo-sophical, or religious significance only distort its function and mean-

---

is no mere flight of literary or artistic fancy. . . ." (*Thespis: Ritual, Myth and Drama in the Ancient Near East* [New York, 1950], p. 5). Though it is undeniable that myth and literature have many differences, it is fair to say that the impulse which inspires literature is no mere flight of literary fancy either.

[31] *Myth and Literature*, pp. 109-11.

[32] *Myth and Reality*, trans. from the French by Willard Trask (New York, 1963), p. 45; *The Sacred and the Profane*, pp. 203-204. For an excellent discussion and criticism of Eliade's views on myth, see Herbert Weisinger, *The Agony and the Triumph*, pp. 206-208.

ing; they avoid understanding myth as it actually functions by seeking to impose on it a dogmatic significance it never had and a mystical meaning it can no longer support.

But the approach of the cultists is by no means the only or the most important development of myth in modern thought and language. Their excessive demands on myth make them incapable of seeing its real potentialities, and their attempts to revive functions of myth which are anachronistic and useless in contemporary society indicate a reaction against recent scientific approaches to myth as a pattern or structure which elucidates human consciousness and behavior. Today when "the sun is too interesting as an object, a source of transformable energies to be interpreted as a god, a hero, or a symbol of passion,"[33] myth can serve to express and clarify man's response and adaptation to a world he attempts to understand mainly through scientific investigation, with less and less interference from fantasy and fear. It was Freud who first recognized that myth could reveal the unconscious conflicts and terrors it displaced with omnipotence. He employed its language as scientific terminology and invented "scientific myths" to describe his discoveries about the nature and development of man.

Fruitful investigations of myth in recent times have been made by Claude Lévi-Strauss who, clearly influenced by Freud, has attempted to discover a structural basis for myth and to work out its "constituent units" or "mythemes," combinations of elements in myth which produce a coherent pattern. His point of view is essentially anthropological, but his insights and conclusions are important to all students of myth and especially to those concerned with psychology or literature. Lévi-Strauss does not restrict his investigation of myths to those found in primitive society. In fact he says, "The mythical value of myth is preserved even through the worst translation." He describes a myth "as consisting of all its versions; or to put it otherwise, a myth remains the same as long as it is felt as such."[34]

In a comparison of psychoanalysis with shamanism, Lévi-Strauss

[33] *Philosophy in a New Key*, p. 279.

[34] *Structural Anthropology*, trans. from the French by Claire Jacobson and Brooke Drundfest Schoepf (New York, 1963), pp. 210-17.

makes some important contributions to a theory of myth, one of the most valuable of which is his suggestion that situations in life may be traumatic because "the subject experiences them immediately as living myth." It is not the actual situation or event that is necessarily painful, but rather the fact that a person experiences it in relation to a "pre-existing structure." He goes on to explain:

> For the neurotic, all psychic life and all subsequent experiences are organized in terms of an exclusive or predominant structure, under the catalytic action of the initial myth. But this structure, as well as other structures which the neurotic relegates to a subordinate position, are to be found also in the normal human being, whether primitive or civilized. These structures as an aggregate form what we call the unconscious.

Lévi-Strauss's conclusion that "the unconscious . . . is always empty," being merely a function which imposes structure upon feelings and memories,[35] is, however, unconvincing. In fact, in his recent book *The Raw and the Cooked*, his attempt to create a "science of mythology" is impeded by his narrow and arbitrary conception of the human mind. In "drawing up an inventory of mental patterns" in order to discover "the laws operating at a deeper level" than the conscious one, he is sometimes so caught up in his own system that he ignores or treats superficially contents of myth that are clearly the product of unconscious drives.[36]

[35] *ibid.*, pp. 202-203.

[36] See, for example, his approach to the theme of incest in the "key myth" of the Bororo Indians, which is the "connecting thread" throughout his investigation. Though the myth deals almost entirely with son-mother incest and the various trials and "mortal danger" the son is ordered to undergo by his father, Lévi-Strauss sees evidence of a "curious indifference to incest" in this myth (*The Raw and the Cooked*, trans. from the French by John and Doreen Weightman [New York, 1969], pp. 1-48). This interpretation is based on the absence in the myth of any apparent guilt on the part of the son, who finally kills his father. Although, on an obvious level, it is possible to regard "the incestuous person . . . as the victim, while the person offended against is punished for having taken revenge or for having planned to do so" (p. 81), it is also fairly clear that the myth narrates the enactment of forbidden unconscious wishes and a difficult escape from "mortal danger" and dreadful punishment and pain through omnipotence. The son survives

There is more empirical evidence to support a structural theory of myth when that theory is based on the assumption that the unconscious contains repressed instinctual drives and memories which express themselves in mythical forms and constructions, and can in turn be depicted consciously in mythical narrative. In studying the reappearance of ancient myth in modern poetry it is possible to see how unconscious drives convert experience into a mythical pattern. Thus, ancient myth can reappear in the report of an everyday event when that event has been transformed in the mind or in words into a narration fitting a mythical pattern of omnipotence, compulsion, or guilt. Since the narrative structure of myth is particularly suited for endless adaptation in the expression of unconscious feelings and drives, it has evolved, like language, to the needs of contemporary society.

In *Civilization and its Discontents*, Freud discusses ancient man's projection of his desire for omniscience and omnipotence on gods who personified his ideal of these characteristics. In today's civilization science and technology have provided for man the means to become "almost . . . a god himself," but the ideal has been only partially fulfilled. Man has become, as Freud brilliantly describes it, "a kind of prosthetic God. When he puts on all his auxiliary organs he is truly magnificent, but these organs have not grown on to him and they still give him much trouble at times." An unwilling prophet, Freud nonetheless predicted one of the apparently insoluble problems of the twentieth century when he spoke of man's inability to achieve contentment in his "Godlike character."[37]

A significant theme of contemporary poetry is this spiritual

---

the ordeals to which his father subjects him through the supernatural aid of animals and insects and a magic wand. He undergoes suspension "in the void" and an attack of vultures who gnaw away his rectum, which he himself restores (p. 36). Lévi-Strauss's judgment that "In the long run, it is the father who appears guilty" (p. 48) is questionable; his death seems his final victimization by his omnipotent son rather than a deserved punishment. For further discussion of this myth and an evaluation of the "limits of the structural approach," from another point of view see Kirk, *Myth, Its Meaning and Functions in Ancient and Other Cultures*, Chapter II.

[37] SE XXI, 91-92.

wretchedness of the "prosthetic God," suspicious of the very instruments of his superiority and helpless against the gods within, the instinctual drives which Freud called "mythical entities,"[38] more powerful than any prostheses and all too eager to take them in hand. Many poets of the twentieth century, in expressing their fears about both the instruments man has perfected and the instincts he has just begun to understand, have employed traditional myth thus transformed into a modern language which can depict both the continuous struggle of the instincts for mastery and the threat of an ancient dream of omnipotence fulfilled.

One of the values of restricting a study of myth to its appearance in ancient Greek and Latin literature, and investigating its various functions in contemporary poetry is that it allows one to observe the continuity of as well as the changes in the form. One need not yearn for a revival of "true" myth; it is very much alive in contemporary music, art, and literature, the chief forms in which it remains vital at present. In twentieth-century poetry myth offers many valuable clues to contemporary thought, to poetic techniques and themes, and finally to its own limitations and powers. In an age whose intellectual endeavors and whose values are determined largely by science and technology, myth continues to function, recording and interpreting the personal and universal history of man's inner life; it is the language of that history, surviving the loss of sacred ritual, the prettifying of poetasters and advertisers, the impassioned attacks by "realists," and the pretensions and distortions of mythologizers—and remaining irreplaceable.

[38] *New Introductory Lectures*, SE XXII, 95.

II

FREUD AND JUNG ON MYTH
The Psychoanalytic Background

SOME years ago the journal *Arion* published a series of answers by well-known writers to its questionnaire on the classics and the contemporary man of letters. In response to a rather involved question as to whether Greece and Rome, which "provided valid cultural myths" in the past, or any "new . . . mythologizations of the ancient world" could "survive our much greater historical knowledge," Iris Murdoch replied with the two words, "Ask Freud."[1] She was speaking for many twentieth-century writers. When Freud took as his epigraph to *The Interpretation of Dreams* the statement in *Aeneid* VII, 312, uttered by Juno, the only major deity in Vergil who retains her instinctual aggression, "Flectere si nequeo superos, Acheronta movebo," he probably could not have predicted the extent to which he was to arouse the gods of the underworld or open the realm of the unconscious to writers of his own time and the future. Yet, in declaring his intention of moving hell itself in his quest for knowledge of the nature of man, Freud reveals the imagination and courage that attracted so many contemporary poets not only to his explorations of the unconscious but to myth, revitalized by his influence into a new form of expression.

Freud's use of the myth of Oedipus to describe and define in concrete terms a psychic conflict common to all men and pathological in some is the most dramatic of the developments that characterize the twentieth-century preoccupation with myth. Of course, Freud's is by no means the only significant contribution to the field. Frazer's

[1] *Arion* III, 4 (Winter 1964), 67.

The Golden Bough opened a new approach to anthropologists and classicists, as well as to poets.[2] Jung's studies of archetypal patterns represent a far more elaborate investigation of myth than either Freud's or Fraser's. Otto Rank and others influenced by Freud developed theories to explain the births of culture heroes and other typical features of ancient myth. Yet the strongest influence on twentieth-century poets' interpretation and use of myth was Freud's; though he did not set out systematically to investigate this field, but used myth occasionally for evidence and illustration in his psychoanalytical writings and exploited its possibilities as a vehicle of expression, myth, like so many areas which Freud touched on only indirectly, was altered forever by his influence. Two pervading changes produced in twentieth-century approaches to myth directly traceable to the writings of Freud and the widespread response to psychoanalysis are the acceptance of myth as an expression of unconscious wish, fear, and instinctual drives, and the use of myth as an analytical device, which can reveal truth through its unique illusions and distortions.

As is well known, Freud found confirmation for his discovery of childhood incestuous desires for one parent and consequent hatred of the other in Sophocles' *Oedipus Tyrannus*, the action of which, he says, can be compared with the process of psychoanalysis in its revelations "with cunning delays and ever-mounting excitement" of the truth of Oedipus' terrible crimes. Freud rejects the explanation that the tragic effect of the *Oedipus Tyrannus* lies in "the contrast between the supreme will of the gods and the vain attempts of mankind to escape the evil that threatens them." He observes that the playwrights of his time producing plays with similar themes failed to affect their audience, while the *Oedipus Tyrannus* continues to move "a modern audience no less than it did the contemporary Greek one." It is the "particular nature of the material" of the play, says Freud, in other words, the myth, to which all ages respond; our dreams indicate that the story of Oedipus is an enactment of unconscious and unfulfilled childhood wishes.[3]

[2] Frazer's influence on myth is discussed below, in Chapter IV.
[3] *The Interpretation of Dreams*, SE iv, 261-62.

Freud employed the mythical material dramatized by Sophocles to substantiate the evidence he had collected from dreams and neurotic symptoms of the existence of what he named the Oedipus complex. His choice of the name is itself a striking indication that for him the myth so perfectly illustrated unconscious drives and guilts that it served as a precise and economical mode of expression, a type of analytic formula. Furthermore, Freud was drawn to the difficult and devious search for truth contained in the story of Oedipus, at least as Sophocles interprets it. This myth, like many others, contains within its fantastic episodes clues to latent truths about human behavior, but, more explicitly than most, it deals with a contest between the yearning for the limited consolations of self-deception and the necessity for self-knowledge, even at the cost of anguish.

In the *Oedipus Tyrannus* Freud was struck by Jocasta's attempt to allay Oedipus' fears of the prophecy that he was doomed to engage in sexual intercourse with his mother by assuring him: "Many men in dreams have lain with their mother. But he to whom these things are as nothing bears his life most easily." To Freud this is "an unmistakable indication in the text of Sophocles' tragedy itself that the legend of Oedipus sprang from some primaeval dream-material which had as its content the distressing disturbance of a child's relation to his parents owing to the first stirrings of sexuality." In asserting, moreover, that it is "the fate of all of us" in childhood to experience the incestuous and murderous wishes toward our parents enacted in the myth of Oedipus, he declares, "Our dreams convince us that that is so."[4]

Throughout Freud's work one finds indications of this interest in the relationship between myth and dreams. In discussing symbols elsewhere in *The Interpretation of Dreams*, he says, "Many of the beasts which are used as genital symbols in mythology and folklore play the same part in dreams: e.g. fishes, snails, cats, mice (on account of the pubic hair), and above all those most important symbols of the male organ—snakes."[5] He sees further similarities in dreams and myths dealing with a child's entry into water; these

[4] *ibid.*, SE IV, 262-64.   [5] *ibid.*, SE V, 357.

he views as a distorted representation of "the delivery of the child *from* the uterine waters," and lists "the births of Adonis, Osiris, Moses, and Bacchus" as examples.[6]

Freud regarded the incident in Homer's Odyssey in which Odysseus appears naked before Nausicaä as related to a dream of anxiety. Commenting on this episode, Freud offers one of his many tributes to the power of poets to evoke remnants of a mythical past which lies buried in the human unconscious: "The deepest and eternal nature of man, upon whose evocation in his hearers the poet is accustomed to rely, lies in those impulses of the mind which have their roots in a childhood that has since become prehistoric." In this passage dream and myth are equated in their power to reveal feelings too painful for conscious awareness: "Suppressed and forbidden wishes from childhood break through in the dream behind the exile's unobjectionable wishes which are capable of entering consciousness; and that is why the dream which finds concrete expression in the legend of Nausicaä ends as a rule as an anxiety-dream."[7]

In the preface to the third edition of *The Interpretation of Dreams*, Freud says that future editions will have to "afford closer contact with the copious material presented in imaginative writing, in myths, in linguistic usage and in folklore,"[8] his main purpose, of course, being the clarification of dreams through such material. In *New Introductory Lectures on Psychoanalysis*, however, he reveals his interest in the elucidation of myths through the insight that dreams provide: "In the manifest content of dreams we very often find pictures and situations recalling familiar themes in fairy tales, legends and myths. The interpretation of such dreams thus throws a light on the original interests which created these themes." Though he is careful to point out that the meanings of myths and legends change in the course of time, he feels that the interpretation of dreams can elucidate "mythological themes in particular." As

[6] *ibid.*, SE v, 401.
[7] *ibid.*, SE iv, 246-47. See also *The Psychopathology of Everyday Life*, SE vi, 107.
[8] SE iv, xxvii.

an example he suggests that "the Labyrinth can be recognized as a representation of anal birth: the twisting paths are the bowels and Ariadne's thread is the umbilical cord."[9]

Freud turned to myths, legends, and fairy tales for material illustrative of basic human instincts, conflicts, and yearnings. The antagonism between Kronos and Zeus, for example, provided, as did the story of Oedipus, dramatic evidence of the inherent rivalry between father and son.[10] Freud's discussion of the Moirai (Fates) in his essay "The Theme of the Three Caskets" is a brilliant analysis of the human need to create myth and the way in which myth functions both to disguise and to expose reality: "The Moerae were created as a result of a discovery that warned man that he too is a part of nature and therefore subject to the immutable law of death." Freud then shows how, in his unwillingness to accept this limitation, man created a myth derived from that of the Moirai, "in which the Goddess of Death was replaced by the Goddess of Love."

He deals with the connection between Aphrodite, Persephone, and the "triform Artemis-Hecate," and remarks, "The great Mother-goddesses of the oriental peoples . . . all seem to have been both creators and destroyers—both goddesses of life and fertility and goddesses of death."[11] The connection between death goddess and love goddess, the goddesses of double function (productivity and destruction), and the various choices in literature (Paris' choice of Aphrodite, Portia's choice of the leaden casket, Lear's choice of Cordelia) is that all reveal the human compulsion to bring about a "wished-for reversal" of reality. "Choice stands in the place of necessity, of destiny. In this way man overcomes death, which he has recognized intellectually. No greater triumph of wish-fulfillment is conceivable. A choice is made where in reality there is obedience

---

[9] SE XXII, 25.

[10] *The Interpretation of Dreams*, SE IV, 256. In this passage Freud says that Zeus "emasculated his father." In the second edition (1909) he added a footnote, indicating his awareness that this version of the story appears in some myths, whereas others tell only of the emasculation of Uranus by Kronos. In *The Psychopathology of Everyday Life*, he discusses his "error" and explains its psychological basis (SE VI, 218-20).

[11] SE XII, 299.

to a compulsion."[12] Though man may use such mythical constructions to obscure the truth, ultimately they offer him insight into the very limitations he sought to avoid in creating them and knowledge of the way his mind functions in its efforts to reform the conditions of life. Freud ends the essay with a discussion of Lear, in which he says, "Eternal wisdom, clothed in the primaeval myth, bids the old man renounce love, choose death and make friends with the necessity of dying."[13]

Freud's interpretations of particular myths are always original and sometimes startling in their revelations about the literary works in which they appear; but his actual references to myth itself are not the main source of his profound effect on the field. His method of probing unconscious conflict through free association, his remarks on fantasy and daydreaming, his discussion of displacement and condensation, the devices employed in dream, his whole approach to the imagination and the non-rational life of the mind—all indicated new uses for myth as a guide for exploring the past of civilizations and individuals and new possibilities for myth as a poetic language.

His essay "Creative Writers and Daydreaming" is especially interesting in this connection. He compares the child at play to the imaginative writer, who "rearranges the things of his world in a new way that pleases him." The adult's substitute for play, says Freud, is fantasy or daydreaming, which is generally erotic or ambitious. His discussion of the relationship of fantasy and time is of utmost importance not only in understanding how man employs fantasy as an ally in his struggle against his most pressing limitation, but also in determining how time operates in myth and poetry:

We may say that it [fantasy] hovers, as it were, between three times—the three moments of time which our ideation involves. Mental work is linked to some current impression, some provoking occasion in the present which has been able to arouse one of the subject's major wishes. From there it harks back to

[12] SE XII, 299. Cf. the discussion of Achilles' choice, above, p. 24.
[13] SE XII, 301.

a memory of an earlier experience (usually an infantile one) in which this wish was fulfilled; and it now creates a situation relating to the future which represents a fulfillment of the wish. What it thus creates is a day-dream or phantasy, which carries about it traces of its origin from the occasion which provoked it and from the memory. Thus, past, present, and future are strung together, as it were, on the thread of the wish that runs through them.[14]

Freud then shows how similar the imaginative writer is to the daydreamer, though he is well aware that the aesthetic quality of the writer's production transforms its nature as well as its effect. In turning to literature based on traditional material, Freud speaks of myths, legends, and fairy tales as a "popular treasure-house," "constructions of folk psychology"; myths, he believes, "are distorted vestiges of the wishful phantasies of whole nations—the *secular dreams* of youthful humanity."[15]

Always the characters, incidents, and symbols of myth and legend are to Freud a source of knowledge about human assumptions, feelings, and drives unexpressed on a conscious level. Recognizing myths as remnants of "archaic modes of thought,"[16] he used them to suggest the persistence of such primitive patterns of thought in the unconscious. Speaking of repressed unconscious wishes in *The Interpretation of Dreams*, he describes them as "immortal," like the "legendary Titans, weighed down since primaeval ages by the massive bulk of the mountains which were once hurled upon them by the victorious gods and which are still shaken from time to time by the convulsion of their limbs."[17]

As early as 1901, in *The Psychopathology of Everyday Life*, Freud suggests that myth, like superstition, expresses "conscious ignorance and unconscious knowledge," and thus is potentially a valuable psychological instrument:

[14] SE IX, 143-48.
[15] SE IX, 152.
[16] "Character and Anal Erotism," SE IX, 174.
[17] SE V, 553.

In point of fact I believe that a large part of the mythological view of the world, which extends a long way into the most modern religions, *is nothing but psychology projected into the external world.* The obscure recognition (the endopsychic perception, as it were) of psychical factors and relations in the unconscious is mirrored—it is difficult to express it in other terms, and here the analogy with paranoia must come to our aid—in the construction of a *supernatural reality,* which is destined to be changed back once more by science into the *psychology of the unconscious.*[18]

This is an early indication of an awareness, which seems to develop throughout Freud's writings, that not only could surviving myth be employed as a clue to the human past but that its methods could be imitated and the process of investigation be reversed: a consciously devised mythological construction could provide a foundation for further exploration and description of the psychical history and continuous inner experience of man.

He perceived in his experience with the delusions of the sick a "mythological method" which he himself was to adapt and transform into a scientific terminology and method. In the revelations of the paranoiac Schreber, who regarded the sun as God or, as Freud interprets it, "a sublimated symbol for the father," and was proud of his ability to "gaze at it without any difficulty," Freud recognized a resemblance to the traditional myth that eagles had the peculiar ability to look directly at the sun, a myth which reflected a totemic origin. Schreber in his illness had "rediscovered the mythological method" which at once expressed his delusion and revealed its nature. For Freud this parallel offered evidence of "a psycho-analytic explanation of the origins of religion" and a clue to understanding individual psychic disorders.[19]

Freud himself created two comprehensive myths, both of which he described as such and employed as scientific structures of the unconscious of the individual and the species. The first, which he develops in *Totem and Taboo* and refers to as his "scientific myth" in

[18] SE VI, 258-59.
[19] "Psycho-analytic Notes upon an Autobiographical Account of a Case of Paranoia (Dementia Paranoides)," SE XII, 54-82.

Group Psychology and the Analysis of the Ego,[20] is that of the primal horde, the sons who banded together to kill and consume the father, whom they then commemorated in a totem meal, "the beginnings of so many things—of social organization, of moral restrictions and of religion." Freud's hypothesis leads him to the conclusion that "in the beginning was the Deed," a clear attempt to replace the Hebrew-Christian conception of "supernatural reality" with a psychological explanation which, he conjectures, has roots in primitive history. His view is that the burden of guilt for the murder of the father is borne by all the descendants of the primal horde, for whom it has become "psychical reality."[21] Thus, a scientific myth both explains and supersedes a religious one.

It is well known that Freud's theory of the primal horde is unacceptable to most anthropologists, and apparently even Freud's defenders do not perceive the essential function of the historical-mythical narrative he describes so effectively. Freud was the first to admit that there is no way of discovering factual evidence of the murder of the primal father by his sons.[22] Such evidence, moreover, is not his real concern. When Freud speaks of his account of the murderous and cannibalistic deeds of the primal horde as a "scientific myth," he is not using the term myth in its popular sense to mean a distortion of the truth; nor is he trying to avoid the problem of defending his position without available evidence. He means exactly what he says: he has invented a method of applying mythical techniques in the service of science to investigate inner or psychical reality.

To call his use of myth "euhemerist"[23] is to oversimplify and reduce one of his most impressive and original techniques. The Euhemerist

---

[20] SE xviii, 135.

[21] *Totem and Taboo*, SE xiii, 140-61.

[22] In *Totem and Taboo* Freud discusses the evolution of his "hypothesis," which derives from theories of Darwin, Atkinson, and Robertson Smith; he apologizes for his "lack of precision," and adds, "It would be as foolish to aim at exactitude in such questions as it would be unfair to insist upon certainty" (SE xiii, *footnote*, 142-43). In *Group Psychology and the Analysis of the Ego* he again refers to the conception of the primal horde as "a hypothesis" and quotes "a not unkind" critic's reference to it as a "Just-So Story" (SE xviii, 122).

[23] Philip Rieff, *Freud, the Mind of the Moralist* (London, 1960), p. 193.

attempts to explain existing myths on the basis of past historical events; he believes that heroes of the past were deified out of gratitude for their accomplishments. This approach is entirely historical, accounting for the existence of myth on a simple, rational basis. Freud, on the other hand, invents a myth in which the narrative or "deed" constructs and explains psychological and historical conditions that could have determined the development of the human psyche. Thus, the myth of the primal horde tells of a "Deed" which helps to elucidate the "*Historical* reality" of infantile murderous impulses.[24] Primitive man's lack of inhibition may have made it possible for him to commit the monstrous murder, whereas the infant is capable only of violent impulses, but for both, deed or wish creates a historical past which determines their future inner experience and their behavior in the external world. Freud's approach to history is not the simple and factual one of the Euhemerist; his scientific myth is a hypothetical case history of the unconscious mind of the human race, in which the memory of all deeds and thoughts is timeless, continuous, and dynamic.

The scientific myth he invented also suggested to Freud the productive role of myth in early society: "The myth, then, is the step by which the individual emerges from group psychology. The first myth was certainly the psychological, the hero myth." Freud envisions the poet setting "himself free from the group in his imagination" through the creation of the hero myth, in which the hero is the poet's idealized self, who alone freed the horde from the tyranny of the primal father. This hero myth is a distortion, "a lie,"[25] but it provides a clue to the history of man's development and a means of release for individual imagination, thought, and artistry.

Throughout his work Freud continued to draw upon existing myth and to adapt its structure and meaning to his own scientific purpose. In *Beyond the Pleasure Principle*, illustrating the point that an instinct is a drive "*inherent in organic life to restore an earlier state of things*,"[26] Freud turns to "a myth rather than to a scientific

[24] *Totem and Taboo*, SE XIII, 161.
[25] *Group Psychology and the Analysis of the Ego*, SE XVIII, 136-37.
[26] SE XVIII, 36.

43

explanation" because the former "fulfills precisely the one condition whose fulfillment we desire."[27] The myth, of course, is Aristophanes' explanation in the Symposium of the origin of the sexual instinct in the strivings of split human beings to unite again.[28]

It was in connection with his theory of the instincts that Freud developed his most brilliant mythical invention, the comprehensive abstractions, Eros and Thanatos. In "Why War?" he refers to "our mythological theory of instincts,"[29] and in *New Introductory Lectures* he writes of the "theory of instincts" as "our mythology." In the latter work he goes on to say, "Instincts are mythical entities, magnificent in their indefiniteness."[30] Freud's use of the word "mythical" in this context has been defended, with some justice, as an indication of his awareness of "the contingent nature of scientific laws and of scientific theory."[31] His rhetorical questions to Einstein: "But does not every science come in the end to a kind of mythology like this? Cannot the same be said today of your own Physics?"[32] do support the view that the mythical for him suggests the theoretical and the abstract. But Freud's earlier interpretation and use of myth and his narrative development of the mythical entities Eros and Thanatos indicate that a mythical frame of reference also provides him with the terminology he requires to describe essential components of man's nature, as old as human life yet never before defined or analyzed.

By employing the language of myth, Freud, like Einstein, creates a symbolic structure—a comprehensive psychological equation—which opens up the possibilities of further scientific knowledge and avoids any suggestion that he is setting down eternal truth. He himself had discovered the scientific implications of the Oedipus myth more than two thousand years after its origin and had retained its

---

[27] SE xviii, 57.

[28] Freud refers to this myth again in *Three Essays on the Theory of Sexuality*, SE vii, 136.

[29] SE xxii, 212.   [30] SE xxii, 95.

[31] Sidney Axelrad, "The Straw Couch: Some Misunderstandings of Freudian Theory and Technique," *The American Journal of Orthopsychiatry* xxvi, No. 2 (April, 1956), 412.

[32] "Why War?" SE xxii, 211.

name as a psychological symbol; other myths had disclosed to him secrets hidden in the unconscious for countless centuries. Having invented the method of using traditional myth as a scientific symbol, he now takes up a conventional figure and concept, Eros, and, aware of its centuries of accumulated connotation, employs it to describe the creative energy of all life. To symbolize the nature of its opposite, the instinct of death, more comprehensive and more terrible than any individual experience or fantasy of death, Freud recreates the ancient figure Thanatos as a mythical construct. He thus invents a new scientific myth, which describes the instincts and suggests their limitless capacity to evade our understanding and control.

Like myths, the instincts in a language of their own tell a story inexpressible merely through rational discourse. Dreams, physical struggle, violence, and tenderness, physiological signs and symptoms, and imaginative creation are only some of the expressions of their power, which, despite the most severe repression, finds an ingenious form of escape. Furthermore, the instincts are mythical because they are the "archaic heritage"[33] of civilization. Like myth, they have a continuous vitality in the history of phylogenetic and individual experience. The instinctual is mythical in its grandeur and its universality; emerging from the "psychical underworld," it makes itself manifest in the "open market-place."[34]

Freud maintains that there are "two essentially different classes of instincts: the sexual instincts, understood in the widest sense—Eros, if you prefer that name—and the aggressive instincts, whose aim is destruction." Aggressiveness turned upon the self becomes "an expression of a 'death instinct.' "[35] Thus, the erotic, or life instinct, and the death instinct, directed either inward or outward, constitute the basic impulses or drives within the human psyche. Freud's "mythical entities," like Lucretius' Venus and Mars, are the insistent energy and force of all animal and human life.

In *Civilization and its Discontents*, a slightly earlier work than *New Introductory Lectures*, Freud uses his own mythical abstrac-

---

[33] *Moses and Monotheism*, SE XXIII, 101.
[34] *New Introductory Lectures*, SE XXII, 110.
[35] *ibid.*, SE XXII, 103-107.

tions and something of the narrative technique of traditional myth to describe the conflict between the insistent demands of the instincts and the inhibitory requirements of civilization. Analyzing the foundation of communal life, he presents his material in mythical terms: "Eros and Ananke [Love and Necessity] have become the parents of human civilization. . . ."[36] Like the all-beneficent God of Hebrew and Christian myth, Eros and Ananke made it possible for man to enjoy the earth. Freud refers to them as "these two great powers" who "were cooperating" as men learned "to live together in a community." He builds the suspense of his narrative as he comments: "Nor is it easy to understand how this civilization could act upon its participants otherwise than to make them happy," and before seeking "from what quarter an interference might arise," he digresses to examine the complex nature of Eros.[37]

Slowly Freud leads up to the great and inevitable struggle between Eros and aggressiveness. Since "the aggressive instinct is the derivative and the main representative of the death instinct," this is actually a conflict between Eros and Thanatos. Freud's depiction of this struggle is stark and dramatic; it is a "battle of the giants that our nursemaids try to appease with their lullaby about Heaven."[38] His tone is tragic as he enlarges on the condition of man, caught forever in this conflict between the two forces that forever define his nature. The "eternal struggle" within him creates the sense of guilt which continually torments him, and is the price he pays for his civilization, which results only when man's deepest aggressive instincts are curbed.[39]

Like a tragic dramatist, Freud offers man no consolation; he ends *Civilization and its Discontents* with the "fateful question" of whether men's "cultural development will succeed in mastering the disturbance of their communal life by the human instinct of ag-

[36] SE XXI, 101. In *Beyond the Pleasure Principle* Freud also mythicizes Necessity, referring to it as "a remorseless law of nature, . . . sublime 'Ανάγχη" (SE XVIII, 45).

[37] SE XXI, 101. Freud's conception of Eros is discussed below in connection with the poetry of Auden.

[38] SE XXI, 122.   [39] SE XXI, 132-33.

gression and self-destruction." The hope is that "eternal Eros" will be a match for his "equally immortal adversary."[40] Freud's "immortals," his mythical adversaries, are the instincts. He uses the mythical method here as an analytical tool for disclosing the nature of warring instincts, but it hardly seems possible to avoid the light these mythical adversaries inadvertently shed on the true nature of earlier ones, such as Venus and Mars and God and Satan, who had similar attributes.

In his essay "The Acquisition and Control of Fire," Freud interprets the myth of Prometheus' punishment for giving fire to man as an expression of instinctual drive and repression. Freud first deals with another myth about Prometheus—the story in Hesiod of how, when men were faced with the problem of sharing a sacrificial animal with the gods, Prometheus aided them by concealing the best parts of a slain ox in its hide and wrapping the bones in fat, in this way tricking Zeus into choosing the less desirable parts of the animal. The gods were thus defrauded. The parallel Freud sees between this myth and the more widely known and more complicated myth of Prometheus' theft of fire suggests to him an explanation of why the Titan was punished for bestowing this gift on mankind. Freud assumes that "in myths the gods are granted the satisfaction of all the desires which human creatures have to renounce." Therefore, "in analytic terms, . . . instinctual life—the id—is the god who is defrauded" through Prometheus' second act of kindness to man, the provision of fire, or, as Freud puts it, "when the quenching of fires is renounced." Freud considers the gratification which results from extinguishing fires through urination a primitive sexual one which had to be renounced for man's attainment of control over fire and his achievement of progress. The myth reveals not only man's reluctant acceptance of the necessity of renouncing instinctual satisfactions but also his recognition of the "indestructibility" of instinctual drives.

The significant point here in connection with Freud's approach to myth is his explicit statement and concrete examples of myth as

[40] SE XXI, 145.

an expression of the instincts. He says, "in the legend, a human desire is transformed into a divine privilege. But in the legend the deity possesses nothing of the characteristics of a super-ego: he is still the representative of the paramount life of the instincts." Prometheus' punishment, moreover, is an expression of the resentment "men driven by their instincts" would inevitably feel at the "instinctual renunciation" of the hero.[41]

Freud made no claim to certainty about either the origin or the essential function of myth. Observing that some myths describe and illustrate instinctual drives and "mental processes,"[42] he speculated on whether this was not a general characteristic. Essentially, however, his contribution to myth lies in his own use of traditional myth to express and elucidate his discoveries about the human psyche, his understanding of the relation between myth and dreams, his conception of unconscious feelings and instincts as mythical in their universality and continuity, and, finally and most broadly, in his exploration of the unconscious mind and the nature and function of dream. In all these ways Freud opened new pathways for scientific studies of myth and poetic adaptations of it.

"The contrast between Freud and myself," says C. J. Jung, "goes back to essential differences in our basic assumptions." Underlying all Jung's assumptions is one which permeates his entire psychology and which certainly is irrelevant to the Freudian conception of human desire and motivation: that modern man is faced with "the necessity of rediscovering the life of the spirit," a term Jung does not define but uses to indicate religious faith in a supernatural agency or power. It is this assumption that determines Jung's approach to myth and his effort to reestablish something of its ancient religious character and function in modern society.

Jung assumes that there is in all men a basic conflict or "collision" between the "natural instincts" and the "spirit," both of which he regards as "powerful forces whose nature we do not know." Religion, he asserts, has a "positive value" because it provides a means of "dealing with the forces of the inner life." Thus, he discusses "cere-

[41] SE XXII, 188-91.   [42] SE XXII, 191.

monial, ritual, initiation rites and ascetic practices" as "techniques for bringing about a proper relation to these forces."

The theory that "psychic energy involves the play of opposites" is developed in connection with the opposition between the bonds of the flesh and the "opposite urge of life, the spirit." Jung regards primitive initiation rites as the first step in "man's advance toward a spiritual life," a continuous process, "the wheel of history" which, he warns, "must not be turned back." Lacking a spiritual base, man's life becomes sterile and neurotic. Jung ends this discussion with an expression of hope for spiritual rebirth: "Ever and again human beings arise who understand what is meant by the fact that God is our father. The equal balance of the flesh and spirit is not lost to the world."[43]

This assumption that man yearns for some spiritual meaning in life—some direction from a supernatural force—is developed more fully in Jung's writings on myth. He feels that poets are in touch with a reality beyond that which the rational mind can perceive, for they have discovered "the spirits, demons, and gods." Poets know "that a purposiveness out-reaching human ends is the life-giving secret for man."[44] In Jung's view psychic truth is actually a step toward spiritual fulfillment, and myth is an instrument which can bring about a union between the unconscious and the supernatural.

Myth is an essential element in Jung's conception of the "collective unconscious," the contents of which are not personal but general, resulting from "the inherited brain-structure. These are the mythological associations—those motives and images which can spring anew in every age and clime, without historical tradition or migration."[45] Another term that Jung uses for mythological associations is "archetypes of the collective unconscious," which he regards as universal patterns of behavior expressed in mythical forms:

[43] *Modern Man in Search of a Soul*, trans. from the German by W. S. Dell and Cary F. Baynes (New York, 1934), pp. 136-42.

[44] *ibid.*, p. 188.

[45] *Psychological Types*, trans. from the German by H. Godwin Baynes (London, 1946), p. 616.

"The archetype . . . is a psychic organ present in all of us."[46] Thus, the collective unconscious is "a universal homogeneous substratum whose homogeneity extends into a world-wide identity or similarity of myths and fairy tales; so that a negro of the Southern States of America dreams in the motives of Grecian mythology, and a Swiss grocer's apprentice repeats in his psychosis, the vision of an Egyptian Gnostic."[47]

Of course, mythical expressions of archetypal experience as they appear in poetry, art, or religion are transformed into "conscious formulas"; even in such forms, however, they provide clues to unconscious experience, and they open an avenue through which man may return to what Jung believes is not only an older but a deeper level of reality. In "The Psychology of the Child Archetype," a chapter in *Essays on a Science of Mythology*, written in conjunction with C. Kerényi, Jung says that "Myths are original revelations of the preconscious psyche, involuntary statements about unconscious psychic happenings; . . . they *are* the psychic life of the primitive tribe, which immediately falls to pieces and decays when it loses its mythological heritage, like a man who has lost his soul." Jung assumes that the urgent demands of the unconscious are satisfactorily expressed in religious experience: "A tribe's mythology is its living religion, whose loss is always and everywhere, even among the civilized, a moral catastrophe. But religion is a vital link with psychic processes independent of and beyond consciousness, in the dark hinterland of the psyche."[48]

It is not only for primitive man that religion performs the function of unifying conscious and unconscious experience; Jung believes that orthodox Christianity can also serve this purpose:

> Dogma takes the place of the collective unconscious by formulating its contents on a grand scale. The Catholic way of life is completely unaware of psychological problems in this sense.

[46] C. G. Jung and C. Kerényi, *Essays on a Science of Mythology*, trans. from the German by R.F.C. Hull, rev. ed. (New York, 1963), p. 79.
[47] *Psychological Types*, p. 624.
[48] *Essays on a Science of Mythology*, p. 73.

Almost the entire life of the collective unconscious has been channeled into the dogmatic archetypal ideas and flows along like a well-controlled stream in the symbolism of creed and ritual. It manifests itself in the inwardness of the Catholic psyche.

Jung deplores the effects of the "enlightened consciousness" of Protestantism, which he holds responsible for the loss of power of traditional Christian symbol and rite and for "the alarming poverty of symbol that is now the condition of our life." In his view, "we are, surely, the rightful heirs of Christian symbolism, but somehow we have squandered this heritage."[49] He regards myth, religion, and unconscious psychological forces as essentially inseparable, since he believes that religion both releases and channels unconscious experience, which is expressed in mythical archetypes.

Jung's definitions of religion include attitudes which seem dissimilar: on the one hand, he describes as religious a general feeling of devotion or allegiance,[50] and on the other, he defines religion as "a careful and scrupulous observation of what Rudolf Otto aptly termed the *numinosum*, that is, a dynamic agency or effect, not caused by an arbitrary act of will." This experience of *numinosum* is involuntary and is "either a quality belonging to a visible object or the influence of an invisible presence that causes a peculiar alteration of consciousness."[51] A third definition suggests that religion is a psychological experience: "That psychological fact which wields the greatest power in your system functions as a god, since it is always the overwhelming psychic factor that is called 'God.' "[52]

These definitions indicate a broad and sometimes ambiguous conception of religion, but they also reveal the essential role of religious experience in the Jungian scheme, his certainty that it is a

---

[49] *The Archetypes and the Collective Unconscious*, trans. from the German by R.F.C. Hull, *The Collected Works of C. G. Jung*, ed. Sir Herbert Read, Michael Fordham, and Gerhard Adler (Bollingen Series XX, New York, 1953-), v. 9, part I, pp. 12-15.

[50] *Psychology and Religion: West and East*, trans. from the German by R.F.C. Hull, *Collected Works*, v. 11, p. 8.

[51] *ibid.*, p. 7.   [52] *ibid.*, p. 81.

"great treasure," which provides "a source of life, meaning, and beauty," and "has given a new splendour to the world and to mankind."[53] For Jung, then, myth is more than a psychological tool, a guide to the psyche and a conveyor of its language. His complicated and sometimes mystical approach to myth is established on a religious base; myth for him is a means not only of regressing to the primitive unconscious but of restoring ancient forms of expression for instinctual drives and adapting ancient functions of myth and rite to what he feels are the requirements of modern man.

Though Jung does not commit himself to either a positive or a negative position on the existence of a deity, his psychology is based on the premise that a "God-image is a complex of ideas of an archetypal nature" and thus "it must necessarily be regarded as representing a certain sum of energy (libido) which appears in projection." The God-image is thus a "psychic organ" intrinsic to the nature of man. In a footnote Jung mentions his awareness that "this proposition has caused much offense," but his explanation for this reaction to his premise indicates that he fails to come to terms with all the implications of his own position. He accounts for objections on the basis that

> people have failed to see that it is a *psychological* view and not a metaphysical statement. The psychic fact "God" is a typical autonomism, a *collective archetype*. as I have later called it. It is therefore characteristic not only of all higher forms of religion, but appears spontaneously in the dreams of individuals. The archetype is, as such, an unconscious psychic image, but it has a reality independent of the attitude of the conscious mind. It is a psychic existent which should not in itself be confused with the idea of a metaphysical God. The existence of the archetype neither postulates a God, nor does it deny that he exists.[54]

The question of the existence of a deity is actually irrelevant to Jung's position, but the significance of his assumption of the psychic

---

[53] *ibid.*, p. 105.

[54] *Symbols of Transformation, An Analysis of the Prelude to a Case of Schizophrenia*, trans. from the German by R.F.C. Hull, *Collected Works*, v. 5, pp. 56-57.

reality of such a concept cannot be underestimated. He assumes that the idea of God is intrinsic to the nature of man, so deeply imbedded in his being as to have instinctual force, a determinant of his nature and its whole development. Jung's entire conception of mythical archetypes must be viewed in relation to this proposition.

Jung examines and analyzes the individual psyche in connection with the general archetypes he has established, since he believes that archetypes "always . . . were the bringers of protection and salvation" as well as the "unfailing causes of neurotic and even psychotic disorders, behaving exactly like neglected or maltreated physical organs or organic functional systems."[55] Thus, myth plays an active role not only in Jung's theory of psychic functioning but in his descriptions and analyses of specific case histories. In his *Symbols of Transformation, An Analysis of the Prelude to a Case of Schizophrenia*, he develops the thesis that the fantasies of an emotionally disturbed young woman are analogous to mythical motifs and patterns of various cultures. Drawing on a vast collection of myths—Egyptian, Greek, Roman, biblical, and others—Jung suggests that the collective unconscious, which is the heritage of all people, both nourishes their creative energy and becomes the source of illness when it is undervalued or denied. This approach characterizes his discussion of fantasies and dreams throughout his writings. His analyses of particular archetypes, moreover, develop his view that the deepest levels of the unconscious can be discovered only through myth and ritual.

Among Jung's chief archetypes are "the *shadow*, the *wise old man*, the *child* (including the child hero), the *mother* ('Primordial Mother' and 'Earth Mother') as a supraordinate personality ('daemonic' because supraordinate), and her counterpart the *maiden*, and lastly the *anima* in man and the *animus* in woman."[56] The ancient figures of Demeter and Persephone are for Jung mythical representations of the mother and maiden archetypes. The Kore figure, he believes, is an archetypal presence in both male and fe-

---

[55] *Essays on a Science of Mythology*, pp. 75-76.

[56] *ibid.*, p. 157. See also *The Integration of the Personality*, trans. from the German by Stanley Dell (New York, 1939), pp. 52-89.

male: in the female she is a "double" figure, both mother and maiden; in the male, she is the anima or "psychic representation of the minority of female genes in a male body."[57] The Demeter-Kore myth, celebrated in the Eleusinian mysteries, has an essential role in the "supraordinate personality," the whole being, including the unconscious elements. This mother-daughter archetype extends the life of woman: "We could therefore say that every mother contains her daughter in herself and every daughter her mother, and that every woman extends backwards into her mother and forwards into her daughter." For Jung this is "the first step towards the immediate experience and conviction of being outside time, which brings with it a feeling of *immortality*." The psychological value and significance of the archetype expressed in the myth of Demeter and Kore is that it binds individual to general life and establishes a continuity within generations of human experience. For Jung, myth and its concomitant ritual are salutary in enlarging human consciousness: "It is immediately clear to the psychologist what cathartic and at the same [time] rejuvenating effects must flow from the Demeter cult into the feminine psyche, and what a lack of psychic hygiene characterizes our culture, which no longer knows the kind of wholesome experience afforded by Eleusinian emotions."[58]

For the male psyche, also, the myth in the form of the anima has value in extending time and thus individual life. The anima is an ambivalent power, "positive one moment and negative the next." In addition, "the anima . . . has 'occult' connections with 'mysteries,' with the world of darkness in general, and for that reason she often has a religious tinge." Since the anima is "outside time," it is "more or less immortal."[59]

Jung describes these archetypes as "active personalities," involved with another group which he calls the *"archetypes of transformation."* These are "typical situations, places, ways, animals, plants, and so forth that symbolize the kind of change, whatever it is."

[57] *Psychology and Religion*, p. 30.
[58] *Essays on a Science of Mythology*, pp. 160-63.
[59] *ibid.*, p. 173.

The process of transformation is salutary; it is achieved when the "conscious and unconscious are interfused, and a decided change of consciousness is brought about." It is, however, fraught with danger, for there is the possibility that the conscious mind will "be drawn completely into the archetype." Jung cites the labors of Heracles as an example of the difficulties encountered at the beginning of transformation. Other symbols suggest the perils of "initiation": early stages are projected in the forms of animals, such as "the serpent, bird, horse, wolf, bull, lion." Images of "cave and sea" portray the unconscious. "The hero and the *puer aeternus* may appear as themes throughout the whole process." Jung distinguishes between the "Christian cross" as a symbol of beginning the process of transformation and "the *cross with equal arms*" which "appears later (as it did in early Christianity)."[60]

The "illumination" which results effects an integration of personality. We are brought "back to ourselves as an actual, living something, poised between two world-pictures and their darkly discerned potencies." This unified self "can claim anything—kinship with beasts and gods, with crystals and with stars—without moving us to wonder, without even exciting our disapprobation." The self transcends the ego since it includes the whole personality and may be called the "God within us." The process of transformation is compared with primitive initiation ceremonies, which Jung calls "transformation mysteries of the greatest spiritual significance." Again he refers to the Eleusinian mysteries as beneficial in offering a means of expressing "unconscious contents" through religious ritual.[61]

[60] *The Integration of the Personality*, pp. 89-95.

[61] *Two Essays on Analytical Psychology*, trans. from the German by R.F.C. Hull, *Collected Works*, v. 7, pp. 228-38. Elsewhere Jung says, ". . . the spontaneous symbols of the self, or of wholeness, cannot in practice be distinguished from a God-image." According to the "empirical findings of psychology, . . . there is an ever-present archetype of wholeness which may easily disappear from the purview of consciousness or may never be perceived at all until a consciousness illuminated by conversion recognizes it in the figure of Christ. As a result of this 'anamnesis' the original state of oneness with the God-image is restored. It brings about an integration, a bridging of the split in the personality caused by the instincts striving apart in different and mutually

Jung's discussion of his chief mythical archetypes exemplifies his general approach to myth as an expression of universal inner experience which demands external manifestation and fulfillment in ritual. In his view, myth usually reveals an unconscious craving for the eternal or superhuman in some form. Most commentators on myth would not argue with Jung's assumption, no doubt derived from Freud, that myth discloses unconscious feelings and desires for powers beyond those of limited mortals. The main features of his approach which are unique and most dramatically opposed to the Freudian view are his description of the mythical archetype as a "psychic organ," his insistence on the use of archetypes as therapeutic agents for the illness of individuals and society, and, perhaps most basic, his premise that the idea of God is a "psychic existent" in all human beings. Jung seeks to establish through his system of psychological archetypes an emotional milieu in which myth may recover the therapeutic powers it exercised in ancient religion.

Whereas Freud attempts to exploit the powers of myth by determining and defining its limitations, by employing it as a scientific language to express the instinctual roots of cravings for and projections of omnipotence, Jung seeks to extend the original mystery of myth by treating it as open-ended, reaching ultimately toward the timeless and the immortal. He yearns for a return to mythical views of physical reality:

> How different was the former image of matter—the Great Mother—that could encompass and express the profound emotional meaning of Mother Earth. In the same way, what was the spirit is now identified with intellect and thus ceases to be the Father of All. It has degenerated to the limited ego-thoughts of man; the immense emotional energy expressed in the image of "our Father" vanishes into the sand of an intellectual desert.[62]

---

contradictory directions" (*Aion, Researches into the Phenomenology of the Self*, trans. from the German by R.F.C. Hull, *Collected Works*, v. 9, part II, p. 40).

[62] "Approaching the Unconscious," *Man and His Symbols*, ed. C. G. Jung, and after his death, M-L. von Franz (Garden City, New York, 1964), p. 95.

According to Jungian psychology, the mythical hero performing superhuman deeds represents the ego conquering the "shadow," that part of the conscious mind which contains unacceptable traits of personality: "In the developing consciousness of the individual the hero figure is the symbolic means by which the emerging ego overcomes the inertia of the unconscious mind, and liberates the mature man from a regressive longing to return to the blissful state of infancy in a world dominated by his mother."[63] Thus, in Jung's view, the mature ego, represented as the hero conquering dragons and monsters, is experienced as exalted, godlike, and invincible. Such idealization is not found in Freud's approach to mythical constructs of heroes of supernatural power: he generally views them as projections of infantile omnipotence or of a struggle to express and control instinctual drives.

For Freud there are neither heroes of supernatural power nor devils within the human psyche. In his description of the merciless struggle between the instinctual drives Eros and Thanatos, myth is tragically demythified. Implicit in Freud's "scientific myth" is the demand that man face the limits of his own nature and his own existence, without the sustenance of projected gods and heroes. Jung, on the other hand, starting with the premise of the god image as an unconscious archetype, demands that myth fulfill its implied promise of superhuman power and knowledge. For him myth is coexistent with man; it is a supernatural element within man's psyche that promises him the fulfillment of all his fantasies of omnipotence, if only he will return to the "ancient and venerable pattern" of investing physical matter with spiritual presences and worshiping them in ritual.[64] Freud sees in myth a special form of symbolic language, one which can express instinctual drives in a narrative form that reveals their operation and function in the human psyche. He thus adapts an ancient language to a new use, revitalizes it, and even creates new forms of it; he is the catalyst of its evolution. Jung seeks to restore the original religious role of myth, a

[63] Joseph L. Henderson, "Ancient Myths and Modern Man," *Man and His Symbols*, p. 120.

[64] *The Archetypes and the Collective Unconscious*, p. 157.

function he justifies on the basis of its roots in psychological need; in so doing he attempts to recreate the visionary or oracular atmosphere of ancient rite.

Unquestionably, the extensive use of myth in all the arts in this century can in large part be attributed to the new possibilities opened to it by the approaches of Freudian and Jungian psychology. Different as these two interpretations are, both view myth as a revelation of unconscious feeling and as a basic vehicle of emotional and aesthetic expression. Poets certainly were drawn to both views. In the works of some twentieth-century poets the influence of either Freud or Jung is clear and explicit, and mythical and other allusions can be traced directly to their writings. Other poets are ambivalent; questioning the validity of Freud's psychology, repelled by his use of myth as a scientific device and by the tragic narratives he himself created, they nevertheless reflect his influence even as they seek to mitigate the force of the instruments he provided.

For some poets the Jungian approach is more promising. The archetypes of the unconscious seem to offer possibilities of a universal and ordered mythical framework which can replace the Hebraic-Christian one. They are also drawn to Jung's suggestion that myth offers the poet a sure means of uniting his own experience with the continuous psychic history of man, and they seem consciously to evoke the mythical archetypes which Jung considered the source of all artistic creation.[65] In still other contemporary poetry, mythical allusions indicate the general influence of both Freud

[65] Commenting on artistic creation, Jung says: "The creative process, so far as we are able to follow it at all, consists in the unconscious activation of an archetypal image, and in elaborating and shaping this image into the finished work." He describes the archetype as "a figure—be it a daemon, a human being, or a process—that constantly recurs in the course of history and appears wherever creative fantasy is freely expressed. Essentially, therefore, it is a mythological figure. When we examine these images more closely, we find that they give form to countless typical experiences of our ancestors. They are, so to speak, the psychic residua of innumerable experiences of the same type. They present a picture of psychic life in the average, divided up and projected into the manifold figures of the mythological pantheon" (*The Spirit in Man, Art, and Literature*, trans. from the German by R.F.C. Hull, *Collected Works*, v. 15, pp. 81-82).

and Jung uneasily combined and often reflecting popular distortions, or, perhaps, of the writings of such less influential but well-known figures as Otto Rank, who developed his own theories regarding the common features of various culture heroes and gods, or C. Kerényi, who applied and elaborated the Jungian method in many books on myth. Psychoanalytic approaches to myth are reflected in contemporary poetry in countless ways; however direct, submerged, combined, or distorted, they have been chiefly responsible for the reincarnation of myth as a new and potent symbolic language.

III

MYTH AND THE UNCONSCIOUS

W. B. YEATS, T. S. Eliot, and Ezra Pound are the earliest major poets who grew to artistic maturity during the period when the new fields of anthropology and psychology were opening hitherto unexplored approaches to myth. W. H. Auden, who was born more than twenty years after Pound and Eliot, was drawn to these disciplines as intrinsic to the intellectual life of his time. All these poets reflect the new awareness that myth is a guide to and expression of unconscious feelings and instincts. They differ, of course, in their choice and interpretation of mythical materials and in their adaptation of these to their individual point of view and poetic idiom. In one respect, however, Yeats, Eliot, and Pound are remarkably similar: each of these poets expresses ambivalence toward the very insights into the unconscious which myth provides him. For Yeats and Eliot, myth offers the promise of a light beyond the enlightenment of self, a hope of eternity—for Yeats in art, for Eliot in the hereafter; for Pound it is an endowment, a charm which leads to the darkness where he can reign as a poetic fallen angel who alone explores chaos. Auden is the only one of these poets whose development reveals a consistent reliance on myth as a clue to the unconscious mind.

Yeats, Pound, and Eliot are roughly contemporaries of Freud and Jung. Yeats was born nine years after Freud and died in the same year. Freud's major psychoanalytic theories and some of Jung's important works dealing with myth were published before Yeats was an established poet. Pound and Eliot, of course, had access to the writings of both psychoanalysts. There is no question that all three poets were aware of the essential ideas of Freud and

Jung, whose influence, along with Frazer's, was chiefly responsible for the break in all the arts with the dominant nineteenth-century "sensuously symbolic or allegorical"[1] approach to myth, and for the emergence of the modern conception of myth as a symbolic structure of unconscious feelings and drives. Furthermore, the poetry of Yeats, Pound, and Eliot, and especially their use of myth, expresses their reaction to the new light shed on the unconscious by Freud and the attempt by Jung to retreat from this light into a mythical realm which ultimately leads back to religious orthodoxy.

W. B. YEATS
Myth as Psychic Structure

Of these three poets Yeats was the most self-conscious in his adaptation of myth not only to poetry but to his personal psychology and to his unique view of philosophy and history. A great deal has been written on myth in Yeats's poetry, and it is unnecessary to add to the summaries, interpretations, and evaluations of the importance of *A Vision* in relation to his poems and plays.[2] But if Yeats's approach to traditional myth and his creation of his own mythology have been treated in detail, no critic has shown that most of Yeats's efforts to build a mythical system constitute an attempt to reach his unconscious and control it by uniting his own being to a structure beyond himself; that, like Jung, he seeks the immortal in the

---

[1] Douglas Bush, *Mythology and the Romantic Tradition in English Poetry* (Cambridge, Mass., 1937), p. xiv.

[2] For discussions of Yeats's use of myth, see Peter Ure, *Towards A Mythology: Studies in the Poetry of W. B. Yeats* (London, 1946); Richard Ellmann, *Yeats: The Man and the Masks* (New York, 1948) and *The Identity of Yeats*, 2nd ed. (New York, 1964); T. R. Henn, *The Lonely Tower, Studies in the Poetry of W. B. Yeats* (New York, 1952); R. P. Blackmur, "W. B. Yeats: Between Myth and Philosophy," *Language as Gesture* (New York, 1953); Morton I. Seiden, *William Butler Yeats, The Poet as A Mythmaker* (East Lansing, Michigan, 1962); Helen Hennessy Vendler, *Yeats's Vision and the Later Plays* (Cambridge, Mass., 1963); Thomas Parkinson, *W. B. Yeats, The Later Poetry* (Berkeley and Los Angeles, 1964); Daniel Hoffman, *Barbarous Knowledge, Myth in the Poetry of Yeats, Graves, and Muir* (New York, 1967).

human psyche but, unlike Jung, once Yeats has built his system, he repudiates it in his poetry.[3] Gradually, in his poems, he makes his way out of his own mythical labyrinth and, with the insight and security he has gained there, is able to face the most painful limitations of everyday reality and to express the horror of old age, decay, and death—indeed, to depict man in his absurd struggle with these indignities as tragic and heroic.

For much of his long life Yeats used myth as both a defense against the power of his own insight and a means of releasing unconscious knowledge in poetry. There are signs of his awareness of this conflict in his early writings, but it took him a lifetime to come to terms with it; finally he employed the energy and pain of this struggle in constructing his greatest poetry.

As early as 1888, in a letter to Katharine Tynan, Yeats, speaking of his own poetry, discloses a remarkable understanding of his "flight" from the very revelations he seeks. He says of his poetry:

> . . . it is almost all a flight into fairyland from the real world, and a summons to that flight. The Chorus to the "Stolen Child" sums it up—that it is not the poetry of insight and knowledge, but of longing and complaint—the cry of the heart against necessity. I hope some day to alter that and write poetry of insight and knowledge.[4]

Yeats's hope is indeed a prophecy, which is fulfilled gradually as he turns from fairy tale to myth. Yeats uses myth in many ways: as a heroic ideal, as an elaborate structure to deny what he here calls "necessity," and, most effectively, as a guide to "insight and knowledge," an interpreter of his longings and dreams which re-

---

[3] Helen Hennessy Vendler discusses Yeats's use of his "symbolic system . . . to make conscious what had been formerly unconscious," but she approaches *A Vision* essentially as an expression "in mythical form of what we are to believe about poetry" and of his "theory of creation" (*Yeats's Vision and the Later Plays*, pp. 18-19; 22-23), rather than as a clue to Yeats's efforts to come to terms with his own unconscious fears and conflicts, which become the material of some of his most significant creation.

[4] *The Letters of W. B. Yeats*, ed. Allan Wade (New York, 1955), p. 63.

vealed limitation in the boast of omnipotence, death in the promise of immortality.

Throughout Yeats's prose and poetry—from his earliest writings to his last ones—he finds analogues in Celtic, Greek, and eastern myth and in mystical doctrine. Some of the analogies are authentic; some he imposes out of a compulsion to forge from the symbolic contents of traditional material his own mythical construction. In the profusion and apparent disorder of mythical allusions in Yeats's work, with their subjective and seemingly haphazard associations, one can discover a consistent thematic and structural development which culminates in the revised version of *A Vision*; for his poetry this mythical structure provides a foundation never entirely below the surface. All of Yeats's adaptations of myth indicate a need to impose order and unity on an apparent anarchy in his own mind and in the universe; he does so by equating individual with universal experience, seeking some eternal element in the human soul. Ultimately his purpose is to use myth as a guide to reality, both unconscious or personal, and historical or general.

Thus, when Yeats sees analogies in Gaelic legend, Greek Orphism, Christian myth, Rosicrucianism,[5] and the vague mysticism of Theosophy, it is because, different as these are in origin and even in function, they are similar in one important respect: all of them express in symbolic form a human longing for regression and continuity, a simultaneous merging with past and future. Yeats used various myths and mystical doctrines to provide narrative and rite for his own mythical structure, which attempts to unite features of all yet is ultimately personal, since his quest for a unifying principle in myth expresses a demand for unity in his own soul and his own art.

In his prose, both autobiographical and critical, Yeats frequently refers explicitly to an awareness that his deepest "insight and knowledge" lie hidden within his unconscious self and can be brought to the surface only in poetry, through the agency of myth. In "The Symbolism of Poetry" he describes "the moment when we are both

[5] Seiden, *William Butler Yeats*, p. 9.

asleep and awake" as "the one moment of creation." He then goes on to recount his experience in writing "a very symbolical and abstract poem." He tells of dropping his pen and, in bending to retrieve it, suddenly remembering dreams of many past nights. At this point he could not recall real events of the previous day; "all my waking life had perished from me." When, "after a struggle," he remembered the ordinary events of his life, the series of dreams, "that more powerful and startling life perished in its turn." He calls this union of dream and creation "a trance"; but his description makes it clear that it was actually a moment of intense communication with his own unconscious mind. He concludes:

> So I think that in the making and in the understanding of a work of art, and the more easily if it is full of patterns and symbols and music, we are lured to the threshold of sleep, and it may be far beyond it, without knowing that we have ever set our feet upon the steps of horn or of ivory.[6]

Yeats here substitutes "steps" for the traditional gates "of horn or of ivory," suggesting a descent into the unconscious through mythical allusion. It is not only the entrance to the realm of dreams that he evokes; it will be remembered that Aeneas passed through the ivory gates when he left the underworld, the realm of the dead. Yeats seems to indicate that when, through the symbolism of art, we are "lured to the threshold of sleep, and it may be far beyond it," perhaps unwillingly, without conscious awareness, we are lured to a knowledge of death, hidden in our own unconscious minds. Another passage from Yeats's prose supports this interpretation: "The knowledge of reality is always in some measure a secret knowledge. It is a kind of death."[7] Of course, Yeats is speaking not of death, but of mortality, of man's deep awareness of the limits which time and his own nature impose upon him. In much of Yeats's poetry, dream and myth provide knowledge of "the buried self,"[8] at once the repository of hidden weakness and terror, and the source of creation.

---

[6] *Essays and Introductions* (London, 1961), pp. 159-60.
[7] *The Autobiography of W. B. Yeats* (New York, 1953), p. 293.
[8] *ibid.*, p. 164.

Repeatedly Yeats deals with the necessity and the difficulty of achieving self-knowledge. In the unfinished *The Poet and the Actress*, he says:

Now the art I long for is also a battle, but it takes place in the depths of the soul and one of the antagonists does not wear a shape known to the world or speak a mortal tongue. It is the struggle of the dream with the world—it is only possible when we transcend circumstances and ourselves, and the greater the contest, the greater the art. . . .

He then goes on to say that in every great play there are characters "who express the dream" and others who "express its antagonist." The dream emerges from deep in the soul; the "antagonist," who uses language "close to that of daily life," struggles against the revelations of the inner world. The dream is expressed in myth:

But it is not only the mere speech that must be heightened, there must be whole phantasmagoria through which the life-long contest finds expression. There must be fable, mythology, that the dream and the reality may face one another in visible array.

Yeats is aware that art produces "ecstasy and that cannot exist without pain," but he can accept this suffering for the freedom which the "images" bring him. He is convinced that "if we left out a single painful fact, we would be unable to believe in those images."[9]

In *Per Amica Silentia Lunae* Yeats reveals his efforts to adapt the recent psychoanalytic work on dream by the "doctors of medicine" to his own quest for self-knowledge through deliberate trance and vision. He seems to be thinking of Freud's *The Interpretation of Dreams* when in "Anima Hominis" he comments on the discovery "that certain dreams of the night, for I do not grant them all, are the day's unfulfilled desire, and that our terror of desires condemned by the conscience has distorted and disturbed our dreams." In his consideration of the general psychological "compromise" between man's desires and the demands of daily reality

[9] Unp. MS. quoted by Ellmann, *The Identity of Yeats*, pp. 105-106.

Yeats expresses remarkable insight into his own motivation for the construction of a visionary system:

> We can satisfy in life a few of our passions and each passion but a little, and our characters indeed but differ because no two men bargain alike. The bargain, the compromise, is always threatened, and when it is broken we become mad or hysterical or are in some way deluded; and so when a starved or banished passion shows in a dream we, before awakening, break the logic that had given it the capacity of action and throw it into chaos again. But the passions, when we know that they cannot find fulfillment, become vision; and a vision, whether we wake or sleep, prolongs its power by rhythm and pattern, the wheel where the world is butterfly.

Clearly it is his effort to create a permanent form for the logic of dream, to provide it with at least symbolic "action," which leads Yeats to set it within a mythical framework. Unwilling to relinquish the knowledge of self and man contained in dream, he challenges the human mind's acceptance of the starvation or banishment of prohibited desires, and goes beyond dream itself to a vision of control which avoids compromise. The vision "compels us to cover all it cannot incorporate, and would carry us when it comes in sleep to that moment when even sleep closes her eyes and dreams begin to dream. . . ." Paradoxically, the vision created to extend and fulfill the powers denied to dream finally leads to awareness of its own and man's essential limitation—impermanence. At the very time when "we are taken up into a clear light and are forgetful even of our own names and actions and yet in perfect possession of ourselves murmur like Faust, 'Stay, moment,' " we "murmur in vain."[10]

Determined to extend that moment which defies compromise, Yeats devised a method of converting dream into trance. In "Anima Mundi" he describes a process that begins with free association and leads to vision: "If you suspend the critical faculty, I have discovered, either as the result of training, or, if you have the gift, by passing into a slight trance, images pass rapidly before you." These images

[10] *Per Amica Silentia Lunae* (London, 1918), pp. 39-41.

66

are "linked by certain associations" and even originate in them. Thus, even "traditional forms and sounds" can "bring up from the 'subconscious' anything you already possess a fragment of." He uses both association and dream to convey him beyond conscious knowledge: "I elaborated a symbolism of natural objects that I might give myself dreams during sleep, or rather visions, for they had none of the confusion of dreams. . . ."[11] Yeats's quest for his unconscious self reaches beyond dream to vision, beyond psychology to a "religious system."[12]

It seems plain that an insistent need to know his "buried self," and a desire to deny or at least mitigate the terrible certainty of mortality that it revealed, impelled Yeats to create a mythical system which would establish the experience of trance and vision in a permanent structure. That system is, of course, presented in its most complete and unified form in *A Vision* of 1925 and in the revised version of 1937. The revised edition especially can be said to reflect Yeats's lifelong absorption in myth; it is his effort to assimilate and synthesize mythical allusion, ritual practice, and mystical doctrine into a commentary on civilization and a guide to the soul of man.

Cleanth Brooks points out that in *A Vision* "the psychology is founded on the conflict of opposites."[13] In this respect, as well as in several others, there is a remarkable resemblance between Yeats's and Jung's approaches to the structure of the human personality, which resemblance probably results not so much from the direct influence of Jung on Yeats as from the fact that both men saw analogues in myths from various and disparate cultures, both employed myth in forging a psychological system, and both sought a link between individual, collective, and, ultimately, eternal life.

A fundamental similarity to Jung emerges clearly in "Anima

---

[11] *ibid.*, pp. 47-49.

[12] *The Letters of W. B. Yeats*, p. 627. The phrase is from a letter that Yeats wrote to his father in June of 1917 (the year during which he was writing *Per Amica Silentia Lunae*), in which he describes that book as "part of a religious system more or less logically worked out. . . ." In the same letter he writes of "gradually getting the disorder of one's mind in order" as "the real impulse to create."

[13] *Modern Poetry and the Tradition* (Chapel Hill, 1939), p. 185.

Mundi," in which Yeats sets forth his theory of the "Great Memory." Here, he seems to reject Freud's emphasis on the personal unconscious[14] in favor of what he calls "Anima Mundi," the collective memory, containing all that is experienced by the living and dead:

> Before the mind's eye, whether in sleep or waking, came images that one was to discover presently in some book one had never read, and after looking in vain for explanation to the current theory of forgotten personal memory, I came to believe in a Great Memory passing on from generation to generation.[15]

The concept of the Great Memory is basic to the structure developed in *A Vision*: it is one way of overcoming the dual limitations of time and physical being, since neither affects the eternal workings of Anima Mundi.

Similar to Jung's "process of transformation," which is "possible only when one allows the ego-consciousness to enter the image," a process he also describes as "*a psychosis brought about by free choice*,"[16] is Yeats's "controlled vision."[17] For Yeats, seance, dream, and vision all served as avenues to the hidden self—especially its past and its future in some eternal manifestation, and *A Vision* is "expression that unites the sleeping and waking mind."[18] Throughout *A Vision* he refers to the "unconscious," sometimes equating it with a past life (p. 229) or with ancestral memory expressed in archetypal myths and symbols (p. 230). At one point he suggests that

[14] In *Moses and Monotheism*, Freud, attempting to reconstruct certain elements of the "repressed" past of the human race, remarks: "It is not easy for us to carry over the concepts of individual psychology into group psychology; and I do not think we gain anything by introducing the concept of a 'collective' unconscious. The content of the unconscious, indeed, is in any case a collective, universal property of mankind" (SE XXIII, 132). From Freud's point of view, the "content of the unconscious" is "collective" not because the unconscious mind contains specific mythical or archetypal motifs or patterns, but because all men possess unconscious instinctual drives.

[15] *Per Amica Silentia Lunae*, p. 50.

[16] *The Integration of the Personality*, pp. 90-91.

[17] Henn, *The Lonely Tower*, p. xiv.

[18] *A Vision* (New York, 1937), p. 23. Unless otherwise indicated all further quotations from *A Vision* are from this edition.

"spirits" play "a part resembling that of the 'censor' in modern psychology" (p. 235).

Often Yeats seems to regard the human unconscious as the eternal element within man. Thus, he speaks of the spirits entering the "'unconsciousness' or incarnate *Daimon*" of the human being; these spirits "so act upon the events of our lives as to compel us to attend to that perfection which, though it seems theirs, is the work of our own *Daimon*" (p. 234). Since the Daimon is also the "unconscious," it is never quite clear whether Yeats regards these presences which "bring us back to the spiritual norm" (p. 234) as existents or as externalizations which give structure and pattern to unconscious experience. He explains that "the words spoken in trance or written in the automatic script . . . belong to the 'unconscious'" (footnote, p. 234), and these alone serve the spirits who instruct him. Elsewhere he quotes the spirit named Leo Africanus, who had come to him in a seance, as saying of himself and his associates, "We are the unconscious as you say or as I prefer to say your animal spirits formed from the will, & molded by the images of Spiritus Mundi."[19] The ambiguity indicates Yeats's association of the unconscious with the supernatural; both are given form and structure through the mythical pattern which Yeats creates.

A Vision contains many references to traditional myth and, occasionally, remarkable awareness of myth as an expression of emotional disturbance, which parallels contemporary psychological investigation. Thus, in describing "Phase Thirteen," Yeats writes (p. 130) of the being

> . . . struggling with the *Body of Fate*, forms of emotional morbidity which others recognize as their own; as the Saint may take upon himself the physical diseases of others. There is almost always a preoccupation with those metaphors and symbols and mythological images through which we define whatever seems most strange or most morbid.

Later on, he mentions the "various legends of spirits that appear under the impulse of moral and emotional suffering" (p. 231).

[19] Unp. letter quoted by Ellmann, *Yeats: The Man and the Masks*, p. 197.

Traditional mythical figures—Leda, Helen, the Sphinx, Achilles, Aeneas, Heracles—are always adapted to the grand pattern of antithesis, regeneration, and transcendence on which *A Vision* is based. Moreover, pervading the whole work is an archetypal image of God, as ambiguous as the spirits of seances, never quite present, yet always within reach in the human psyche or in the universal framework. Like Jung's "God-image," the deity is in Yeats a "psychic organ," whose presence is felt in the Thirteenth Cycle, which "may deliver us from the twelve cycles of time and space" (p. 210). This God is by no means the conventional Christian deity. He may be "the absolute idealization of the psychic life of mankind,"[20] or merely a symbol of unending psychic energy, the antithetical continuous and regenerative powers of the universe struggling against the human limitation of death.

Like Jung, Yeats is drawn to the traditional symbol of quaternity and, to a greater degree, the symbol of perfection—the sphere or the Great Wheel.[21] Another similarity is Yeats's use of mythical archetypes to designate qualities of the human personality. The *"Four Faculties"* into which Yeats divides the human character, *"Will* and *Mask, Creative Mind,* and *Body of Fate"* (p. 73) are described as "not the abstract categories of philosophy" but "the four memories of the *Daimon* or ultimate self" of a man (p. 83). Thus, the Daimon, the unconscious, contains in its vast and troubled memory archetypes which express man's will, his conception of what he ought to be, his thought processes, and his external involvements, all struggling together, like the anima, shadow, mask, and other archetypes of the Jungian scheme, participating in the buried life of each individual as well as in the collective unconscious of the species.

The similarity between Jung's and Yeats's approaches to myth helps to elucidate Yeats's concept of the human soul, which is the

---

[20] Seiden, *William Butler Yeats,* p. 123.

[21] See C. G. Jung, *Two Essays on Analytical Psychology,* p. 108, and *The Integration of the Personality,* pp. 41, 106. One can find further references to these symbols throughout Jung's work.

main subject of *A Vision*. Though Yeats also deals with history and the question of immortality, the real importance of *A Vision* lies in his approach to the psychology of man and to the universal forces which impinge on his existence: time, chance, and fate. *A Vision* is a mythology to the extent that the structure and operation of the Great Wheel, the phases, cycles, gyres, the Four Faculties, and all the rest of Yeats's strange machinery, comprise an attempt to control and order the unconscious mind of man and to describe its function in the universal scheme of mutability and recurrence. The parallels between *A Vision* and the psychological writings of Jung are not really surprising: in their treatment of the human psyche, and especially of myth as a revelation of unconscious drives, both men represent a fairly widespread reaction to the religious skepticism so pervasive in the intellectual and scientific movements of the early twentieth century and explicitly set forth in the new psychology of Freud. Jung counters with a direct attack; Yeats, questioning, ambivalent, now believer, now skeptic, neither entirely accepting nor ignoring the revelations of the new sciences of anthropology and psychology, creates his own universal and personal order, which includes a temporal and timeless habitat for the soul, yet he never ceases to doubt the validity of his own design.

There have been various explanations and interpretations of Yeats's rather wistful comment near the end of *A Vision* as, hoping to "know all" and "find everything in the symbol," he instead feels that "nothing comes—though this moment was to reward me for all my toil" (p. 301). After this expression of despair, he finds relief in recalling "the *thirteenth sphere* or cycle which is in every man and called by every man his freedom. Doubtless, for it can do all things and knows all things, it knows what it will do with its own freedom but it has kept the secret" (p. 302). Richard Ellmann suggests that the "last two pages" of *A Vision* describe the

system's anti-self. All the determinism or quasi-determinism of *A Vision* is abruptly confronted with the Thirteenth Cycle which is able to alter everything, and suddenly free will, liberty, and deity pour back into the universe.

It is, according to Ellmann, Yeats's final triumph over "his father's scepticism" and "his own."[22] This analysis seems somewhat too simple when one considers the complexity of Yeats's concept of God and the ambiguity of the entire system of *A Vision*. Yeats's last remarks in *A Vision* reflect the compulsive self-questioning of a lifetime, the despair at limitation, the fearful search into the contents of his own dreams and his own psyche, and the final qualified hope in a self-created immortality compounded of eternal dream and superhuman knowledge.

In this last section of *A Vision* Yeats confesses, "I have felt the convictions of a lifetime melt though at an age when the mind should be rigid, and others take their place, and these in turn give way to others" (p. 301). If the Thirteenth sphere or cycle offers an answer, it is only an ambiguous one, providing a God who is essentially an inhabitant of the human unconscious, relating past to future, individual life to that of the species. Yeats envisions the "*Spirit*" of man engaged in a process of "*Dreaming Back*," turning dreams into knowledge (p. 226). The Thirteenth Cone or Sphere provides "*Teaching Spirits*" who "substitute for *Husk* and *Passionate Body* supersensual emotion and imagery; the 'unconscious' or unapparent for that which has *disappeared*." It is these "*Teaching Spirits*" who "conduct the *Spirit* through its past acts" and even sometimes "through those in past lives" (p. 229). The process of gaining immortality consists of an unrestrained search through dream and past experience for a knowledge of man which exceeds time and space and unites the individual soul to all the emotional and spiritual life of mankind. If Yeats's thirteenth sphere provides a deity, it is not the deity of "our exhausted Platonism and Christianity" (p. 230), but the image of an immortal self in his own unconscious, which, once acknowledged and built into a mythical system, allowed Yeats to face the "secret knowledge" of death which motivated its creation.

---

[22] *Yeats: The Man and the Masks*, p. 282. Seiden's thesis that, had Yeats known the Orphic Mysteries better than he did, they "would probably have fulfilled his mythological yearnings" (*William Butler Yeats*, p. 224) seems to me naive and unsupported by the evidence of either Yeats's life or his work.

Yeats's use of certain mythical themes in his poetry, especially in connection with the implied or stated system of *A Vision*, reveals even more precisely this double nature of myth: the construct of superhuman power created out of human weakness, despair, frustration, and chaos. Yeats says in *A Vision*, "Upon the throne and upon the cross alike the myth becomes a biography" (p. 273). Perhaps, one may add, in the poem as well.

Long before Yeats devised his mythical system, he frequently used traditional Celtic and Greek myth in his poetry, and expressed varying attitudes toward it as a symbolic device. Obviously, in trying to find his way as a poet, Yeats was aware that myth could serve him. The question was how was it to be adapted to the problems and conflicts of his own time and to the more pressing conflicts of his own life. In *Responsibilities* (1914) two short poems express apparently contradictory attitudes toward myth. "The Realists" is addressed to those who underestimate the value of myth:

> Hope that you may understand!
> What can books of men that wive
> In a dragon-guarded land,
> Paintings of the dolphin-drawn
> Sea-nymphs in their pearly wagons
> Do, but awake a hope to live
> That had gone
> With the dragons?[23]

Yeats's defense of myth in the form of a rhetorical question suggests an interesting function of the mythical dragons and of myth itself. The dragons, he says, are gone, taking hope with them. These dragons represent a past in which men

> . . . lived in a world where anything might flow and change, and become any other thing; and among great gods whose passions were in the flaming sunset, and in the thunder and the thunder-shower. . . . They worshipped nature and the abundance

---

[23] *The Collected Poems of W. B. Yeats* (New York, 1958). All quotations from Yeats's poetry are from this edition.

of nature, and had always, as it seems, for a supreme ritual that tumultuous dance among the hills or in the depths of the woods, where unearthly ecstasy fell upon the dancers, until they seemed the gods or the godlike beasts and felt their souls overtopping the moon; and, as some think, imagined for the first time in the world the blessed country of the gods and of the happy dead. They had imaginative passions because they did not live within our own strait limits, and were nearer to ancient chaos, every man's desire, and had immortal models about them.[24]

The dragons, the "god-like beasts," belong to an idealized emotional past, in which feeling freely expressed itself in identification with fabulous creatures, the projections of "imaginative passion." The organized ritual worship which supported such feelings and encouraged their expression is gone, and with it man's hope of immortality, of exceeding the "strait limits" of reality. Only in "books" which depict a land still "dragon-guarded" can such hope be reestablished; it is a hope to experience again "ancient chaos," the deep past which then merges with the future in "immortal models." Yeats's "hope to live" is a desire for the expression in some lasting and ordered form of chaotic unconscious wishes to exceed the limits of daily inhibition, indeed, of mortality itself. Only myth, he suggests, can provide such hope.

Yet "A Coat," the last poem in the volume, repudiates myth, or at least "old mythologies":

> I made myself a coat
> Covered with embroideries
> Out of old mythologies
> From heel to throat;
> But the fools caught it,
> Wore it in the world's eyes
> As though they'd wrought it.
> Song, let them take it,
> For there's more enterprise
> In walking naked.

[24] W. B. Yeats, "The Celtic Element in Literature," *Essays and Introductions*, p. 178.

Perhaps the essential point of the poem is indicated in the rhymed words, "embroideries" and "mythologies." More and more in his later poetry Yeats is to turn from a romantic, idealized mythology, which evokes a bygone realm of unbridled pleasure in the easy mingling of men with gods, "embroidering" the chaos of the unconscious with pastoral exaltation. Instead he employs myth as a device for achieving and expressing knowledge of himself, an experience he here envisions as "walking naked."

In "Lines Written in Dejection," composed shortly after this poem, Yeats at fifty sees himself in "a solar phase,"[25] in which he must relinquish all the mythical associations of the moon:—"dark leopards," "wild witches," "holy centaurs of the hills." The "Banished heroic mother moon" takes with her all that seems magical and comforting in myth. The poet resents his self-imposed demands for greater realism, projecting them on "the embittered sun"; actually, as these demands on himself become more intense, Yeats's use of myth becomes increasingly complicated and original.

"Ego Dominus Tuus," a dialogue between *Hic* and *Ille*, terms as neutral and general as *Ego* and *Id*, presents an explicit treatment of the conflict between primary and antithetical qualities within every man. Though *Hic* and *Ille* are sometimes regarded as separate characters,[26] their very names and even more the intimacy of their dialogue indicate that they represent conflicting personalities within a single man—the primary, or solar, concerned with objective reality, and the antithetical, or lunar, seeking in his own soul a knowledge of unconscious forces, which include an "opposite" self more difficult to perceive and to know than the obvious and aggressive *Hic*. This "opposite" is the Mask, which can be summoned only through the "help of an image." It is the side of himself that he has "handled least, least looked upon"; it is a conveyer of truth through artifice.

It is interesting that *Hic* also claims to seek self-knowledge. Indeed, he asserts, "And I would find myself and not an image." But the self he seeks is a conscious, objective being to be discovered in action; it excludes the "tragic war" that results from continuous in-

---

[25] John Unterecker, *A Reader's Guide to William Butler Yeats* (New York, 1959), p. 139.
[26] *ibid.*, p. 147.

ner conflict. The poet now accepts this war, which must exist within the "blind, stupefied hearts" of all who would be "wise" in "their writings." Furthermore, he knows that the wisdom that emerges from this struggle can express itself only indirectly, through a mask, which provides the essential image or myth through which the unconscious speaks.

In another dialogue, "The Phases of the Moon," the characters Owen Aherne and Michael Robartes, who appear in both versions of *A Vision* as well as in several of Yeats's poems and stories, speak of the poet, inside his tower, reading, seeking "in book or manuscript / What he shall never find." The two characters are, of course, projections of two sides of the poet's own being; representing his deepest insight forcing itself upon the self-conscious intellectual poring over his manuscript of *A Vision*, they are two aspects of the mask which communicates through the myth of a poem—or specifically, in this poem, in Robartes' long explanation of the twenty-eight phases of the moon. These phases describe the cycle of human incarnations, the primary and antithetical periods of man's existence and history.

Yeats combines the mythical and the actual in depicting the twelfth phase:

> Eleven pass, and then
> Athene takes Achilles by the hair,
> Hector is in the dust, Nietzsche is born,
> Because the hero's crescent is the twelfth.

This phase and the two that follow it illustrate Yeats's essentially psychological approach to history, a subject which will be developed later (below, Chapter V), but which must be mentioned briefly here. The lines quoted above, which summarize the action of the *Iliad*, suggest that the heroic and tragic phase of human personality is also the symbol of an historical era. When "Athene takes Achilles by the hair," she merely restrains the outward expression of his wrath;[27] Achilles, continuing to rage inwardly, withdraws from the

[27] In *The Resurrection*, the Greek says: "When the goddess came to Achilles in the battle, she did not interfere with his soul, she took him by his yellow hair." (W. B. Yeats, *Wheels and Butterflies* [London, 1934], p. 121.)

Trojan War, a decision that results in the succession of tragic events terminating in the violence and anguish of his return and the death of Hector. The heroic phase of personality, myth, and history are all seen as one. In the thirteenth phase the soul is "at war / In its own being," and in the fourteenth it begins "To die into the labyrinth of itself"; it is approaching the fifteenth phase, one of pure spirit or knowledge, acquired only after "loneliness" and "terror."

It is in the "moon's light" of this fifteenth phase in "The Double Vision of Michael Robartes" that Yeats's spokesman comes to terms with two important symbols: the Sphinx and the Buddha. Yeats was to comment on this poem in *A Vision* in a passage dealing with the conjunction of Jupiter and Saturn in the fifteenth sphere. He considers these two conjunctions "the outward-looking mind, love and its lure, contrasted with introspective knowledge of the mind's self-begotten unity, an intellectual excitement," and he recalls: "In certain lines written years ago in the first excitement of discovery I compared one to the Sphinx and one to Buddha" (pp. 207-208).

In "The Double Vision of Michael Robartes" the image of the Sphinx is adapted to the scheme which Yeats was devising for *A Vision*, but the mythical figure also retains its associations with the classical past. The Sphinx is seen "in the mind's eye," as is the Buddha, and between them is a girl dancing. The Sphinx is described:

> One lashed her tail; her eyes lit by the moon
> Gazed upon all things known, all things unknown,
> In triumph of intellect
> With motionless head erect.

She is confident, majestic, and entirely self-sufficient; since she possesses knowledge unattainable to man, except through an agonizing struggle within his own soul, her gaze seems not only a triumph but a challenge. The Buddha, in contrast, is sad:

> That other's moonlit eyeballs never moved,
> Being fixed on all things loved, all things unloved,
> Yet little peace he had,
> For those that love are sad.

Neither Sphinx nor Buddha responds to the dancer between them, nor does she, in her perfect beauty, notice them. Each has a completeness and sufficiency in his or her own existence because, unlike human beings, they have no need of each other. They exist as symbols in the poet's memory and are part of the Great Memory.

In the last section of the poem the speaker realizes that the dancing girl is a recurrent dream which he has at last remembered. She has been released from his "unremembering nights," from dreams that even unrecalled had so powerful an effect upon him that he felt himself "undone" by Helen of Troy:

> As though I had been undone
> By Homer's Paragon
>
> Who never gave the burning town a thought;
> To such a pitch of folly I am brought,
> Being caught between the pull
> Of the dark moon and the full,
>
> The commonness of thought and images
> That have the frenzy of our western seas.

Traditional myth is interpreted in accordance with the pattern later recorded in *A Vision* as symbols emerge from the realm of dream, the unconscious mind. The Sphinx, the Buddha, and the dancing girl identified with Helen are symbols of a knowledge of past and present, of beauty, and love in all its sadness and potential destruction contained in the unconscious and finally released in the fifteenth sphere. This sphere, in which physical life is impossible, symbolizes knowledge and beauty, toward which man struggles; unattainable in life except in elusive dream, it is expressible in art. Yeats ends his poem gratefully; his mythical system has provided a means for seizing and holding this wisdom: he has

> arranged it in a song
> Seeing that I, ignorant for so long,
> Had been rewarded thus
> In Cormac's ruined house.

Dream and myth dominate the poems of this period. In "Towards Break of Day" Yeats records his wife's mythical dream and his own, marveling at the symbols that link them to each other. In another poem, "Demon and Beast," he tells of moments of escape from "That crafty demon and that loud beast" which torment him "day and night." These symbols of "hatred" and "desire" within his being may cause conflict and pain, but, ironically,

> every natural victory
> Belongs to beast or demon,

and therefore they offer knowledge and "mastery of natural things."

The Sphinx appears again in "The Second Coming," once more a symbol of buried knowledge, disinterested and "pitiless." The beast symbol also reappears, as does the reference to dream, but in this poem it is a "nightmare" vision that Yeats records. The poem is, of course, a prophecy of a new age, a "Second Coming," the poet twice exclaims, as if trying to avoid the "vast image out of *Spiritus Mundi*," a "nightmare" composed of the Sphinx, "the indignant desert birds," and the "rough beast, its hour come round at last." Thus, the Christian myth of prophetic hope is displaced by a vision of despair, an interpretation that Yeats's mythical design derives from contemporary events. The hope of the second coming of Christ, which has comforted "twenty centuries," seems a mockery when confronted by the eyes of the Sphinx, a "gaze blank and pitiless as the sun," for her prophecy, as she slowly moves, bearing her knowledge of the ancient past into the chaotic future, is that the "rough beast" of anarchy will be resurrected. Yeats again imposes his personal vision, emerging from the realm of nightmare and ancient prophecy, formed by the design of the Great Wheel and the turning gyres, upon history, and he assumes that the "darkness" and the half-human demons with which he has contended threaten all mankind.

Yeats's study and adaptation of myth have carried him a long way from his early heroic and pastoral idealizations, yet the despair of "The Second Coming" is neither a lasting nor a final expression of the insight he gained through the mythical design he constructed.

In "The Second Coming" ancient mythical images cast a prophetic shadow of chaos and destruction on the future. In "On a Picture of a Black Centaur by Edmund Dulac" they seem to threaten the poet's very sanity; at the same time the images, which in this poem are all connected with the figure of the centaur, provide release for imaginative and creative power. In his *Autobiography* Yeats recalls that he "thought all art should be a Centaur finding in the popular lore its back and its strong legs." He expected strength and vitality in legend and myth, but little did he realize how deeply into his own soul myth would lead him. Nor, indeed, "not having the courage of [his] own thought," did he foresee "the growing murderousness of the world."[28]

"On a Picture of a Black Centaur by Edmund Dulac," which is said to be a "composite image" of two paintings—Dulac's and one by Cecil Salkeld[29]—actually seems to reflect Yeats's characteristic symbolic depiction of inner experience more than any pictorial model. In the first lines, this experience is described as frightening: the poet has allowed himself to be drawn into the centaur's realm, half bestial and violent; he has been "driven half insane" by his quest —through vision, seance, and myth—for knowledge of self beyond that usually granted to man, perhaps beyond his own courage to accept. The bizarre quality of his imagination is expressed in the image of the "horrible green parrots," whose "green wing" sends him desperately to gather "old mummy wheat / In the mad abstract dark." Through the contrast between the two phrases Yeats creates a moving reminiscence of his efforts to understand and control the darkness of his unconscious mind by fitting his own conflicts and perceptions into some system of ancient lore—hopefully as productive as the fabled growth of wheat grains among the coverings of Egyptian mummies.

Now he feels he is freer. Less obsessed by images and more accepting of the knowledge they offer, he can produce "full-flavoured wine." This wine, he says, comes

[28] *The Autobiography of W. B. Yeats*, pp. 117-18.
[29] Henn, *The Lonely Tower*, p. 243.

> out of a barrel found
> Where seven Ephesian topers slept and never knew
> When Alexander's empire passed, they slept so sound.

His is an art as rich as aged wine and as powerful to lead one deep into the realm of the buried self, which emerges from sleep and dream to renewed vitality. He bids his own creative impulse within his unconscious mind:

> Stretch out your limbs and sleep a long Saturnian sleep;
> I have loved you better than my soul for all my words,
> And there is none so fit to keep a watch and keep
> Unwearied eyes upon those horrible green birds.

One is reminded of Yeats's description of creation as "the moment when we are both asleep and awake,"[30] and of other similar remarks, among them the comment in *On the Boiler*: "The old Irish poets lay in a formless matrix; the Greek poets kept the richness of those dreams and yet were completely awake.[31] The last lines of this poem suggest that the poet, now confident of the richness of his own creative spirit and also of his rational and poetic powers of control, is indeed both sleeper and watcher, dreamer and creator.

It is with this essential confidence that in "The Tower" Yeats turns to "Images and memories" of the past to seek answers to his questions about old age and impending death. He begins by questioning his own "troubled heart" about "this absurdity . . . this caricature, / Decrepit age." He turns to memories of the past and "images, in the Great Memory stored," among them the myth of a "Translunar Paradise" created by man. These seem to help him to formulate from his own experience a concept of eternity fashioned from "memory" and "dream," words used again and again in this poem:

> I have prepared my peace
> With learned Italian things
> And the proud stones of Greece,

[30] See above, pp. 63-64.
[31] *On the Boiler* (Dublin, 1939), p. 28.

> Poet's imaginings
> And memories of love,
> Memories of the words of women,
> All those things whereof
> Man makes a superhuman
> Mirror-resembling dream.

Here Yeats deals explicitly with the relation between dream, the yearning for immortality, and the images created from both, which the poet uses to construct his only challenge to "the wreck of body" and the "slow decay of blood."

In "Sailing to Byzantium," another of the many poems in which Yeats comes to terms with the limitations of age, he creates his symbols of immortality—a mythical bird singing in a mythical land. In flight from the country of the young—Ireland, the present, sensual, limited experience—the poet imagines that he has thus left behind him the limitations of time, age, and human frailty. Every reader of Yeats's poetry is familiar with the passage from *A Vision* (p. 279) beginning, "I think if I could be given a month of Antiquity and leave to spend it where I chose, I would spend it in Byzantium a little before Justinian opened St. Sophia and closed the Academy of Plato. . . ." This seems to Yeats the ideal period because he believes that "in early Byzantium, maybe never before or since in recorded history, religious, aesthetic and practical life were one." The passage is extremely important as background for the symbolic city in "Sailing to Byzantium," for it suggests a city united in a "vast design, the work of many that seemed the work of one, that made building, picture, pattern, metal-work of rail and lamp, seem but a single image." It is thus the symbolic city of the artist to which the poet sails in his escape from old age and the threat of death.

Equally important in understanding "Sailing to Byzantium" is the next paragraph in *A Vision*, which has not been sufficiently emphasized in relation to the poem. Continuing his imaginary reconstruction of life in the ancient city, Yeats says (p. 280) that there all of life reflected the splendor of the spirit:

The ascetic, called in Alexandria "God's Athlete," has taken the place of those Greek athletes whose statues have been melted or broken up or stand deserted in the midst of the cornfields, but all about him is an incredible splendour like that which we see pass under our closed eyelids as we lie between sleep and waking, no representation of a living world but the dream of a somnambulist. Even the drilled pupil of the eye, when the drill is in the hand of some Byzantine worker in ivory, undergoes a somnambulistic change, for its deep shadow among the faint lines of the tablet, its mechanical circle, where all else is rhythmical and flowing, give to Saint or Angel a look of some great bird staring at miracle. Could any visionary of those days, passing through the Church named with so un-theological a grace "The Holy Wisdom," can even a visionary of today wandering among the mosaics at Ravenne or in Sicily, fail to recognize some one image seen under his closed eyelids?

To Yeats Byzantium clearly represents no "living world" but a mythical realm within the unconscious mind of the artist. I have earlier discussed Yeats's conception of creation as "the moment when we are both asleep and awake." Elsewhere he says, "I cannot explain it, but I am certain that every high thing was invented in this way, between sleeping and waking. . . ."[32] Thus, the splendor of Byzantium, which seems to him an image seen "between sleep and waking," the "dream of a somnambulist," is an image of immortality emerging from the unconscious mind of the artist, freed from the "secret knowledge" that accompanies it, the awareness of death. Byzantium in its very structure denies death; the "single image" of its "vast design" is that of immortality, and the "somnambulistic" vision it frees is the yearning for and imagining of eternal life, realized in the very existence of this splendid city.

In "Sailing to Byzantium" Yeats adapts to his own "vast design" an old theme, the artist's conviction that his *monumentum aere perennius* will insure victory over death. More vividly and more in-

[32] *The Cutting of an Agate* (New York, 1912), p. 78.

tensely than any other poet who has treated this theme Yeats presents a contrast between the external reality of the "dying animal" and the inner conviction of immortality in the "artifice of eternity." In fact, the poem imitates the process of creation; as the image of immortality emerges into consciousness, despair, old age, and decay are overcome, and in the proud merging of poet and bird the "somnambulistic" vision is actualized in the poem. The poet envisions himself as the golden bird set on the "golden bough," singing "Of what is past, or passing, or to come." This is the realization in song or verse of the image of immortality known to the Byzantine "Saint or Angel" with his "look of some great bird staring at miracle." The golden bird or poet, since finally they are one, translates the "look" of the "Saint or Angel," or the silent bird with which they are compared, into song and thus articulates the image of eternity which exists under the "closed eyelids" of "any visionary" or artist.

It is hard to take seriously Sturge Moore's objection that the "goldsmith's bird is as much nature as a man's body, especially if it only sings like Homer and Shakespeare of what is past or passing or to come. . . ."[33] Moore seems to miss the point that being "out of nature" does not imply a simple rejection of life; it is a state exceeding the *natural* limits in that it rearranges time and challenges death. In nature, past, present, and future are merged only in the individual human unconscious; beneath the surface of daily experience and rational thought, the desire to overreach the usual limits of time teases the imagination in dream and fantasy.[34] The golden bird, however, has captured in the essential quality of its form and its song the merging time of past, present, and future; it is an objective realization, an imposition upon nature, of the artist's compulsion to overcome his most disturbing natural limitation.

The chief importance of Moore's remarks is that Yeats himself took them seriously enough to reply that his poem "Byzantium" resulted from this criticism.[35] "Byzantium," which was written in

[33] Quoted by Curtis Bradford, "Yeats's Byzantium Poems: A Study of Their Development," *PMLA*, LXXV (March, 1960), 118.

[34] See above, Chapter II, pp. 39-40.

[35] Bradford, "Yeats's Byzantium Poems: A Study of Their Development," 118-19.

1930, three years after "Sailing to Byzantium," does indeed further develop the theme and symbolism of the earlier poem. As Unterecker points out, " 'Byzantium' . . . is written from the point of view of the initiate who watches the uninitiated, unpurged spirits arriving"[36] in the eternal realm of Byzantium. The quality of the mythical city is established by the "image" the poet describes of "man or shade, / Shade more than man, more image than a shade." This is the spirit of man freed from reincarnation ("For Hades' bobbin bound in mummy-cloth / May unwind the winding path"). The ancient image of Hades, adapted to Yeats's system, is particularly appropriate for the idea of immortality he establishes. It is a land of the dead which always recalls the living, and in its confines shades achieve various degrees of freedom from the bounds of nature. The freed spirit in "Byzantium" declares:

> I hail the superhuman;
> I call it death-in-life and life-in-death.

It is significant that the two are merged. Life is not renounced for immortality; instead, immortality is imposed on nature, for the superhuman, life, and death, like all of time, are merged.

Once again the bird is a symbolic representation of this state. In this poem Yeats explicitly relates the bird to his conception of Byzantine splendor in *A Vision*:

> Miracle, bird or golden handiwork,
> More miracle than bird or handiwork,
> Planted on the star-lit golden bough,
> Can like the cocks of Hades crow,
> Or, by the moon embittered, scorn aloud
> In glory of changeless metal
> Common bird or petal
> And all complexities of mire or blood.

Here the bird not only stares "at miracle," but is itself the miracle. Artist, "handiwork," and vision of immortality are one, planted on the "golden bough," which Aeneas plucked before entering Hades

---

[36] *A Reader's Guide to William Butler Yeats*, p. 217.

and which, according to Sir James Frazer's view, accepted by Yeats, was plucked by each aspirant seeking the role of King of the Wood or spirit of fertility and renewal. Yeats's mythical system has incorporated the knowledge of death; the "golden bough," which provides entrance to Hades, has become the resting place of the miraculous bird. Like the freed spirits, the bird has faced death and, in the perfection of its form and knowledge, has conquered it. The "miracle" of the work of art, the poem itself, has overcome the "bitter furies of complexity" within the "troubled heart" of the poet.

Having achieved this inner victory, Yeats could not rest content in it. The poems of his last years reveal him still struggling with his own conflicts: his desire for some form of immortality and his recurrent skepticism, his conviction that there are essential order and meaning in life and his observation of only chaos and change. Yeats's later prose comments on myth and his use of it in his poems indicate these attitudes, but they chiefly reflect a more realistic approach to myth, an awareness that it is, in the end, a guide to the labyrinth within his own being, a guide both he and the characters of his poems finally desert.

In the "Introduction" to *The Resurrection* Yeats mentions "a certain myth" with which he has been "preoccupied" for years. He is obviously referring to *A Vision* and, lest he be misunderstood, he adds, "I do not mean a fiction, but one of those statements our nature is compelled to make and employ as a truth though there cannot be sufficient evidence."[37] The compulsion to know and express his conflicts and terrors through myth is abundantly clear in *A Vision* and in many of Yeats's major poems. Elsewhere he says, ". . . nor is mythology mere ostentation, mere vanity if it draws me onward to the unknown; another turn of the gyre and myth is wisdom, pride, discipline."[38] One of the most interesting ways in which myth operates in some of Yeats's later poems is that, as it uncovers the "unknown," it provides the "wisdom, pride, and discipline" required to face its terrors.

In "Her Vision in the Wood" there is a remarkable shift from

[37] *Wheels and Butterflies*, p. 101.
[38] *The Words Upon the Window Pane* (Dublin, 1934), p. 4.

mythical to real experience. The poem begins in an atmosphere of myth. The speaker, a woman "Too old for a man's love," stands in a wood at midnight, "in rage / Imagining men." She wounds herself in order to "assuage" the greater pain of lovelessness. Then, as she stands looking at her "wine-dark nail," she has a vision which immediately recalls the myth of Adonis: a group of women enter carrying "a litter with a wounded man," and they sing of the fallen year-god wounded by a boar. At first the speaker identifies with the mythical procession and sings with them of the wounded god. When he looks into her eyes, however, unseen by the stately mythical ladies, she falls and shrieks, for she knows that this torn body is "no fabulous symbol," but her lover, her "heart's victim and its torturer." No longer seeking to assuage the pain of reality by either self-induced ritual pain or mythical belief, she faces her old age, her aloneness, her grief, and finally the limitations of love itself. The mythical vision discloses the extent of her rage at her own old age and incapacity for love, and of her fury at the "beast-torn wreck" she sees as her lover, no longer idealized as a god who will be reborn but revealed as a victim of the wounds lovers inflict on themselves and each other. The vision is an expression of her most intense and most honest feelings about desire, old age, and death; thus, it must finally be a vision of "no fabulous symbol" but of her own human soul and her "bitter-sweet" experience in love.

The poet's search for reality becomes a rejection of all myth in "Meru," which is named for the most famous of the holy mountains in India. Here Yeats takes the point of view of the hermits who live on this mountain or on Everest, and he questions not only myth but all systems of thought and all of man's ephemeral creation. He says that man,

> despite his terror, cannot cease
> Ravening through century after century,
> Ravening, raging, and uprooting that he may come
> Into the desolation of reality . . .

As Yeats declares, "Egypt and Greece, good-bye, and good-bye,

Rome!" he gives up reliance on all myth and all abstract thought which in the past offered meaning and security. He is himself seeking "the desolation of reality."

Yet he returns to myth, though he now continues to peer beyond it for new approaches to truth. The very title of "News for the Delphic Oracle" is ironic; the poet will inform the oracle, the ancient source and voice of all wisdom, of the true nature of the mythical eternity. In the first stanza Yeats pictures "all the golden codgers," among them Pythagoras, Plotinus, and Oisin, chosen by "Manpicker Niamh," sighing along with the water and wind in a kind of idyllic boredom. Ellmann's explanation of Yeats's addition of his own hero Oisin to the ancient figures in the afterworld is that "Yeats is half-satirizing his early work, *The Wanderings of Oisin*,"[39] but it seems more likely from the context of the poem that what Yeats is satirizing is his own earlier heroic interpretation of myth.

In the second stanza Yeats adds further details about the afterlife unknown to the Delphic oracle:

> Those Innocents re-live their death,
> Their wounds open again.

Memory and suffering enter paradise, as the innocent souls are borne by "brute dolphins," who finally "pitch their burdens off." Sacred rite and suffering merge in this strange place, where ancient Hades seems imposed on Christian paradise.

All of this leads to the third stanza, in which Yeats clearly intends to shock the oracle with his new version of an old myth:

> Slim adolescence that a nymph has stripped,
> Peleus on Thetis stares.
> Her limbs are delicate as an eyelid,
> Love has blinded him with tears;
> But Thetis' belly listens.
> Down the mountain walls
> From where Pan's cavern is
> Intolerable music falls.

[39] *The Identity of Yeats*, p. 284.

> Foul goat-head, brutal arm appear,
> Belly, shoulder, bum,
> Flash fishlike; nymphs and satyrs
> Copulate in the foam.

Conventional, idealized mythical figures are revealed for what they are: Thetis, best known as the bereaved, weeping nymph-mother of Achilles, hears in her "belly" the "intolerable music" of Pan—a signal for sexual release. In mythical terms Yeats depicts the essential quality of sexuality, and the marvel is that he is able at once to suggest its intuitive nature, its violence, and its beauty. The real details of physical love intensify the universal symbols of nymph and satyr, as they reveal new facets of these traditional mythical figures. This sensuality, Yeats indicates, is also part of the afterlife, which in this poem seems closer to the recurring experience of generations than it does to any orthodox version of paradise.

Yeats's ironic examination of myth continues in "The Circus Animals' Desertion," in which he again looks back at the images he used in his former poetry:

> Those stilted boys, that burnished chariot,
> Lion and woman and the Lord knows what.

The majestic Sphinx, wise and menacing in the earlier poetry, is here reduced to "Lion and woman"; in the next stanza Oisin is made ridiculous in the phrase "led by the nose." Yeats continues to mock his own "allegorical dreams," declaring that

> Players and painted stage took all my love,
> And not those things that they were emblems of.

Concerned by his lifelong involvement in dream, myth, and symbol, he wonders whether these were not an escape from rather than a key to reality. In the question with which he begins his last stanza and the answer he himself provides he justifies both dream and myth even as he finally deserts them:

> Those masterful images because complete
> Grew in pure mind, but out of what began?
> A mound of refuse or the sweepings of a street,

Old kettles, old bottles, and a broken can,
Old iron, old bones, old rags, that raving slut
Who keeps the till. Now that my ladder's gone,
I must lie down where all the ladders start,
In the foul rag-and-bone shop of the heart.

The images have emerged from all the ugliness, destruction, and pain of reality, to which they finally return the poet. Now, the "ladder" removed, unsupported by myth or image, he looks at "the foul rag-and-bone shop of the heart," unquestionable evidence of his own mortality and the source of all that would surely be immortal in his poetry.

In a late essay on "Modern Poetry," Yeats declares, "I think profound philosophy must come from terror." He speaks of an "abyss" under us, into which all our "inherited convictions" must drop. Then he says, "Whether we will or no we must ask the ancient questions: Is there reality anywhere? Is there a God? Is there a Soul? We cry with the Indian Sacred Book: 'They have put a golden stopper into the neck of the bottle; pull it! Let out reality!' "[40] As so often throughout his prose and poetry, Yeats describes his lifelong search for the reality of his own nature and the nature of man through a mythical tale.

EZRA POUND
The Voice from Hades

Though myth is as basic a mode of expression for Ezra Pound as it is for Yeats, no two poets have conveyed through its use greater differences in their approach to their art, to their own feelings, and to myth itself. Whereas Yeats's conception and adaptation of myth evolve through a lifetime of questioning and ordering, Pound's approach, from early in his career to the present, is static and declamatory. Yeats's use of traditional myth and of his own mythical construct leads ultimately to self-discovery and self-revelation; Pound's repeated references to mythical themes and his identifica-

[40] *Essays and Introductions*, pp. 502-503.

tion with mythical figures expose unacknowledged and chaotic feelings beneath the mask of authority.

Yeats's remarks on Pound's poetry reflect an essential distaste for the disorder which characterizes it:

> When I consider his work as a whole I find more style than form; at moments more style, more deliberate nobility and the means to convey it than in any contemporary poet known to me, but it is constantly interrupted, broken, twisted into nothing by its direct opposite, nervous obsession, nightmare, stammering confusion; he is an economist, poet, politician, raging at malignants with inexplicable characters and motives, grotesque figures out of a child's book of beasts.

Curiously, Pound's self-indulgence or, as Yeats describes it, his "loss of self control"[41] is essentially impersonal. Between his feelings and his subject Pound imposes many mythical personae. It seems almost inappropriate to include Pound's poetry in a discussion of myth and the unconscious, since no poet has used myth as a more effective barrier to self-revelation. Yet, perhaps in spite of himself, the mythical voices Pound adopts, especially the voice from Hades, expose a chaos within the speaker deeper and more threatening than even the rage he projects on the people and the societies he judges and condemns.

Some of Pound's comments on myth indicate a recognition of its power to reach and transmit unconscious feelings. In an early essay, "Psychology and Troubadours," he describes myth as a means of both explicating and disguising "psychic experience." His approach is both psychological and aesthetic:

> I believe in a sort of permanent basis in humanity, that is to say, I believe that Greek myth arose when someone having passed through delightful psychic experience tried to communicate it to others and found it necessary to screen himself from persecution. Speaking aesthetically, the myths are explications

[41] *The Oxford Book of Modern Verse,* ed. William Butler Yeats (New York, 1936), p. xxv.

of mood: you may stop there, or you may probe deeper. Certain it is that these myths are only intelligible in a vivid and glittering sense to those people to whom they occur. I know, I mean, one man who understands Persephone and Demeter, and one who understands the Laurel, and another who has, I should say, met Artemis. These things are for them *real*.[42]

Pound considers poetry "a sort of inspired mathematics, which gives us equations . . . for the human emotions." Mythical allusions and ritual effects can be regarded as forms of such equations; one can "speak of these equations as spells or incantations."[43] Absent from modern society, myth and ritual remain in the mind of man; Pound asks rhetorically whether "a modern Eleusis [is] possible in the wilds of a man's mind only?"[44] In Pound's poetry myth exposes the "wilds" of the unconscious mind in a manner at once unique and impersonal. Both his need "to communicate" and his compulsion "to screen himself" are projected on a series of personae, closely related in their expression of feeling through mythical descents to the underworld.

The persona of the *Homage to Sextus Propertius* results from Pound's imposition of his own attitudes on his imaginary alter-ego of the first century B.C. Even this, the most realistic of the many personae Pound adopts, has an arrogance, a sense of his own omnipotence, absent in the poetry of Propertius but characteristic of the personae of Pound's later poetry.[45] Pound's own explanations of his adaptation of the role of Propertius were made in self-justification. In a letter written in 1919, defending himself against the harsh criticism of the well-known classicist William Gardner Hale, Pound says that "there was never any question of translation, let alone

---

[42] *The Quest*, IV, No. 1 (October 1912), 43-44.
[43] *The Spirit of Romance* (1910; reprint, New York, 1968), p. 14.
[44] *Guide to Kulchur* (1938; reprint, New York, 1968), p. 294.
[45] The question of the value of Pound's *Homage* as an imitation is irrelevant here. Various critical appraisals of the *Homage* as translation or imitation are discussed in J. P. Sullivan's *Ezra Pound and Sextus Propertius* (Austin, Texas, 1964). Though I cannot agree with Sullivan's view that the *Homage* is valuable as a translation, it is interesting as an imitation in which the modern poet differs markedly in tone and point of view from the ancient poet he adapts to his own purpose.

literal translation. My job was to bring a dead man to life, to present a living figure."[46]

The question this last sentence raises, and it is not meant facetiously, is which dead man, Propertius or Pound? Surely Pound's use of Propertius to create a persona for himself can hardly have been motivated simply by the altruism implied in the statement "to bring a dead man to life"; furthermore, the *Homage* is but the first of many examples which indicate that it is from the world of the dead that Pound speaks most truly. One of Pound's comments on *Hugh Selwyn Mauberley* is relevant not only to that poem but to the body of his work; Pound says, "Mauberley buried E.P. in the first poem: gets rid of all his troublesome energies."[47] Throughout his poetry, Pound gets himself buried; he deadens his own troublesome identity and his personal desires and conflicts through his empathy with either a poet he invokes from the dead or the shades he summons in his versions of Hades. Out of this failure of emotion, this frigidity of his own spirit and his consequent identification with a voice from a mythical realm of the dead, there emerges a persona which releases a curious combination of feelings—rage, contempt, despair, and longing for power and immortality—often expressed in a chaotic and exaggerated form which ultimately suggests the coldness and rigidity of their source.

It is obviously not the process of imitation in itself that conveys the sense that Pound is joining the dead rather than identifying with a living voice from the ancient past. The fusion of two worlds and two minds through poetic imitation always raises the questions: What is the poet seeking in his ancient source? How does he view him? And how is the ancient poet revitalized or transformed in the modern version? Pound partially answers these questions in a second defense of the *Homage* in a later letter:

I may perhaps avoid charges of further mystification and wilful obscurity by saying that it presents certain emotions as vital to me in 1917, faced with the infinite and ineffable imbecility of

[46] *The Letters of Ezra Pound, 1907-1941*, ed. D. D. Paige (New York, 1950), pp. 148-49.
[47] In a letter to Thomas E. Connolly to which Connolly refers in "Further Notes on Mauberley," *Accent*, XVI, 1 (Winter, 1956), 59.

the British Empire, as they were to Propertius some centuries earlier, when faced with the infinite and ineffable imbecility of the Roman Empire. These emotions are defined largely, but not entirely, in Propertius' own terms.[48]

Most readers of Propertius have not thought of him as primarily a poet to whom one turns for "emotions" in response to "the infinite and ineffable imbecility of the Roman Empire." But most students of the ancient poets have not considered them, as Pound does, "antiseptics." He goes on to repeat, "They are almost the only antiseptics against the contagious imbecility of mankind."[49]

It is perhaps unnecessary to say that for the majority of his readers Propertius is primarily a love poet. He is also regarded as the Roman poet "most profoundly influenced and inspired by thoughts of death and the underworld."[50] That Pound diminishes the intensity and importance of the love motif in the *Homage* is generally accepted; his approach to the obsessive concern with death is less obvious and more significant.

J. P. Sullivan's defense of Pound's ironic treatment of both love and death in the poems of Propertius is based on Pound's discovery of "ironical play" or *logopoeia*[51] in these poems. This "refined mode of irony," Sullivan believes, is intrinsic to Propertius' approach to his beloved and to myth and ritual, and justifies Pound's ironic imitation of serious themes. Nonetheless, even Sullivan admits that "this note in Propertius in no way invalidates the more serious poems on death and his real passion for Cynthia."[52]

No doubt there is irony in Propertius, but this is only one quality in a poet who is chiefly known for his ability to convey passion, disappointment, hope, and dread as immediate experience. The main subject of Propertius' elegies is love as a battle, a kind of warfare to which he repeatedly dedicates himself. He dwells on the pain of longing and betrayal as well as on the surpassing pleasures

---

[48] *The Letters of Ezra Pound*, p. 231.
[49] *ibid.*, p. 113.
[50] *Sexti Properti Opera Omnia*, ed. H. E. Butler (London, 1905), p. 8.
[51] *Literary Essays of Ezra Pound*, ed. T. S. Eliot (New York, n.d.), pp. 25, 33.
[52] *Ezra Pound and Sextus Propertius*, pp. 67-73.

of love, and both are almost always connected with his strange attraction to and dread of death. Love is related to death in its boundlessness and in the inability of lovers to bear separation, in the lover's need to die for love, and, most significantly, in fantasies of the beloved mourning the poet after his death. In Propertius' elegies not only love but art reaches toward death for its culmination and definition. The poet imagines himself offering his work to Persephone; he will be known as the poet who "served one love" (II, 13 B).[53]

It is from this perspective as a dedicated lover and poet that Propertius views contemporary political and military affairs, sometimes expressing regret that, involved as he is in his own limited realm, he cannot engage in the larger world of war or even write in the epic manner, and at other times being mildly ironic about the external struggles of state, which only a poet can immortalize. Of course, the poet who says that "conquered nations are of no value in the realm of love" (II, 7, 6) and that he will not join the expedition to Parthia but will gladly cheer the victors on the Via Sacra (III, 4) is ironic, but his irony is gentle, humorous, and, most important, directed as much at the poet "telling of lovers' battles on a narrow couch" (II, 1, 45) as at the pompous Roman political and military establishment.

Surely this mildly ironic approach to Roman affairs in a few poems does not suggest that Propertius is attacking "the infinite and ineffable imbecility of the Roman Empire." The poems of the fourth book, in which he celebrates the history and traditions of Rome, are sufficient evidence that, though Propertius gently mocked contemporary leaders and events, and felt removed from the political and military affairs of his time, he certainly was not the angry and cynical poet Pound describes.

Pound's *Homage* and, indeed, the body of his prose and poetry

[53] In referring to and quoting from the elegies of Propertius, I have used *The Elegies of Propertius*, ed. H. E. Butler and E. A. Barber (Oxford, 1933). I have, however, used the variant "ad infernas" (instead of "at inferna") in III, 5, 14, since it appears in *Catulli Tibulli Propertii Carmina* recensuit Lucianus Mueller (Lipsiae: Teubner, 1892), the text Pound used. See Sullivan, *Ezra Pound and Sextus Propertius*, p. 96. All translations, unless otherwise noted, are mine.

indicate that he was attracted more to Propertius' involvement with death than to his scorn for Roman imperialism. Pound was drawn to the feeling in Propertius that all of life is qualified by death, and even love by the imagination of decay. Ironically, even Propertius' conviction of the immortality of his verse emerges from his ever-present awareness of death, for, he insists, "after burial-rites a name is more esteemed by men" (III, 1, 23-24). It is in the atmosphere of Hades, which pervades the elegies and with which Pound begins the *Homage*, that his kinship with Propertius is established; for Pound this persona becomes a means of expressing his disapproval of ancient and modern society and of forging his own poetic ideals in opposition to its values.

The first section of the *Homage*, an imitation of Propertius' III, 1 and 2, begins with an invocation to the "Shades of Callimachus, Coan ghosts of Philetas."[54] It is interesting that Pound intensifies the appeal for identification with the poets who now inhabit Hades and thus suggests the atmosphere of the underworld. In the line Pound imitates: "Callimachi Manes et Coi sacra Philetae" (III, 1, 1), Propertius appeals to the shade of Callimachus and that of Philetas and to the "sacra," the rites for the dead; thus, when he says in the next line: "in vestrum, quaeso, me sinite ire nemus," the reader is aware that the grove he wishes to enter is a consecrated place where the dead are honored. Pound calls up many shades and adds "ghosts"; since he omits "rites," his second line: "It is in your grove I would walk," suggests a wood in Hades inhabited by shades and ghosts, all of whom express the spirit of the dead Callimachus and Philetas. For both poets, of course, these two lines are a declaration of allegiance, for Propertius to the artistry of the Alexandrian poets whom he mentions a number of times throughout the elegies, and for Pound certainly less to Callimachus and Philetas specifically than to the artistic integrity they represent for Propertius.

Having entered their "grove," Pound freely interprets Propertius' declaration that many poets can add to the glory of Rome and his prophecy that "Bactra will be the boundary of her empire," but he

---

[54] *Homage to Sextus Propertius, Personae* (New York, 1926), pp. 205-30. All references to the *Homage* are to this edition.

will be honored after his death for singing in his own way, writing love elegies rather than epics. In Pound's version, the poets who write of Rome's triumphs are "Annalists"; they are also "Celebrities" who "will belaud Roman celebrities." His tone throughout his combined version of the first two elegies of the third book is mainly ironic. Whereas Propertius is solemn in his frequent assertions that his work will outlast death, Pound almost always, in a word or a phrase, suggests a contrast between what is valued by society and the eternal value of art. Only at the end does he directly and movingly state his belief in "genius" as a "deathless adornment." Having allied himself with the shades and ghosts who inspired Propertius, Pound departs from his Latin source to attack the "celebrities" and those who admire "a frigidaire patent," only to return ultimately to an assertion of his own immortality. He demands, moreover, not only eternal fame, as does Propertius, but "a complete elucidation of death," which would free the living poet from the limitations imposed by society and his own nature.

In section VI Pound combines passages taken from various elegies of Propertius to create a structure that reflects his own emotional need. He begins by imitating line 17 of II, 13 B: "Quandocumque igitur nostros mors claudet ocellos," which he interprets as: "When, when, and whenever death closes our eyelids." Still dwelling on death, Pound now turns to lines 13-16 of III, 5:

> haud ullas portabis opes Acherontis ad undas:
>   nudus ad infernas, stulte, vehere rate.
> victor cum victis pariter miscebitur umbris:
>   consule cum Mario, capte Iugurtha, sedes.

In Pound's version the passage becomes:

> Moving naked over Acheron
> Upon the one raft, victor and conquered together,
> Marius and Jugurtha together,
>   one tangle of shadows.

The consciousness of personal mortality leads to reflections on the death of political enemies and especially on the deadening of all conflict in "one tangle of shadows."

Pound then adapts a passage on contemporary affairs from another elegy. He turns to the first six lines of III, 4, in which Propertius optimistically anticipates a Roman victory in Parthia; in Pound's version this becomes an ironic attack on imperialism, ancient and modern:

> Caesar plots against India,
> Tigris and Euphrates shall, from now on, flow at his bidding,
> Tibet shall be full of Roman policemen,
> The Parthians shall get used to our statuary
>   and acquire a Roman religion. . . .

Pound then repeats with variations his comment on Marius and Jugurtha in Hades:

> One raft on the veiled flood of Acheron,
>   Marius and Jugurtha together.

The rest of Section VI is an imitation of Propertius' II, 13 B, from which Pound's first line is derived, an elegy in which the poet foresees his own death, describes the mourning for him, and discusses his role as a poet of love.

Pound's use of Propertius in this section of the *Homage* illustrates what I have suggested is typical of his adaptation of the myth of Hades. Beginning with a line in which Propertius imagines his own death, Pound then moves on to a passage from another poem in which the shades of Hades exist denuded of personality and thus without conflict. His voice then emerging from the realm of the dead, he abruptly turns to contemporary (Roman and by implication his own society's) political and military affairs, expresses his contempt, and returns to Hades, in which he foresees his own immortality. Even this hope is qualified, the emotion muted by the atmosphere of the underworld:

> In vain, you call back the shade,
> In vain, Cynthia. Vain call to unanswering shadow,
>   Small talk comes from small bones.

Pound's *Homage* does not reflect either Propertius' intense joy in love or his terror of death; love in the *Homage* is a game, death more a symbol of the muted spirit than real extinction. Even Propertius' traditional assertion that his poetry will be immortal is qualified by Pound's irony. The persona of Propertius served Pound as a means by which he could express his conception of the artist alienated from the values of a society he despised, and, more important, it served as an "antiseptic," purifying the poet's feelings so that they emerge as the impersonal expression of one of his "elaborate masks."[55] Certainly the persona of Propertius helps to control Pound's anger in the *Homage*, where it is a mere suggestion of the fury and contempt of his later work.

In *Hugh Selwyn Mauberley* Pound employs a less congenial mask. Having arranged for his own burial to "get rid of all his troublesome energies," he allows himself to speak through the desiccated form of Mauberley, a disillusioned minor artist defeated by the insensitivity of his age. In a letter to Felix Schelling, Pound says: "(Of course, I'm no more Mauberley than Eliot is Prufrock. Mais passons.) Mauberley is a mere surface. Again a study in form, an attempt to condense the James novel."[56] One of the main critical controversies in regard to *Mauberley* has concerned the question of the speaker or speakers of the separate poems. The most convincing position is that of Thomas Connolly, who argues that "Mauberley is the speaker of the first thirteen poems and ... except for the direct quotation in Poem IV of the 'Mauberley' section, the entire series of poems in the second section is in the third person and represents the dismissal of Mauberley by the hostile world of letters."[57] Pound is never directly present in the poem; he emerges, after his symbolic or emotional death, in the aloofness, rage, and contempt of his persona, "mere surface" reactions to the very real problems *Hugh Selwyn Mauberley* touches on.

The first poem "E.P. Ode Pour l'Election de Son Sepulchre"[58] sets the mood of the whole series. This is a curious epitaph; while it de-

---

[55] Ezra Pound, *Gaudier-Brzeska, A Memoir* (1916; reprint, New York, 1960), p. 85.

[56] *The Letters of Ezra Pound*, p. 180.

[57] "Further Notes on Mauberley," p. 60. For a different point of view, see John J. Espey, *Ezra Pound's Mauberley, A Study in Composition* (Berkeley and Los Angeles, 1955).

[58] *Hugh Selwyn Mauberley, Personae*, pp. 185-204. All references to *Mauberley* are to this edition.

scribes an ineffectual poet, "Wrong from the start," who "passed from men's memory in *l'an trentiesme*," it also identifies the dead poet as a heroic figure, a Capaneus and, even more important, an Odysseus. Capaneus, one of the Seven against Thebes, declared in his pride that not even Zeus could stop him and was killed by the god's thunderbolt on the walls of the city. He is thus a hero destroyed by the intensity of his desires, which surpass the limits imposed by social and religious authority. Pound's reference to Capaneus, which stands a clause in itself, surrounded by semicolons, is obliquely autobiographical. The speaker, the mannered and condescending Mauberley, attempts to assimilate Pound into his own ineffectual struggle against a coarse society by identifying him with an "out of date" literary past. In spite of himself, however, Mauberley reveals the poet's heroic energy, which has been destroyed by society and emerges now only in rather patronizing mythical allusions to his virtue.

The technique is even more effective when he identifies E.P. as an Odysseus figure:[59]

> His true Penelope was Flaubert,
> He fished by obstinate isles;
> Observed the elegance of Circe's hair
> Rather than the mottoes on sun-dials.

As Odysseus, E.P. is the only man who dares to listen to the Sirens' song, part of which Pound quotes here from the *Odyssey* (XII, 189): "ἴδμεν γάρ τοι πάνθ᾽ ὅσ᾽ ἐνὶ Τροίη" ("For we know all the things that have been in Troy"). Like Odysseus, he has known gods and strange adventures among men, but his goal was artistic truth: "His true Penelope was Flaubert." Experience and knowledge were to lead to his realization of the integrity and selflessness of a Flaubert

---

[59] Hugh Witemeyer discusses the development of the "poet-as-Odysseus" in some detail in his recent book *The Poetry of Ezra Pound, Forms and Renewal, 1908-1920* (Berkeley and Los Angeles, 1969), pp. 161-76. Though I am unconvinced by some of Witemeyer's correlations, e.g., the "failed minor artists" compared with "the crewmen of Odysseus," or the "stylist" in Section X reaching "a sort of Ithaca," his general discussion of the Odysseus myth in *Mauberley* is extremely suggestive and interesting.

in poetry. All the curiosity and energy of Odysseus, which Pound feels are his own characteristics, are deadened by the time and the society in which he lives. The poet dies unmourned and unremembered; he then emerges, an emotional shade in the form of Hugh Selwyn Mauberley, a persona incapable of absorbing or expressing E.P.'s passion or his energy; his passion is thus perverted in sexual impotence and fantasy, his energy in rage; only his technical mastery remains intact. Pound is no doubt right when he says that Mauberley is not he, but the cynical and angry Mauberley expresses attitudes and feelings that remain within him after Pound has written the epitaph for part of his own soul. There is perhaps more autobiography in this poem than Pound intended.

In the twelve poems that follow, Mauberley develops the contrast between his own memories and ideals and the hideous values of a world he is forced to inhabit. In most instances allusions to ancient Greek and Roman poets or myths represent a beauty and dignity no longer known or admired in the twentieth century. As if to accentuate his aloneness, the speaker slips into the ancient languages; his allusions become more difficult as he is increasingly unwilling or unable to communicate with the members of his society.

In the first three poems, the contrasts between the grace and nobility of ancient civilization and the "tawdry cheapness" of the contemporary world are indicated in some fairly obvious allusions. A stanza from III is typical:

> The tea-rose tea-gown, etc.
> Supplants the mousseline of Cos,
> The pianola "replaces"
> Sappho's barbitos.

Mauberley rejects modern Christianity along with commerce, and in his despair cries out:

> O bright Apollo
> τίν᾽ ἄνδρα, τίν᾽ ἥρωα, τίνα θεόν,
> What god, man, or hero
> Shall I place a tin wreath upon!

Many critics have noticed the ironic pun based on the similarity of sound in the repeated Greek word meaning "what" and the English word "tin." Pound has changed the order of the words he has taken from Pindar's Olympian II and made another slight change to emphasize this pun, which suggests a schoolboy's gleeful mockery and interferes with any intense response the reader may have to the evocation of the ancient poet. In general, Mauberley is rather irritating in his references to the heroic qualities of the ancient world; too often he uses them as if they were acquisitions which he exhibits as evidence of his own taste and culture.

Mainly, however, allusions to ancient myth reveal his weakness. This is especially true of references to Venus and Eros, which Pound uses to develop the theme of the "Mauberley" section, where Mauberley's life and career are viewed by a society unsympathetic to his aspirations and his failure. This failure is essentially an emotional one; he is incapable of experiencing or expressing love except in retrospective fantasy. In the second poem of the "Mauberley" section this theme is emphasized in a series of Greek words, and culminates in Mauberley's bitter acknowledgment of the power of Eros. The epigraph in French, signed "Caid Ali" who is Pound himself,[60] asks rhetorically what those who cannot understand poetry and music can possibly know about love. Mauberley, who prides himself on being the superior aesthete, is actually incapable of experiencing any deep feeling. His emotional failure is at the root of his failure as an artist. He has abstracted a part of himself which observes his own repressed desires and feelings, and he allows himself only the narcissistic satisfaction of lamenting his loss.

The first stanza records his sole attempt to experience love:

> For three years, diabolus in the scale,
> He drank ambrosia,
> All passes, ANANGKE prevails,
> Came end, at last, to that Arcadia.

It is ANANGKE, necessity—actually the necessity or compulsion of

---

[60] See Espey, *Ezra Pound's Mauberley*, p. 51.

his own personality—that puts an end to this love affair. His nostalgia for his lost "Arcadia" is essentially self-conscious:

> He had moved amid her phantasmagoria,
> Amid her galaxies,
> NUKTIS 'AGALMA. . . .

The quality of the love affair is indicated through stylized language, combining allusions to Bion and Henry James.[61] The whole experience is centered around Mauberley's image of himself as the "ornament of night," a bright Eros about to be extinguished. And so he is, not by any external force, no matter how he inveighs against the demands of the age, but by his own hesitant and fearful reaction to sexual desire:

> Drifted . . . drifted precipitate,
> Asking time to be rid of . . .
> Of his bewilderment; to designate
> His new found orchid. . . .
>
> To be certain . . . certain . . .
> (Amid aerial flowers) . . . time for arrangements—
> Drifted on
> To the final estrangement. . . .

The sexual motif is expressed indirectly, through the word "orchid," which, as John Espey points out,[62] is derived from ὄρχις (testicle). What Pound calls the "surface" is composed of "aerial flowers," but it is derived from an instinctual force hidden yet present, like the Greek root of the word "orchid." It is the demands of his own instinctual drives that Mauberley recognizes and finally rejects. More important than his beloved is his compulsion "To sift TO AGATHON from the chaff," to be certain that in giving of himself, he loses nothing of his exalted self-image and his illusion of creative power, his "fundamental passion."

[61] *ibid.*, pp. 47-52.
[62] *ibid.*, p. 51.

The last three stanzas of the poem describe the full implications of his rejection of love:

> He had passed, inconscient, full gaze,
> The wide-banded irides
> And botticellian sprays implied
> In their diastasis;
>
> Which anaesthesis, noted a year late,
> And weighed, revealed his great affect,
> (Orchid), mandate
> Of Eros, a retrospect.
>
> . . .
>
> Mouths biting empty air,
> The still stone dogs,
> Caught in metamorphosis, were
> Left him as epilogues.

Botticelli's image of the goddess of love in his painting *The Birth of Venus* is evoked to depict Mauberley's avoidance of the passion revealed in the gaze of the lady and, even more important, repressed in his own soul. In his memory love is "purified" or dehumanized as he associates it with an aesthetic experience. He becomes aware of this "anaesthesis," this deadening of normal feeling, only a year later in "retrospect" when Eros, long imprisoned, demands his price. Tormented by unexpressed desire, Mauberley is identified with the dog of Cephalus and the monster he pursued, both transformed into marble (Ovid, *Metamorphoses*, VII), forever "biting empty air" in their impotence. The great power of Eros, underestimated and denied, now exists as a monstrous stone force of repression and denial within him.

In the first section of *Hugh Selwyn Mauberley*, the death of the spirit or the emotions is attributed to a cold and unresponsive society; in the second, it is recognized as a slow and barely perceptible suicide. It is this theme that unites the two sections; as speaker or subject, the persona of Mauberley reveals a deadness within the soul and the rage and despair which this hell within projects on the living. Slowly Mauberley retreats from the demands of the age into an "Olympian *apathein*"; then he removes himself even further from reality and, drifting into a fantasy realm of sea and islands, he goes to his death.

He leaves behind one poem, "Medallion," in which a woman singing is compared first with a portrait painted by Bernardo Luini and then with the Venus Anadyomene "in the opening / Pages of Reinach." Mauberley has reduced his lady to a footnote reference and has summoned the goddess of love from a scholarly volume. This is his last attempt to recover feelings long dead, but the poem, like Mauberley, is all surface and manner; it is more an epitaph than a love poem. *Hugh Selwyn Mauberley* ends as it began: with death. The persona, having emerged speaking an epitaph for the dead poet E.P., who, he claims, was destroyed by a hostile society, now also dies. At the end Mauberley and E.P. are really one, for both are victims less of society than of their own spiritual and emotional frigidity.

The image of death discloses repression and rage in the unconscious mind of the persona most effectively in *The Cantos*, where the myth of Hades is basic to the structure of the poem. *The Cantos* begins with a journey to Hades, where Pound's persona, Odysseus, performs the appropriate rites for summoning the shades of the dead in order to obtain their counsel; throughout *The Cantos*, moreover, periodic allusions and returns to Hades establish the connection between the dead and the living, the hidden past and the demanding present.

In "A Packet for Ezra Pound," Yeats describes the plan of *The Cantos* as follows: "There will be no plot, no chronicle of events, no logic of discourse, but two themes, The Descent into Hades from Homer, a Metamorphosis from Ovid, and, mixed with these, mediaeval or modern historical characters."[63] Pound, in a letter to his father, also emphasizes the combination of two main mythical themes with history. His outline of *The Cantos* is that of a "fugue":

A.A. Live man goes down into world of Dead
C.B. The "repeat in history"

[63] *A Vision*, p. 4.

B.C. The "magic moment" or moment of metamorphosis, bust
thru from quotidien into "divine or permanent world."
Gods, etc.[64]

Both mythical themes, the descent and the metamorphosis, have
been discussed by previous commentators,[65] but there has been no
analysis of their primary functions or of their essential relationship.
The descent is used mainly to release the voice of the chief persona
and to establish his claim to superhuman authority; the series of
metamorphoses creates an atmosphere of magic produced by the poet's imitation of rituals of renewal as he imposes his own concept
of order on the chaos of history. We shall deal here with the descent
motif as it is developed through the persona of Odysseus; the theme
of metamorphosis will be discussed later in connection with myth
and ritual.

A fruitful approach to Pound's use of the myth of Odysseus is that
of Forrest Read, who regards *The Cantos* "as a modern Odyssey,
following with varying degrees of exactness the experience of Odysseus as Ezra Pound sees it. The narrator of the poem follows the
trail of Homer's wanderer, seeking the way home." In Read's view
the narrator of the poem is "Pound as Odysseus" or "Odysseus-
Pound," who can learn only by suffering and whose essential "edu-
cation" takes place in Hades. Read considers the importance of the
Odysseus motif in *The Cantos* mainly structural, and says that "the
Odysseus myth orders the experience Pound undergoes as he travels
through the Land of the Dead and comes forth a different man."[66]
There is no question that a recognition of the narrator as Odysseus-

---

[64] *The Letters of Ezra Pound*, p. 210.

[65] For the descent, see especially Hugh Kenner, *The Poetry of Ezra Pound*
(Norfolk, Connecticut, 1951); George Dekker, *The Cantos of Ezra Pound*
(New York, 1963), especially pp. 35-39; and Forrest Read, "A Man of No
Fortune," *Ezra Pound, A Collection of Critical Essays*, ed. Walter Sutton
(Englewood Cliffs, New Jersey, 1963), 64-79. For the myth of metamorphosis,
see Sister M. Bernetta Quinn, *The Metamorphic Myth in Modern Poetry*
(New Brunswick, N. J., 1955), pp. 14-48. Other essays on Pound's use of myth
can be found in *New Approaches to Ezra Pound*, ed. Eva Hesse (Berkeley
and Los Angeles, 1969).

[66] "A Man of No Fortune," pp. 64-71.

Pound helps to reveal the structure of *The Cantos*, but this is only the first step in understanding how the narrator and his mythical background elucidate the meaning of the poem as a whole. Further analysis of Pound's persona in *The Cantos* and his emergence from and returns to Hades will disclose assumptions and feelings which determine the poet's approach to history, ethics, and the problems of contemporary man—the themes of his poem. The Odysseus figure of *The Cantos* represents not only the poet's conscious search for experience and knowledge; as Odysseus plans his journeys, enters, and leaves the underworld, he conveys the darkness of its atmosphere and the pain of its inhabitants. If *The Cantos* "is the diary of a mind,"[67] it is the figure of Odysseus who suggests something of its unconscious conflicts.

The Cantos begins with Pound's translation of Andreas Divus' Latin version of the "Nekuia," the descent into Hades in *Odyssey* XI. Even more explicitly than in his earlier works, Pound here suggests through his initiatory ritual—an imitation of Odysseus' summoning of the shades—that his own personality has merged with the spirits of the insubstantial dead. In the first Canto the poet, like Odysseus, seeks from the shades of the dead knowledge unattainable to most living men. The chief, though not the only, source of such knowledge is Tiresias, who appears near the end of this Canto. Here his prophecy is incomplete; in a line and a half Pound summarizes some of the essential prophetic passages spoken by Tiresias in Homer, but he leaves out a good deal. Homer's Odysseus pays but one visit to Hades where, despite pain and fear, he learns much about his past and future. Then he returns to and remains in the world of the living. But Pound's Odysseus will return to Hades many times. The journeys of Pound's Odysseus persona to the underworld are always interrupted and unfinished, for in *The Cantos* the ancient mythical realm of Hades, which incorporates suffering and knowledge, fear and power, is clearly the hell within.

In the mind of the Odysseus persona Hell is ever present; beneath the surface of all his experience its lessons remain. Like the ancient Hades of epic, it is the realm of heroes, gods, and prophets, with

[67] Noel Stock, *Reading the Cantos* (London, 1967), p. 104.

whom he identifies, and also the hideous and frightening depths where human souls endure the memories of their crimes. Pound's delineation of Hades is by no means restricted to Cantos XIV and XV, which are generally considered the "Hell Cantos." In these, hell is externalized more than anywhere else in *The Cantos* as a foul and noisome region inhabited by the corrupters of contemporary political, social, and cultural life. From the point of view of the persona, this is, as T. S. Eliot describes it, "a Hell for the *other people*";[68] yet it is fixed in his memory even as he emerges into the sunlight:

> Ἥλιον τ᾽ Ἥλιον
> > blind with the sunlight,
> Swollen-eyed, rested,
> > lids sinking, darkness unconscious. (XV, p. 67)[69]

Pound places greater emphasis than Homer does on Circe's role in sending Odysseus on his journey to the underworld. In the *Odyssey*, Circe merely informs Odysseus that he must undertake the voyage and offers him assistance and advice about libation and sacrifice to the dead. In *The Cantos*, however, Circe appears repeatedly, always representing sexual pleasure and fertility rooted in, and inevitably leading to, the land of the dead.

It is not only Circe who figures as a destructive enchantress in *The Cantos*. She is one of a series, the one most closely related to the persona, who, like the Odysseus of Homer, protects himself against her power to reduce men to swine, though he cannot escape her command that he descend to Hades. Another mythical figure who functions repeatedly as a symbol of beauty, influence, and destruction is Helen, who appears for the first time in Canto II:

> And the wave runs in the beach-groove:
> "Eleanor, ἐλέναυς and ἐλέπτολις!"
> > And poor old Homer blind, blind, as a bat,

---

[68] *After Strange Gods* (London, 1934), p. 43.

[69] *The Cantos* (*1-95*) (New York, 1956). All references to Cantos 1-95—*A Draft of XXX Cantos, Eleven New Cantos, The Fifth Decad of Cantos, Cantos LII-LXXI, The Pisan Cantos*, and *Section: Rock Drill*—are to this edition, in which the pages of each section are numbered separately.

Ear, ear for the sea-surge, murmur of old men's voices:
"Let her go back to the ships,
Back among Grecian faces, lest evil come on our own,
Evil and further evil, and a curse cursed on our children,
Moves, yes she moves like a goddess
And has the face of a god
   and the voice of Schoeney's daughters,
And doom goes with her in walking,
Let her go back to the ships,
    back among Grecian voices."   (p. 6)

In this Canto Eleanor is the powerful godlike woman who has both historical and mythical significance. She may be Eleanor of Aquitaine and she certainly is Helen of Troy. She is the woman whose beauty drew Odysseus and the other Greeks to the Trojan battlefield, the prelude to his ten years of wandering and his descent into hell.

In describing her Pound uses the first and the third words of a line (671) from Aeschylus' *Agamemnon*, in which the chorus inveighs against Helen, calling her "ἑλέναυς, ἕλανδρος, ἑλέπτολις" ("ship-destroying, man-destroying, city-destroying"). Pound combines allusions to Aeschylus and Homer to suggest the prototype of the alluring and destructive woman whose evil influence seems to consume not only Greek lives but the creative power of "poor old Homer, blind, blind, as a bat" and the hearts of the old Trojans to whom she points out the Greek leaders from the walls of Troy (*Iliad* III, 154 ff.). To them she is cursed and beautiful, evil and godlike.

In Canto VII Eleanor is more clearly delineated as both Eleanor of Aquitaine and Helen of Troy:

Eleanor (she spoiled in a British climate)
Ἕλανδρος and Ἑλέπτολις, and
  poor old Homer blind,
  blind as a bat,
Ear, ear for the sea-surge;
  rattle of old men's voices.   (p. 24)

Here the exalted and cursed woman is again a historical figure as well as Homer's godlike and Aeschylus' baleful Helen, man-destroying and city-destroying. Further on in the same canto Pound repeats the entire line from Aeschylus, emphasizing the role of the powerful and death-dealing woman throughout history. His persona, having ascended from Hades, views history past and current—extending from the Trojan War into medieval Britain, and finally into the chaotic present. Floating through time—legendary, historical, and present—these female presences emerge as Pound repeats the familiar quotation with variations of his own. In Canto XX Helen appears again, a perennial influence on man and his history, present in the Renaissance and contemporary worlds, whose inhabitants repeat the pathetic wish of the Greek elders: "Neestho, le'er go back. . . ."

Helen, or some form of the beautiful and destructive female, part goddess and part demanding and chaotic biological principle, dominates the external and inner world of *The Cantos*:

> Chiefest of these the second, the female
> Is an element, the female
> Is a chaos
> An octopus
> A biological process. . . .   (XXIX, p. 144)

The Odysseus persona, moving through the earth, past and present, is always aware of this "element," this "chaos," as he emerges from the arms of Circe to descend into hell, where he seeks knowledge and power. In Cantos XXXIX and XLVII, Pound quotes passages from the Circe episode in *Odyssey* X, which occurs before the visit to Hades and thus before the opening scene of *The Cantos*. The expected sequence of natural and even literary time is suspended[70] as

---

[70] For an extended and useful discussion of cyclical time in *The Cantos*, see Daniel Pearlman's *The Barb of Time* (New York, 1969). Pearlman is less effective, however, in establishing his main point: that the conflict between "poetry and history, Spirit and Time," is "the central one of the *Cantos*" (p. 85) and is finally resolved in *The Pisan Cantos* in a vision of "a social paradise on earth" (p. 287). The antagonism in *The Cantos* between these two forces can hardly be considered a "major dramatic conflict" (p. 23) since through-

various experiences with Circe and descents into Hades merge in the mind of the speaker.

Canto XXXIX begins with a depiction of Circe's magical and sexual powers—her evil drugs, her beautiful voice, and the sounds and textures of her sensuous, overpowering realm. Pound then quotes in Greek a passage from the *Odyssey* (X, 490-95), in which Circe informs Odysseus that he must undertake a journey to Hades in order to seek the advice of Tiresias. This is followed by a brief allusion to Hathor, an Egyptian sun-goddess afloat on the sea in a box, a quotation in Italian from Dante's *Paradiso* (XXIII, 129), in which Mary is praised by a heavenly chorus singing in a circle of light, and a reference to Glaucus in Ovid's *Metamorphoses* (XIV). Both Hathor and Mary are associations that follow from and enlarge on the image of Circe, the exalted and powerful goddess. Belonging to different cultures and representing different kinds of power, both female figures extend the limits of time and place as Odysseus prepares for his journey below. Glaucus, who was also directly involved in Circe's magic, returns us to Odysseus' particular experience.

Pound now echoes a scene earlier in Book X of the *Odyssey* than the one mentioned above, in which Circe tells Odysseus of his obligation to visit Hades. Employing a few Greek words, which he both quotes and transliterates, Pound suggests the intrinsic relationship in the mind of his persona between the experience of love and the descent into the land of the dead:

> Discuss this in bed said the lady
> Euné kai philoteti ephata Kirkh
> Εὐνῇ καὶ φιλότητι, ἔφατα Κίρκη
> es thalamon
> Ἐς θάλαμόν. . . .   (p. 44)

The first three Greek words are taken from *Odyssey* X, 335; Circe, amazed at Odysseus' power to resist her enchantment, asks him to become her lover, saying that in the act of love they may come to trust one another. The words Pound quotes, "εὐνῇ καὶ φιλότητι,"

---

out the poem the omnipotent persona reverses, extends, and controls time to suit his vision of self, society, and history.

III

express the act of love concretely and abstractly; the phrase can be translated literally "in bed and in love." On one level Circe is thus asking merely for the intimacy of the sexual embrace. But the word εὐνή also means one's last bed, or the grave. In Pound's version, at least, the word is surely used to suggest that the first embrace of Circe prefigures the journey to Hades with which Odysseus' visit to her will end. Pound reinforces this meaning by using as his next two lines a quotation and a transliteration of a phrase which occurs in *Odyssey* X, 340: "ἐς θάλαμόν," "into the bedroom." The word θάλαμος also has overtones of death; it is used in various combinations to mean the regions below or the grave. Soon after she suggests that they become lovers, the Circe of *The Cantos* demands, "Been to hell in a boat yet?" (p. 45). Pound's Odysseus persona, like his earlier Mauberley, resists love, accepts it briefly and unwillingly, and leaves it for the realm of the dead. The chief difference between the two is that the persona of *The Cantos* has not lost his interest in the world of men and contemporary events. Fortified by his periodic journeys to Hades, he views the external world with eyes that have known the dead and a depersonalized spirit charged with the energy of hate.

In the Cantos that follow Circe's invitation to love and Hades, Pound inveighs against the crimes of past and contemporary history and what he regards as their essential cause: usury. He insists that the corruption of the economy infects individual and personal experience:

> Usura slayeth the child in the womb
> It stayeth the young man's courting
> It hath brought palsey to bed, lyeth
> between the young bride and her bridegroom
> CONTRA NATURAM
> They have brought whores for Eleusis
> Corpses are set to banquet
> at behest of usura.　　　　　　　(XLV, p. 24)

The hero-persona has returned from hell filled with this knowledge of sickness and despair. Like Tiresias, he warns of corruption which contaminates the state. He sneers, moreover, at those who interpret current history differently:

> And if you will say that this tale teaches . . .
>   a lesson, or that the Reverend Eliot
>   has found a more natural language . . . you who think
>   you will
>   get through hell in a hurry. . . .   (XLVI, p. 25)

There is obviously no logical justification for this simplistic attribution of all the crimes of history to one main cause—ill-understood and scarcely explained—or for the intensity of the poet's rage at and hatred of those he feels are responsible for it. Usury for Pound is not simply an economic institution; it becomes the focus of his wrath because it represents a quality of hell visible and active on earth, which he alone recognizes for what it is: a disease destroying the fertile spirit of man. A repression of nature and thus opposed to her principles, it results only in death. Its proponents are creatures of hell:

> Semi-private inducement
> Said Mr RothSchild, hell knows which Roth-schild. . . .
>   (XLVI, p. 27)

In the same Canto, having listed various examples of the crimes of "hyper-usura," the "monumentum" modern civilization has built to testify to its wealth and corruption, Pound declares:

> I have set down part of
> The Evidence. Part / commune sepulchrum
> Aurum est commune sepulchrum. Usura, commune sepulchrum.
> helandros kai heleptolis kai helarxe.
> Hic Geryon est. Hic hyperusura.   (pp. 28-29)

Pound's two main literary and mythical references in this passage are extremely important in elucidating his attitude toward usury, which here is associated not only with death but with love that corrupts and destroys. The first two transliterated Greek words are taken from the passage in Aeschylus' *Agamemnon* mentioned above, in which the chorus cries out that Helen is "ἑλέναυς, ἕλανδρος, ἑλέπτολις." This quotation, which, we have observed, Pound has employed several times earlier in *The Cantos* in connection with women, has a climactic force here, for it brings together two major and obsessive themes of *The Cantos*: the use of man's love and his creative capacities for destruction and death by women of beauty and power, and the corrosive effects of usury, through which the profiteer gains without producing. The usurer and the enchantress are alike in that they use what they have not produced; they profit from the creativity of others, and they end by destroying what they envy and exploit. Pound applies the last two words of Aeschylus' line, "man-destroying" and "city-destroying," to usury and adds, perhaps to retain the association of the powerful parallel construction, his own word "helarxe," or "government-destroying." The association with Helen suggests that usury, like love, lures man to deceptive and sterile pleasure, which leads ultimately to hell. The idea is then developed in the next line in the allusion to Geryon, the triple-headed or triple-bodied monster who represents usury in Dante's *Inferno* (XVII). His form in Dante includes the characteristics of human being, beast, and reptile. In *The Cantos*[71] the monstrous figure reinforces the triple threat of usury conveyed by the three Greek words. Usury is hell on earth, the visible product of death and hell within the human mind, represented by Hades throughout the poem. Shifting from Greek to Latin, from Helen to Geryon, Pound associates usury with the beautiful, the destructive, the fraudulent, and the monstrous—with love and death.

In his visits to hell, the Odysseus persona, to whom we return in the next Canto (XLVII), gains knowledge of this manifestation of death in life, hell on earth. Through his association with the dead, moreover, he feels he has gained mastery over the needs and conflicts which drive men to depend on those who destroy them; he emerges with a sense of superiority to the follies of the unenlightened, which permits him to rage, like the prophets and gods, at the shortcomings of the world of men.

[71] See also Canto LI, p. 45.

At the beginning of Canto XLVII Odysseus is again told by Circe
that he must visit Hades in order to gain knowledge from Tiresias,
who is thus described in the first line in a translation of *Odyssey*
X, 494-95: "Who even dead, yet hath his mind entire!" Repeatedly
Pound emphasizes the wisdom of the dead seer:

Eyeless that was, a shade, that is in hell
So full of knowing that the beefy men know less than he. . . .

(p. 30)

The message of Pound's Tiresias differs from that of Homer's; in
Canto XLVII the seer twice warns Odysseus: "By this gate art thou
measured." Judged in hell, he is also reminded:

By Molü art thou freed from the one bed
  that thou may'st return to another. . . .   (p. 31)

Never entirely possessed by Circe, he must return to his wife and
his real task; Pound echoes Hesiod (*Works and Days*, 383ff.) as
the shade of Tiresias commands the Odysseus persona to devote himself to cultivation, to the works and laws of nature.

 Immediately upon his ascent, in the next Canto (XLVIII), there
follows another furious attack on usury and its evil effects on civilization. This pattern of descent and bitter returns to earth—marked
by violent denunciations of past and present history—leads to the
culmination of the persona's experience in *The Pisan Cantos*, where
hell, past, and present history become one.

 The lines

ΟΫ ΤΙΣ, ΟΫ ΤΙΣ? Odysseus

the name of my family.   (p. 3)

near the beginning of Canto LXXIV convey the deepest and most
personal motif of *The Pisan Cantos*. Combining two episodes in
Odysseus' experience with the Cyclops—his initial use of the trick
name Noman and his final proud assertion of his identity—the question, "ΟΫ ΤΙΣ, ΟΫ ΤΙΣ?" suggests Pound's loss of identity as a
human being in the prison camp, and the answer, "Odysseus /
the name of my family," his return to his original superhuman persona

115

for assurance and self-discovery. Throughout most of *The Pisan Cantos* Pound retains his identification with Odysseus, sometimes in the role of "OΥ ΤΙΣ / OΥ ΤΙΣ / I am noman, my name is noman," and at others, as the proud hero who, having explored hell, is "wise as the gods."

The Odysseus persona of *The Pisan Cantos* interprets the literal hell of his daily experience in an army prison as if it were the visible construction of all he has known in the Hades of his soul up to this point. Here are present Tiresias, the powerful and terrible goddesses, the insubstantial shades, as well as the daily indignities of prison life. There is, however, one significant new element: for the first time in *The Cantos* the poet allows himself to express intense feelings other than anger and hate: he writes of his sadness, fear, pain, and yearning for love.

Imprisoned in a literal hell, denied the usual human satisfactions by bars and guards, he allows himself to feel and express direct, intense emotions; imagining the possibility of death as a punishment, he praises the potentialities of life. At one point, apparently emerging from a fantasy of love, he declares: "Le Paradis n'est pas artificiel / States of mind are inexplicable to us." This is followed by a chorus of weeping: "δακρύων δακρύων δακρύων" (LXXVI, p. 38), a word he later repeats in both Greek and English letters as he asks, "Will I ever see the Giudecca again? / or the lights against it . . ." (LXXXIII, p. 110).

In *The Pisan Cantos* Pound's depiction of inner conflict and suffering is personal; the speaker does not separate himself from those who endure the darkness and pain of hell:

> dry friable earth going from dust to more dust
>   grass worn from its root-hold

and he asks:

> is it blacker? was it blacker? Νύξ animae?
> is there a blacker or was it merely San Juan with a belly ache
>   writing ad posteros
> in short shall we look for a deeper or is this the bottom?

(LXXIV, p. 16)

Images of Hades are here direct expressions of his own experience and suffering:

> How soft the wind under Taishan
>> where the sea is remembered
> out of hell, the pit
> out of the dust and glare evil
>> Zephyrus / Apeliota
> This liquid is certainly a
>> property of the mind
> nec accidens est   but an element
>>>> in the mind's make-up. . . .
>>>>>> (LXXIV, p. 27)

He sees himself as one of those "who have passed over Lethe"; and Tiresias remains the symbol of the dead soul who "Still has his mind entire," but Pound is now chiefly preoccupied with his own mind's changing moods and attitudes:

> When the mind swings by a grass-blade
>> an ant's forefoot shall save you
> the clover leaf smells and tastes as its flower
>
> The infant has descended,
>> from mud on the tent roof to Tellus,
> like to like colour he goes amid grass-blades
>> greeting them that dwell under XTHONOS   ΧΘΟΝΟΣ
> ΟΙ ΧΘΟΝΙΟΙ;   to carry our news
>> εἰς χθονίους   to them that dwell under the earth,
> begotten of air, that shall sing in the bower
>> of Kore,   Περσεφόνεια
> and have speech with Tiresias, Thebae. . . .
>>>>>> (LXXXIII, p. 111)

The underworld is now not only the realm of knowledge for the omnipotent poet and seer, apart from and superior to human frailty; it is also the repository of the secrets of the earth—"O GEA TERRA."

Throughout *The Pisan Cantos*, woven through the depiction of a real prison, which is also the visible structure of an inner hell, is the theme of love as the sole preserver and healer. If hell is the "night of the soul," the externalization of suffering beyond pain, and the projection of an image of omnipotence deep in the mind of the persona, it has never quite extinguished the traces of love which memory now revitalizes as he struggles to survive. Pound repeats this theme many times:

> nothing matters but the quality
> of the affection—
> in the end—that has carved the trace in the mind
> dove sta memoria. . . .   (LXXVI, p. 35)

Like a memory trace, this idea reappears, either in words similar to those above, "nothing counts save the quality of the affection" (LXXVII, p. 44), or more fully developed:

> What thou lovest well remains,
>   the rest is dross
> What thou lov'st well shall not be reft from thee
> What thou lov'st well is thy true heritage
> Whose world, or mine or theirs
>   or is it of none?
> First came the seen, then thus the palpable
>   Elysium, though it were in the halls of hell,
> What thou lovest well is thy true heritage. . . .
>   (LXXXI, pp. 98-99)

Pound dissociates himself briefly from his persona, the explorer of hell, to write his own love song; it is more direct and more honest than Mauberley's but it is essentially a memory of an emotion straining against the barriers to feeling which created an inner hell and against the real prison to which his own life has delivered him. Love may be an "Elysium" in the "halls of hell," but Elysium has left its trace only in nostalgia and yearning. The main persona of *The Cantos* is most deeply involved in projecting the chaotic rage fostered by the hell he has constructed within and has come to know in the reality of his daily life.

In *Rock-Drill* and *Thrones,* Pound returns to this theme: love remaining alive in the depths of hell. Perhaps in spite of himself, in *Rock-Drill*, especially in Canto 90, he is most explicit in contrasting the "dulled edge beyond pain," the depersonalized realm of Hades, with the nostalgia for love. He appeals to the Sibyl:

> Sibylla,
>   from under the rubble heap
>   m'elevasti
>   from the dulled edge beyond pain,
>   m'elevasti
>   out of Erebus, the deep-lying
>   from the wind under the earth,
>   m'elevasti
>   from the dulled air and the dust,
>   m'elevasti
>   by the great flight,
>   m'elevasti. . . .   (p. 66)

But even love is not entirely free from the inhibitions, imposed by Erebus, the "deep-lying" realm of dulled consciousness. In Canto 93, Pound asks plaintively: "Shall two know the same in their knowing?" and then he grows apprehensive:

> You who dare Persephone's threshold,
> Beloved, do not fall apart in my hands.   (p. 91)

Throughout the last six cantos of *Rock-Drill* love is related to the ancient ceremonies of renewal at Eleusis, and the beloved, like Persephone, experiences love and death as one. Finally, even as Pound insists that love has "stirred my mind out of dust," he qualifies his own reassurance with ironic mockery of love itself:

> You are tender as a marshmallow, my Love,
> I cannot use you as a fulcrum.
>   You have stirred my mind out of dust.   (p. 92)

At the end of *Rock-Drill*, Pound returns to his lonely Odysseus persona, struggling to survive the storm sent by the gods. In this contest he is aided by the sea-nymph Leucothea. This section of *The*

Cantos ends with two quotations from *Odyssey* V, the first, translated into English, describes Leucothea: "mortal once / Who is now a sea god"⁷² (*Odyssey* V, 334-35) and her words to Odysseus: "νόστου / γαίης Φαιήκων" (ll. 344-45): "Your way to the land of the Phaeacians." Odysseus, to some extent, repeats the experience of Leucothea's transformation into a deity, since she endows him with superhuman powers. She gives him an immortal veil so that he may overcome the violence of the elements and the frailties of his own nature. *Rock-Drill* ends with the persona once again assuming his identity as the lone, omnipotent, wise Odysseus, setting out to explore the world above and below the earth.

The first two lines of *Thrones*:⁷³ "Κρήδεμνον . . . / κρήδεμνον . . ." recall the magic veil, and the third line, "and the wave concealed her," a translation of *Odyssey* V, 353, describes the disappearance of Leucothea after she has helped Odysseus. The Odysseus persona then recalls his adventure with another goddess, Calypso: "& on the hearth burned cedar and juniper . . ." (*Odyssey* V, 59-61), and he again wanders through history. Raging at politicians and usurers, he is chaotic, frantic, and often barely coherent. He moves from European medieval and Renaissance to American history, interspersing his attacks with references to the gods of the underworld (e.g. "Manes Di," 97, p. 34) and to the goddess Leucothea ("Leucothea gave her veil to Odysseus," 98, p. 36). He evokes the powerful goddesses and women who lead men to the underworld: Circe, Persephone, Aphrodite, and Helen. Here, as throughout *The Cantos*, Pound attempts to set up a standard of order adapted from ancient Greece and ancient China, but his persona, wandering between hell and history, continues to express the chaotic associations that result from muted feelings distorted into hate and rage.

In one of his recent Cantos (CXIII),⁷⁴ Pound repeats a line he had used earlier in *Thrones* (106, p. 107): "God's eye art 'ou," but in the later passage he adds the warning: "do not surrender per-

---

⁷² Probably Pound also recalled Propertius' II, 26 A, 10: "iam dea, Leucothoe!"

⁷³ *Thrones, 96-109 de los cantares* (New York, 1959). All references to Cantos 96-109 are to this edition.

⁷⁴ *Drafts and Fragments of Cantos CX-CXVII* (New York, 1968).

ception." It is hard not to believe that he addresses himself in this line and that he describes his own still troubled search for light in the last lines of the passage:

Out of dark, thou, Father Helios, leadest,
but the mind as Ixion, unstill, ever turning.   (p. 20)

Like Ixion, tortured in hell, Pound measures reality through the darkness of his own perception. The shift from Odysseus to Ixion suggests that the persona who sought knowledge in Hades has been trapped there by his own arrogance and rage.

T. S. ELIOT
The Retreat from Myth

For T. S. Eliot, Pound's hell, at least his depiction of it in Cantos XIV and XV, though "in its way admirable," lacks the essential component of evil. "Mr. Pound's Hell," Eliot says, "for all its horrors, is a perfectly comfortable one for the modern mind to contemplate and disturbing to no one's complacency." These critical comments disclose less about Pound's mythical construction of the horrors of modern society than they suggest about Eliot's own "mythical method." His most revealing remark in this connection is that "a Hell altogether without dignity implies a Heaven without dignity also." Eliot's dissatisfaction with Yeats's approach to myth is based on the same criterion: regarding him as an "equally interesting example of the modern mind," Eliot remarks on Yeats's use of "folklore, occultism, mythology and symbolism, crystal-gazing and hermetic writings," and concludes that Yeats's was the "wrong supernatural world. It was not a world of spiritual significance, not a world of real Good and Evil, of holiness or sin, but a highly sophisticated lower mythology."[75] Here Eliot clearly indicates that the "mythical method" which he had recommended in an earlier essay as "a step toward making the modern world possible for art,"[76] can be effective only when it expresses the Christian ethos.

Certainly pagan myth and Christian theology are often connected

[75] *After Strange Gods*, pp. 43-46.
[76] See Chapter I, p. 26 and footnote 27 to that chapter.

in his own poetry, but it is not the mere presence of the two that is particularly new or interesting. Both have been abundantly explicated and discussed, but no one has elucidated the unique way in which they function in his poetic development. In his early poetry, ancient myth is one of his most important means of conveying unconscious feelings and drives. It creates an essential thematic and stylistic quality of *The Waste Land*: the suggestion and evocation of unconscious conflicts which are never fully expressed or resolved. At the very moment when a mythical persona discloses or a mythical image implies deep human emotion or experience, these are diverted into a Christian framework of sin, suffering, and potential repentance through allusions to or imitation of traditional ritual. In *The Waste Land* myth functions chiefly in relation to ritual, a subject that will be developed more fully in the next chapter. However, a significant clue to the purpose and nature of Eliot's ritual effects must be sought in his use of myth to convey man's struggle and failure to gain self-knowledge—a conflict resolved only in the conversion of personal into religious experience, the transformation of mythical insight into ritual observance.

There is no doubt that Eliot considered myth a means of reaching beneath the level of present and conscious experience. In a review of Stravinsky's *Le Sacre du printemps*, he says: "In art there should be interpenetration and metamorphosis. Even the Golden Bough can be read in two ways: as a collection of entertaining myths, or as a revelation of that vanished mind of which our mind is a continuation."[77] His conception of poetry, moreover, is based on the assumption that it contains and expresses unconscious levels of experience:

What I call the "auditory imagination" is the feeling for syllable and rhythm, penetrating far below the conscious levels of thought and feeling, invigorating every word; sinking to the most primitive and forgotten, returning to the origin and bringing something back, seeking the beginning and the end. It works through meanings, certainly, or not without meanings

[77] "London Letter," *Dial*, LXXI (October 1921), 453.

in the ordinary sense, and fuses the old and obliterated and the trite, the current, and the new and surprising, the most ancient and the most civilized mentality.[78]

Eliot employs myth as well as sound to probe "far below the conscious levels of thought and feeling," but, in doing so, he does not seek any new insight into human emotion, suffering, conflict, or aspiration. In fact, he avoids such revelation when it seems about to emerge, for his aim is to disclose not human but "supernatural realities." The conflict implicit in "The Love Song of J. Alfred Prufrock" and *The Waste Land* is stated directly in a critical essay written some years after these poems: "Either everything in man can be traced as a development from below, or something must come from above. There is no avoiding that dilemma: you must be either a naturalist or a supernaturalist." For Eliot there is no real choice: "If you remove from the word 'human' all that the belief in the supernatural has given to man, you can view him finally as no more than an extremely clever, adaptable, and mischievous little animal."[79] It is this view of man that consistently determines Eliot's approach to myth: to the "lower mythology" which for him expresses man's cleverness and adaptability and, at best, his dissatisfaction with his limited nature and his yearning for completion "from above," and to the more advanced mythology of Dante, which offers the "pure vision" of the supernatural.[80]

Even as early a poem as "Prufrock," written years before Eliot's formal conversion to the Anglican Church, has an implicit Christian point of view. The Hell of Dante sets the mood of the poem through the epigraph spoken by Guido da Montefeltro. The lines

> If I thought that I were making
> Answer to one that might return to view
> The world, this flame should evermore cease shaking.

[78] "Matthew Arnold," *The Use of Poetry and the Use of Criticism* (London, 1933), pp. 118-19.

[79] "Second Thoughts About Humanism," *Selected Essays, 1917-1932* (New York, 1932), p. 397.

[80] "Dante," *The Sacred Wood* (1920; reprint, London, 1964), pp. 162-63.

But since from this abyss, if I hear true,
None ever came alive, I have no fear
Of infamy, but give thee answer due.[81]

establish not only the fact that Prufrock, like Guido, is trapped in Hell, but that Hell—which Eliot, in an essay on Dante written in 1929 but certainly illuminating in relation to "Prufrock," defines as "not a place but a *state*"—is the mythical structure beneath the ordinary details of Prufrock's memories and fantasies. To Eliot, "man is damned or blessed in the creatures of his imagination as well as in the men who have actually lived; . . . Hell, though a state, is a state which can only be thought of, and perhaps only experienced, by the projection of sensory images."[82] Prufrock is damned by the creatures of his own imagination, all of whom are projections of his own narcissism and despair.

These are expressed mainly in realistic terms, but beneath the streets and drawing room lies the mythical underworld transformed by a Christian perspective into a state extremely uncomfortable "for the modern mind to contemplate." The myth is almost totally submerged in this poem but, as Prufrock talks to himself, the rituals which rise to the surface of his consciousness in distorted and even comic form clarify the mythical structure of his "visions and revisions."[83] For Eliot a true Hell implies the existence of Heaven; thus Prufrock, immobilized by neurotic terror in the hell of his own soul, gropes toward the "overwhelming question," the possibility that the world he knows has some meaning beyond its present chaos and despair. Like many of Eliot's personae, Prufrock is a quester, but his acceptance of his damnation precludes his possibility of escape. In the epigraph Guido da Montelfeltro says he will respond to a question only because he assumes the seeker is doomed. Prufrock approaches the overwhelming question without belief or hope; in the end he is tormented not by his society or his way of life, but by

[81] *The Divine Comedy*, I: *Hell*, trans. Dorothy L. Sayers (Harmondsworth, Middlesex, 1949), p. 241.

[82] "Dante," *Selected Essays, 1917-1932*, pp. 211-12.

[83] "The Love Song of J. Alfred Prufrock," *Collected Poems 1909-1962* (New York, 1963). All quotations from and page references to Eliot's poetry are from this edition.

a mythical ideal which has replaced his brief and unrealized glimpse at the possibility of heaven: the "mermaids singing, each to each," teasing the lonely inhabitant of hell with a suggestion of joy he cannot experience. Prufrock's interior monologue, his brief and pathetic effort to unite his timidity and desire, his apathy and yearning, in a fantasy of love, leads him to the overwhelming question, which implies a "world of spiritual significance" that can be encountered only through religious ritual; in Chapter IV it will be demonstrated that Prufrock's retreat from this one possibility of action, which is, of course, symbolic, is the key to his final damnation.

In "Mr. Apollinax" Eliot uses ancient myth to suggest submerged personal feelings within the individual which have an unacknowledged effect on human society. There is, in this poem, neither revelation for the characters nor resolution in ritual, merely the ominous and ironic indication that a hidden world, "submarine and profound," confronts us even as we turn away from its meaning. Mr. Apollinax, whom Grover Smith identifies as Bertrand Russell,[84] is far more than an individual portrait. Admired, as the epigram indicates, for his paradoxes, he is himself an embodiment of the paradox of man: Fragilon and Priapus, inventive mind and wild, demanding body. The essential character of Mr. Apollinax emerges from his unconscious in mythical images. At a tea party in the United States, the new world, he reminds us of the most ancient and continuous elements of the human soul—lust and violence, both expressed in images of superhuman aspiration. He contains all that is man, in his formation and development, his inheritance from the past, and his life in the present.

Much is revealed in his laughter, with which the poem begins:

> When Mr. Apollinax visited the United States
> His laughter tinkled among the teacups.

This is his social manner, but soon the deeper self emerges:

> He laughed like an irresponsible foetus.
> His laughter was submarine and profound
> Like the old man of the sea's

[84] *T. S. Eliot's Poetry and Plays* (Chicago, 1956), p. 32.

Hidden under coral islands
Where worried bodies of drowned men drift down
    in the green silence,
Dropping from fingers of surf.

Now his laughter bursts upon the pretentious tea party as the very
force of life—elementary, pre-human, rich as a sea-god's and suggestive of beauty and death. The observer imagines Apollinax's head
"rolling under a chair." He sees it "grinning over a screen / With
seaweed in its hair." After the wild laughter, Apollinax exhibits a
grin of vast experience and pleasure. The final mythical image he
suggests is of a centaur:

I heard the beat of centaur's hoofs over the hard turf
As his dry and passionate talk devoured the afternoon.

Even his intelligent and rational conversation conveys the force of
his unconscious drives. The centaur implies more than the obvious
presence of the human and animal in man; it is a projection of the
desire to transcend conflict in fusion, to impose human reason on
animal power. The integrity of Mr. Apollinax lies in the very qualities that shock his hosts: "He must be unbalanced," they conclude.
They are neither informed nor enlightened by his presence, but his
vitality disturbs them.

Mr. Apollinax, "clever, adaptable, and mischievous," is Eliot's most
elegant and attractive mythical creation of "natural" man; Sweeney,
his most repulsive. Like Apollinax, Sweeney is characterized both as
an individual and a representative of continuous instinctual drives,
the unconscious forces in man and society. The initial shock on
reading the epigraph of "Sweeney Among the Nightingales"—
"ὤμοι, πέπληγμαι καιρίαν πληγὴν ἔσω," the cry of the dying
Agamemnon in Aeschylus' tragedy—preceding "Apeneck Sweeney,"
soon wears off as Eliot convinces one that Sweeney participates in
mythical experience as authentic as that of Oedipus or Agamemnon. F. O. Matthiessen refers to Eliot's comment that "all he consciously set out to create in 'Sweeney Among the Nightingales' was
a sense of foreboding." Matthiessen sees "wider implications" in the

"sympathetic feeling for Sweeney" created by the suggestion that his fate will be similar to Agamemnon's.[85] Actually, Eliot's statement contains "wider implications" than Matthiessen's interpretation of it or the poem. The complicated mythical structure of "Sweeney Among the Nightingales" creates "a sense of foreboding" not only about the fate of Sweeney but of mortal life. Implicit in the myths of Oedipus, Agamemnon, Orion, and the horned gate is the inevitability of violence and destruction as part of man's experience on earth. Sweeney, the prototype of the most basic human drives, neither restrained by social, nor tempered by spiritual, experience, is closer than most men to the primitive, destructive forces which myth delineates. "Among the nightingales," he embodies the knowledge of conflict and death which Oedipus possessed near the end of his life, as he rested in a grove sacred to the Furies and listened to the song of the nightingales (*Oedipus at Colonus*, l. 18). Sweeney "guards the hornèd gate" because this awareness, unconscious and universal, is present in true dreams.

The poem suggests the preparation for Sweeney's murder by "Rachel *née* Rabinovitch" and "the lady in the cape." As Sweeney sits with them in a cafe, he grows suspicious, and soon he leaves. For the moment he is spared, but the last two stanzas make it clear that he is indeed destined to act out a mythical role as the victim of treachery and violence:

> The host with someone indistinct
> Converses at the door apart,
> The nightingales are singing near
> The Convent of the Sacred Heart,
>
> And sang within the bloody wood
> When Agamemnon cried aloud
> And let their liquid siftings fall
> To sustain the stiff dishonoured shroud.

The song of the nightingales, the symbol of recurrence in the title and the poem, first associated with the suffering and knowledge of

---

[85] *The Achievement of T. S. Eliot*, 3rd ed. (New York, 1958), p. 129.

Oedipus, now seems to echo the tranquillity of the convent and to suggest the permanence of its values. These exist, however, within a world of continuous hatred and violence, which still contains "the bloody wood" where kings were killed who exemplified in myth what Sweeney enacts in contemporary society.

The Waste Land marks the height and essentially the end of Eliot's use of classical myth in his poetry to symbolize individual and general unconscious feeling and conflict. In later poems he does employ classical myth, though more sparingly, and he combines pagan allusions with Christian ones, but never again is myth so intrinsic to the theme and structure of his poetry. In the "Notes" to *The Waste Land* Eliot informs the reader that Tiresias, "although a mere spectator and not indeed a 'character,' is yet the most important personage in the poem, uniting all the rest. . . . What Tiresias *sees*, in fact, is the substance of the poem." Eliot's emphasis on the sight of the blind prophet is a perhaps unnecessary indication that it is his insight, his awareness of what lies beneath his and others' conscious perception, that unifies all the elements of the poem.

Yet it is not the myth of Tiresias but the Grail legend that provides the dominant symbolism of *The Waste Land*. Eliot's references in the "Notes" to Jessie Weston's *From Ritual to Romance* and Frazer's *The Golden Bough*, and to the "great anthropological interest" of Ovid's tale of Tiresias' metamorphosis from male to female and his return to his original state, suggest that in his view it is their connection with ancient religious rituals that unites the Greek myth and the medieval legend. More important perhaps is Tiresias' power to see, comprehend, and predict what is dark to other men. His is the unconscious mind of the poem, containing secret knowledge of male and female, gods and mortals, past and future. It is he who perceives the structure of the Grail legend beneath the surface of modern society.

Eliot's use of Jessie Weston's interpretation of the Grail legend as his main symbol of a quest for some source of recovery from the sterility of modern life has been discussed by many critics, whose chief aim has been to explain his various and sometimes cryptic allusions.[86] In so doing they seem to have missed important thematic and structural elements of the poem that are directly related to Eliot's choice of a legend which, at least as Miss Weston interprets it, originates in ancient fertility rites with their attendant myths and is later adapted to Christian myth, symbol, and ritual observance. In adapting this legend, Eliot employs symbols which emerge from its ancient mythical origins to depict modern man's dissatisfactions and inner struggles; his mythical commentary is ironic and tragic, offering neither consolation nor resolution, only the conversion of suffering into a ritual quest for divine sustenance.

In discussing certain similarities in Eliot's and Jung's use of myth, Elizabeth Drew sees a parallel in Eliot's concept of rebirth and Jung's "archetype of transformation." The "I" of *The Waste Land*, she says, "is agonizingly aware, in the imprisonment of his personal waste land, that the possibilities of rebirth cannot be dismissed as an historical anachronism; that the truth of the experience is eternally present and that the living of it plunges the whole man into a process of disintegration and conflict." Miss Drew also reveals similarities in the images used by Jung and Eliot to symbolize unconscious experience, especially the image of water.[87] These parallels are interesting but not surprising since both Jung and Eliot use traditional mythical and literary sources; moreover, in *The Waste Land* Eliot is not quite consciously straining toward a religious position similar to that which is the basis of Jung's psychology. Miss Drew assumes, as does Jung, that the "change of consciousness" brought about through the archetypes of transformation effects "an integration of

[86] See, for example, Grover Smith, *T. S. Eliot's Poetry and Plays*; Cleanth Brooks, "The Waste Land: Critique of the Myth," *Modern Poetry and the Tradition*, pp. 136-72; and George Williamson, *A Reader's Guide to T. S. Eliot*, 2nd. ed. (New York, 1966).

[87] *T. S. Eliot: The Design of His Poetry* (New York, 1949), pp. 63-65. Miss Drew approaches the body of Eliot's poetry from a Jungian point of view as exemplifying an "integration of the personality" (p. xiii). Other studies of Eliot from the perspective of Jungian psychology are: Genevieve W. Foster, "The Archetypal Imagery of T. S. Eliot," *PMLA*, LX (June 1945), 567-85; and P. W. Martin, *Experiment in Depth, A Study of the Work of Jung, Eliot, and Toynbee* (New York, 1955).

personality." Actually, it can be shown that the mythical experience depicted in *The Waste Land* is similar to the Jungian plunge into archetypal consciousness because it leads not to self-knowledge or the resolution of personal conflict, but to a transformation of uncertainty into faith, of human weakness into reliance on supernatural omnipotence. Such a transformation may provide "integration," but only through a belief that the self can merge with a divine principle.

This process evolves gradually in the mythical structure of the poem, which is first indicated in the epigraph spoken by the Sibyl of Cumae in the *Satyricon* of Petronius. The prophetess is associated with the most ancient and honored of rituals, yet in the context of the *Satyricon* and in the story told by Trimalchio, whom Eliot quotes, she is debased both by the scornful attitude of the narrator and the particular myth he tells. The Sibyl, hung in a jar, responds to the children who ask her what she wants, "I wish to die." This is the Sibyl who led Aeneas to the underworld, where his spirit was restored and his dedication to his mission renewed. Now, in a degenerate time, her powers limited, she can only wish for death. The epigraph creates the atmosphere of cynicism and despair with which *The Waste Land* begins; the old rituals of renewal, like the Sibyl who once assisted in their performance, have been tainted by the weakness and corruption of man.

Thus April, the month of rebirth, is "the cruellest month," promising renewal and indeed "breeding / Lilacs" but along with them "Memory and desire." As the earth stirs, man becomes aware of a drive for renewal within his own soul, a yearning to overcome the limitations of his separate being and to feel himself reborn as the earth is restored. Yet his memories and experience seem to deny such fulfillment. Eliot's first allusion to a religious source in this poem is explicit: he refers in a note to Ezekiel 2 and Ecclesiastes 12 in connection with lines 20 and 23, but in the entire passage from line 19 to line 30, he echoes the preacher and the prophet to intensify and extend the feelings of sterility and despair which darken man's memory and his life in the present.

Momentarily, the possibility of human love, "the hyacinth girl," seems to offer salvation, but the very symbol in which this hope is expressed reveals its limits. The "hyacinth garden" calls to mind Frazer's description of both the mythical figure Hyacinth as representative of "the vegetation which blooms in the spring and withers under the scorching heat of the summer sun" and the "sad flower" which was "an omen of death."[88] Eliot suggests that human love cannot offer fulfillment, for it is itself involved with and subject to death.

The protagonist of *The Waste Land* then turns to a new source of regeneration, a contemporary and debased form of an old myth and ritual, "the lower mythology" of the fortune teller. The Tarot pack, originally used "to predict the rise and fall of the waters which brought fertility to the land,"[89] is now employed by Madame Sosostris, the "famous" and tainted clairvoyante. After telling the protagonist that his is the card of "the drowned Phoenician Sailor," she announces that she cannot find the "Hanged Man," whom Eliot associates "with the Hanged God of Frazer," a figure sacrificed in various forms and cultures so that his spirit might insure fertility to the earth and its inhabitants. She offers the advice, "Fear death by water," but does not see the connection between the missing "Hanged Man" or god and the prophetic meaning of the "drowned Phoenician Sailor" for the protagonist.

Like most prophetic statements, this one is ambiguous and cryptic, revealing as much about the character of the recipient as about his fate. The prophecy confirms the protagonist's fear of death and at the same time reveals his yearning to participate in a rite of rebirth. Since the hanged god is not to be found in his society, he himself will imitate the prototypal sacrificial figure, drowning only to be recovered, dying to be reborn. This is the first hint of a wish to merge with divinity, which is later realized in the poem. The prophecy is fulfilled in Part IV in the drowning of Phlebas the Phoenician, "a type of fertility god,"[90] with whom the speaker identifies as

[88] *The New Golden Bough, A New Abridgment of the Classic Work by Sir James Frazer,* ed. Theodore H. Gaster (New York, 1959), pp. 320-21.

[89] Jessie L. Weston, *From Ritual to Romance* (1920; reprint, New York, 1941), p. 76.

[90] Brooks, *Modern Poetry and the Tradition,* p. 142.

sacrificial victim and example. Only after this "death by water" does the "Hanged God" appear; in a note Eliot associates him with "the hooded figure in the passage of the disciples to Emmaus in Part V," a clear indication that he is also Christ.

The continual merging of characters with one another and all of them with the speaker or protagonist is intrinsic to the theme of *The Waste Land*. Eliot emphasizes this technique in a note: "Just as the one-eyed merchant, seller of currants, melts into the Phoeni-cian Sailor, and the latter is not wholly distinct from Ferdinand Prince of Naples, so all the women are one woman, and the two sexes meet in Tiresias." Since, moreover, all the figures merge in the mind of Tiresias, they are all part of a universal consciousness whose fate is projected in the symbols of the Tarot pack.

Among these is "the man with three staves," whom Eliot associ-ates "quite arbitrarily with the Fisher King." His role in *The Waste Land* reflects Jessie Weston's theory that he is "the essential centre" of the entire ritual of fertility on which the Grail legend is based, "a being semi-divine, semi-human, standing between his people and land, and the unseen forces which control their destiny."[91] It is to-ward the maimed Fisher King, who symbolizes "the Divine Prin-ciple of Life and Fertility,"[92] combining the attributes of ancient fertility god and Christian healer, that the quest of the protagonist is directed. Jessie Weston points out that in many versions of the Grail legend the duty of the hero is to ask the proper question of the Fisher King: in one version he asks "concerning the Grail," in another "whom it serves." When the proper question is asked, the maimed king is healed and thus the land is restored; when the question is not asked, the king remains sick or dies, and the land suffers.[93] Questions about the meaning of their own lives or of life itself are implicit in the conflict and despair of the protagonist and the other characters of *The Waste Land*. These feelings expressed in myth throughout the poem are ultimately enacted in a ritual quest for the restoration of health to man and the earth.

The unfulfilled desire for human love symbolized in the allusion

[91] *From Ritual to Romance*, p. 129.
[92] *ibid.*, p. 108. [93] *ibid.*, pp. 13-15.

to the myth of Hyacinth has already been discussed. Other mythical references repeat and intensify this experience. In Part II the failure of romantic love is revealed in human society on both its highest and lowest cultural and economic levels. In the first scene Eliot evokes Shakespeare's most magnificent description of Cleopatra and alludes to Vergil's Dido, only to flatten and demythify the composite portrait. This lady, "Belladonna," has all the external trappings of a great queen and none of her mythical power. The symbol of overwhelming physical beauty and sexual appeal is itself reduced in this portrait of a modern upper-class woman, nervous, frightened, vainly seeking some purpose in her superficial life. She is surrounded by reflections of her own despair:

> Above the antique mantel was displayed
> As though a window gave upon the sylvan scene
> The change of Philomel, by the barbarous king
> So rudely forced; yet there the nightingale
> Filled all the desert with inviolable voice
> And still she cried, and still the world pursues,
> "Jug Jug" to dirty ears.
> And other withered stumps of time
> Were told upon the walls; staring forms
> Leaned out, leaning, hushing the room enclosed.

In this representation even the myth of Philomel has lost its power and its dignity. Its ancient meaning—the conversion of pain to beauty, death to perennial life—is gone: in the past the nightingale may have "Filled all the desert with inviolable voice," but now it sings, " 'Jug Jug' to dirty ears." It is one of the "withered stumps of time." The myth serves a double purpose here: it expresses one of the themes of *The Waste Land*, the effect of the sterility of modern life on traditional values, and, more important, it suggests the inadequacy of myth to do more than depict contemporary apathy and despair. Eliot presents the Philomela myth in a static picture "displayed" over an "antique mantel"; it does not function either to reveal or to transcend the sources of alienation and spiritual death. The woman whose home it adorns asks, "What shall I do now?

What shall I do? . . . What shall we do tomorrow? / What shall we ever do?" The mythical exposure of violation and sterility ends in a frantic quest.

In "The Fire Sermon," another scene reveals the failure of human love to provide sustenance in a sterile world. Here the presence of Tiresias, who announces that he "Perceived the scene, and foretold the rest—" suggests the depth of unconscious agony beneath the sordid and trivial life of the typist and her "carbuncular" lover, but the seer offers no revelation. The young woman looks not at her inner self, but "in the glass":

> Hardly aware of her departed lover;
> Her brain allows one half-formed thought to pass:
> "Well now that's done: and I'm glad it's over."

The consciousness of Tiresias drifts away from the mechanical sound of the gramophone to music which evokes an enchanted world of love and beauty: "This music crept by me upon the waters." As he incorporates the character Ferdinand, remarking on a song of Ariel in *The Tempest* (l. 391), he brings this memory to the contemporary city. It leads him away from the ugliness he has witnessed to a place

> Where fishmen lounge at noon: where the walls
> Of Magnus Martyr hold
> Inexplicable splendour of Ionian white and gold.

The mythical seer whose mind encompasses all the suffering of the waste land seeks the "fishmen" and the church, a scene of momentary relief and a suggestion that even in the barren "city" and its maimed inhabitants there is a remnant of "splendour" and hope.

The music continues in the sound of the river, which Eliot mythicizes; three "Thames-daughters," like the Rhine-daughters of the *Götterdämmerung*, sing of the failure of love, of violence and ugliness, all without meaning:

> I can connect
> Nothing with nothing.

The shift from this mythical scene of unrelieved despair to a quotation from St. Augustine's *Confessions* and the Buddha's Fire Sermon, which Eliot compares with the Sermon on the Mount, serves as a religious commentary on man's sin, suffering, and possible repentance.

In the last two sections of *The Waste Land* the central myth of sterility and rebirth is expressed almost entirely through allusions to and imitation of ritual. Like all the action of *The Waste Land*, this takes place within the consciousness of the protagonist who merges with all the characters as the impotent Fisher King, waiting for the proper question. The rich and varied mythical structure of the poem reveals man's inability to understand or resolve his central conflicts; the poetic reconstructions of ritual (which are discussed in the next chapter) indicate that his only possibility of salvation lies in the enactment of a symbolic quest.

The study of Greek and Roman myth as a vehicle expressing unconscious conflict in Eliot's poetry properly ends with *The Waste Land*. Though some allusions to ancient myth occur in connection with Christian ritual in his later poems, and Greek mythical themes and characters are the essential structural background of most of his plays, he did not use pagan myth extensively in the poetry he wrote after his conversion to the Anglican Church. In certain respects, Eliot rejected the full implications of myth even as he used it in his early poetry; here mythical figures and symbols express yearning for love and purpose and the pain of impotence and frustration within men's souls, but these feelings reveal little about the nature of human beings, except their need for "something outside themselves."[94]

In using myth Eliot neither sought nor attained insight into his own unconscious mind, as did Yeats; nor does myth develop in Eliot's poetry, as it does in Yeats's, into an instrument for approaching the deepest and most fearful aspects of inner and external reality. For Eliot myth essentially provides "an escape from emotion . . .

[94] T. S. Eliot, "The Function of Criticism," *Selected Essays, 1917-1932*, p. 15.

an escape from personality."[95] In an essay on Matthew Arnold, in which he comments on the statement: "Poetry is at bottom a criticism of life," Eliot remarks: "At the bottom of the abyss is what few ever see, and what those cannot bear to look at for long. . . . We bring back very little from our rare descents."[96] Classical myth was for a time a guide to the "abyss" for Eliot, but he could use it effectively only as an impersonal means of expression, which inevitably led to imitation of traditional ritual.

W. H. AUDEN
Myth as Analytic Instrument

The technique Eliot employs in his most important early poetry, of diverting unconscious drives symbolized in myth into rites of devotion, depicts the urgency of his need to escape the demands and implications of psychological conflict; the fulfillment of this need is reflected in his allusions to Christian dogma and his increasing use of ritual effects in his later poetry. In the work of W. H. Auden, who, at least on the surface, followed a similar path, seeking a Christian solution to the problems of man in contemporary society, classical myth discloses deeper and more subtle levels of conflict and suffering, which occur in a very different crisis of disbelief; and it is an essential element in his poetic expression of a religious resolution. In discussing the contemporary poet's awareness of the usefulness of myth, Auden says:

> He knows, too, that in poetry all dogmas become myths; that the aesthetic value of the poem is the same whether the poet and/or the reader actively believe what it says or not. He is apt then to look around for some myth—any myth, he thinks, will do—to serve the same purpose for himself. What he overlooks is that the only kind of myth which will do for him must have one thing in common with believed dogma, namely, that the relation

---

[95] T. S. Eliot, "Tradition and the Individual Talent," *Selected Essays, 1917-1932*, p. 10.
[96] *The Use of Poetry and the Use of Criticism*, p. 111.

of the former to the poet, as of the latter to the soul, must be a personal one.[97]

In this passage Auden reveals a good deal about his own poetic development, in which a union of intellectual, psychological, and technical elements is always present and evident. For Auden myth has served as a major and continuous mode of expression and always as a deeply personal one. His use of myth, moreover, indicates a consistency and continuity within all the diversity of his thought and poetic form. From his early work to the present day, in the persona of classical healer and in that of Christian poet-preacher, Auden has employed myth and ritual to suggest through the body of his work a definition of his poetry as public, ceremonial, and efficacious in alleviating emotional and spiritual disorder.

In his poetry of the late thirties, myth reveals man's lonely struggle with the unconscious forces of his own nature unaided by faith in any supernatural power; in the poetry written after his conversion to Christianity, "dogmas become myths" as he attempts to understand and control the unconscious drives revealed in myth through Christian faith and devotion. When Christian dogma becomes his ultimate psychological reality, he adapts and converts it to mythical expression.

Auden's approach to myth and ritual was influenced by his knowledge of the works of Freud and, to a much lesser extent, those of Jung. In employing myth as an expression of the unconscious, Auden, like Freud, exploits its possibilities as an analytic tool; it is an instrument of fantasy, most effective in exposing the irrational; even as it creates illusion, it shatters it. Unlike Yeats, Auden did not begin by contesting the insight that myth provided. For him there was no initial "flight into fairyland." Yeats created a mythical structure as both a defense against and a unique means of releasing unconscious insight and knowledge; Auden, relying on a scientific structure provided by the new psychology, approached myth as a guide to unconscious drives in man and society.

Practically every commentator on Auden has noticed the psycho-

[97] "Yeats as an Example," *The Kenyon Critics*, p. 111.

logical basis of his thought throughout his prose and poetry, which results in part from his broad knowledge of psychology, biology, and anthropology. Monroe Spears speaks of the combination in Auden's poetry of "the didactic, diagnostic impulse of the rational mind with the deep, magical, emotional, irrational impulse (or compulsion) to fantasy." According to Spears, Auden's "problem is to keep the power and magic of the fantasy while making it accessible and meaningful, to make it, in short, diagnostic."[98] An analysis of Auden's development as a poet will indicate that he solved this problem by uniting two apparently contradictory realms of experience through his use of myth. In so doing Auden relies on ancient literature and on his readings in anthropology and psychology, especially Freud, but his approach is neither traditional, clinical, nor scholarly, for he makes of ancient myth his own symbolic language.

Though Auden's use of myth to reveal unconscious feelings and conflict is varied and extensive, it manifests itself in four main modes: he employs large mythical concepts or "entities"; he mythicizes the scene and atmosphere of contemporary life; he alludes to well known mythical figures or legends, which provide a background of feelings and associations to which he relates a contemporary experience; he relies for contrast or irony on the reader's memory of specific mythical references in the works of ancient poets.

In his early work, *Paid on Both Sides: A Charade* (1930), *Poems* (1930), the second edition of *Poems* (1933), and *The Orators* (1932), Auden does employ myth, but he relies far more on general mythical and legendary figures and ideas and on dream images than on specific mythical references; furthermore, though there are hints of some mythical concepts, such as Eros and the quest, these are not yet fully developed. His use of myth is not nearly so extensive nor is it so intrinsic to his thought as it is in the poems of the later thirties, the forties, and the fifties. For example, myth is really imposed on the theme of "Since you are going to begin today,"[99] which Spears

[98] Monroe K. Spears, *The Poetry of W. H. Auden, The Disenchanted Island* (New York, 1963), p. 60.

[99] The poem is III in *Poems* (London, 1930) and in the revised edition, *Poems* (London, 1933) and *Poems* (New York, 1934); it is reprinted in *The*

describes as "an address to the doomed bourgeois by Dame Kind, or the Life Force, explaining how and why he is to be superseded."[100] It was not until Auden prepared the 1945 edition of his *Collected Poetry* that he gave this poem the title "Venus Will Now Say a Few Words," apparently attempting to characterize the speaker more exactly while retaining her quality as a life force. The *persona* of the poem, however, remains a generalized mythical figure—secure, powerful, and exultant—and the title does little to strengthen her identity.

Elsewhere in the early poems there are references to "the dragon's day, the devourer's"[101] and to many "ghosts,"[102] but these are all general, creating a dream-like mood or a suggestion of legend or myth somewhere in the background, but certainly not of major importance in the language or its associations. Only as Auden matures as a poet does myth become significant to him as a symbolic language.

A good deal of critical attention has been paid to two mythical concepts which appear again and again in Auden's poetry, the Quest and Eros. The first has been analyzed by many critics,[103] and in general needs little further explication except in connection with particular mythical allusions.[104] It will be discussed more extensively in rela-

---

Collected Poetry of W. H. Auden (New York, 1945). Since *The Collected Poetry* is most accessible to readers, quotations are, whenever possible, taken from and page references made to this volume.

[100] *The Poetry of W. H. Auden*, p. 32.

[101] XVI, *Poems* (1930 and 1933); "1929" in *Collected Poetry*.

[102] For example, "And ghosts must do again / What gives them pain," XXVII, *Poems* (1933); "What Do You Think?" in *Collected Poetry*; "ghost's adversity," XVIII, *Poems* (1930 and 1933), "This One" in *Collected Poetry*;

> And the heart changes,   But this was never
> Where ghost has haunted,   A ghost's endeavor
> Lost and wanted.   Nor, finished this,
>   Was ghost at ease . . . ,

XVII, *Poems* (1930 and 1933), "Pur" in *Collected Poetry*.

[103] See Spears, *The Poetry of W. H. Auden*, especially p. 138ff.; Richard Hoggart, *W. H. Auden* (London, 1957), pp. 11, 18-22; and Herbert Greenberg, *Quest for the Necessary* (Cambridge, Mass., 1968), pp. 83-116.

[104] See below, pp. 162-70; 251-55.

tion to Auden's use of ritual in the next chapter. Auden's view of Eros, however, though it has often been treated, has never been satisfactorily explained.

Spears's discussion of Eros in Auden's poetry oversimplifies both his conception and its expression in the poems. He sees it as appearing in three phases: "In the early verse, love or Eros is conceived of generally in Freudian terms as including both ego- and object-love, the urge to self-preservation and preservation of the species, as well as sexual love; Eros opposes (but sometimes combines with) the other basic drive, Thanatos, the death-wish or the destructive instinct." The second phase, which Spears assigns to the poems of *On This Island* (which first appeared in 1936 under the title *Look Stranger!* and with its new title in 1937), is one in which Eros seems to him separable from love; Eros, according to Spears, is now "seen as selfish, crooked, and bad," as opposed to love which is "unselfish and social."[105] In the third and Christian phase Eros, "being selfish, tends toward evil," and opposes Agape, "selfless Christian love, divine as opposed to human."[106]

There is no doubt that Eros is a concept of diverse meaning in Auden's poetry, but this diversity is far more complex than is indicated in Spears's simple division. One can hardly use the term Eros in any meaningful sense to describe Auden's concept of love in the early poems. Though in a general and rather superficial way,

---

[105] *The Poetry of W. H. Auden*, pp. 124-25.

[106] *ibid.*, p. 135. Stephen Spender also oversimplifies Auden's interpretation and use of Freud. In developing the point that the idea of "Symptom and Cure" pervades Auden's poetry, Spender describes the Cure as "At one time Love, in the sense of Freudian release from inhibition; at another time a vaguer and more exalted idea of loving; at still another the Social Revolution; and at a yet later stage, Christianity." This is a distortion of Auden's approach to love, Freud, and Christianity. Spender is, however, correct in his conclusion that "the direction of Auden's poetry has been towards the defining of the concept of Love" ("W. H. Auden and His Poetry," in *Auden, A Collection of Critical Essays*, ed. Monroe K. Spears [Englewood Cliffs, N. J., 1964], 28). A more convincing discussion of Auden's concept of Eros can be found in Herbert Greenberg's *Quest for the Necessary*, pp. 61-62, 85.

love—the term Auden does use—is based on the Freudian Eros, in these poems it actually designates simpler, less ambiguous feelings and experiences than Freud describes. In Auden's early poems love is usually a general term, sometimes implying brotherly love[107] and at other times personal or physical love. It may also be a creative force opposing physical and psychological sickness, but it does so far more automatically than Freud suggests and certainly with none of the ambiguity he finds inevitable in Eros, either as a natural force or as an individual experience.

The key to Eros in Auden, as in Freud, lies in the fact that it is a mythical term and concept. Though in depth and significance the Freudian Eros goes far beyond the ancient mythical figure of the god of love, it includes his ambivalent nature, his capacity to bring suffering and pleasure, to cause destruction and death, and to inspire creation. In ancient literature Eros is at once a child god and a childish one, and also a powerful productive force. Freud says that his approach to Eros derives from Plato's definition of the concept in the *Symposium*. In his "Preface" to the fourth edition of *Three Essays on the Theory of Sexuality*, Freud reminds his readers "how closely the enlarged sexuality of psychoanalysis coincides with the Eros of the divine Plato,"[108] and elsewhere he says that he employs the term "exactly in the sense in which Plato uses the word 'Eros' in his *Symposium*."[109]

Plato's Eros, the child of Poros, or Plenty, and Penia, or Poverty, is foolish, poor, and rough, but he is also courageous and strong, wise and resourceful. Sometimes he flourishes and at other times he is unsatisfied. He is an ambivalent figure, a mean between good and evil; Eros can be a "philosopher," but he can also be "a dreadful enchanter." Surely Freud is conscious of these opposing characteristics when in *Civilization and its Discontents* he says that "we are never so defenceless against suffering as when we love, never so helplessly unhappy as when we have lost our loved object or its

---

[107] Joseph Warren Beach, *The Making of the Auden Canon* (Minneapolis, 1957), p. 24.

[108] SE VII, 134.   [109] "Why War?" SE XXII, 209.

love."[110] In his discussion of Eros as a parent of civilization he concludes that only a "small minority are enabled by their constitution to find happiness, in spite of everything, along the path of love." These, he goes on to say, are people who do not depend on a beloved object for their satisfaction but who instead transfer their need and capacity for love to mankind as a whole, "transforming the instinct into an impulse with an *inhibited aim*."[111] His example of such a person is St. Francis of Assisi. As will be illustrated below, the Freudian Eros diverted and inhibited becomes for Auden Agape.

Love directed toward an object is restricted and complicated by the demands of civilization. As Freud says, "in the course of development the relation of love to civilization loses its unambiguity." He then deals with the ways in which love opposes the "interests of civilization" and the many ways in which civilization curbs the development of individual sexuality and love.[112] Indeed, the entire body of Freud's work is concerned with this problem: the difficulty of the fulfillment of the love instinct and the illness which results from its suppression in both individuals and society.

For Freud, Eros exists side by side with death, with which it is continually engaged in warfare, but which is by no means its only enemy. The capacity of Eros to cause suffering results in part from its own nature: pain, dependence, and loss are intrinsic to it, the variety and extent of its power threaten organized life, and possibly "not only the presence of civilization but something in the nature of the function itself . . . denies us full satisfaction and urges us along other paths."[113] Eros is further complicated and modified by its use of the very drive which opposes it, the death instinct. In the form of external aggressiveness, the death instinct is "pressed into the service of Eros, in that the organism [is] destroying some other thing, whether animate or inanimate, instead of destroying itself." Freud goes on to say that "the two kinds of instinct [Eros and Death] seldom—perhaps never—appear in isolation from each other, but are alloyed with each other in varying and different proportions."[114]

[110] SE xxi, 82.   [111] SE xxi, 101-102.   [112] SE xxi, 103ff.
[113] SE xxi, 105.
[114] SE xxi, 119. See also *The Ego and the Id*, SE xix, 41.

Eros, threatened by the death instinct, employs it for the preservation of life, yet is itself modified by this alloy. Freud suggests that sadism is the clearest example in which "the death instinct twists the erotic aim in its own sense and yet at the same time fully satisfies the erotic urge."[115] Other manifestations of the close relationship between these opposing drives are less obvious but ever present in human life.

In adopting as his own the Freudian Eros, Auden slowly came to apprehend it as the complex and ambiguous force Freud explored and described. Auden's early poems emphasize the inherent strength of Eros in its opposition to death, but it is only in his mature work that he recognizes love as an instinctual drive which can most accurately be delineated through a mythical or legendary image. Furthermore, the struggle of Eros against social and political as well as personal adversaries suggested to Auden its intrinsic relationship to other basic needs denied by a repressive society. In his essay "Psychology and Art," which appeared in 1935, he says, "Both Marx and Freud start from the failures of civilization, one from the poor, one from the ill. Both see human behavior determined, not consciously, but by instinctive needs, hunger and love." At this point, Auden feels that despite their basic disagreement "both are right."[116] There is no question that Auden was more deeply influenced by Freud than he was by Marx, and certainly his subsequent development and his conversion to Christianity indicate that both influences were modified by his individual view of and response to the problems of human life, yet he never ceased to be concerned with the issues he summarizes so concisely in this essay.

Throughout *On This Island*, Auden deals with the theme of love, sometimes in connection with hunger ("Hunger and love in their variations"[117]) and at other times as the dominant instinctual force in man's life, never entirely free of death. Love is presented in a variety of forms and experiences, and in some poems does convey

[115] SE XXI, 121.
[116] *The Arts Today*, ed. G. Grigson (London, 1935), p. 19.
[117] XXI, *On This Island* (New York, 2nd ed., 1937); "A Bride in the 30's" in *Collected Poetry*.

the complexity of the Freudian Eros. Though Auden does not use the term Eros in the poems of this volume, his approach to the theme of love reveals a deeper understanding of the instinct Freud describes than do his earlier poems; moreover, in *On This Island* Auden begins to develop his unique poetic adaptation of Eros as a mythical concept. In so doing he is concerned not with a distinction between Eros and love but rather with the various and subtle ways in which this drive manifests itself in the personal and social life of man; rarely free of the effects of guilt, loss, hunger, and aggression, it nonetheless offers him his only chance of survival.

In the "Prologue" ("Perhaps" in *Collected Poetry*), love is asked to "display its power," to inspire man with renewed strength and courage; but in other poems of *On This Island* Auden expresses his awareness of the limits of love's nature and power, its involvement with guilt and death. He speaks of the "tyrannies of love" in II, "Out on the lawn I lie in bed," and knows that love is threatened by hunger and aggression ("A Summer Night 1933" in *Collected Poetry*):

> Soon, soon, through dykes of our content
> The crumpling flood will force a rent
>   And, taller than a tree,
> Hold sudden death before our eyes
> Whose river dreams long hid the size
>   And vigours of the sea.

Auden's imagery—"flood," "river dreams," "vigours of the sea"—suggests the connection between man's personal life and the evolving life of external nature.

Many of the poems of *On This Island* contain dreams in which mythical figures appear as symbols. Auden generally invents these mythical types: "the stocky keepers of a wild estate";[118] "the smiling grimy boy at the garage"; "the physician, bridegroom and incendiary,"[119] all of whom are involved in the struggle between the compulsion to sickness and violence and the yearning for love. Some-

[118] X, *On This Island*; "Not All the Candidates Pass" in *Collected Poetry*.
[119] XI, *On This Island*; "Nobody Understands Me" in *Collected Poetry*.

times, however, he turns to traditional myth to express the complex nature of love, which he wishes to establish as a standard of civilized life. In "Here on the cropped grass" (XVII) Auden sets an experience of personal love within the environment of "Gross Hunger" in the outside world:

> Europe grew anxious about her health,
> Combines tottered, credits froze,
> And business shivered in a banker's winter
> While we were kissing.

He then looks back to past civilizations:

> Like the cupped hand of the keen excavator
> Busy with bones, the memory uncovers
> The hopes of time. . . .

Ancient Greek civilization for him is associated with the "laws of love":

> Small birds above me have the grace of those who founded
> The civilization of the delicate olive,
> Learning the laws of love and sailing
> On the calm Aegean. . . .

No sooner has he spoken of love than the image of the hawk comes to his mind, "the symbol of the rule by thirst." Love, here depicted as flourishing in ancient Greece, which itself became a pervading myth for western civilization, approaches the Freudian Eros, though Auden does not yet use that name; it is the generator of life and inspirer of law, but threatened throughout man's history by hunger and aggression. In the present it is further threatened and finally defeated by man's pride in his technological achievement; man has become what Freud calls the "prosthetic God." He is, Auden says, heir to the "unbounded vigours of the instrument." The "bones of war" declare:

> . . . we assumed their power to be our own,
> Believed machines to be our hearts' spontaneous fruit. . . .

145

In XXV, "Casino," suggesting that the rituals of gambling have become the only religion of twentieth-century man, Auden describes the loneliness of those who "in the rites of disbelief are joined." With this sad scene he contrasts the world of external nature—rivers, mountains, and birds. Then he comments:

> But here no nymph comes naked to the youngest shepherd;
> The fountain is deserted; the laurel will not grow;
>   The labyrinth is safe but endless, and broken
>   Is Ariadne's thread.

> As deeper in these hands is grooved their fortune: "Lucky
> Were few, and it is possible that none were loved;
>   And what was godlike in this generation
>   Was never to be born."

The failure of myth to ring true indicates a failure of imagination and a failure of love. There is more horror in the "safe but endless" labyrinth, offering neither challenge nor hope, than in the mythical labyrinth where the "godlike" Theseus faced and killed the Minotaur. The myth tells of a heroic struggle with and conquest of the monstrous and the destructive and of the release from toil and danger, guided by the thread of love. Love in the ancient myth offers the way out of the labyrinth. The generation in which "none were loved," however, never face the danger of the beast-man, but instead wander endlessly in a labyrinth which they have not the courage to investigate or the incentive to leave.

Yet the gods have not entirely deserted this generation. Man has a choice, says Auden, though it may be an unconscious one (XXI; "A Bride in the 30's" in Collected Poetry):

> But the heart repeats though we would not hearken:
> "Yours is the choice to whom the gods awarded
>   The language of learning and the language of love,
>   Crooked to move as a moneybug or a cancer
>   Or straight as a dove."

146

The "language of learning and the language of love" provide the only cure for the disease of contemporary life. In a familiar role of poet as physician Auden calls attention to what "the heart repeats." At this point it is his only prescription.

Another Time (1940) and *The Double Man* (which in the English edition was called *New Year Letter,* 1941) again deal with this theme: the struggle of love to exist and to preserve a measure of health in a sick society. In these volumes Auden's conception of love is a deeper and broader one than in the earlier poems; it is indeed the Freudian mythical entity Eros, a term Auden now uses to designate the complex nature of love and continually considers and redefines in his exploration of the possibilities and limits of human life and his own role in history and society.

In his poem "In Memory of Sigmund Freud" Auden refers to Eros as a creative force. Freud himself is depicted as almost a mythical figure, surrounded to the end by "shades that still waited to enter / The bright circle of his recognition." His enemy is a mythicized Hate, who rejoices in his death:

> Only Hate was happy, hoping to augment
> His practice now, and his shabby clientèle
>   Who think they can be cured by killing
>   And covering the garden with ashes.

Eros too is explicitly mythical in this poem:

> Sad is Eros, builder of cities,
> And weeping anarchic Aphrodite.[120]

In eulogizing Freud, Auden simplifies Eros, employing it, as Freud certainly did not, as an unqualified symbol of civilization; in this form it seems suited to its role as chief mourner for Freud who established its place in modern thought.

Other poems of this period suggest that Eros is a more ambiguous concept, expressing as much the ills of society as the creative force which produced it. One of the most moving of these poems is "Sep-

[120] *Another Time* (New York, 1940); also in *Collected Poetry.*

tember 1, 1939" in which Auden uses the first person singular to express his despair at the "anger and fear" of a world at war and to suggest the possibility of deliverance from "the error bred in the bone"—limited though his means may be—through love and creation, which are in the end the same. False worship of a "psychopathic god" has "driven a culture mad." Auden sees men and women constantly avoiding their unconscious childish yearnings and fears:

> Lest we should see where we are,
> Lost in a haunted wood,
> Children afraid of the night
> Who have never been happy or good.

Like children in a fairy tale, alone and fearful of woods full of monsters, each of us searches not for "universal love / But to be loved alone." Auden indicates that love is too often a limited, infantile need, but he goes on to assert that it is also creative energy and power. It is the only answer to sickness, war, and death. The poet turns to himself, to his own creative powers, to seek a love deeper than the infantile self-love which is so destructive:

> All I have is a voice
> To undo the folded lie,
> The romantic lie in the brain
> Of the sensual man-in-the-street
> And the lie of Authority
> Whose buildings grope the sky:
> There is no such thing as the State
> And no one exists alone;
> Hunger allows no choice
> To the citizen or the police;
> We must love one another or die.
>
> Defenceless under the night
> Our world in stupor lies;
> Yet, dotted everywhere,

> Ironic points of light
> Flash out wherever the Just
> Exchange their messages:
> May I, composed like them
> Of Eros and of dust,
> Beleaguered by the same
> Negation and despair,
> Show an affirming flame.[121]

Auden omitted the first of these two stanzas from the version of this poem in *Collected Poetry*. Critics have found various explanations for the omission,[122] but there seems to be no real justification for it except perhaps Auden's personal feelings about the poem. The omission does not change the theme of the poem or the poet's point of view. It merely removes a powerful development of the struggle between love and death and reduces the impact of the last stanza. The repetition of the word, "lie," which finally rhymes with "die," suggests the urgency of the only available alternative: love turned from the self to others. We are struck by the frailty of the voice pleading for love in the face of all the organized illusions created to avoid the admission of its absence, but we are also impressed by the strength of conviction of the lonely participant in despair who at the same time takes on the role of healer. Eros may be limited by man's childish narrowness of vision and by his need for self-delusion, but it is the only creative force against the power of death. Eros in this poem both includes and exceeds the selfish, narrow love of self which is destructive to man, for it is also the "affirming flame" of creation and of life itself.

Once again in V, "Oxford," Auden wrestles with the limitations of love, its selfishness and apparent impotence. He speaks of "Eros Paidagogos" who "Weeps on his virginal bed." Nature loves only

---

[121] *Another Time*, pp. 100-101.

[122] Spears says Auden omitted the stanza "presumably because it seemed too explicit and facile" (*The Poetry of W. H. Auden*, p. 155). See also Beach, *The Making of the Auden Canon*, pp. 50-52. Auden has withdrawn the entire poem from more recent collections of his poetry.

itself, and "Eros must hate what most he loves." Eros here can be neither part of the mindless self-love of nature nor free of its own involvement with destruction. In fact, throughout the poem love is involved with death:

And over the talkative city like any other
Weep the non-attached angels. Here too the knowledge of death
Is a consuming love. . . .

In all its forms Eros is limited, by its own ambiguous nature and by its association with aggressiveness or the instinct of death, to which it is irrevocably attached.

"New Year Letter,"[123] dated January 1, 1940, contains a more extensive and more hopeful picture of Eros in its various creative functions:

To set in order—that's the task
Both Eros and Apollo ask;
For Art and Life agree in this
That each intends a synthesis,
That order which must be the end
That all self-loving things intend
Who struggle for their liberty
Who use, that is, their will to be.   (p. 266)

Eros, like Apollo, is a principle of order in a chaotic universe. Self-love here transcends narcissism in that it becomes the will to exist and to flourish. In a later passage, however, Auden is again ambivalent about the productive quality of Eros. It is a hazardous power, perverting Logos, or law:

. . . sterile and diseased by doubt,
The dwarf mutations are thrown out
From Eros' weaving centrosome.   (p. 288)

The biological terminology suggests the intuitive nature of Eros, qualifying all of man's logical schemes for the perfect state, his hope for "millennium" itself.

[123] *New Year Letter* (London, 1941), published in the United States under the title *The Double Man* (New York, 1941); *Collected Poetry*, pp. 265-316.

These varying attitudes toward Eros do not indicate inconsistency in Auden's thinking, nor does his revelation of the havoc brought by Eros presuppose a condemnation. At this point Auden is not judging the instinct; he is seeking to understand it as a primary component of man and of civilization, for it is man's capacity to deal with Eros which to a large extent determines his character and the nature of his society. In Part III of the poem Auden again speaks of Eros in an extended passage concerning man's inability to accept "love's volition." Thus, we blame politicians

> For all those customs that frustrate
> Our own intention to fulfill
> Eros's legislative will. (p. 305)

But Eros' capacity to civilize is, after all, no greater than the collective ability of individual men to love. Each man, if he is honest, says Auden, knows all too well how he fails in this respect:

> Even true lovers on some bed
> The graceful god has visited
> Find faults at which to hang the head,
> And know the morphon full of guilt
> Whence all community is built,
> The cryptozoön with two backs
> Whose sensibility that lacks
> True reverence contributes much
> Towards the soldier's violent touch. (p. 305)

Through the mythical entity Eros, Auden indicates the inevitable unity of individual and social life, "the graceful god" and the creative principle of the universe. Both are continually threatened by violence; both are all too fragile in their struggle against man's propensity to self-delusion and vanity. Auden sees man as "craving language and a myth"; without purpose and order Eros leads only to anarchy.

The last section of "New Year Letter," beginning "O Unicorn among the cedars," which is a prayer, reveals the speaker's need for a more rational and stronger presence than man to control and organize human instinctual and intellectual forces in the service of civilization. Images used in earlier poems, here repeated with significant changes and united in an appeal to a spiritual power, indicate that Auden, having relinquished his early idealized conception of love and having come to grips with the ambiguous and frightening mythical "indefiniteness" of Eros, turns for support to a deity who, he hopes, will provide the clarity of purpose which man lacks. He addresses this deity in many forms, among them:

> O sudden Wind that blows unbidden,
> Parting the quiet reeds, O Voice
> Within the labyrinth of choice
> Only the passive listener hears,
> O Clock and Keeper of the years. . . .　　　(p. 315)

In "September 1, 1939" Auden had examined his role as man and poet composed of "Eros and of dust" with only a "voice" to combat organized deceit and violence; this lonely and objective appraisal was itself an assertion of strength and an implied definition of poetic eloquence in the twentieth century. But it was a position he could not maintain. In "New Year Letter" no human voice seems sufficient, and he turns to the "Voice" of a deity to inspire his own.[124] This "Voice" is heard within the labyrinth, a mythical allusion Auden had previously used to indicate despair —the labyrinth "safe but endless" of "Casino"—and has brought to mind earlier in "New Year Letter" when he asks, rhetorically, what man, having experienced the horror of the last ten years of poverty and war throughout the world, "will not feel blind anger draw / His thoughts toward the Minotaur," the monster enclosed in the labyrinth. Continuing the image, Auden depicts man's desperate hope as he takes "an early boat for Crete" to "add his small tidbit to the rest" (p. 273). The words "last tidbit" describing man's combat with the monstrous forces which threatened the ancient world and have become more ingenious and more hideous in the modern one disclose how little he expects to result from

---

[124] This passage is perhaps the best clue to Auden's omission of the eighth stanza of "September 1, 1939" and his subsequent withdrawal of the poem.

any effort of defense. The conclusion of this poem conveys Auden's feeling that only when the labyrinth contains the "Voice" of the deity is it a "labyrinth of choice."

Both mythical images, Eros and the labyrinth, recur in the "Epilogue" to "New Year Letter" ("Autumn 1940" in *Collected Poetry*), in which Auden more openly than ever before turns from an acceptance of the merely physical universe, where Eros and Thanatos wage their eternal struggle, to a belief in an eternal Christian deity. The poem begins with a return from the unconscious—the "timeless world"—to the "world of time," everyday reality, which the "ego" rejects. It is indeed a frightening prospect to awaken to: a world of "shadows with enormous grudges," of poverty, "tribulation and death." Auden asks if, forced to face this world each morning,

> Will the inflamed ego attempt as before
> To migrate again to her family place,
>> To the hanging gardens of Eros
>> And the moons of his magical summer?
>
> But the local train does not run any more,
> The heretical roses have lost their scent,
>> And her Cornish Hollow of tryst is
>> Swarming now with discourteous villains
>
> Whom father's battered hat cannot wish away,
> And the fancy-governed sequence leads us all
>> Back to that labyrinth where either
>> We are found or lose ourselves forever.

Eros, though attractive in its promise of vitality and pleasure, is tainted, and only the absolute offers continuing security. In the labyrinth either, passive, we are found by a Christian God, or, seeking our own solution in action, we "lose ourselves forever." In this allusion Auden evokes the dual qualities of the ancient labyrinth of Crete, as religious and ritual center and as scene of imprisonment and brutality. For the ancient Cretans and Athenians the labyrinth was a center of religious experience in which was enacted yearly a ritual of slaughter and human sacrifice.[125] Auden fuses the image of Eros and that of the labyrinth in reject-ing the violent and destructive elements associated with both and demanding that the experience of love and the ritual of religion be free of man's aggression and hatred. Thus, he again demands a "labyrinth of choice," in which ambivalence is removed by faith. The threat of "glaciers," a recurring image in Auden's poetry, which "glitter in the chilly evening," and the awareness that "death is probable" now make a belief in the creative energy of the am-biguous instinctual Eros insufficient. The premonition of chaos contained in secular myth can be controlled only by traditional religion and rite:

> Let the lips do formal contrition
> For whatever is going to happen. . . .

In Auden's poetry Eros does not achieve its full Freudian in-stinctual and mythical implications until the beginning of his con-version to Christianity. Then he can no longer maintain his earlier belief in the power of Eros, since its association with suffering and conflict and its tie with Thanatos seem to preclude optimism or even acceptance. For reassurance Auden gropes toward a new ideal —Agape. The new struggle in his poetry is indeed between Eros and Agape, but while the mythical concept Eros deepens in scope and depth with each new question and challenge, the religious ideal Agape seldom seems to provide the final answers Auden sometimes patiently, and at other times desperately, seems to hope it will offer.

"Kairos and Logos," which first appeared in 1941, is, as Spears points out, "a meditation on the significance of the incarnation,"[126] in which Auden develops the theme that man, constantly pressed by his awareness of time, can come to terms with his limitations only by accepting a Christian God, whose love imposes order and removes the ever-present fear of death. Since nature provides

---

[125] See C. N. Deedes, "The Labyrinth," *The Labyrinth, Further Studies in the Relation between Myth and Ritual in the Ancient World*, ed. S. H. Hooke (New York, 1935), 27-29.
[126] *The Poetry of W. H. Auden*, p. 192.

only a "chthonic love, / Destroyer of cities and the daylight order," men are "time-obsessed." In the world of ancient Rome, which "worshipped an aesthetic order," only the Christian knew that "eternal order" defeats time and death, and prayed, "O Thou who lovest, set its love in order." Thus, Christ is asked to remove from Eros, the "chthonic love," its taint of imperfection, to diminish the force of Thanatos, to which Eros is ever bound in conflict.

Throughout the poem Auden expresses, perhaps more effectively than ever before, man's sense of aloneness in a world apprehended entirely through his own perspective and defined by his own limitations. Part IV especially is a lament on the theme:

> We are imprisoned in unbounded spaces,
> Defined by an indefinite confusion.

In a passage reminiscent of an earlier one in "Casino," he asks plaintively:

> Where are the kings who routed all confusion,
> The bearded gods who shepherded the spaces,
> The merchants who poured gold into our lives?
> Where the historic routes, the great occasions?
> Laurel and language wither into silence;
> The nymphs and oracles have fled away.

The legendary and mythical order no longer exists; in the "cold and absence" remaining Auden finds his answer in faith in man's purpose in the universe: "Our presence is required by all the spaces" (*Collected Poetry*).

Purpose implies order, which at this point is the highest value. Eros, the bearded gods, indeed all of myth, seem to Auden as disorderly and fickle as man himself; they are only a symbolic language expressing the limited nature of material reality: "Laurel and language wither into silence. . . ."

The same disappointment in the promise of classical humanism is expressed in "For the Time Being," a Christmas Oratorio.[127]

---

[127] *For the Time Being* (New York, 1944); also published in London, along with "The Sea and the Mirror" in the same year; *Collected Poetry*, pp. 405-66.

In Part I the Semi-Chorus asks rhetorically:

> Can great Hercules keep his
> Extraordinary promise
> To reinvigorate the Empire?   (p. 407)

Hercules embodies the power and courage of humanity, but also
its imperfection, especially its capacity for brutality and its propensity to despair. Thus, the answer, implicit in the question, is

> Utterly lost, he cannot
> Even locate his task but
> Stands in some decaying orchard
> Or the irregular shadow
> Of a ruined temple, aware of
> Being watched from the horrid mountains
> By fanatical eyes yet
> Seeing no one at all, only hearing
> The silence softly broken
> By the poisonous rustle
> Of famishing Arachne.   (p. 407)

Auden's depiction of the state of the classical world, disheartened
by the failure of its own symbols, recalls the personal despair he
describes in the poems written just preceding and at the beginning
of his conversion to Christianity. His need for an order and a direction that Eros cannot provide is mirrored in a decaying society
in which no voice is heard, only the sound of Arachne, whose pride
led her to defy the goddess Athene, and whose punishment suggests the fate of all who work without purpose, forever suspended
in despair. This rejection of a purely human drive or ideal as an
answer to death is contained in the declaration, "We who must die
demand a miracle" (p. 411). Ancient myth, at the same time that
it expresses man's yearning for immortality, reveals all too clearly
his limited human condition; the secular myth of Eros conveys
only man's continuous and painful contest for survival.

The section "The Massacre of the Innocents" contains a long
prose monologue by Herod, who exposes the shortcomings of the

enlightened "liberal" solutions to the threat of irrationality and violence in the past and present, and admits:

> Reason is helpless, and now even the Poetic Compromise no longer works, all those lovely fairy tales in which Zeus, disguising himself as a swan or a bull or a shower of rain or what-have-you, lay with some beautiful woman and begot a hero. For the Public has grown too sophisticated. Under all the charming metaphors and symbols, it detects the stern command, "Be and act heroically"; behind the myth of divine origin, it senses the real human excellence that is a reproach to its own baseness. (p. 457)

Myth now serves only to disclose human longing and human failure. Thus, the very language of myth is debased by a civilization which cannot measure up to the heroic contests of its own mythical inheritance: "Idealism will be replaced by Materialism. Priapus will only have to move to a good address and call himself Eros to become the darling of middle-aged women" (p. 458). This in a severe rejection of Eros, the mythical entity and the creative drive. The impotence of the humanist, depending on his own resources, is expressed in the figure of Herod, in his analysis of the failures of mere rationalism, and finally in the debased role he envisions for the great mythical entity Eros. Mere sensuality can take the god's name for it has usurped his high function.

In "For the Time Being" myth creates the atmosphere of decay and despair in which Auden envisions the Incarnation as the one possibility of transcending the limitations of material existence. This religious position is maintained and developed in "The Sea and the Mirror,"[128] which Auden wrote shortly after "For the Time Being." He describes "The Sea and the Mirror" as "A Commentary on Shakespeare's *The Tempest*"; employing Shakespeare's characters in roles he imagines for them after the action of the play, he creates a dramatic contrast between the enchantment of art, the reality of ordinary life, and the possibility of a deeper reality in dedication to

[128] *Collected Poetry*, pp. 349-404.

religious belief. Auden is here concerned with the relationship of art to magic and the nature of magic itself. Prospero, who leaves the enchanted island for the real world, where "I can really believe I shall die" (p. 352), defines magic as "the power to enchant / That comes from disillusion" (pp. 353-54). Dissatisfaction with the limitations of human power, the disorder of ordinary life, drove him to seek strength in magic, but it is disillusion which creates its power.

Caliban makes the most significant comment on the mythical or magical, which Auden, like Prospero, denounces at this stage as he approaches what he considers a truer understanding of reality. Again the figure of Eros appears as ambiguous, limited, attractive on the surface but ultimately savage and destructive. Caliban represents the audience as he asks Shakespeare:

> Are we not bound to conclude, then, that, whatever snub to the poetic you may have intended incidentally to administer, your profounder motive in so introducing Him to them among whom, because He doesn't belong, He couldn't appear as anything but His distorted parody, a deformed and savage slave, was to deal a mortal face-slapping insult to us among whom He does and is, moreover, all grossness turned to glory, no less a person than the nude august elated archer of our heaven, the darling single son of Her who, in her right milieu, is certainly no witch but the most sensible of all the gods, whose influence is as sound as it is pandemic, on the race-track no less than in the sleeping cars of the Orient Express, our great white Queen of Love herself? (p. 383)

He expresses the audience's indignation at the playwright who has thrust Eros (Him) in the form of Caliban, the principle of nature or reality, into the realm of art. Eros or Cupid, as Auden calls him later on in Caliban's speech (p. 394), is sentimentalized by the audience in their daily lives; they see him as the conventional Cupid, "all grossness turned to glory, . . . the nude august elated archer of our heaven" and his mother Venus as "our great white Queen of Love herself." In art, however, he appears only as "His distorted parody, a deformed and savage slave," Caliban, the son of the Devil and the witch Sycorax. Of course, the image of Cupid that the audience rejects is his true face; the face of savagery and destruction avoided in life asserts its hideous vitality in art. This is Eros in all its brutality, who is worshiped as the principle of love by those who would see only its attractive and deceptive appearance.

The members of the audience console themselves with the prospect of reestablishing Cupid in his conventional role once they have left the play, but then they are confronted with another outrage. Ariel has been allowed to enter the real world. If it is dangerous to allow life to intrude upon art, it is even more frightening to imagine art challenging the smooth deceptions of everyday experience. Ariel released from the confines of poetry can create havoc.

In a curious way Auden equates the two figures. Caliban exposes the superficial and comforting image of Cupid to which the principle of Eros has been reduced, with all its tragic ambiguity removed; Ariel, released on the world, will break down fences, seduce wives, and rob banks. Both challenge deceptions and false comforts; both express the vitality and creativity of Eros, as well as its insistent and sometimes overwhelming force.

Caliban, finally speaking for Auden, indicates that neither Ariel nor Caliban represents an ultimate symbol of truth or reality. As Cupid ("O Cupid, Cupid, howls the whole dim chorus, take us home." p. 394), Caliban leads only to fantasies of childhood, idealization, self-pity, and dependence. Once again Auden reduces the image of Eros by uniting it with that of the minotaur:

> O take us home with you, strong and swelling One, home to your promiscuous pastures where the minotaur of authority is just a roly-poly ruminant and nothing is at stake, those purring sites and amusing vistas where the fluctuating arabesques of sound, the continuous eruption of colours and scents, the whole rich incoherence of a nature made up of gaps and asymmetrical events plead beautifully and bravely for our undistress. (p. 394)

This minotaur may seem benign but, in league with Eros, he represents self-indulgence, delusion, and finally chaos.

Rejecting also the escape that Ariel provides into an oversimplified Platonic realm of ideas, Caliban then indicates that any attempt to discover reality must include a consciousness of divinity. The artist is concerned with man's "estrangement from the truth," but he "is doomed to fail the more he succeeds, for the more truthfully he paints the condition, the less clearly can he indicate the truth from which it is estranged." Even revealing the "gap between what you so questionably are and what you are commanded without any question to become" is dangerous since the very acceptance of the gap can become a substitute for "contrition and surrender." The only valid solution for the artist is the possibility that he will not succeed, that "some unforeseen mishap will intervene to ruin his effect" (pp. 399-400).

This is Auden's strongest denial of the creative power of man: Eros is reduced to Cupid, keeper of an infantile Eden, and the artist is defined as a faithful worshiper only when he fails in creation. Auden demands of the artist a love for mankind greater than his love for his craft and purer than nature alone—Eros, violent and soiled, driving toward survival and creation—can provide.

It is against this idealized conception of love that Eros now is continually measured and finally reduced in Auden's view to mere narcissism, dangerous because it manifests itself not only as a personal quality in man but as a universal human drive. "In Sickness and in Health" (*Collected Poetry*) deals with the difficulty of attaining love unqualified by man's unconscious selfishness and violence. All too aware of "Those inarticulate wastes where dwell / Our howling appetites," Auden warns those who claim to understand the nature of love:

> O let none say I Love until aware
> What huge resources it will take to nurse
> One ruining speck, one tiny hair
> That casts a shadow through the universe. . . .

The difficulty of achieving love that is neither narcissistic nor destructive manifests itself in the well known symbols of Tristan and Don Juan; denial and indulgence, apparently so different, are actually the same. The *Liebestod* of Tristan and Isolde can only

> conjure up their opposite,
> Don Juan, so terrified of death he hears
> Each moment recommending it. . . .

Auden now interprets Eros as love perverted by death. Thanatos determines its nature, and "Nature by nature in unnature ends." The aggressive thrust of Eros may seem to promise beauty and productivity, but its energy is used for destruction, and its effect is universal:

> The lovers of themselves collect,
> And Eros is politically adored:
> New Machiavellis flying through the air
> Express a metaphysical despair,
> Murder their last voluptuous sensation,
> All passion in one passionate negation.

Once again Auden suggests that the only force that can check the destructive power of Eros lies outside nature; it is divine love, "O Essence of creation," and he prays that this divine influence may produce love which is faithful and honest. He is convinced that man's psychological limits, determined by the biological forces Eros and the death instinct, which are never entirely separated, can be transcended only by a superhuman power. The mythical entity Eros, which for so long dominated Auden's poetry, has become a symbol of the cynicism and despair produced by instinctual drives, unless they are directed by the Christian Agape, a mythical concept untainted by human need or human failure. Yet Auden continues to use classical myth to represent unconscious drives and conflicts. Though no one myth ever again assumes so obsessive or consistent a role as Eros in his poetry, myth remains for him a magic instrument of poetry and an analytic tool to disclose the nature of that magic ("New Year Letter," p. 290):

> So, hidden in his hocus-pocus,
> There lies the gift of double focus,
> That magic lamp which looks so dull
> And utterly impractical
> Yet, if Aladdin use it right,
> Can be a sesame to light.

Commenting on Auden's *The Age of Anxiety*[129] in connection with his own musical interpretation of it, Leonard Bernstein says that "most of the poem takes place" in the "realm of the unconscious."[130] The theme and structure of *The Age of Anxiety*, which Auden subtitles "A Baroque Eclogue," have been discussed at length by Monroe Spears, who points out that the "genre is the Quest, in which everyman seeks spiritual knowledge."[131] However, Auden's use of the eclogue form and of myth has not been treated. A study of these techniques is essential in reading *The Age of Anxiety*, for it elucidates Auden's method of disclosing unconscious conflicts and drives through an ironic play on traditional forms. Through the use of various myths, moreover, Auden unites the three realms of the traditional or pastoral, the historical or contemporary, and the personal or unconscious.

The eclogue, which traditionally combined various levels of experience—country and city, nature and artifice, poetry and politics, naïvete and sophistication—is particularly appropriate to Auden's subject: the quest for perennial values in a chaotic society. The characters, like the shepherds of pastoral, combine a childlike yearning for a simple life in an idealized natural setting with the sophistication acquired through experience they can never really shed. Eden for the jaded is provided by the liquor consumed in a Third Avenue bar on All Souls' Night during the second World War.

The four characters—strangers to each other—at first reveal their aloneness and fear in their self-absorption and fantasies. Quant "had spent many hours one winter in the Public Library reading for the most part—he could not have told you why—books on Mythology. The knowledge gained at that time had ever since lain oddly around in a corner of his mind like luggage left long ago in an emergency by some acquaintance and never reclaimed" (p. 4). This knowledge emerges as, in the language of myth and the symbols of dream, he speaks of unconscious longings and terrors. Malin, "a Medical In-

---

[129] *The Age of Anxiety* (New York, 1947); published in London in 1948.
[130] Jacket of Col. ML 4325.
[131] *The Poetry of W. H. Auden*, pp. 230-40.

telligence officer, trying to recapture the old atmosphere of labora-
tory and lecture hall" (p. 5), is the most explicit in defining the quest
for faith. Rosetta, a Jew, is a department store buyer, but she has a
"favorite day-dream," a pastoral landscape, a detective story Eden
(p. 5). Emble, an anxious young man who left college to enlist in
the Navy, speaks of the sea in symbolic terms, as that which promises
or fulfills the goal of the quest.

Quant speaks to his mirror image; Malin introduces the eclogue
motif as he thinks bitterly that man's "greenest arcadias have ghosts
too" (p. 8). Rosetta retreats to the idealized setting of her fantasy
world. As Emble regards the others, he imagines them as

> Eyeing the door, for ever expecting
> Night after night the Nameless One, the
> Smiling sea-god who shall safely land
> Shy and broad-shouldered on the shore at last,
> Enthusiastic, of their convenient
> And dangerous dream. . . .   (pp. 10-11)

In this poem Auden frequently employs myth to express a common
dream. Here, through the figure of the "smiling sea-god," Emble
defines for himself the submerged universal fantasy of strength,
beauty, hope, and omnipotence, "convenient" for retreat, "dangerous" in its delusion of superhuman power and control, which comes
to the surface only when drink has released unconscious longings.
But the common dream is interrupted by the reality of a radio broadcast "compelling them to pay attention to a common world of great
slaughter and much sorrow" (p. 11), and the four characters of the
drama begin to share their quest.

Part II, which is called "The Seven Ages," consists of an analysis
of the seven ages of life made familiar by Shakespeare, which Auden
regards as the seven divisions of man's quest for love and a sense of
his own value in a universe without apparent order or meaning. In
all the ages dreams and fantasies conflict with reality; they disclose
feelings hidden beneath the stock responses of daily life and they
point up the meager returns of the struggle for love and achieve-

ment. Often these are expressed in the language of myth. For example, in the Third Age, which deals with sexual love, Quant describes his fantasy of a "voyage to Venus Island."

It is a dreadful place, which suggests Hades rather than an island of love, a "savage shore where old swains lay wrecked / Unfit for fable" (p. 36). For the reader who has followed Auden's use of the figure and symbol of Eros throughout his earlier poetry, the passage has a particular horror:

> cupids on stilts,
> Their beautiful bottoms breaking wind,
> Hunted hares with hurricane lanterns. . . .   (p. 36)

In this passage Auden indicates that the productive principle of love, repressed and distorted, can manifest itself only in vulgarity and narcissism; cupids on stilts bear only a faint and tragic resemblance to Eros. The erotic has been entirely tainted—reduced to the ridiculous or the sick. Even more powerful is Auden's depiction of

> Gentlewomen with dejected backs
> And raw fingers morosely stitching
> Red flannel scivvies for heroic herms.   (p. 36)

The great herms of antiquity, stones with a human head of the god Hermes and a phallus representing fertility, were sacred objects placed on roads and before houses to provide guidance to travelers and to assure productivity. Thus, the refined obscenity of the prudish ladies is far more treacherous than it appears; mild and dejected, without wrath or conviction, they express the values of a society which regards love and creation as obscene and which ignores, distorts, or denies their power.

As a symbol of fertility in antiquity Hermes is often united with Aphrodite; here he joins with her to represent obscenity, despair, and disease. The goddess finally appears:

> Primroses, peacocks and peachtrees made
> A fair foreground but fairer there, with
> An early Madonna's oval face
> And lissom limbs, delighting that whole

> Degraded glen, the Goddess herself
> Presided smiling; a saucy wind,
> Plucking from her thigh her pink wrapper
> Of crêpe-de-chine, disclosed a very
> Indolent ulcer. (pp. 36-37)

Through the figures of ridiculous Cupids and a diseased Venus Auden expresses his despair at and contempt for the popular fantasy of love. Recalling his tragic recognition of the limitations of Eros in "Kairos and Logos" and "New Year Letter," one is struck by the cynicism of his tone and attitude in this poem. Auden dissects his mythical figures; his approach is detached and censorious, his anger cold. This change in attitude is reflected in his method of using myth. In the earlier poetry Eros, as a mythical concept, is broad, ambiguous, and powerful; here the erotic is depicted in concrete terms, a combination of traditional mythical figures and symbols and horrible details of everyday reality: bottoms breaking wind, scivvies, and an ulcer. Auden infects dream and fantasy, which, emerging in conventional mythical terms, express perennial need and desire, with the disease of modern life, for this, he feels, is pernicious to all dream.

Quant continues to speak in mythical terms. In the fifth age he says that man is the same in all times; history is "a continuous Now" (p. 44). His evidence is taken from classical myth which, he declares, lies beneath all of the present in man's unconscious and his memory. "Who closes his eyes" sees all the ancient world: "temples, tombs, and terminal god." These are his "myths of Being," which are "there always." "Man's Memory" is composed of "etruscan landscape" and the myths of Narcissus, Polyphemus, Orpheus, and others (pp. 45-46). Though these myths express essential elements of our history and character—our "Being"—our awareness of them lies beneath the surface of our lives; we see the "myths of Being" only when our eyes are closed, and we impose on them the distortions of our daily compromises.

In the Seventh Age, imagining the approach of death, the characters draw comfort from fantasy. Quant addresses Rosetta as a "peregrine nymph," and, maintaining the tone and language of pastoral, asks her to "delight" her "shepherds" with a "route / Into hope and health" (p. 55). Her answer introduces the journey or quest of the next section, "The Seven Stages," which many undertake but few complete. All, she says, start out with hope, but the mythical image and the pun she uses belie her facile statement:

> ... all start out with the hope of success,
> Arm in arm with their opposite type
> Like dashing Adonis dressed to kill
> And worn Wat with his walrus moustache. ...   (p. 56)

"The Seven Stages" is a search for "that state of prehistoric happiness which, by human beings, can only be imagined in terms of a landscape bearing a symbolic resemblance to the human body" (p. 57). The four characters enter a kind of dream world induced by alcohol and go through seven stages of a quest for the idealized innocence of childhood. They fail in this attempt to find peace, for at the end of their journey they cannot muster the spiritual resources to go beyond the values of "the world from which their journey had been one long flight" (p. 96). Yet the darkness in which their quest begins "dissolves" for a while, and the search they make into themselves elucidates memories and longings they formerly had repressed or dismissed. They come upon water, mountains, valleys, maritime plains, ports, and a city, and beneath the surface of landscape and metropolis they seek the meaning of all they see as symbol.

The sixth stage, which ends at the hermetic gardens, a sensuous and disturbing setting, deals with the need for sexual love. Malin protests:

> To know nature is not enough for the ego;
> The aim of its eros is to create a soul,
> The start of its magic is stolen flesh.   (p. 86)

This is the only instance in which Auden uses the word "eros" in *The Age of Anxiety*, and he uses it in a technical sense, not capitalized as in his earlier poems or with mythical meaning. Indeed, the whole point of these lines is to transform the Freudian concept of Eros. Auden now uses eros as love which has a spiritual goal; its aim goes beyond nature to the creation of a soul. Thus, it has religious purpose and direction.

But the characters of this drama are not to achieve spiritual love or peace. The charm of the hermetic gardens "seems an accusation" (p. 88). The remembrance of their past experience in love makes them ill, and they leave the gardens. They enter a "labyrinthine forest and vanish down solitary paths" (p. 90), each alone with his sorrowful recognition of failure in the search for love. In the last stage of their journey at the edge of a forest they come to a desert, where they ask, "Is triumph possible? If so, are they chosen?" (p. 93). The questions imply a choice beyond mortal love, and the characters discover their inability to exceed their ordinary, limited selves. They cannot choose spiritual salvation and thus are thrust back into the world they left for this fantasy quest.

They awake from their dream, which they cannot "recall exactly" (p. 99), but the effects of their descent into the unconscious have not entirely left them. Emble and Rosetta have drawn together, "conscious of some sweet shared secret which it might be dangerous to remember too well" (pp. 99-100). They all go off to Rosetta's apartment.

The fourth part, "The Dirge," deals briefly with the despair of the characters at their recognition of nature's lack of order and purpose and man's folly and childishness. It contains their lamentation for "some semi-divine stranger with superhuman powers, some Gilgamesh or Napoleon, some Solon or Sherlock Holmes" who in the past rescued man and nature "for a brief bright instant from their egregious destructive blunders" (p. 103). He is "Our lost dad / Our colossal father" (p. 104), but since he is mortal, his influence is momentary and ultimately ineffectual. The hero belongs to the world of myth; he represents mankind's yearning for the omnipotent father; thus, in his absence

> In the high heavens,
> The ageless places,
> The gods are wringing their great worn hands
> For their watchman is away, their world-engine
> Creaking and cracking.   (p. 106)

The mythical gods are projections of the unconscious anxieties and longings of mankind, which faith in "some semi-divine stranger" can temporarily relieve; myth expresses man's need for order and meaning, but it cannot fulfill his quest for ultimate purpose in the universe.

In Part IV, "The Masque," which takes place in Rosetta's apartment, Auden returns to the theme of the quest for love; allusions to Venus as the mythical symbol of sexual union and creation are again significant in his development of this motif. Malin builds "a little altar of sandwiches" to the goddess of love, and his invocation is a mockery of the Lucretian Venus as the creative principle of the universe and of Auden's own adaptation of the Freudian Eros in his earlier work:

> Hasten earthward, Heavenly Venus,
> Mistress of motion, Mother of loves.
> A signal from whom excites time to
> Confused outbursts, filling spaces with
> Lights and leaves. In pelagic meadows
> The plankton open their parachutes;
> The mountains are amused; mobs of birds
> Shout at fat shopkeepers: "Shucks! We are free.
> Imitate us—"
>
> (pp. 111-12)

The passage is a light and mocking imitation of the opening of the *De Rerum Natura*. Malin's invocation, like that of Lucretius, asks Venus to fill all creation with her presence. Some of the details and language are similar; thus the difference in tone is striking. Lucretius asks Venus to visit all of nature and to infuse all things with life: for her the earth will bring forth flowers, the ocean will "laugh," the heavens will "glow with light." The birds, the seas, the mountains, and plains will feel her influence. Though Auden speaks of Venus' beneficent effect on meadows, mountains, and birds, his language indicates his ironic point of view. Instead of Lucretius' word *ridet*, "laughs," he has "is amused"; the birds are in "mobs"; the vulgarity of their speech reflects the limitations of the freedom they claim: "Shucks! We are free. Imitate us—"

For Lucretius, the materialist who denies the influence of the gods on man, Venus is a symbol of the creative principle of nature, and for him the symbol is sufficient. To Auden, on the other hand, Venus as merely a symbol of love and creation, limited by man's desires and perceptions and yet regarded as the creative principle of the universe, is a false god; the worship of her is a sacrilege, for she offers no ultimate purpose or reality. The figure of Venus symbolizes the acceptance of instinctual drives as the basis of love and creation, and in his mockery of Venus, Auden includes the whole humanistic tradition, which claims no need of an ultimate authority or God. Personal love inspired by Venus is doomed to failure. Emble and Rosetta express their love for each other in mythical terms, which Auden again uses in mockery:

> She   The snap of the Three
> said: Grim Spinning Sisters' Spectacle Case
>   Uphold our honors.
>
> He   The Heavenly Twins
> said: Guard our togetherness from ghostly ills.   (p. 114)

The hope of permanence expressed in these myths is belied by Auden's ironic tone.

Venus is once more treated with ridicule as Auden suggests that man's attempt to gain security by guarantees, promises, and social reform are all means of avoiding his need for spiritual salvation. Venus, as nature, becomes a kind of legislator, who promotes the welfare of animals and crops:

>   since Venus has now
>   Agreed so gladly to guarantee
>   Plenty of water to the plants this year,
>   Aid to the beasts, to all human demands
>   Full satisfaction with fresh structures
>   For crucial regions.   (p. 119)

Part VI, the "Epilogue," takes place in the street. Quant and Malin part, each man instantly forgetting the other, each alone with his reflections. At the end of the poem Malin expresses its theme: man's quest for and self-denial of the only security available to him: a belief in God. This conflict emerges as one between an unconscious wish for ancient mythical and ritual observance and an awareness, however slight and unheeded, of the existence of a Christian deity:

> Our passions pray but to primitive totems
> As absurd as they are savage. . . .   (p. 136)

Yet man waits, "unawares for His World to come" (p. 138).

In *The Age of Anxiety* Auden assumes that man's primitive unconscious drives are contained in dreams and myths; these are the pastoral illusion, the alcoholic fantasies centered around Venus and other mythical figures which the characters share. When man attempts to set in order the chaotic world of external nature and human society and the inner chaos of his own feelings, he sometimes turns to a religion equally unsatisfying: "Yet the grossest of our dreams is / No worse than our worship" (p. 136), says Malin in his last reflections. Without any real hope for man's salvation, caught himself in a life and a society without direction, Malin is yet convinced of the existence of a merciful God.

Throughout the poems of *Nones, The Shield of Achilles, Homage to Clio,* and *About the House,* Auden continues to employ figures and incidents from classical myth to disclose the unconscious conflicts and drives, the unknown motives and forces that govern individuals and society. In these volumes he increasingly communicates his pleasure in mingling mythical allusions with colloquial language and contemporary references. Myth is now a familiar language to Auden, and he adapts it with a special grace to the conversational didacticism characteristic of his manner in this period. He has used the ancient gods as guides to the darkness of the unconscious; accepted as such, they become part of his household, and even in apparently light and familiar poetry he never loses sight of the psychological underworld where he discovered the meaning of myth and made it his own instrument.

In "Prime," the first poem of *Nones,*[132] Auden uses the commonplace experience of awakening in the morning to suggest that each

---

[132] *Nones* (New York, 1951); published in London in 1952.

day is a rebirth in which the psyche emerges from the unconscious
—depicted through classical myth—to a conscious awareness of reality and an acceptance of the Christian myth of man's fall. Speaking
in the first person, he describes the process of awakening:

> the kind
> Gates of the body fly open
> To its world beyond, the gates of the mind,
> The horn gate and the ivory gate
> Swing to, swing shut, instantaneously
> Quell the nocturnal rummage
> Of its rebellious fronde, ill-favored,
> Ill-natured and second-rate,
> Disenfranchised, widowed and orphaned
> By an historical mistake:
> Recalled from the shades to be a seeing being,
> From absence to be on display,
> Without a name or history I wake
> Between my body and the day.

During sleep he descends into the hell of the unconscious, a shade
experiencing true and false dreams, yet from this mythical journey
he awakes refreshed, momentarily "Adam still previous to any act."
Before long, however, he is aware that Paradise is lost and he faces
the day conscious that he bears the taint of mortality:

> this ready flesh
> No honest equal but my accomplice now
> My assassin to be. . . .

The mythical world of the dead, which Auden interprets as the realm
of dreams, is thus carried into the day. In sleep, without will or purpose, he faces his mortal nature; awake, he interprets it in Christian
terms, imposing meaning on the "nocturnal rummage" by conscious
will.

This tense union of the mythical or unconscious and the willed or
purposeful is described in many of the poems of *Nones*, in which
gods, heroes, and furies lurk beneath the surface of daily life, refuting
"antimythological myths," mocking facile solutions to social problems,

and suggesting that even the hope of personal fulfillment is a delusion. In "Song" the "Furies" wait "With claw and dreadful brow" for a pair of lovers embracing; Capri is a "jealous, sometimes a cruel god," who "defends the cult of Pleasure" ("Ischia").

"The Managers" describes the leaders of the present as rigid, colorless men who dare not "behave like genuine Caesars" or "be frank about the world." Dehumanized, they work continually, "Reducing to figures / What is the matter, what is to be done." But all their compulsive efforts, their "papers" and "discussions," their denials of their own appetites and passions, cannot eliminate human dissatisfaction and craving, which upsets their careful schemes:

> And, behind their backs bent over some report,
>   On every quarter,
> For ever like a god or a disease
>   There on the earth the reason
> In all its aspects why they are tired, the weak,
>   The inattentive, seeking
> Someone to blame. . . .

In a striking double simile Auden conveys the power of the "weak," who are "inattentive" to the plans of the managers. The equation of a "god" and a "disease" expresses the urgency of unconscious or unacknowledged desires and terrors which persist in society and weaken the barriers the managers erect to deny their existence. The disease that results from unfulfilled yearning and unanswered need for love and purpose, like an ancient god, continually threatens the euphemisms and surface reassurances of organized repression. This depiction of unacknowledged but persistent human frailty and questioning as "a god or a disease" exemplifies one of Auden's main uses of myth—specific or general—in this period, to express the conflict and pain of modern life denied by the smooth bureaucrats.

Throughout the poems of *Nones* the search for Christian faith is motivated by the psychological revelation expressed in myth. Opposing the deceptive and repressive city is the mythical underworld which, as it exposes man's weakness, makes him question the stock responses of his society and demand of mortal life a meaning which the city cannot provide. In "Under Sirius," Fortunatus, a citizen of ancient Rome in its "dog-days," apathetic and depressed by his inability to find any real faith or purpose in life, is warned:

> How will you answer when from their qualming spring
>   The immortal nymphs fly shrieking
>   And out of the open sky
> The pantocratic riddle breaks—
>   "Who are you and why?"

The questions rise from the spring of ancient myth; the answers which Auden requires, however, can come only from the revelation of Christianity.

In the title poem, "Nones," Auden deals with the crucifixion from the point of view of the average man, regarding and reacting to it. The event was "What we knew to be not possible," for it was predicted "By wild hermits, by shaman and sybil / Gibbering in their trances." The apparently impossible, predicted by seers and interpreters of pagan myths, is, of course, the central reality of Christian man's life. Preceded by the warnings of mythmakers, it is reported as myth by bystanders:

> All, if challenged, would reply
> —"It was a monster with one red eye,
>   A crowd that saw him die, not I—."

The transformation of Jesus into the figure of the monstrous Cyclops expresses the compulsion to turn away from the actual event. Yet if the description of what took place is false, the mythical transformation contains its own truth: the unseeing participants and observers, in spite of themselves, disclose their fears and their violence; as they "mythify" they unconsciously convert the crucifixion, which has just taken place, back into the "gibbering" of "shaman and sybil." In so doing they lay bare their weakness, their desire to avoid the meaning of what they have seen and done. The event is returned to the symbolic expression of prophecy, to a myth which conveys the bystanders' questioning of reality, their uneasy feeling that some monstrous episode must be faced, and their denial of the Christian answer which, Auden insists, "waits for" them, however they may seek to escape, throughout their lives.

In both *The Shield of Achilles* and *Homage to Clio,* Auden continues to employ ancient myth to uncover the presence of unconscious drives in daily experience, but in these volumes myth is more closely tied with ritual than ever before in his work; it is also used to develop his conception of history and of time. Since these subjects are treated in later chapters, *The Shield of Achilles* and *Homage to Clio* will be discussed more fully below. There are, however, several poems in these volumes in which a general mythical figure or a specific classical myth is used in a new way to express the urgency of the unconscious forces in man and nature.

Thus, in the initial poem in *The Shield,*[133] "Winds," Auden addresses the "Goddess of winds and wisdom," a generalized mythical figure who clearly symbolizes the unconscious. He asks her to be present when the poet "Unconsciously invokes" her, for he hopes to feel her presence in order to perform "every verbal rite" fittingly. The poem begins with a reminder that

> Deep below our violences,
> Quite still, lie our first Dad, his watch
> And many little maids. . . .

Yet the "boneless winds," free and unpredictable, remind the poet that man, violent and tainted, was yet chosen to receive the love of God. This love manifests itself in the winds, which Auden depicts as a goddess. He thus creates his own mythical concept—a fusion of the unconscious creative power he has always longed to envision without its destructive component and the Christian element of divine love. He has created his own Muse, as wind, as a presence in the woods, and, perhaps most magnificently, as Gaea, Mother Earth herself.

In "Precious Five," which appeared in *Nones,* Auden, instructing his five senses, tells the tongue to praise "the Earthly Muse," and in the "Ode to Gaea," in *The Shield* volume, he fulfills this command with tenderness and respect for what he calls the "Nicest daughter of Chaos." Regarding the earth from the air, Auden says, "Now that

---

[133] *The Shield of Achilles* (New York, 1955); also published in London in 1955.

we know how she looks, she seems more mysterious" but "less approachable" than she did as the occasion and object of myth. His treatment of Gaea is a remarkable fusion of two apparently contradictory views: he regards her with the detached attitude of a scientific observer and at the same time he approaches her more intimately as he adapts her ancient mythical role to his own purposes as a twentieth-century man and poet.

Throughout the poem earth is the mother; with her "old / Grand style of gesture," yet Auden also says:

And Earth, till the end, will be herself; she has never been moved
Except by Amphion. . . .

On its obvious level the statement implies that the earth responds neither to man's dream of Eden nor to his fantasies of human perfectibility. But this is the actual earth, not Gaea, whose spirit invests it. She can be moved only by Amphion, the marvelous harper whose music moved the stones that formed the walls of Thebes. Thus, the earth is at once the natural world of Homer, unconcerned, simply there, and the mythical realm of musician and poet, who use her to build the ideal city. Ironically, the earth can be perceived and enjoyed only by those who can feel her mythical presence in the reality of her waters, mountains, woods, and plains. This mythical presence is a Muse, practical, sometimes tough and contemptuous of man's self-deceptions; it is the Muse who turns man's eyes on the real world, allowing him to perceive the grandeur of creation and the possibilities of his voice to reveal and praise it.

Studying earth and sky, seeking evidence of the ancient past from the modern perspective of an airplane, Auden is always aware that

Tempting to mortals is the fancy of half-concerned
Gods in the sky, of a bored Thunderer who turned
From the Troy-centred grief to
Watch the Hippemolgoi drink their milk,

And how plausible from his look-point: we may well
Shake a weak fist one day at this vision, but the spell
Of high places will haunt us
Long after our jaunt has declined. . . .

This reference to a passage at the beginning of *Iliad* XIII indicates how continuous is the yearning for a mythical order, however remote from daily experience. Zeus, like Gaea, removes himself from man's agony and, if he reminds us that the sky is uninvolved in our concerns, as is the earth, the myth of his presence remains and assumes a new function: Zeus, like Gaea in this poem, challenges on the one hand our fantasies of omnipotence and on the other our facile acceptance of the mere surface of material reality.

The "Ode to Gaea" exemplifies an approach to myth which is developed in *Homage to Clio*.[134] Auden now employs myth as a means of rediscovering daily reality—incident, history, and time. Clio, he says, is the "Muse of the unique / Historical fact," in contrast with Aphrodite and Artemis, goddesses of the natural world. In her function in human society the figure of Clio suggests that myth defines man's role in history and clarifies his contest with time.

In the volume *About the House*,[135] in which Auden writes with ease and humor of his life in middle age—his friends, his pleasures, his discomforts, his habits—he uses myth less frequently than before. Still it appears, sometimes unexpectedly adapted to the most mundane of daily occurrences. "Et in Arcadia Ego" is Auden's most direct statement in this volume that myth, though apparently absent from the mechanized, tamed surface of modern life, remains, as do unconscious drives, part of everyday experience. He asks, "Who, now" can conceive of the earth as

> the screeching
> Virago, the Amazon,
> Earth Mother was?

Then, looking further at the world around him, he asks again:

> As for Him:
> What has happened to the Brute
> Epics and nightmares tell of?

---

[134] *Homage to Clio* (New York, 1960); also published in London in 1960.
[135] *About the House* (New York, 1965); published in London in 1966.

But the superficial calm of daily life is reality only for those who can "manage not to see" myth and nightmare acted out in everyday public and private experience. The adult's arrogant disregard of nature and the child's intuitive knowledge of violence remind us that the monstrous remains unacknowledged in our minds and acts.

Auden's most recent extensive use of myth as a vehicle for exploring the unconscious mind is in *The Bassarids, Opera Seria with Intermezzo in One Act,* [136] written in collaboration with Chester Kallman. Employing the myth of Dionysus as it appears in Euripides' *The Bacchae,* Auden and Kallman create an original poetic drama which revitalizes the myth and its associations accumulated for centuries. Their range in exploring and interpreting the myth of Dionysus is enormous. As their tone shifts from tragic to comic, from ironic to burlesque, they seem to uncover layer by layer the traces of instinct and memory in the unconscious mind. Essentially, their depiction of Dionysus, the god of wine, productivity, ecstasy, and even frenzy, is similar to that of Euripides—and equally ambiguous. Like him they suggest that Dionysus, who represents the aggressive and sometimes violent forces of the unconscious, can be denied only at a dreadful cost. In *The Bacchae* he is both benevolent and destructive; he releases the productive and joyous spirit of man, and he kills those who deny him. The Dionysian spirit has nothing to do with justice: it is as intense, powerful, fertile, and destructive as nature itself.

The Dionysus of *The Bassarids* is all these things, and he is also what he appears to be: "a rather affected adolescent, his affectation that of Byronic languor" (p. 24), the "dear / New God" (p. 40) of Tiresias, the prophet who is dressed as an Anglican archdeacon, and the Sir Bacchus of the Intermezzo. The languid adolescent, the new god, whom Tiresias rationalizes as merely a symbol of wine (pp. 25-26), and the mythologized Bacchus are conventional disguises and at the same time convenient denials of the force of instinctual drives. As languid adolescent, Dionysus is almost unrecognizable;

---

[136] *The Bassarids, Opera Seria with Intermezzo in One Act* (Mainz, Germany, 1966).

as Tiresias' god of wine or as Sir Bacchus, he is reduced to the absurd. Yet beneath these disguises and denials lie his potential fertility and violence.

Auden and Kallman play with myth, using it on many levels as they probe into the darkness of the Dionysian realm. In *The Bassarids*, as in *The Bacchae*, Dionysus arrives in Thebes to establish his worship in the land of his mother Semele; in *The Bassarids*, however, as the name implies, the chorus consists of both Maenads and Bacchants. Cadmus, "the embodiment of legendary age" (p. 6), is skeptical and cautious; he does not want to believe in the power of this new god who is his divine grandson as Pentheus is his mortal one. His hesitation is expressed in apparent reason:

> Could I but *know*: Who
> *Is* Dionysus?   (p. 9)

To Agave he cries out, "I beg you, / Think . . ." and "half to himself" he repeats, "Think" (p. 10). The failure of this attempt to come to terms with the reality of the Dionysian presence by rational means is all too apparent in Cadmus' slow realization of the danger of the god and in his inability to prevent the disasters that follow.

Tiresias, on the other hand, accepts Dionysus all too readily. He is the new fashionable god. Tiresias does perceive the threat of Dionysus to those who oppose him, but he smooths down his fear with a facile acceptance which does not allow for a real awareness of the violence and terror inherent in the god. Tiresias accepts Dionysus on a superficial religious level, attempting to fit him into the Olympian scheme of things. The women, Agave and her sister Autonoe, respond to him on more than one emotional level; he offers them sexual release, and he suggests a spiritual force and vitality absent in their lives.

Pentheus, the figure who is most threatened by the god, at first entirely denies his power or his influence. He refers to Dionysus as "Nothing," and is determined to worship the "True Good" which "is one" (pp. 22-23). Failing to defeat Dionysus by torture, he finally yields to his own submerged desires as he falls under the spell of the god.

At this point the authors introduce the Intermezzo, which consists mainly of a brilliant play on myth. As Pentheus, under the influence of Dionysus, gazes into Agave's mirror, he sees a "representation of a Boucher-like garden, with statues of mythological groups," and Agave and Autonoe "dressed as 'Marie Antoinette' Shepherdesses" (p. 37). When the Captain of the Royal Guards comes in, the two women compete in their efforts to seduce him. Tiresias enters, with fawn-skins draped over his clothing, and carrying a thyrsus. Shocked by the women's open display of their desire for the Captain, Tiresias suggests a charade to "act out" their passion:

> It would never do
> To divulge what's true
> Of kin and kith
> Too nakedly
> In Arcady:
> We must find a Myth
> To drape it with.
> Now let me see. . . .   (p. 40)

The charade, a play within the play, is a falsification of myth, a mythological fantasy to "drape" or conceal and decorate the harsh and fearful truth contained in the myth of Dionysus and Pentheus. The characters exhibit their shallow interpretation of the Dionysian spirit as they act out this charade, a mythological episode entitled "The Judgment of Calliope," in which Venus and Proserpine compete for the love of Adonis. The episode, from the point of view of Pentheus, the spectator or voyeur, is an enactment of his own long repressed lascivious desires, and, from the actors' point of view— Agave as Venus, Autonoe as Proserpine, the Captain as Adonis, and Tiresias as Calliope—an expression of their absurd and indecent reduction of the erotic drive to a competition for sexual adventure. Neither Pentheus nor the actors, however, are allowed to remain in this fantasy. He is to take the role of voyeur a second time, but on this occasion he is forced into the action and destroyed by it.

After the Intermezzo, Pentheus is led by Dionysus deeper into the agony of his own unconscious feelings as the god persuades him to dress as a woman so that, unrecognized, he may spy on the revels of the Maenads on Mount Cytheron. There, the Maenads, warned by a voice that a trespasser observes their ritual, discover Pentheus. Though he pleads for mercy, Agave does not recognize her son, and he is murdered. The long series of No's in response to Pentheus' appeals (pp. 55-56) conveys the blindness of frenzy. Deeper than the love Agave and Autonoe played at is the rage they now express as they murder Pentheus.

The Bassarids return triumphantly to Thebes, led by Agave, who proudly carries the head of Pentheus in her arms, believing that it is the head of a lion cub. Slowly Cadmus forces her and Autonoe to face what they have done. Autonoe characteristically denies her role in the murder, claiming that Agave forced her to participate. Agave pleads for death. The Bassarids also deny their responsibility. All turn from the terrible memory of their own violence.

Dionysus banishes Cadmus, Agave, and Autonoe, and orders that the palace be burned. The god has taken his vengeance, and now he leaves Thebes in ruins. At the end "two enormous primitive fertility idols of an African or South Seas type" (p. 67) are seen on Semele's tomb, worshiped by the Bassarids. What remains of Dionysus' presence is thus a symbol of the erotic drive, testifying to his powers of fertility and built on the ruins of those who denied him. In *The Bassarids* Auden and Kallman return to a theme which Auden never really relinquished: the ambiguous creative drive—in the earlier poetry depicted as Eros, here as Dionysus—hideous when repressed or disguised and tainted with death even in its productivity and beauty.

IV

MYTH AND RITUAL

THE GOLDEN BOUGH
Rite as Social Expression

Though many of Sir James Frazer's methods and conclusions in *The Golden Bough* have been discredited by more recent work in anthropology and classical studies, his name and *The Golden Bough* itself are still considered intrinsic to the revolutionary conceptions of man and society which emerged in the late nineteenth and early twentieth centuries. The question of how Frazer's work could have contained so much that was erroneous and at the same time have been so valuable need not be answered here. Perhaps any study of his influence is itself an answer. Nor need we consider all the scholarly techniques and evidence which have been employed to disprove the basic thesis of *The Golden Bough*. What is important is that Frazer and several other literary anthropologists at the turn of this century approached myth as a key to social behavior, exploring the relation of myth to ritual and seeking through both a deeper understanding of human society than had been available to their predecessors. Unquestionably, Frazer discovered behind ancient and primitive rites assumptions and patterns of thought and feeling that persist in some form throughout man's social history. For this reason students of myth as it appears in the poetry of the twentieth century cannot neglect him.

It is now well known that the theory which supplied the title of Frazer's most famous work was incorrect: we no longer believe that the priest at Aricia was the King of the Wood who embodied its life spirit, and that in this vicinity the golden bough was a symbol of supernatural power, like the bough that Aeneas plucked before entering Hades. Still, Frazer's reconstruction of the role of the priest at Aricia, though fallacious, was fruitful both in indicating

181

a ritual of replacement common in ancient kingship and in revealing some of the mysteries inherent in the golden bough which Vergil
adapted from ancient ritual to literary purposes.

The events Frazer imagines as taking place in the sacred grove of
Diana in Aricia near the "calm water" of the Lake of Nemi[1] probably never occurred, but most scholars today would accept his general
view that in prehistoric times many kings had the sacred role of
priests, that for their people they embodied a spirit of fertility and
a principle of recurrence, and that they were replaced in ceremonies
that included ritual slaying and rebirth. Furthermore, though it is
now generally accepted that the "golden bough at Aricia had nothing whatsoever to do with that borne by Aeneas on his journey to
the nether-world,"[2] Frazer's approach to the golden bough as a symbolic and magic object has a general validity; at Aricia it may have
been merely the "suppliant's branch"[3] (a more modest but nonetheless potent object), but certainly in the *Aeneid* it reflects centuries
of belief in the magical powers invested in mistletoe, which was
thought capable of helping man to overcome the limitations of
mortality.

Though Frazer's approach to the nature and origins of myth is
tentative and sometimes inconsistent, among his important contributions are evidence of the relationship of myth to ritual practice
and his exploration of rite as a key to hidden levels of human feeling
and social need. His depictions of ritual slaughter, homeopathic
magic, and ceremonial dance are so effective that he seems to recreate the emotion and atmosphere of the actual ancient or primitive
ceremony. One of the most powerful and influential sections of *The
Golden Bough* deals with the subject of the death and rebirth of
ancient gods, whom Frazer views rather narrowly as embodiments
of the spirit of corn or other vegetation. Among these are Adonis,
Attis, Osiris, Dionysus, Demeter, and Persephone. Frazer gives de-

---

[1] *The Golden Bough*, one-volume abridged edition (1922; reprint, New
York, 1948), p. 1. Unless otherwise noted, all references to *The Golden
Bough* are to this edition.

[2] Theodore H. Gaster, ed., *The New Golden Bough*, p. 668.

[3] *ibid.*, p. 667.

tailed descriptions of rites performed in their honor, dwelling on the principle of death and rebirth, and the displacement of "magical theory" by religious belief (p. 324). He traces the story of Dionysus from his birth as the child of Zeus and Persephone, his metamorphosis into a bull whom the Titans slaughtered, and his rebirth, through various versions of the myth, indicating the related rituals of rending and consuming animal representatives of the god and the wild ceremonies performed to insure his powers of fertility (pp. 386-92). Frazer also tells the myth of Demeter and Persephone, which he derives from the Homeric *Hymn to Demeter*. From his point of view the "whole poem leads up to the transformation scene" in Eleusis, where the goddess converts the barren earth into a field of corn, and "teaches . . . her mystic rites" (p. 394).

In *The Golden Bough* ancient Greek myth and modern examples of primitive practice and worship are mingled to establish evidence for Frazer's theory. Anthropologists have objected to Frazer's lack of discrimination in accepting the accounts of primitive worship provided by tourists and missionaries. He has also been criticized for the inconsistency of his approach to the origins of myth: he begins with the theory that myth is derived from ritual practice, then goes on to suggest that myth merely explains natural occurrences; he also takes a euhemerist position, and sometimes he combines all of these views.[4] His approach is sometimes more literary than scientific, reflecting his own excitement, uncertainty, and pleasure in speculation and discovery. The various editions of *The Golden Bough* indicate his willingness to correct himself, to grow and change even through his own errors.

Perhaps Frazer's very capacity to see many possibilities for the origin of myth, his speculative and essentially imaginative approach, his capacity to conjure up the scene and atmosphere of ritual, and his deep feeling for—despite his rational objection to—the hidden fears and open superstitions these myths and rituals elucidated all made him so attractive to the literary mind. His descriptions of ancient ritual observances, moreover, recreate both the emotional

4 Stanley Edgar Hyman, *The Tangled Bank: Darwin, Marx, Frazer, and Freud as Imaginative Writers* (New York, 1962), pp. 240-41.

intensity of the participants and the stylized, aesthetic qualities of the ceremonies. Thus, the related myths seem to take on new vigor, as if released from centuries of literary decoration. In his description of festivals in honor of Adonis, for example, Frazer tells how the mourning women "with streaming hair and bared breasts, bore the image of the dead Adonis to the sea-shore and committed it to the waves." Then he comments, "Yet they sorrowed not without hope, for they sang that the lost one would come back again" (p. 335). The myth, like Adonis himself, is renewed through Frazer's style and his feeling for the vital role of ritual in ancient life.

Despite Frazer's occasional expressions of contempt for the superstitions prevalent in primitive society and still remaining beneath the surface of civilized life, his aim—to disclose customs and attitudes of the past and thus enlighten his own age—is a scientific one. Nonetheless, readers were drawn to the atmosphere of enchantment which he so effectively recreated; his King of the Woods and the other mythical figures and ceremonies he described suggested to both literary scholars and poets new approaches to ancient texts and fresh possibilities for mythical allusion and ritual effects in poetry.

Frazer was not, of course, the only literary anthropologist of his period whose discoveries helped to bring about new explorations of myth. He owed a great deal to the writings of W. Mannhart and W. Robertson Smith, whose influence and aid he acknowledged. Furthermore, Frazer's work on myth was, to some extent, supported and developed in the writings of Gilbert Murray, Jane Harrison, and others, whose emphasis on the ritual origins of myth resulted in new and controversial interpretations of ancient drama. It was, however, *The Golden Bough* that directly or through intermediate sources suggested the possibility of transforming ancient and primitive rites into a poetic language which could express contemporary feelings and attitudes.

This effect is plain in Yeats's early career in his interpretation of Celtic nature myth, and later in his preoccupation with the dying god motif; moreover, Yeats's interest in magic, myth, and ritual throughout his life can, to some degree, be traced to his reading of *The Golden Bough*. Yeats is by no means the only poet whose work

184

reflects the spell of *The Golden Bough*. T. S. Eliot pays tribute in his notes to *The Waste Land* to Jessie Weston's *From Ritual to Romance*, which derives its main thesis from Frazer, and to Frazer himself. The new emphasis on ritual, moreover, had a deeper influence on the work of Yeats, Eliot, and many other poets than direct references to myth and ritual can indicate. Not only have ancient social customs and rites which recall the primitive communities of *The Golden Bough* reappeared as metaphors in modern poetry, but the many attempts to revive stylized, ceremonial effects have created a type of poem that imitates and creates the illusion of ritual. Thus, in studying the use of ritual in modern poetry, one must consider both the prevalence of consistent or repeated allusions to ancient rites and the imitation of ritual techniques through words and rhythm; the effect of both is seen in structure, language, and theme.

W. B. YEATS
Prophecy and Control

In Yeats's poetry, evocations of ritual are usually directly connected with his use of myth, primarily Celtic in his early poems and, in his later ones, the structure composed of Greek and other mythologies found in *A Vision*. In his notes to *The Wind Among the Reeds* he explains his use of Celtic myth and ritual on the basis of his reading "Rhys' *Celtic Heathendom* by the light of Fraser's *Golden Bough*." In these early poems his attempts to evoke the old ritual contest between summer and winter, "death battling with life,"[5] seem self-conscious and strangely (for Yeats) impersonal. He is trying—perhaps too hard—to discover a mythological basis for unity in Irish life and thought. But his quest is actually a more personal one than this early poetry indicates. His essays of the period suggest that Celtic mythology is but one aspect of a unity he is attempting to forge from myth, rite, and magic, as a basis for his own art. In "The Celtic Element in Literature," Yeats says: "Matthew Arnold asks how much of the Celt must one imagine in the ideal man of genius. I prefer to say, how much of the ancient hunters and fishers

[5] *Collected Poems*, p. 450.

and of the ecstatic dancers among the hills and woods must one imagine in the ideal man of genius?"[6] It is not the Celtic so much as the ancient, primitive, and ecstatically ritualistic with which Yeats wishes to identify as a poet.

His essay "Magic," written a few years later, is even more explicit on this subject. Having declared his belief in magic and the "power of creating magical illusions," Yeats introduces as one of his "doctrines" the concept of the "great memory," of which "our memories are a part," and which "can be evoked by symbols." After describing some personal experiences as well as dreams to illustrate the operation of magic through symbols, he declares, "I cannot now think symbols less than the greatest of all powers whether they are used consciously by the masters of magic, or half unconsciously by their successors, the poet, the musician and the artist." The creator is thus the spokesman for "the supreme Enchanter,"[7] and employs the devices of myth, dream, rite, and symbol to forge his own magic.

This magic leads beyond rational consciousness to the forgotten past and the unknown future, and one of its main instruments of prophecy and control is ritual. For Yeats dance is "a supreme ritual" which promotes "unearthly ecstasy";[8] in *A Vision* and in his poetry he uses dance in a variety of ways but almost always with a ritualistic connotation. It is, moreover, a ritual of transcendence, for the movements of a dance, stylized and perfect, usually symbolize superhuman skill and knowledge. The dancer achieves control over nature; the silent, moving figure transcends the language in which he is described.

References to dance in *A Vision* suggest the writer's actual experience of illumination[9] and synthesis as he approaches the mystery of

[6] *Essays and Introductions*, p. 184.

[7] *ibid.*, pp. 28-52.

[8] *ibid.*, p. 178. I have not discussed Yeats's use of ritual dance in his plays because any consideration of its important function in them would necessarily be too lengthy to be included in a book limited to poetry.

[9] For a discussion of dance as "the prelude to the enlightenment symbolized by the Fifteenth Phase," see Helen Vendler, *Yeats's Vision and the Later Plays*, pp. 35-36.

existence. In the first edition the Great Wheel is described as originating in the dance of the "Four Royal Persons," who are further depicted as "the King, the Queen, the Prince and the Princess of the Country of Wisdom." They have come "to explain human nature" to the Caliph of Bagdad, and they "reveal all in a dance." In accordance with the rule the Caliph has established, they are executed because he finds them "unintelligible." When the Caliph learns that, while awaiting death, "each dancer said to the executioner: 'In the Name of Allah, smooth out the mark of my footfall in the sand,'" he realizes that there is "some great secret in the marks of their feet." After these markings are explained by their teacher, Kusta ben Luka, the Caliph says, "I now understand human nature; I can never be surprised again."[10]

Yeats's suggestion that his geometrical symbols emerge from the secret markings of an ancient ritual dance helps to establish his authority in *A Vision* of 1925 as the recipient of transcendent knowledge and power. He is the interpreter of religious myth and ritual; like Kusta ben Luka, he appears with "his book of geometrical figures," which are unintelligible to the uninitiated. When, in the 1937 edition of *A Vision*, Yeats feels free to reveal that his "teachers" appeared through his wife's automatic writing and her speech while she was asleep (pp. 9-10), he no longer attributes the origin of the Wheel to the mysterious dancers, though he does refer to his earlier use of this story (p. 80). Now that he can describe his wife's and his own extraordinary initiation into "every completed movement of thought or life" (p. 81), he no longer requires the tale of the ritual dance to establish his role as the communicant of extraordinary illumination.

Yeats does use dance elsewhere in both versions of *A Vision* to symbolize knowledge or understanding beyond ordinary experience or expression. The "revelation of truth" is described in *A Vision*

---

[10] *A Vision* (London, 1925), pp. 9-10. In his poem "The Gift of Harun Al-Rashid" (1923), Yeats attributes the first expression of the patterns of *A Vision* to the wife of Kusta ben Luka; the sage says that it was she who "marked out those emblems on the sand / That day by day I study and marvel at. . . ."

of 1925 as "an intellectual ecstasy"; the spirit freed by its apprehension of "good and evil," by its control over love itself, as in an illuminating "dream," can accept "the most horrible tragedy" as "a figure in a dance" (pp. 229-31). One of Yeats's most powerful adaptations of dance as a symbol of revelation in *A Vision* of 1937 occurs in his discussion (p. 240) of the *Thirteenth Cone* as liberated consciousness:

> The *Thirteenth Cone* is a sphere because sufficient to itself; but as seen by Man it is a cone. It becomes even conscious of itself as so seen, like some great dancer, the perfect flower of modern culture, dancing some primitive dance and conscious of his or her own life and of the dance.

The simile of the dancer conveys Yeats's conception of an inner fusion of primitive feeling and intuition with modern intellectual awareness. It is a state "sufficient to itself" because it partakes of the past and death, it deals with the secret pain of "unconsciousness," and it relates such knowledge to life—or full inner experience (pp. 230-40). The dancer, always aware of the theoretical and visible qualities of the dance throughout its historical development yet free to explore every possibility of movement within its laws, symbolizes this complicated, independent, and perfect flowering of consciousness.

In Yeats's poetry dance also symbolizes the fusion, balance, and harmony of extraordinary insight or knowledge. The cat Minnaloushe, in "The Cat and the Moon," takes on superhuman power and knowledge as, troubled by the light of the moon, she performs a ritual dance. In doing so, she achieves union with the moon, which performs in its own "courtly fashion":

> When two close kindred meet,
> What better than call a dance?

In fact, "the moon may learn" a "new dance turn" from this inspired creature, animal, human, and superhuman at once, in its ritual dance, "Alone, important and wise."

The dancer in "The Double Vision of Michael Robartes" emerges from the Great Memory as a symbol of beauty and knowledge beyond reason. The girl who "had outdanced thought" symbolizes in her ritual dance a vision of "perfection" and control within the human unconscious mind which can emerge only in dream, myth, and ritual. As the myth provides language for this vision, the ritual dance enacts it in motion.

Even in the angry and despairing "Nineteen Hundred and Nineteen," dance implies that there is some order, some meaning, within the apparent anarchy of world, civil, and personal conflict. The mood of the poem reflects that of post-war Europe and strife-torn Ireland:

> Now days are dragon-ridden, the nightmare
> Rides upon sleep. . . .

The poet now doubts that there is any permanence: "gone are Phidias' famous ivories," and those "who can read signs" know that neither their art nor their honor will survive in a "mighty monument." Yeats then asks, "But is there any comfort to be found?" Ironically, it is the very appearance of the nightmare images—the dragons lingering from troubled sleep to haunt the days—in a ritual dance which implies that some order is possible:

> When Loie Fuller's Chinese dancers enwound
> A shining web, a floating ribbon of cloth,
> It seemed that a dragon of air
> Had fallen among dancers, had whirled them round
> Or hurried them off on its own furious path;
> So the Platonic Year
> Whirls out new right and wrong,
> Whirls in the old instead;
> All men are dancers and their tread
> Goes to the barbarous clangour of a gong.

The dragon, hideous in nightmare, is beautiful in the fury of the ritual dance. In "the barbarous clangour of a gong," to which all men dance, chaotic feelings are channeled into rhythm and pattern, and the continuous movement and recurrence of life are reestablished. This pattern does not diminish the violence, pain, and despair of the age, nor does it relieve the suffering of the observer; the only "comfort" it provides is that it fixes the conflict and disorder of the present within a pattern that includes past and future. The dancers act out "the Platonic Year," in their movement, merging past with future time, whirling out "new right and wrong," only to restore "the old instead."

Ritual dance symbolizes a deeper synthesis of experience and even a transcendence of the pattern of repetition in "Byzantium":

> At midnight on the Emperor's pavement flit
> Flames that no faggot feeds, nor steel has lit,
> Nor storm disturbs, flames begotten of flame,
> Where blood-begotten spirits come
> And all complexities of fury leave,
> Dying in a dance,
> An agony of trance,
> An agony of flame that cannot singe a sleeve.

> Astraddle on the dolphin's mire and blood,
> Spirit after spirit! The smithies break the flood,
> The golden smithies of the Emperor!
> Marbles of the dancing floor
> Break bitter furies of complexity,
> Those images that yet
> Fresh images beget,
> That dolphin-torn, that gong-tormented sea.

This ritual fire-dance, in which "spirits" and "flames" are almost indistinguishable, is clearly a purification; it is described as "Dying," as an "agony of trance," from which the spirit emerges released from the necessity of reincarnation. Having established his mythical symbol of immortality in the miraculous bird on the "golden bough," Yeats then creates a ritual enactment of the process of achieving this state, as "Spirit after spirit" dances away the agony of a lifelong awareness of death.

Both "I Am of Ireland" and "The Dancer at Cruachan and Cro-

Patrick" suggest the actual rhythm and movement of ritual dance. Each of the dancers in these poems, in an exalted mood, celebrates an ideal. In "I Am of Ireland," which is based on a fourteenth-century English poem,[11] the refrain seems to be spoken by a dancing woman, pleading for communion in ritual:

> *"I am of Ireland,*
> *And the Holy Land of Ireland,*
> *And time runs on," cried she.*
> *"Come out of charity,*
> *Come dance with me in Ireland."*

The alternate stanzas, spoken by a man who refuses to join her, set her exalted dance against ordinary experience. He is unmoved by her compulsion to outdance time and thus express an image of holiness and permanence. St. Cruchan in "The Dancer at Cruachan and Cro-Patrick" also creates reverence through dance. He tells of how he moved in praise of God: "Acclaiming, proclaiming, declaiming Him," the dancer achieved union with men, animals, and all of nature.

In "Crazy Jane Grown Old Looks at the Dancers" dance is a dream image, conveying in ritual form the extremes of love and hate, tenderness and violence, which may characterize sexual experience. The speaker Crazy Jane expresses her yearning for love in dream through a ritual dance which portrays in stylized form all the ambivalence of love ordinarily disguised or denied:

> I found that ivory image there
> Dancing with her chosen youth,
> But when he wound her coal-black hair
> As though to strangle her, no scream
> Or bodily movement did I dare,
> Eyes under eyelids did so gleam;
> *Love is like the lion's tooth.*

[11] See Walter E. Houghton, "Yeats and Crazy Jane: The Hero in Old Age," *The Permanence of Yeats*, ed. James Hall and Martin Steinmann (New York, 1950), 379n.

> When she, and though some said she played
> I said that she had danced heart's truth,
> Drew a knife to strike him dead,
> I could but leave him to his fate;
> For no matter what is said
> They had all that had their hate;
> *Love is like the lion's tooth.*
>
> Did he die or did she die?
> Seemed to die or died they both?
> God be with the times when I
> Cared not a thraneen for what chanced
> So that I had the limbs to try
> Such a dance as there was danced—
> *Love is like the lion's tooth.*

The ritual dance is no mere play, though "some" who would deny their own feelings pretend that it is; the speaker declares, "I said that she had danced heart's truth," as she describes the woman dancer acting out a ritual murder. In the last stanza Yeats articulates the questions implicit in ritual action:

> Did he die or did she die?
> Seemed to die or died they both?

The ritualistic sound created by the repetition of short clauses and the word "die" as well as the inversion of word order suggest the emergence of hidden fears and desires in compulsive, stylized action. The answer, which is actually an expression of the speaker's own violence, hatred, and longing for love, can be accepted as natural only in "such a dance as there was danced," in which conflicting feelings achieve unity and harmony.

Dance is the most widely known of the rituals that Yeats employs as poetic symbols. Even when he uses more specific and localized rituals, however, in adapting them to his own design, he invests them with broad implications. Thus, he fits the ritual rape of Leda by the swan into the pattern of antithesis and recurrence on which *A Vision* is based. In that work Yeats describes (p. 268) the cycle from 2000 B.C. to A.D. 1 as follows:

I imagine the annunciation that founded Greece as made to Leda, remembering that they showed in a Spartan temple, strung up to the roof as a holy relic, an unhatched egg of hers; and that from one of her eggs came Love and from the other War. But all things are from antithesis, and when in my ignorance I try to imagine what older civilization that annunciation rejected I can but see bird and woman blotting out some corner of the Babylonian mathematical starlight.

Yeats refers to this antithesis of love and war, which is so similar to Freud's conception of Eros and Thanatos, many times in *A Vision*; the figure of Leda possessed in violence and love represented for him the union of these two apparently opposing feelings both on a personal and a universal level. The mythical rape, he implies, lies beneath the surface of all creation, which is always a struggle against the destructive elements inherent in the self and the universe. Yeats alludes to the Leda myth many times in his poetry: the beauty and splendor of Maud Gonne emerge through a comparison of her with Leda in "His Phoenix" and "Among School Children"; a curiously heroic quality of sleep is suggested in "Lullaby" by Yeats's description of sleeping mythical figures, among them Leda and the great swan. All of Yeats's references to the myth evoke its ritual connection, but none so significantly as the sonnet "Leda and the Swan." In this poem he actually reconstructs the ritual; in fact the entire poem describes it:

> A sudden blow: the great wings beating still
> Above the staggering girl, her thighs caressed
> By the dark webs, her nape caught in his bill,
> He holds her helpless breast upon his breast.
>
> How can those terrified vague fingers push
> The feathered glory from her loosening thighs?
> And how can body, laid in that white rush,
> But feel the strange heart beating where it lies?

193

> A shudder in the loins engenders there
> The broken wall, the burning roof and tower
> And Agamemnon dead.
>   Being so caught up,
> So mastered by the brute blood of the air,
> Did she put on his knowledge with his power
> Before the indifferent beak could let her drop?

Yeats alternates between detailed description of the rape and questions expressing Leda's fear and awe, as she, a mortal, is "caught up" in the ritual act which, for all its terror, promises godlike knowledge and power. This ritual rape symbolizes the inextricable union of the forces of creation and destruction operating on all levels of experience. On the simplest level, of course, the intercourse of Leda and the swan symbolizes the union of violence and tenderness, which Yeats considered characteristic of sexual love. But no experience, in his view, is merely personal, and this mythical rape perfectly exemplifies his idea that "all things are from antithesis." The children Leda will bear represent, even more than she, the antithetical violence and love which characterize their conception, and which are the basis of all experience, individual and historical.

Yeats's use of questions to present Leda's point of view intensifies the ritual atmosphere of the poem. The questions indicate both her resistance to and participation in the prophetic experience imposed upon her by the forces of the universe embodied in the god as swan. Only when she submits to the ritual encounter with these forces has she the possibility of putting on "his knowledge with his power." In the last two lines of the poem the aim and nature of this and all ritual—the enactment of a human desire to comprehend and control the sources of creation—are expressed in a question which suggests perennial yearning, uncertainty, and ritual quest.

The ritual to which Yeats was most drawn throughout his life was that of the dying and reborn god: Adonis, Attis, Osiris, and Dionysus. It was not only Frazer's *The Golden Bough* but other works, such as Thomas Taylor's *Dissertation* and Nietzsche's *The*

Birth of Tragedy,[12] which reinforced Yeats's inclination to consider ritual the ultimate act of control—over death itself. Yeats employs ritual rebirth as a motif most often in his drama; in his poetry, where it occurs less frequently, it is nonetheless important as theme and symbol.

"Two Songs From a Play," the first of which appears at the beginning and the second at the end of Yeats's brief drama *The Resurrection*, celebrate Dionysus and Christ as year-gods, slain only to be reborn. In both the play and the songs Yeats emphasizes the similarity of the two gods as figures in a common ritual of resurrection. The two stanzas of the first song are recreations of known mythical and ritual occurrences: the first, the death of Dionysus as it is described in Frazer; the second, the prophetic utterance of the Sibyl of Cumae as Vergil imitates it in the fourth, or Messianic, eclogue. Both deal with recurrence: the god will be reborn; the golden age and Astraea will return.

The first stanza of the second song describes the "fabulous, formless darkness" in which "Christ was slain," an act which

> Made all Platonic tolerance vain
> And vain all Doric discipline.

This ritual murder, like the earlier repeated ones of Dionysus and other gods, discloses the naivete of the philosophers in assuming that they could overcome the irrationality of the human soul with reason and discipline. In "Two Songs" Yeats is less concerned with the theme of resurrection than with ritual as an acting-out in symbolic form of the perennial "fabulous darkness" of man's being. His use of ritual helps to explain the last stanza, which was added some years after the first publication of the "Songs." It has been criticized because "its insistence upon . . . all things as man-made is slightly out of key with the insistence of the rest of the two songs on divine miracle."[13] Such a view ignores Yeats's ambivalent attitude toward ritual in both the play and the songs. In *The Resur-*

[12] See F.A.C. Wilson, *W. B. Yeats and Tradition* (London, 1958), pp. 58-62.
[13] Ellmann, *The Identity of Yeats*, p. 262.

rection, after much argument about and expression of disbelief in the divinity of Jesus, a revelation comes to the Greek, who finally accepts and understands the words of Heraclitus: "God and man die each other's life, live each other's death."[14] God and man are thus inseparable; the ritual for Dionysus or Jesus is ultimately an expression of man's desperate effort to extend his own life through the death and rebirth of a god. Yet, attempting to "live" in this "death," he recognizes his own role in the ritual and faces the agony that

> Everything that man esteems
> Endures a moment or a day.
> Love's pleasure drives his love away,
> The painter's brush consumes his dreams;
> The herald's cry, the soldier's tread
> Exhaust his glory and his might:
> Whatever flames upon the night
> Man's own resinous heart has fed.

Yeats brilliantly unites this last stanza with the rest of the two songs through the phrase "Man's own resinous heart." In the first stanza of Song I, it is the "heart" of Dionysus that is torn from his side in a ritual slaughter; at the end of the second song we realize that the ritual centered around the heart of the god, to whom the resinous pine was sacred,[15] is actually "fed" or inspired by the "resinous heart" of man, who enacts his awareness of death and his yearning for rebirth in his identification with the maimed and risen year-god.

In "Vacillation," Yeats alludes to Attis, a god whose function is similar to that of Dionysus, since the rituals in his honor include death and resurrection. From Frazer certainly, and perhaps other sources, Yeats learned the various myths attached to Attis' name and the bizarre rituals observed by his priests. One myth records that Attis, like Adonis, was slain by a boar; another that, driven mad by Cybele, he castrated himself. Frazer describes rituals in honor of Attis in which a pine tree was carried into the sanctuary

[14] *Wheels and Butterflies*, p. 128.   [15] *The Golden Bough*, p. 387.

of Cybele and given the reverence of a deity. To its stem an image
of Attis was tied, and ceremonies including wild dances and blood
sacrifices were held both to mourn and to resurrect the god.[16]

Yeats refers to Attis in the second section of "Vacillation," a long
poem in seven parts which are united by the theme the title indicates: the speaker's vacillation between religious belief and skepticism, desire for immortal life and acceptance of the fact that "all
things pass away." Yeats begins by declaring:

> Between extremities
> Man runs his course;

and ends his first stanza by asking, "What is joy?" In the second
stanza he adapts the tree sacred to Attis to his own conception of
opposites or "antinomies":

> A tree there is that from its topmost bough
> Is half all glittering flame and half all green
> Abounding foliage moistened with the dew;
> And half is half and yet is all the scene;
> And half and half consume what they renew,
> And he that Attis' image hangs between
> That staring fury and the blind lush leaf
> May know not what he knows, but knows not grief.

The tree is recognizable as both the pine of Attis and the "burning
tree" described in the *Mabinogion*, which Yeats quotes in "The
Celtic Element in Literature": "They saw a tall tree by the side
of the river, one half of which was in flames from the root to the
top, and the other half was green and in full leaf."[17] In "Vacillation," the tree symbolizes opposition: the natural "green" part is
ephemeral, subject to death; the supernatural, flaming part suggests
eternal consumption and renewal. Yeats then presents a ritual ceremony in which "Attis' image" is hung between the two parts, unit-

[16] *ibid.*, pp. 348-49. See also A. Norman Jeffares, *A Commentary on the
Collected Poems of W. B. Yeats* (Stanford, 1968), p. 362, for other possible
sources of this myth and ritual.

[17] *Essays and Introductions*, p. 176.

ing death with eternal life, assuring immortality. He who performs this rite "knows not grief," but he "May know not what he knows." It is a curious ritual of avoidance; the participant denies his knowledge of death and thus avoids grief, and in so doing he identifies with the castrated and immortal god.

This is one but not the final means of resolving the extremities with which the poem deals. Ultimately Yeats finds his resolution in "man's blood-sodden heart." Though throughout the poem he reiterates his yearning for a belief in immortality, he ends by declaring, "Homer is my example and his unchristened heart." Both pagan and Christian ritual lead the poet back to the memory of a "crowded London shop" where, alone in his "fiftieth year," his "body of a sudden blazed" with an unexpected "happiness." Like the "resinous heart" in the song discussed above, the blazing body seems to be the ultimate source of the divine image—the flaming tree, renewed even as it is consumed; but the poet, finally identifying with a "conqueror" crying out to "battle-weary men," rejects this consolation:

> What's the meaning of all song?
> "Let all things pass away."

A ritual for a year-god again leads the participant back to the reality of her own feelings in "Her Vision in the Wood." In the previous chapter I discussed the development in this poem from mythical to real experience, accomplished through the speaker's involvement in ritual, first a private one and then in communion with a band of women who mourn the year-god Adonis. In a solitary ritual of grief for the loss of youth and love, the woman wounds herself. This attempt to assuage her pain with a "lesser pang" is a rite that symbolically transforms her "blood" into "wine," that "might cover / Whatever could recall the lip of lover," and leads her to a vision of a more formal ritual of grief for a lost god, pain thus being converted into hope, death into rebirth. She joins a band of "stately women" moving to music in a stylized procession, like figures in a Quattrocento painting or on an ancient coin. Suddenly the "beast-torn wreck" on the litter they carry looks at her and, recalling through his gaze the real experience of love, she can no longer continue one with the mourners who remain "forever young" in their perennial rite. She breaks through the ritual mourning with its promise of renewal, and recognizes love and death for what they are; the "fabulous symbol" is gone, and the speaker is alone in her unrelieved grief.

Here Yeats employs ritual as a means of confronting the reader with conflicting and all but unbearable emotions. Ironically, ritual enacts the human desire for comfort, for belief in rebirth and immortality, only to expose all the more dramatically the frailty and skepticism that lie behind the ritual act. He uses a similar technique in a poem on a very different theme; in "Parnell's Funeral," where he associates the dead Parnell with an ancient god, the rite he evokes to exalt the hero only exposes the extremity of the need for godlike qualities and the impossibility of fulfilling this need in a barbaric time:

> The rest I pass, one sentence I unsay.
> Had de Valéra eaten Parnell's heart
> No loose-lipped demagogue had won the day,
> No civil rancour torn the land apart.
>
> Had Cosgrave eaten Parnell's heart, the land's
> Imagination had been satisfied,
> Or lacking that, government in such hands,
> O'Higgins its sole statesman had not died.
>
> Had even O'Duffy—but I name no more—
> Their school a crowd, his master solitude;
> Through Jonathan Swift's dark grove he passed, and there
> Plucked bitter wisdom that enriched his blood.

Yeats depicts the urgency of the need for heroic virtue by repeating the bizarre fantasy of eating the hero's heart. Twice he insists that this rite should have been performed; then he shatters his own fantasy. Interrupting himself, he says, "But I name no more—" He concludes his poem imagining Parnell's life and his end in ritual terms; like the solitary Swift, Parnell passed through the "dark grove," there achieving "bitter wisdom that enriched his blood," a knowledge of the bounds of man's nature and the compromises of society so profound that it finally leaves the hero alone, unable to communicate his insight or to express it in action.

In Yeats's poetry ritual enacts an inner vision of permanent beauty, harmony, or courage, and in some of his poems the reader, like a participant in the transcendent experience of a rite, is involved in the creation of the miraculous—the dance or the work of art which unites opposing forces and defies time itself. In other poems, however, the contrast between the vision of immortality or perfection, which the rite enacts, and human mutability and failure creates a dramatic tension which is only partially resolved in the protagonist's or speaker's "bitter" acknowledgement of his own and man's limitations.

EZRA POUND
Rebirth and Reversion

Ritual is an even more important element of Pound's poetry than it is of Yeats's; neither ambivalent nor skeptical about the power of ritual to restore vitality to the earth and spiritual transcendence to man, Pound claims the authority of seer and god as he establishes his poetic version of hell and paradise. Pound's *Cantos* begins with a ritual ceremony in which his Odysseus persona summons the dead; this introduces not only the chief mind and voice of *The Cantos* but the characteristic Poundian evocation and adaptation of ancient ritual. Pound's use of the myth of the descent into Hades has been discussed in Chapter III; in this chapter the descent will be examined in connection with several other rituals—especially those of metamorphosis and restoration—which Pound employs throughout *The Cantos*. His allusions to ancient rites and his imitations of ritual effects extend the mythical background he creates for his persona, connecting the actual world he inhabits with the historical past and the mythical realm of the dead.

For the Odysseus persona the descent is a ritual of self-renewal; his compulsive returns to Hades restore his sense of surpassing knowledge and power. There he associates with the prophet Tiresias and he learns the true nature of what he considers the most consuming evil of civilization: usury. The double quality of this ritual—the painful quest and the restorative effects—are suggested several times in *The Cantos*. In Canto I Pound describes the rites in detail: the "sickly death's-heads," and the "Dark blood" flowing in sacrifice; he also tells of the "impetuous impotent dead" held off by the Odysseus persona until he can speak with Tiresias, and the shade of his old comrade Elpenor, "Unwept, unwrapped in sepulchre, . . . / Pitiful spirit." From this "joyless region" (pp. 3-4) the persona emerges inspired by his ritual descent to summon and judge man and history.

The recurrent evocations of Hades usually contain some ritual element either intrinsic to the descent itself—libation, sacrifice, questioning of and promises to dead spirits—or related to other traditional rites. In Canto XXXIX, as the Odysseus persona is about to set out on his journey to Hades, he is urged on by a last question from Circe, "Been to hell in a boat yet?" The next passage, an imitation of a fertility rite, provides the answer, suggesting the experience of death and rebirth to follow. Pound combines Latin, Chaucerian and modern English, and transliterated Greek to create a ritual chant for the renewal of the year. In dance and song a chorus declares: "Fac deum!" "Est Factus." A new spring is being born. Like an ancient rite, Pound's chant celebrates sexual fertility as part of the process of natural rebirth:

> His rod hath made god in my belly
> Sic loquitur nupta
> Cantat sic nupta. . . .   (pp. 45-46)

Pound's persona here partakes in two ancient rituals which are united—the descent and the festival dedicated to restore the fruitfulness of the earth, yet if the Odysseus persona returns to the present with a renewed sense of his own power, it is with little hope for the productivity of his society. His participation in ritual seems to offer not the expected assurance of general fertility and prosperity; instead it intensifies his rage and despair at the world he sees around him. This inversion is characteristic of Pound's use of rite. Traditionally, ritual is a communal experience, acting out a desire for continuity; for Pound it becomes an individual demand for reversion, for return to a past he himself constructs out of fragments of ancient Greek, Oriental, and more recent European and American history.

Like Jung and others who seek in myth and ritual the possibility of restoring a modern approximation of ancient religious practice, Pound is continually drawn to the Eleusinian mysteries. In his view, as in Jung's, the ritual worship at Eleusis promoted a respect for mystery which nourished communal life and the arts. In *Guide to Kulchur*, Pound says: "Eleusis did not distort truth by exaggerating the individual, neither could it have violated the individual spirit. Only in the high air and the great clarity can there be a just estimation of values."[18] This "great clarity" is not achieved by reason, but by acceptance and promotion of "mysteries," which are essential elements of poetry:

> Great intelligence attains again and again to great verity. The Duce and Kung fu Tseu equally perceive that their people need poetry; that prose is NOT education but the outer courts of the same. Beyond its doors are the mysteries. Eleusis. Things not to be spoken save in secret.[19]

Thus Pound equates mystery, truth, ritual, and poetry, all of which could be combined through participation in ancient rites of rebirth such as were practiced at Eleusis. In Pound's view the modern world has violated the tradition of Eleusis. Usury, which exploits and destroys the productive spirit of man, is chiefly responsible: in

[18] *Guide to Kulcher*, p. 299.
[19] *ibid.*, pp. 144-45.

Canto XLV, after a long denunciation of usury, which he calls "CONTRA NATURAM," Pound declares:

> They have brought whores for Eleusis
> Corpses are set to banquet
> at behest of usura. (p. 24)

In Canto LI he repeats the denunciation in the same terms:

> Usury is against Nature's increase.
> Whores for Eleusis. . . . (p. 44)

Sterile union with a whore has replaced the ritual sexuality of Eleusis. Modern man, according to Pound, forsakes ritual—union of the mystical with the sexual, the achievement of a sense of power through identification with the immortal—for cheap and facile pleasure. Contrasting with these two denunciations of contemporary sterility are the examples of "Kung and Eleusis" (Canto LII, p. 4; Canto LIII, p. 18), the Confucian philosophy and the ancient Greek ritual merging in Pound's mind as symbols of productivity.

Allusion to the Eleusinian mysteries is only one of the many means by which Pound evokes rituals of dying and reborn gods throughout *The Cantos* to establish his spiritual and ethical standards. The suggestion of rebirth through mystery and magic is also conveyed through his adaptation of the myths and rituals associated with such deities as Persephone and Demeter, who figured in the Mysteries, and other year-gods such as Adonis, who, like the Odysseus persona, are reborn through their experience of death.

Critics have interpreted the presence of these figures in *The Cantos* as evidence of Pound's concern with natural and social regeneration,[20] but this view indicates only a recognition of the general and fairly obvious attributes of year-gods. A close study of their

[20] See especially Hugh Kenner, *The Poetry of Ezra Pound*; Forrest Read, "A Man of No Fortune"; M. L. Rosenthal, *A Primer of Ezra Pound* (New York, 1960); and Guy Davenport, "Persephone's Ezra," *Arion*, vol. 7, No. 2 (Summer 1968), 165-99. This essay is reprinted in *New Approaches to Ezra Pound*.

myths and rituals as Pound uses them will reveal that he sees little worthy of renewal in contemporary man and civilization; in fact, he uses the rituals associated with Adonis, Demeter, and Persephone in *The Cantos* to declare his allegiance to an idealized past which he has himself constructed. For Pound rebirth is a return—not to an actual past, but to an image of a perfect civilization, which can be described only in myth and summoned only in ritual.

The connection which Pound establishes early in *The Cantos* between his Odysseus persona and rituals of renewal is repeated throughout the poem. It is perhaps the most important element in his conversion of ancient rituals of renewal to what may be called his rituals of regression. In Canto XLVII the Odysseus persona is directly related to Persephone and Adonis. Having been told by Circe that he must go "to the bower of Ceres' daughter Proserpine" and that he must "sail after knowledge," he sets off for Hades. Suddenly the scene shifts from the Homeric underworld to a ritual in honor of Adonis, the beloved of Aphrodite. The myths of Adonis and Persephone are similar in many respects: both are loved by powerful deities, who symbolize opposite poles of the most basic human experience—love and death; both die and are mourned; both return to life for six months of the year. Clearly Adonis and Persephone were originally agricultural gods whose death and rebirth symbolize the cyclic rebirth of natural life.

Pound associates rituals connected with these deities with the descent of his Odysseus persona who, as he enters Hades, partakes in a chant celebrating Adonis:

> Καὶ Μοῖραι τ' Ἄδονιν
> *Kai* MOIRAI' ADONIN
> The sea is streaked red with Adonis,
> The lights flicker red in small jars.
> Wheat shoots rise new by the altar,
>   flower from the swift seed. (pp. 30-31)

All of nature is invested with the fertile spirit of Adonis as Odysseus also participates in a descent and a return. After this imitation of a ritual chant to the year god, we are brought back to Odysseus' experience with Circe, and then with Scylla. At one point Pound fuses these adventures of Odysseus with the life and death cycle of Adonis:

> Yet hast thou gnawed through the mountain,
>> Scylla's white teeth less sharp.
> Hast thou found a nest softer than cunnus
> Or hast thou found better rest
> Hast'ou a deeper planting, doth thy death year
> Bring swifter shoot?
> Hast thou entered more deeply the mountain?   (p. 32)

Just as the death of the god is only the prelude to his rebirth and with it the renewal of nature, so the descent of the Odysseus persona into Hades is the preparation for his return to earth with new vigor and wisdom. Through ritual he is invested with the omnipotence and omniscience of deity.

The sexual references also support this identification: Pound exploits the conventional ancient connection between sexuality and the fertility of the earth to develop his persona's experience and control of love and sexuality. Repeatedly Odysseus must leave Circe for Hades. Throughout *The Cantos*, moreover, beautiful and destructive women and goddesses suggest an intrinsic relationship between love and death. In this canto, Odysseus, like a fertility god, is asked in a series of rhetorical and ritualistic questions whether his descent into Hades will not produce a deeper satisfaction and a richer reward than the sexual experience with which it is compared. The sexual union of Adonis with Aphrodite precedes his death and his rebirth as a powerful deity; for Persephone love and death are one, also the prelude to her reign as a goddess of fertility. Now the Odysseus persona is identified with these two great forces of nature. The canto ends with another chant to Adonis, as the Odysseus persona emerges from Hades, renewed and freed from the limited human experience of love and the finality of death.

In the next canto, having returned to everyday reality, he immediately focuses on the most mundane of human concerns—money—but his tone, his references, and, most important, his denunciations of past and present society and the corrective values he suggests in this and subsequent cantos indicate that the speaker has taken on the omnipotence of a god, demanding a return to a world he has himself created. The beginning of Canto XLVIII abruptly breaks the atmosphere of magic and ritual with which the previous canto ended. The tone is argumentative:

> And if money be rented
>> Who shd pay rent on that money?
>> Some fellow who has it on rent day,
>>> or some bloke who has not?　　　(p. 34)

There follow some chaotic allusions to historical figures and events, mixed with private associations that seem to have little relevance except to point up the speaker's dissatisfaction with past and contemporary life. This passage ends with a characteristic anti-Semitic outburst:

> Bismarck
> blamed american civil war on the jews;
> particularly on the Rothschild
> one of whom remarked to Disraeli
> that nations were fools to pay rent for their credit. . . .
>> (pp. 34-35)

Immediately following this speculation on the relation of Jews, money, and credit to war, Pound introduces three lines which link this Canto with the one preceding it:

> Δίγενες
> DIGENES: lost in the forest; but are then known as leopards
> after three years in the forest; they are known as "twice-born."
>> (p. 35)

The term Δίγενες, which Pound corrects as δίγονος (twice-born) in the Author's Errata, immediately evokes the god Dionysus, who in one of his forms was a vegetation deity and thus, like Adonis, experienced ritual death and rebirth. Pound introduces the god and the leopard, which is sometimes regarded as his companion or an animal form he took, to contrast what he regards as ultimate values with the decadent institutions of his own sociey. His use of this incantation from the mythical past as a commentary on the events of history reminds us that all is being viewed by his Odysseus persona, who is also twice-born.

Pound continues this contrast in the next canto where he opposes the modern way of life, based upon usury, to an idealized ancient one which combines the values he sees in ancient China and ancient Greece. In the modern world:

> State by creating riches shd. thereby get into debt?
> This is infamy; this is Geryon. (p. 39)

A translation of a Chinese ritual chant via its Japanese transcription conveys the standards which Pound regards as eternal:

> Sun up; work
> Sundown; to rest
> Dig well and drink of the water
> dig field; eat of the grain
> Imperial power is? and to us what is it?

> The fourth; the dimension of stillness.
> And the power over wild beasts. (p. 39)

The simple, direct commands dealing with basic aspects of life—dawn, sundown, work, and rest—followed by and combined with the suggestion of Dionysian mystery and power imply universal ethical and religious values.

One of Pound's assumptions is that "the true base of credit" is "the abundance of nature / with the whole folk behind it" (Canto LII, p. 3). He sometimes pauses to give traditional instruction, taken from Hesiod or Chinese philosophy, about the care of the soil, but essentially nature to him is a divine principle with metamorphic powers of renewal, and it can be influenced only through ritual observance. In *The Cantos* ritual is always the enactment of a return to a mythical condition of life in which man—and especially the poet, the persona, the speaker of truth—participates in divine powers of metamorphosis and endless renewal. In Canto LII Pound translates a long didactic passage from Li-Ki (*Collected Ritual*);[21] here the poet as priest of nature conveys the rituals to "the whole folk," that is, those who share his religious vision of a reversal of time and history:

> Know then:
>> Toward summer when the sun is in Hyades
> Sovran is Lord of the Fire
>> to this month are birds.
> with bitter smell and with the odour of burning
> To the hearth god, lungs of the victim
>> The green frog lifts up his voice
>>> and the white latex is in flower
> In red car with jewels incarnadine
>> to welcome the summer
> In this month no destruction
>> no tree shall be cut at this time
> Wild beasts are driven from field
>> in this month are simples gathered.   (p. 4)

The example of ancient ritual worship is intended to turn man away from contemporary commercial institutions, rivalries, and values, which culminate in international warfare, and to engage him in the only "true" conflict, the struggle between "light and darkness." Pound evokes this traditional contest:

>> Month of the longest days
> Life and death are now equal
>> Strife is between light and darkness
> Wise man stays in his house
>> Stag droppeth antlers
> Grasshopper is loud,
>> leave no fire open to southward.

---

[21] Title as translated by James Robert Hightower, *Topics in Chinese Literature* (Cambridge, Mass., 1962). The *Li-Ki* is a collection of ritual texts dealing with ceremonies for various occasions.

Various astrological signs indicate that the "Lord of the fire is dominant," and a sacrificial rite is necessary:

> To this month is SEVEN,
>> with bitter smell, with odour of burning
> Offer to the gods of the hearth
>> the lungs of the victims
> Warm wind is rising, cricket bideth in wall
> Young goshawk is learning his labour
>> dead grass breedeth glow-worms.   (p. 5)

The rewards man gains from participating in this ancient and eternal ritual are a recognition of and identification with the essential principle of recurrence. Thus, he becomes one with the "glow-worm" emerging from "dead grass" as he joins forces with the hearth-god he worships. It is the poet or in *The Cantos* his spokesman, the Odysseus persona, who teaches this principle as he participates in the rites expressing his religious and personal devotion.

By frequent allusions to Persephone and Demeter and to ceremonies in their honor Pound evokes the sacramental atmosphere of the Eleusinian rites. The goddesses, especially Persephone, become agents of the poet's fantasy; he identifies with their powers of restoration when he demands a magical conversion of society to his own ideals of labor and worship. In a recent study of Pound's use of Persephone, Guy Davenport emphasizes her importance as a goddess of renewal in Pound's poetry. Davenport sees her as "the spirit of natural metamorphosis" and "the promise of rebirth."[22] This is, of course, her conventional role as a mythical figure, and to a certain extent she functions in this way in *The Cantos*. But it must be remembered that her power of renewal is related to her role as goddess of the dead. She has converted her imprisonment by death into control over it; she now can restore what death has apparently destroyed. In *The Cantos* Persephone is a creative principle but, if she is a goddess of renewal, it is not nature that she restores but the poet's sense that he can understand and control its laws.

His Odysseus persona encounters her both on earth and in the

[22] "Persephone's Ezra," *Arion*, 176-77.

underworld. He first discovers her in the meadow from which she is later abducted by Hades. The meeting is the climax to a long passage imitating fertility rites in honor of Dionysus, various nymphs, Hermes, and Athene. Persephone functions here as a guide to the potential fertility of the earth:

> Koré through the bright meadow,
> > with green-gray dust in the grass:
> "For this hour, brother of Circe."
> Arm laid over my shoulder,
> Saw the sun for three days, the sun fulvid,
> As a lion lift over sand-plain;
> > > and that day,
> And for three days, and none after,
> Splendour, as the splendour of Hermes. . . .
> > > > > (XVII, pp. 78-79)

Greeting Odysseus as Circe's "brother," a relationship which implies that he shares her divine attributes and her magical powers, Persephone reveals to him a vision of life unknown in the world he scorns. This is, of course, a Poundian Eden, ever fertile and splendid, reflecting the influence of no human being, only that of divine presences.

Persephone is again part of a ritual of rebirth in *The Pisan Cantos*, where Pound mingles the names and details of daily life in a prison camp with references to the ancient fertility gods Priapus, Pomona, Silenus, Iacchos—who was identified with Dionysus—Demeter, and Persephone. The Odysseus persona summons these gods and recalls their rituals. This inner experience is described in ceremonial language which contrasts with the army slang of conversation and the harsh depiction of daily activity. The fertility gods, like his identity as Odysseus, are the prisoner's solace, for they inhabit the inner realm of freedom which he restores for himself.

In Canto LXXIX Pound imitates the Eleusinian rites:

> Ἴακχε, Ἴακχε, Χαῖρε, AOI
> > "Eat of it not in the under world"
> > See that the sun or the moon bless thy eating

Κόρη, Κόρη, for the six seeds of an error
or that the stars bless thy eating

      O Lynx, guard this orchard,
      Keep from Demeter's furrow

This fruit has a fire within it,
      Pomona, Pomona
No glass is clearer than are the globes of this flame
what sea is clearer than the pomegranate body
      holding the flame?   (p. 68)

The call to Iacchos and the reference to Persephone's eating of the
pomegranate seeds indicate that this is a ritual enactment of the
death of Persephone. There follow long passages of ritual question
and answer, and the appearance of the bassarids, Priapus, and finally
Aphrodite, the goddess "terrible in resistance." Persephone's descent
and death are celebrated by gods and men because her death is only
the prelude to her assumption of power over the productivity of the
earth. This is the beginning of her metamorphosis from life to death,
to eternal and recurring rebirth in which the Odysseus persona will
participate.

The metamorphic rituals of Eleusis provide the scene and atmosphere for what Pound calls in his outline of *The Cantos* "the
'magic moment' or moment of metamorphosis," in which he can
achieve his own "permanent" reality. As his persona's suffering, his
weeping (the repeated δακρύων), is identified with Demeter's
mourning the death of her beloved daughter and thus the dying of
the natural world in the barrenness of the earth, so his faith in survival and his vision of recovery come through association with Persephone. In Canto LXXXIII, he again envisions himself saved, like
an infant, or a wasp born in his cell, descending,

      greeting them that dwell under XTHONOS   ΧΘΟΝΟΣ
ΟΙ ΧΘΟΝΙΟΙ; to carry our news
     εἰς χθονίους   to them that dwell under the earth,
begotten of air, that shall sing in the bower
      of Kore,   Περσεφόνεια
and have speech with Tiresias, Thebae. . . .   (p. 111)

The two apparently contradictory yet traditional features of Hades which Pound has adapted for his own purposes are here directly related. In his fantasy the Odysseus persona escapes from the literal hell of his army prison through a ritual descent to the ancient underworld, where heroes convert suffering to knowledge and gods conquer death through renewal. Inspired by the wisdom of Tiresias and the metamorphic powers of Persephone, he identifies with the eternal recurrence of nature:

> A fat moon rises lop-sided over the mountain
> The eyes, this time my world,
> > But pass and look *from* mine
> > > between my lids
> > > > sea, sky, and pool
> > > > alternate
> > > > pool, sky, sea. . . .   (p. 113)

Renewed, he again ascends to earth, a free and powerful wanderer, holding in his memory all ancient and modern history.

In *Rock-Drill*, especially in the last six cantos, in a ritual of renewal based on Pound's conception of the rites of Eleusis, the freed persona restores other suffering shades to new life through love. He calls for an Eleusinian "procession," with "banners" and "flute tone" to celebrate the emergence of the dead from Erebus. Like Odysseus, the persona has encountered the mythical heroines Tyro and Alcmene in the underworld, but, imbued with the spirit of the Eleusinian mysteries, he exceeds Odysseus in power, raising these inhabitants of hell so that they are "no shades more. . . ." The "love" which transforms these shades into "lights" (90, pp. 68-69) flows from the spirit of Eleusis; exceeding the limits of human love, it restores life to the dead.

As he becomes more firmly identified with what he considers the divine metamorphic powers of nature, the Odysseus persona is aided by a natural force, Leucothea, who was herself metamorphosed into a nature goddess. Pound emphasizes this metamorphosis, repeatedly

referring to her origins as the mortal daughter of Cadmus, even as
she exercises her divine powers in aiding Odysseus:

> As the sea-gull Κάδμου θυγάτηρ said to Odysseus
> KADMOU THUGATER
>   "get rid of parapernalia" ...   (91, p. 75)[23]

In the Homeric passage which Pound imitates (V, 337-38; 343),
Leucothea is compared, not identified, with a seagull. Through the
slight change from simile to metaphor, Pound suggests her metamorphosis not only from mortal to goddess but to one who is part
of the natural world of sea and sky. Whereas in the *Odyssey* Leucothea tells Odysseus to rid himself of his garments and his raft so
that he can swim to the land of the Phaeacians, in *The Cantos* she
advises the Odysseus persona to "get rid of parapernalia," a general
term which suggests that he leave behind all the values and trappings of limited and tainted modern life as he pursues divine power
and vision.

In *Thrones* Pound tries to establish his vision of an ideal past
through references to many ancient civilizations. Ranging through
the Byzantine Empire, ancient China, Egypt, and Greece, the Odysseus persona imagines a realm whose values are based on labor, family loyalty, and ritual observance. In his frantic quest for permanence
and piety he continues to receive the aid of the goddess Leucothea,
who parts with him in the first lines of *Thrones*, but not before she
has inspired him with her magic power; like Circe, she reappears
at crucial moments in the persona's journey through time. Canto 96
begins with a reference to Leucothea's veil, and a bit later on in the
same canto Pound declares, "After 500 years, still sacrificed to that
sea gull" (p. 6). In Canto 98 we are again told, "Leucothea gave her
veil to Odysseus" (p. 36). Then, later in the same canto, Pound introduces a second mythical figure named Leucothoe (or Leucothea)[24]

[23] Pound refers again to Leucothea's origins in Canto 93, p. 83 and Canto
95, p. 104; and in *Thrones*, Canto 98, p. 37; Canto 102, p. 80; Canto 109,
p. 126.

[24] Usually Pound distinguishes between the two figures by his spelling:
the sea-nymph of the *Odyssey* is Leucothea and Ovid's heroine is Leucothoe.

who also experienced metamorphosis. He associates her tale with
that of the sea-nymph Leucothea to intensify the ritual or religious
background of his Odysseus persona's quest:

> And that Leucothoe rose as an incense bush
> —Orchamus, Babylon—
>   resisting Apollo.
> Patience, I will come to the Commissioner of the Salt Works
>   in due course.
> Est deus in nobis.   and
>   They still offer sacrifice to that sea-gull
> est deus in nobis
>   Χρήδεμνον
> She being of Cadmus line. . . .   (p. 37)

"That Leucothoe," daughter of Orchamus, appears in Ovid's *Metamorphoses* IV, where the story of Apollo's love for her is told. At
first she resisted, then accepted the embraces of the god. When Clytie,
a rival for the love of Apollo, informed Orchamus that his daughter
had been the mistress of Apollo, Orchamus, to punish Leucothoe,
buried her in the earth, covering her body with a mound of sand.
Apollo sprinkled the body and the soil with nectar, causing a bush
bearing frankincense to rise from the earth. Thus, Leucothoe is
transformed from a dead girl to a living shrub, which can "touch
the upper air," by the power of the sun-god, or as Ovid describes
him, "mundi oculus." Pound emphasizes Leucothoe's metamorphosis as he repeats his description of the other Leucothea's appearance
as a seagull, since both metamorphoses symbolize for him the potential divinity in mortals—"Est deus in nobis." In the mind of the
persona the "incense bush" of the Ovidian Leucothoe is the site of
a sacred ritual celebrating her metamorphosis, and, turning to the
Leucothea of Homer, he insists, "They still offer sacrifice to that seagull," suggesting the perennial significance of her metamorphosis
in continuous ritual observance. The persona identifies with the

---

On occasion, however, he refers to the sea-nymph as Leucothoe; see, for
example, Canto 95, pp. 104-105.

magical conversion of both figures, especially the Leucothea of the *Odyssey*, whose veil (κρήδεμνον) has become his talisman.

Pound refers to it again in Canto 100, once more adapting a passage from the *Odyssey* (V, 458-62), in which Homer describes Odysseus at the end of his struggle to survive the storm finally arriving at the mouth of the river from which he can reach shore. Translated literally the Homeric passage says: "But when he recovered and his spirit returned to his breast, then he released the veil of the goddess and allowed it to fall into the river that mingled with the sea. A huge wave bore it down the stream, and quickly Ino raised it in her loving right hand." Pound's version is:

> and he dropped the scarf in the tide-rips
>
> KREDEMNON
> that it should float back to the sea,
> and that quickly
> DEXATO XERSI
> with a fond hand
> AGERTHE.... (pp. 68-69)

Pound's use of Homer here is extremely interesting. He omits a good deal, including the presence of Ino (Leucothea), who is directly suggested only through her scarf or veil (KREDEMNON). The transliterated phrase DEXATO XERSI (in her right hand) in Homer refers to Leucothea, but in Pound's passage could refer to either Odysseus or the goddess or both. The last transliterated word AGERTHE (ἀγέρθη, returned) is taken from the beginning of the Homeric passage; it occurs in line 458, in which Homer says that the spirit of Odysseus *returned* to his breast. Pound moves the word to end of the passage he adapts, where it follows the reference to Odysseus' dropping or Leucothea's lifting the veil. It seems certain that he thus deliberately fuses the acts and feelings of Leucothea and Odysseus. The effect of his omissions, his emphasis on the three transliterated Greek words, and his compressions is itself metamorphic. Using these devices Pound unites goddess and hero or persona in one magically endowed being, and thus creates his own "verbal rite."

He produces a similar effect by fusing the stories of Leucothea and Leucothoe into one ritual act: Canto 102 begins with the declaration:

> This I had from Kalupso
>
> who had it from Hermes. . . .

Speaking as the Odysseus persona, confidant of Calypso, he returns to the metamorphosis of Leucothoe:

> Leucothoe
> rose as an incense bush,
>
> resisting Apollo,
>
> Orchamus, Babylon
> And after 500 years
>
> still offered that shrub to the sea-gull,
> Phaecians,
>
> she being of Cadmus line. . . .   (p. 80)

The two women metamorphosed into goddesses are fused in Pound's mind in a ritual in which the shrub that rose from Leucothoe's body is offered to the seagull Leucothea. Later on in the same canto he suggests that the ritual is internalized:

> But with Leucothoe's mind in that incense
> all Babylon could not hold it down.   (pp. 81-82)

At the end of *Thrones* Ino's metamorphosis is again implied as Pound twice refers to

> INO Ἰνώ   Kadmeia
> [. . .]
> Καλλιαστράγαλος Ino Kadmeia . . .   (109, p. 126)

as a reminder of the ritual transformation of a patron goddess of his persona, with whom he has shared the experience of overcoming mortal limitation and attaining divine powers.

Throughout *The Cantos* Pound attempts to achieve what he calls a "bust thru from quotidien into divine or permanent world." In *Thrones* he is most explicit in expressing both his image of himself as a creator who challenges the limits of mortality and his identification with those who seek superhuman knowledge and power. In Canto 102 he declares in transliterated Greek and English:

OU THELEI EAEAN EIS KOSMOU
> they want to burst out of the universe ... (pp. 82-83)

and again in Canto 105:

> οὐ θέλει ἔην εἰς κόσμον
> but from at least here is the Charta Magna
> I shall have to learn a little greek to keep up with this
> but so will you, drratt you.
> "They want to bust out of the kosmos".... (p. 102)

In establishing his "divine" world Pound adapts traditional myths and rituals of metamorphosis to his conception of renewal. The mind of his Odysseus persona contains and controls past and present history; using this as his material, he seeks to forge his own myth of creation. Like God, he imposes his own order—a reversal or suspension of time, a regression to earlier economic, agricultural, social, and religious practices—on what he considers the chaos of man's errors and evil. He would recreate man through a continual ritual of renewal in which "quotidian" labor, customs, and even emotions are invested with magical value.

Returning to Persephone in *Thrones*, Pound speaks of her in ritual questions:

> AND was her daughter like that;
> Black as Demeter's gown,
> eyes, hair?
> Dis' bride, Queen over Phlegethon,
> girls faint as mist about her?

and in the next line, declares:

> The strength of men is in grain. (106, p. 104)

Simultaneously the bride of death and its ruler, the figure of Persephone reminds us that men's reliance on grain is not merely a practical means of survival; it is a conquest of death. Pound's mythical and ritualistic depiction of natural productivity, his constant allusions to "grain rite" in ancient China and ancient Greece are actually details from his own grand creation of a mythical realm continually renewed in the mind of the persona who is both hero and poet. In his identification with the ritual metamorphoses of Persephone, Adonis, Dionysus, Leucothea, and the other gods who inhabit *The Cantos*, the persona asserts his own capacity to impose his inner vision of perfection upon a damaged world.

Perhaps because it is based on anger and despair at man's history and contempt for his values, this vision cannot tolerate skepticism. In *Thrones* Pound criticizes Yeats's continual questioning and revision of his own mythical and philosophical structure:

> Uncle William frantically denying his
> *most* intelligent statements (re/every individual soul,
> per esempio). . . .   (97, p. 28)

In Yeats's poetry adaptations and imitations of ritual are enactments of both man's yearning for permanence and order and his recognition that these exist only as mythical ideals in his memory and his fantasy. The "individual soul" wavers between belief in its own vision and denial of the "fabulous symbol" it creates. For Yeats ritual is primarily a poetic device for expressing the "fabulous darkness" within man himself. In his poetry, if ritual dramatizes man's fears and denials of death through his enactment of rebirth and his image of a limitless existence, it also discloses the human source of his visions of eternity.

Yeats's use of ritual to depict inner drama and conflict threatens Pound's static and dogmatic position. Though Pound rejects established religion as infected with commercialism and other bourgeois vulgarity, his use of ritual reveals him as essentially a religious poet. To him Ovid's *Metamorphoses* is a "sacred book,"[25] clearly because it describes continual transformations from suffering to acceptance, from death to forms of eternal life. Though Pound insists that he would restore society through ritual worship of the divine principle

[25] *The Letters of Ezra Pound*, p. 183.

in nature, in *The Cantos* his approach to this end is neither optimistic nor practical. Emerging from a self-imposed emotional Hades, his persona employs the stylized action and traditional associations of ritual as a means of releasing a Messianic vision of animistic nature and personal immortality.

T. S. ELIOT
Fulfillment through Sacrifice

Eliot, like Pound, uses rite for the poetic construction of a religious vision, but ritual allusions and effects in his poetry function differently from those in *The Cantos*. Ritual for Pound provides a framework for the extension and magnification of his self image; for Eliot it is the product and evidence of "self-sacrifice, a continual extinction of personality."[26] In Eliot's poems, as in Yeats's, ritual expresses the dramatic tension that results from shifting perceptions of and responses to reality; but Yeats's quest ultimately leads inward to "heart's truth," Eliot's beyond man to a "pure vision" of eternity. Ritual is an important key to stylistic and thematic change and development in Eliot's poetry: suggestions and adaptations of rites in "The Love Song of J. Alfred Prufrock" are informal and ironic, revealing psychological conflict and compulsion; in later poems ritual effects clearly imitate traditional Christian prayer and ceremony.

In "Prufrock," allusions to ritual indicate that the speaker seeks more than acceptance by a beloved or society. His neurotic compulsions and probings are only pathetic manifestations of a deeper quest for meaning and order in an apparent chaos. Like all rituals, Prufrock's is centered around an "overwhelming question" about the nature of man in relation to God and the universe.

Unable to enact his search within the security of established rite, Prufrock turns it on himself in an inner drama. This begins with an imagined quest involving an overwhelming question and a lady. He turns away from the first: "Oh, do not ask, 'What is it?'" but it continues to tease and haunt him in his fantasy of unfulfilled love. Throughout his inner monologue, details of the sordid and

[26] "Tradition and the Individual Talent," *Selected Essays 1917-1932*, p. 7.

superficial life around him reinforce his timidity and uncertainty; yet ritual associations intrude, demanding an involvement for which he is inadequate. As he thinks:

> There will be time, there will be time
> To prepare a face to meet the faces that you meet;

he recalls the ancient ritual of destruction and renewal:

> There will be time to murder and create,
> And time for all the works and days of hands
> That lift and drop a question on your plate. . . .

The changing of social masks reminds him of older and deeper change, when new gods rose from the murder of old ones, and with them, new hope from the symbolic control of decay and despair, when the day was given to labor, as indicated by Hesiod, in the order prescribed by nature and rite. Thus, the question he imagines dropped on his plate is not only a sign of his neurotic insecurity but a recurrence of the eternal question of man's role in the universe. If it evokes "visions," these lead only to "revisions," as the unfulfilled need for meaning and security within the framework of an ordered universe expresses itself in personal compulsions. The questions and considerations become narcissistic and ridiculous:

> "Do I dare?" and "Do I dare?"
> Time to turn back and descend the stair,
> With a bald spot in the middle of my hair—

because in his time and place essential questions seem inappropriate:

> Do I dare
> Disturb the universe?

Unable to "presume," he returns to the fears and inhibitions that characterize his daily behavior. Beneath these lies a desperate longing for salvation:

> But though I have wept and fasted, wept and prayed,
> Though I have seen my head [grown slightly bald]
> > brought in upon a platter
> I am no prophet—and here's no great matter. . . .

220

The rites of fasting and praying are fruitless; his momentary identification with John the Baptist ends in self-ridicule which only partially disguises his terror.

The climax of Prufrock's monologue is a long series of subordinate clauses, beginning with the petty rituals of daily life and ending with a ritual drama of rolling the universe toward the overwhelming question and rising from the dead provided with all the answers:

> And would it have been worth it, after all,
> After the cups, the marmalade, the tea,
> Among the porcelain, among some talk of you and me,
> Would it have been worth while,
> To have bitten off the matter with a smile,
> To have squeezed the universe into a ball
> To roll it towards some overwhelming question,
> To say: "I am Lazarus, come from the dead,
> Come back to tell you all, I shall tell you all"—

But such a vision would be rejected by the lady:

> "That is not what I meant at all.
> That is not it, at all."

Having accepted his failure in the role of prophet acting out a resurrection, he imagines himself a buffoon, chanting a childish rhyme full of despair:

> I grow old . . . I grow old . . .
> I shall wear the bottoms of my trousers rolled.   •

The lady, whom we see only through the focus of Prufrock, cannot comprehend the nature of his quest and thus is oblivious to any spiritual meaning love might have. Prufrock's love song, like his image of the lady, emerges from the hell in which he is damned, longing for but incapable of participating in a rite of restoration. His hope of escape from his inner hell lies neither in self-knowledge nor action; in his brief "vision" of fulfillment, personal conflict is submerged in a ritual quest for religious certainty. He can imagine a release from the torment of his own thoughts and feelings only as Lazarus, returning to tell "all."

The first of Eliot's personae who can envision salvation only in "self-sacrifice," Prufrock alone is damned forever to a personal hell. The protagonist of *The Waste Land* reflects a more ambivalent state as he develops gradually, encompassing the various characters who merge into one consciousness. In the previous chapter I indicated that the mythical structure of the poem, in revealing the sterility of modern society and the futility of man's search for meaning in his personal life, offers neither explanation nor resolution; it merely leads to a ritual quest, the goal of which is the merging of the individual with a divine essence. By allusion to and imitation of rituals centered around the Grail legend—though not exclusively these—Eliot again depicts an inner quest, a search within the unconscious mind for evidence of a divine principle within man and the universe. This quest uncovers man's degradation of traditional rite, especially in his violation of the meaning of love and sexuality, which results in the impotence and despair symbolized in his role of the Fisher King, maimed and waiting to be healed of his wound.

The first question that the protagonist asks of himself:

> What are the roots that clutch, what branches grow
> Out of this stony rubbish?

begins the ritual quest. He seeks growth and recurrence, and he finds within himself only stone and decay. The reply, echoing Ezekiel and Ecclesiastes, offers no solution, but it gives the aloneness and fear of the protagonist meaning within a religious context. The horror of sterility is intensified:

> And the dead tree gives no shelter, the cricket no relief,
> And the dry stone no sound of water.

and there is a hint that alleviation is possible only if the full extent of man's limitations is enacted and thus accepted:

> Only
> There is shadow under this red rock,
> (Come in under the shadow of this red rock),

And I will show you something different from either
Your shadow at morning striding behind you
Or your shadow at evening rising to meet you;
I will show you fear in a handful of dust.

Allusions to pagan rituals follow: the recollection of "the hyacinth garden," a quest for love that produced neither insight nor joy, Madame Sosostris, the debased prophet, who foresees more than she realizes, and the meeting with Stetson, which is a ritual encounter.

The protagonist's questions:

"That corpse you planted last year in your garden,
"Has it begun to sprout? Will it bloom this year?
"Or has the sudden frost disturbed its bed?"

clearly refer to the traditional ritual burial of a fertility god and the expectation of rebirth, but here, though the protagonist is certain of the burial, he has doubts about the new bloom. He warns his former comrade:

"Oh keep the Dog far hence, that's friend to men,
"Or with his nails he'll dig it up again!"

Eliot's note indicates that the first two lines echo the Dirge in Webster's *The White Devil*. It is well known that Eliot changes Cornelia's reference to the wolf as foe to the Dog as friend. Many ingenious explanations of the lines have been offered,[27] none of which seems entirely satisfactory. Regarded in the context of Cornelia's distracted lamentation and concern that the soul of her son be received by the Church, Eliot's lines convey a desperate hope that the corpse will indeed "sprout" if only the proper rituals are observed. The warning to Stetson is a plea that the Dog be regarded in its ancient role of fertility spirit (hence the capitalization), not given the liberty of its modern urban one of "friend to men," for as such it is a destroyer of ceremony. In this double role the Dog

---

[27] See, for example, Drew, *T. S. Eliot, The Design of His Poetry*, pp. 74-75; Williamson, *A Reader's Guide to T. S. Eliot*, pp. 134-35; Smith, *T. S. Eliot's Poetry and Plays*, pp. 78-79.

hovers over the ancient rite and the modern scene, suggesting ritual mana and prohibition.

The encounter sets the mood for the fulfillment of the prophecies of Madame Sosostris, which begins with the appearance of Bella-donna. A sad descendant of mythical queens, she embodies the degeneration of ritual and ceremony. The metamorphosis of Philo-mel provides vulgar decoration for her home. With "her hair / Spread out in fiery points," she seems a prophetess about to speak: "Glowed into words, then would be savagely still," but her message is: "My nerves are bad tonight." When her frantic questions de-manding purpose in life are answered only by her husband's images of sterility and death, she turns to a meaningless and barren ritual: "And we shall play a game of chess."

The protagonist's quest exposes the debased patterns of human love in this episode and the one following it, in which illness, decay, and abortion exemplify sterility. In Part III his identification with Phlebas the Phoenician and the Fisher King emerges through allu-sions to water, the archetypal symbol of fertility which is itself now barren: "The nymphs are departed." The protagonist describes himself on the Thames, fishing:

> But at my back in a cold blast I hear
> The rattle of the bones, and chuckle spread from ear to ear.
>
> A rat crept softly through the vegetation
> Dragging its slimy belly on the bank
> While I was fishing in the dull canal
> On a winter evening round behind the gashouse
> Musing upon the king my brother's wreck
> And on the king my father's death before him.

In the allusion to Marvell, Eliot removes any implication of eternity that "winged chariot" may lend to time; the "cold blast" of death surrounds the fisherman, who performs his ritual quest for a "Life symbol of immemorial antiquity"[28] in a hostile and sterile environ-ment. As he fishes, he mourns the death of kings, evoking the oldest

---

[28] Weston, *From Ritual to Romance*, p. 119.

of ritual murders. His identification with Ferdinand here indicates a faint possibility of restoration, since his father Alonzo is, of course, alive. But in the passage that follows:

> White bodies naked on the low damp ground
> And bones cast in a little low dry garret
> Rattled by the rat's foot only, year to year.

death is omnipresent and unrelieved. The bitterness and pain of the protagonist are enacted in the parody of a spring rite which follows, involving Sweeney as Actaeon and Mrs. Porter as Diana:

> But at my back from time to time I hear
> The sound of horns and motors, which shall bring
> Sweeney to Mrs. Porter in the spring.
> O the moon shone bright on Mrs. Porter
> And on her daughter
> They wash their feet in soda water
> *Et O ces voix d'enfants, chantant dans la coupole!*

Eliot's note refers to a passage in Day's *Parliament of Bees* which deals with Actaeon's discovery of Diana bathing in a spring. Diana, who was both a fertility goddess and a goddess of chastity, and Actaeon are clearly mythical remnants of figures in ancient rites of renewal. The "spring" of the wasteland, deadened by "horns and motors," brings Sweeney to Mrs. Porter as the ultimate vulgarization of such rites, which are further mocked in the street ballad Eliot imitates and in the line quoted from Verlaine's *Parsifal*, in which the voices of children are heard by the knight after he has healed the king. Eliot's ironic use of the line following the mock rite discloses the anguish of a quest in which the protagonist discovers the most debased and infantile distortion of the meaning of ritual in his own soul. This experience is echoed in the next four lines in the sound of the nightingale performing its own coarse rite, as before "to dirty ears," projecting the protagonist's feelings on external nature.

In this section as in "A Game of Chess," the failure of human love is exposed in relation to sexuality, associated in ancient rite with the fruitfulness of the earth and now with barrenness and perversion. Mr. Eugenides, described by Madame Sosostris as the "one-eyed merchant," appears in "the brown fog of a winter noon." Cleanth Brooks, relying on Jessie Weston's suggestion that the mystery cults connected with the Grail legend were transmitted by Syrian merchants,[29] views Mr. Eugenides as "a rather battered representative of the fertility cults: the prophet, the *seer* with only one eye."[30] His one eye is also a symbol of the sexually maimed, and his homosexual proposal to the protagonist is a corrupt and sterile debasement of ritual sexuality.

As Tiresias, the protagonist participates in another fruitless sexual experience; perceiving the typist and her lover embracing, he recalls all the suffering of the past he has witnessed in Thebes and in the realm "of the dead." His consciousness drifts away from these sterile encounters as he approaches "Lower Thames Street." Near the church of Magnus Martyr he identifies with the "fishmen" who "lounge at noon." The mythical voices of the river, the Three Thames-daughters, sing of the degeneration of the waters, the traditional symbol of rebirth, as the Rhine daughters in the *Götterdämmerung* sing of night now lying on waters which were clear when the bright Rhinegold glittered within them. Eliot employs this association of the lament of the maidens over the loss of the magic beauty and power of the Rhinegold to indicate that the corruptions of modern life—the "Oil and tar" on the Thames—are only a sign of a deeper source of despair, the loss of symbolic and ritual potency to promote fertility and rebirth. The river songs of sexual adventure that follow are further evidence of the sterility that results when spiritual resources are absent from external and human nature.

Section III ends with quotations from St. Augustine and the Buddha's Fire Sermon, which become part of a ritual of repentance, to which the corruption of man and nature have led. On the basis of Eliot's note referring to his use of these quotations: "the collocation of these two representatives of eastern and western asceticism, as the culmination of this part of the poem, is not an accident,"

[29] *ibid.*, p. 160.
[30] Brooks, *Modern Poetry and the Tradition*, p. 153.

Brooks regards "the various scenes of 'The Fire Sermon'" as "the sterile burning of lust," which can be checked only by asceticism.[31] Certainly the scenes of sterile sexuality in *The Waste Land* convey the horror of lust without love, and the lines:

> Burning burning burning burning
> O Lord Thou pluckest me out
> O Lord Thou pluckest
>
> burning

are a plea for release from fruitless sexual desire, but within the context of the poem they also reveal the burning soul turning in its shame, impotence, and despair to a consciousness of divinity.

The yearning for such solace is expressed in the identification with Phlebas the Phoenician in "Death by Water," where the protagonist enacts another of the prophecies of Madame Sosostris in a ritual of "self-sacrifice." The drowning of Phlebas is like the commitment "to the waves" of an ancient fertility god, but in "Death by Water" there is no "joyous celebration of his resurrection."[32] The anguished "burning" within the soul of the speaker drives him to this sacrifice in his quest for divine sustenance; this is a cleansing, an escape from the bonds of his desire and frustration, a rite of renewal which is continued and extended in Part V.

"What the Thunder Said" begins with allusions to ritual sacrifice that are clearly Christian: the agony of Christ in the garden of Gethsemane and his crucifixion. Furthermore, "the Hanged Man," whom Madame Sosostris could not find and whom Eliot identifies as the "Hanged God of Frazer," emerges as Christ in this section. The first lines recreate the tension and drama of ritual:

> After the torchlight red on sweaty faces
> After the frosty silence in the gardens
> After the agony in stony places
> The shouting and the crying
> Prison and palace and reverberation
> Of thunder of spring over distant mountains . . .

[31] *ibid.*, p. 157.
[32] Weston, *From Ritual to Romance*, p. 44.

but, as in "Death by Water," there is no resolution in joy. The ritual deaths occur again and again, but there seems little promise of resurrection:

> He who was living is now dead
> We who were living are now dying
> With a little patience. . . .

In the dryness of the desert among "mountains of rock without water," hearing "dry sterile thunder without rain," the quester prays for water. As he does so, he becomes one of the two men to whom Christ appeared on the road to Emmaus. His presence is indicated in a series of questions as the quest reaches its climax:

> Who is the third who walks always beside you?
> When I count, there are only you and I together
> But when I look ahead up the white road
> There is always another one walking beside you
> Gliding wrapt in a brown mantle, hooded
> I do not know whether a man or a woman
> —But who is that on the other side of you?
>
> What is that sound high in the air
> Murmur of maternal lamentation
> Who are those hooded hordes swarming
> Over endless plains, stumbling in cracked earth
> Ringed by the flat horizon only
> What is the city over the mountains
> Cracks and reforms and bursts in the violet air
> Falling towers
> Jerusalem Athens Alexandria
> Vienna London
> Unreal. . . .

Like the disciples on the journey to Emmaus, the speaker does not recognize the hooded figure; yet he is aware of his influence as he asks ritual questions concerning "maternal lamentation," a traditional response to the sacrifice of deity, and the effect of the presence of Christ on the "hooded hordes" and on the decaying cities, "unreal" because they reflect no values or spirit. Amid this chaos the protagonist approaches the Chapel Perilous, "an adventure which . . . is fraught with extreme peril to life." A part of the Grail legend, the journey to this Chapel, which sometimes includes a visit to a Perilous Cemetery, is considered the quester's initiation into the mysteries of death and eternity.[33] This lonely and frightening portion of the quest in *The Waste Land* describes the protagonist's deepest experience of the quality of decay and death; here there are no mitigating details of streets or drawing rooms, only "the tumbled graves" and "the empty chapel." As in some of Yeats's later poems, ritual action brings the participant to a full consciousness of the reality of physical death. For the protagonist of *The Waste Land*, however, the experience is an impersonal one; for him a confrontation with death does not intensify or elucidate human love, loss, and suffering as it does for the personae of Yeats. Instead, it leads to a possibility of release from the dryness and sterility of human life, as rain opens the way for a ritual exchange with the thunder.

The commands of the thunder, which speaks for God, are taken by the protagonist as questions about his own and his contemporaries' spiritual condition. At the first command, "Give," he remembers

> The awful daring of a moment's surrender
> Which an age of prudence can never retract
> By this, and this only, we have existed
> Which is not to be found in our obituaries. . . .

This answer recalls Prufrock's repeated "Do I dare?" and indicates that the protagonist of *The Waste Land*, despite his pessimism and despair, has gone deeper and farther in his quest than the earlier persona. He has dared to surrender himself, if only in moments, to desire for human love, which has proved fruitless but has driven him to surrender to a divine voice and presence. It seems his one

[33] *ibid.*, pp. 165-74.

answer to death. To the command, "Sympathize," he can respond
only from the "prison" of his aloneness; his "circle closed on the
outside," he is released briefly in "aethereal rumours" or dreams.
The last command, "Control," is answered by a dream or fantasy
of assurance and quiet power over a boat, the sea, and a beloved, but
it has never been realized: "your heart would have responded. . . ."

The Waste Land ends with the protagonist's total identification
with the Fisher King. All the characters merge in this last scene
in which he sits and waits for the fruitful question, which will release him from impotence and pain:

> I sat upon the shore
> Fishing, with the arid plain behind me
> Shall I at least set my lands in order?

The world of men is an "arid plain," and he has left it behind him.
That part of the quest is over. The whole of The Waste Land is
the fulfillment of a prophecy first uttered by a tainted prophet in
a barren time. As the meaning of the prophecy unfolds, the protagonist realizes that neither human love, society, nor history offers
spiritual renewal; in the end the quester is left with a yearning to
merge with divinity, which has been the cause of his torment and
now seems the only source of comfort in his soul. The quest has
not fulfilled his need, but it has defined it. The question, "Shall I
at least set my lands in order?" indicates his removal from the decaying world around him, for which he sings a contemptuous dirge,
a childish song that is a remnant of "the primitive rite of the foundation sacrifice":[34] "London bridge is falling down falling down falling down. . . ." His further quest lies not in human civilization but
through purgatory and true metamorphosis. In the quotation *Quan-
do fiam uti chelidon*, from the *Pervigilium Veneris*, followed by
the plea "O swallow swallow," the protagonist uses the myth of
Philomela and Procne once again to express a desire for rebirth
and renewal. In a note Eliot suggests a comparison between this
and his earlier use of the myth. The symbol of the nightingale in

[34] Smith, *T. S. Eliot's Poetry and Plays*, p. 97.

Parts II and III reveals only vulgarity and sexual sterility; the present reference to the swallow that Procne became reflects its use in the *Pervigilium Veneris* as a symbol of spring and song. Like the protagonist, the myth itself is restored as it is removed from human society.

At the end of the poem the protagonist is totally isolated from his society; as he waits for spiritual renewal, he may seem an inspired madman: "Hieronymo's mad againe." He listens not to the men around him, but to the sounds of ritual renewal so far removed from his own society that they are uttered in Sanskrit, the actual language of early rites of fertility and the language of a god. Rites connected with the Grail legend, both in its origins in fertility cults and its adaptation to Christian symbolism, convert sexual impotence and psychological aimlessness into symbolic acts of sin and penitence in *The Waste Land*. The very ambiguity of the legend, which encompasses the most primitive acts of ritual murder and mystical elements of Christian worship, provides Eliot with a dramatic structure for the conflict he sees within the consciousness of modern man and society. That drama is enacted in quest, in discovery of spiritual and physical death, and finally in the penitence and tense expectation of the worshiper.

Nowhere else in Eliot's poetry is pagan ritual as basic a structural element as it is in *The Waste Land*; in his later poetry, when references to pagan myths and rituals occur, they are employed principally in the context of Christian rite, which becomes a more important source and model. Nonetheless, a brief glance at some of his adaptations of games, dance, and other remnants of primitive worship to the predominantly Christian tone of some of his later poetry will reveal qualities of his thought and poetic technique hitherto unexplored.

In his discussion of "The Hollow Men" George Williamson says that the poem's "most devastating irony is formal: the extension of game ritual into liturgical form."[35] The use of childish or game

[35] *A Reader's Guide to T. S. Eliot*, pp. 160-61.

ritual is a familiar technique in Eliot's poetry; its effectiveness in "Prufrock" and *The Waste Land* has been discussed above. What is new in "The Hollow Men" is that the explicit ironic connection between the ritual of play and that of both pagan and Christian worship expresses the theme of the poem. This connection is not merely the rather simple one that Williamson sees: "as children make a game of make-believe out of Guy Fawkes so we make a similar game out of religion,"[36] for it expresses the emotional dryness and sterility characteristic of Eliot's personae and the effort to break out of this paralysis through ritual or symbolic action.

The first epigraph, "Mistah Kurtz—he dead," from Conrad's *Heart of Darkness*, alludes to the spiritual death of a man destroyed by the evil within him; even alive, Kurtz is "a shade," a "Shadow," a creature of hell. He is a "hollow sham," a man "hollow at the core." "A penny for the Old Guy," the second epigraph, refers, of course, to the dummy Guy Fawkes, a modern version of the ancient straw figure burned in effigy to rid the land of misfortune. The two figures—Kurtz and Guy Fawkes—are related in that both serve as projections of the fear and anger of their society. From Kurtz, Marlow learns of man's inclination to evil, and in death Kurtz is like an ancient scapegoat, a symbol of the corruption that must be expiated. The persona of "The Hollow Men" identifies with these figures and through them expresses the deadness he feels is present in his own soul and in the men around him.

The poem begins with a declaration that the speaker and his fellow men are assuming the role of scapegoats in a ritual of expulsion:

> We are the hollow men
> We are the stuffed men
> Leaning together
> Headpiece filled with straw. Alas!

This symbolic role reflects a desperate spiritual condition, which can be alleviated only by total self-sacrifice. The hollow men identify

[36] *ibid.*, p. 155.

so deeply with the scapegoat figure that their deadened souls no longer suffer the loss or feel the anger they represent:

> Those who have crossed
> With direct eyes, to death's other Kingdom
> Remember us—if at all—not as lost
> Violent souls, but only
> As the hollow men
> The stuffed men.

The speaker sees himself through the "direct eyes" of those who have experienced actual death and release from mortality in the "other Kingdom" as "hollow" and "stuffed," their scapegoat, not a fellow soul in eternity. Contrasted with the "Kingdom" of the peaceful dead is his own: "death's dream kingdom," the realm of dream where he is haunted by the "eyes" which interpret his spiritual state. The unconscious mind, the source of dream, is projected as the "dead land" which the hollow men inhabit.

Sections III and IV depict the emotional state of the speaker through the development of this image of "the dead land." His psychological aridity is enacted in rituals performed by the dead:

> This is the dead land
> This is cactus land
> Here the stone images
> Are raised, here they receive
> The supplication of a dead man's hand
> Under the twinkle of a fading star.

The suffering of the deadened spirit is never expressed directly; it is instead converted into rituals which symbolize longing for release and the inability to achieve it:

> At the hour when we are
> Trembling with tenderness
> Lips that would kiss
> Form prayers to broken stone.

233

The only hope of "empty men" lies in the "eyes" of those they envision existing in "death's other kingdom." Ironically these eyes, which communicate the one possibility of salvation, belong to the dead—but only to those who have transcended mortality. Within the "dead land" of the hollow souls these "eyes" represent the divine principle, which Eliot, like Jung, considers inherent in the unconscious mind of man. Immediately following the depiction of the eyes

> As the perpetual star
> Multifoliate rose
> Of death's twilight kingdom
> The hope only
> Of empty men.

there is an abrupt shift in tone as the hollow men engage in a childish game, a parody of their role as participants in a ritual of expulsion:

> *Here we go round the prickly pear*
> *Prickly pear prickly pear*
> *Here we go round the prickly pear*
> *At five o'clock in the morning.*

The circle game, an absurd ceremony for a worthless object, suggests the infinite futility they feel, the uncertainty of their purpose and their hopes.

This ritual of despair is repeated in various ways throughout the last section of the poem, interrupted by fragments from the Lord's Prayer, a contrasting rite in which the impotent and despairing cannot participate, though these snatches express their unconscious knowledge of and yearning for union with a divine principle. The symbol of their spiritual deadness in this section is the "Shadow":

Between the idea
And the reality
Between the motion
And the act
Falls the Shadow   *For Thine is the Kingdom*

234

Between the conception
And the creation
Between the emotion
And the response
Falls the Shadow
                                                Life is very long

Between the desire
And the spasm
Between the potency
And the existence
Between the essence
And the descent
Falls the Shadow
                                For Thine is the Kingdom

For Thine is
Life is
For Thine is the

This is the way the world ends
This is the way the world ends
This is the way the world ends
Not with a bang but a whimper.

Throughout these stanzas action—symbolic, creative, and sexual—
is arrested by a compulsion toward self-destruction or death, an inner experience portrayed as the "Shadow," insubstantial as the dying
Kurtz, "unsteady, long, pale, indistinct, like a vapor exhaled by the
earth," and as powerful as he to destroy vitality and hope. The reminder "Life is very long" only increases the feeling of desperation.
The last stanza, another imitation of a childhood game, describes
the final and meaningless ritual sacrifice of the hollow men; their
corrupt world ends not with symbolic violence or destruction, but
with the pathos of an infantile "whimper." Haunted by the faintest
promise of spiritual survival in the broken ritual of the Lord's Prayer,
they are denied even the fulfillment of scapegoats in a sacrificial rite.

Clearly Eliot conceives of "self-sacrifice," the "continual extinction
of personality," as more than a matter of tone or point of view; like

the poet, his protagonists go through a "process of depersonalization." The merging of characters into figures enacting a ritual in "Prufrock," *The Waste Land*, and "The Hollow Men" expresses a central theme of his poetry: Eliot conceives of the effort toward fulfillment not only for the artist but for man in general—however despairing—as "a continual surrender of himself as he is at the moment to something which is more valuable."[37] As he grows firmer in his religious convictions, Eliot refers less often to pagan ritual death and rebirth and more to Christian liturgy. For him, as for Dante, Christianity provides "a mythology and a theology" which allow for "expansion into pure vision."[38] The surrender of the self realized poetically and enacted ritually in "Ash Wednesday," the *Ariel Poems*, and "Choruses From 'The Rock,' " can be analyzed only in relation to Christian dogma and rite, which are not the subject of this book.[39] In *Four Quartets*, however, Eliot's most powerful expression of the theme of "self-sacrifice," echoes and remnants of pagan rite—especially dance—are of some importance. These are blended with adaptations of Christian prayer, incantatory effects, colloquial and philosophical language, as the poet seeks to capture and define the timeless element in history and in time itself. Paradoxically, this most plainly autobiographical work is the one in which Eliot develops most clearly the theme of "depersonalization," his means to fulfillment as a Christian man and maturity as a religious poet.

The subject of *Four Quartets*, according to Helen Gardner, is "religious experience, . . . how the mind comes to discover religious truth: truth which interprets for us our whole experience of life."[40] Yet in this work neither Eliot's tone nor language is primarily that of Christian worship. There are brief sections which imitate prayer or evoke ceremony but, essentially, Eliot attempts to reveal the consciousness of the supernatural within the human mind, not as it is manifest in public worship but as it emerges in private exploration

---

[37] "Tradition and the Individual Talent," *Selected Essays 1917-1932*, pp. 6-7.
[38] "Dante," *The Sacred Wood*, pp. 162-63.
[39] The most comprehensive treatment of Eliot's use of Christian myth and ritual can be found in Genesius Jones, O.F.M., *Approach to the Purpose* (New York, 1964).
[40] *The Art of T. S. Eliot* (1950; reprint, New York, 1959), p. 61.

and illumination. If *Four Quartets* is autobiographical, it deals with a man's response to and interpretation of time, loss, death, and the hope of eternity.

At the beginning of "Burnt Norton," Eliot explores the consciousness of time within man's soul, the interweaving of memory with speculation on "What might have been," with present and with future; at the end of the first section, he says:

> Time past and time future
> What might have been and what has been
> Point to one end, which is always present.   (p. 176)

It is this "end" that he seeks to capture in its eternal presence through the ritual and image of dance. The abstract concept of time and the challenge of its conquest ("Only through time time is conquered.") are transmitted in the movement and stillness of dance:

> The dance along the artery
> The circulation of the lymph
> Are figured in the drift of stars
> Ascend to summer in the tree
> We move above the moving tree
> In light upon the figured leaf
> And hear upon the sodden floor
> Below, the boarhound and the boar
> Pursue their pattern as before
> But reconciled among the stars.   (p. 177)

Like Yeats, Eliot sees in dance the visible expression of forces so deep within man that they determine his nature and destiny. Both poets use the ritual quality of dance movements to suggest a pattern of recurrence or permanence in human experience. There are, however, important differences in their approach to and use of this symbol. Yeats employs dance to depict the harmony, knowledge, and control which he feels exist within the unconscious mind of the seer and the poet and which emerge only in dream, myth, and ritual. In "Byzantium," the ritual fire-dance symbolizes the poet's capacity to synthesize and transcend material existence and ephemeral ex-

perience. Here spiritual transcendence is essentially personal and
artistic. Furthermore, in Yeats's poetry the movements of dance enact "heart's truth," exposing the deepest ambivalence of man's physical nature. In "Crazy Jane Grown Old Looks at the Dancers," the
ritual dance transcends ordinary experience because in controlled
and harmonious movements it can unify the unacknowledged con-
tradictions of violence and love that continually exist within man's
being. Eliot's emphasis on "stillness" is the key to his interpretation
of dance and to his divergence from Yeats in the poetic adaptation
of ritual movement. In his essay "Four Elizabethan Dramatists,"
Eliot describes the dancer transcending dance itself, as between his
movements the deepest and most impersonal expression of a life force
emerges: "The difference between a great dancer and a merely com-
petent dancer is in the vital flame, that impersonal, and, if you like,
inhuman force which transpires between each of the great dancer's
movements."[41] In "Burnt Norton," Eliot uses the vacuum of empty
space and absence of sound that must exist within the pattern of
dance to create time "always present," time conquered through the
awareness of stillness and silence in the context of sound and movement.

Both Yeats and Eliot rely on the tradition that ritual dance expresses a desire to transcend human limitation, but Yeats's dancer
overcomes weakness and terror through the enactment of its conquest by art or love, Eliot's through a control over time which foreshadows eternity. The knowledge of such control is intrinsic not
only to the dancer but to all men whom he symbolizes: "the dance
along the artery" contains the pattern of man's physical nature, but
it also expresses his inherent yearning to transcend it:

At the still point of the turning world. Neither flesh nor fleshless;
Neither from nor towards; at the still point, there the dance is,
But neither arrest nor movement. And do not call it fixity,
Where past and future are gathered. Neither movement from
    nor towards,
Neither ascent nor decline. Except for the point, the still point,
There would be no dance, and there is only the dance.   (p. 177)

[41] *Selected Essays 1917-1932*, p. 95.

In "East Coker," the poet's search within himself for a conception of eternal time takes him back to the land of his ancestors: "In my beginning is my end." There he evokes the past—"what has been"—in his exploration of the finite and the continuous, both of which are expressed in the image of dance. The traditional dance of villagers around a bonfire reflects the rhythm of life—the seasons, the constellations, and the sexual acts of human beings and animals. Since it enacts only recurrence, this dance ends in "Dung and death." The realization that the "dancers are all gone under the hill" intensifies the poet's consciousness of darkness and death: "They all go into the dark. . . ." Only when he allows himself this awareness of death, do we know that the dance of the villagers is merely part of the ritual control over nature:

> I said to my soul, be still, and let the dark come upon you
> Which shall be the darkness of God.

He waits, as in a darkened theater or an underground train, until finally the stillness of his soul receives a sense of the eternal:

> Wait without thought, for you are not ready for thought:
> So the darkness shall be the light, and the stillness the
>   dancing   (pp. 183-86)

Only when the dance is internalized as a vision of motion within the stillness of eternal time is "what has been" redeemed from death.

This internalization of ritual as symbolic knowledge of the eternal within the darkness of man's mind is developed in connection with the river in "The Dry Salvages." The river is first presented as a god:

> I do not know much about gods; but I think that the river
> Is a strong brown god—sullen, untamed and intractable. . . .

This god, "almost forgotten" by city-dwellers, exists in nature,

> Keeping his seasons and rages, destroyer, reminder
> Of what men choose to forget.

Official worship is denied him:

> Unhonoured, unpropitiated
> By worshippers of the machine, but waiting, watching and
>   waiting.

but his "rhythm" persists in human experience: "in the nursery bed-room," in "the smell of grapes on the autumn table," and in other signs of the changing seasons. "The river is within us, the sea is all about us" (p. 191); both have their gods and voices, symbols of the essential rhythm and ritual of creation, change, recurrence, and per-manence, which are intrinsic to man and nature. The energy of the sea and its endless powers of regeneration, its existence beyond time as man reckons it, only increase the poet's sense of man's ephemeral nature and his limited perspective. Creation itself, with all its change and death, seems to contain devotion:

> Where is there an end to the drifting wreckage,
> The prayer of the bone on the beach, the unprayable
> Prayer at the calamitous annunciation?

Without a ritual of devotion to the sources and rhythms of life, man is lost in time, his "unattached devotion which might pass for de-votionless" a cause of dissatisfaction and pain. When he can view the "bone's prayer" as one to "Death its God," and thus accept death as part of the rhythm of rebirth, he is able to attach his devotion to the "Prayer of the one Annunciation" (pp. 193-94) as intrinsic to all creation.

Thus, Section IV includes and synthesizes the changing, the re-current, and the perennial in one ritual of Christian devotion. The poet, addressing the "Lady," who is, of course, the Virgin, asks for her prayers on behalf of men subject to the violence of the sea and the women who wait for them. Finally, he asks her to pray for those whom the sea has killed, who can no longer hear "the sound of the sea bell's / Perpetual angelus." Denied the call to the ritual of An-nunciation in the perennial rhythms of nature, they can be reached only by the "Queen of Heaven" (pp. 197-98).

Having established the necessity of accepting what he considers to be the only true myth and ritual by means of which man can finally cope with his sense of limited time, Eliot now rejects the "lower mythology" employed by men impelled by their "curiosity" about "past and future." He who "clings to that dimension" has no escape from time:

> But to apprehend
> The point of intersection of the timeless
> With time, is an occupation for the saint—
> No occupation either, but something given
> And taken, in a lifetime's death in love,
> Ardour and selflessness and self-surrender.

The saint's apprehension of the timeless point represents the culmination of the strivings of all men, who can reach only "the moment in and out of time" in their quest for permanence. The theme of "selflessness and self-surrender," so important in all of Eliot's poetry, is here developed in relation to an understanding of and approach to timelessness. Self-realization, which for Eliot is "self-sacrifice," cannot be attained by the resolution of human conflict or the fulfillment of desire; it can be achieved only by turning away from such distractions of the past and hopes for the future to "prayer, observance, discipline, thought and action," the aim of which is a glimpse of "past and future . . . conquered, and reconciled" (pp. 198-99) in a vision of eternity.

In "Little Gidding" Eliot returns to the image of dance, which he uses in connection with fire—"the vital flame" that he earlier associated with dance—to symbolize purification as a Christian and fulfillment as a poet. In a place "Where prayer has been valid," where death has been a means to life in eternity,

> the communication
> Of the dead is tongued with fire beyond the language of the living.

In prayer the poet strains toward the transcendent element of language informed by the experience of "the timeless moment." If the theme of "Little Gidding" is "the redemption of men and nations from the fire of hell by the fire of purgation and from the fire of purgation by the fire of love,"[42] this redemptive fire is as much a refiner of language as it is of man's soul. Eliot uses an imaginary meeting with "a familiar compound ghost," who has the "look of some dead master," no doubt at least in part Yeats, to probe for the

---

[42] Smith, *T. S. Eliot's Poetry and Plays*, p. 288.

continuous or the eternal element of his own talent. The ghost's depiction of the bitterness of old age recalls the anger and energy of Yeats's contest with time:

> First, the cold friction of expiring sense
> Without enchantment, offering no promise
> But bitter tastelessness of shadow fruit
> As body and soul begin to fall asunder.
> Second, the conscious importance of rage
> At human folly, and the laceration
> Of laughter at what ceases to amuse.
> And last, the rending pain of re-enactment
> Of all that you have done, and been; the shame
> Of motives late revealed, and the awareness
> Of things ill done to others' harm
> Which once you took for exercise of virtue.

As the poet accepts the ghost's disenchantment, he also blends with him, having become both himself and "someone other," to gain from the purgatorial dialogue insight into the timeless properties of words; the ghost's last admonition contains a promise of immortality expressed in the symbolic fusion of fire and dance reminiscent of Yeats's "Byzantium":

> From wrong to wrong the exasperated spirit
> Proceeds, unless restored by that refining fire
> Where you must move in measure, like a dancer.

Both act and word are continually involved in a process of consummation through destruction, fulfillment through sacrifice, birth through death. The pattern of dance—formal, precise, containing stillness in the control and order of movement—is the final achievement of language and conduct purged of psychological conflict or individual suffering. Thus, the words of the poet "dancing together" in a ritual of prayer, incantation, and self-sacrifice create his "epitaph" (pp. 201-208), his mortal testimony to the existence of eternal time.

W. H. AUDEN
". . . homage by naming"

Though Eliot objected to the notion that poetry can serve as "a substitute for religious faith,"[43] and he describes the "disturbance of our quotidian character which results in an incantation" as a creative experience, quite different from a religious or "mystical" one,[44] Christian rite and poetic incantation do merge and become almost indistinguishable in some of his later poetry. A similar distinction has been made by Auden, who is more explicit than Yeats, Pound, or Eliot about the connection between poetry and rite, and whose own use of ritual does disclose a unique perception of and approach to man and external nature rather than evoking the traditional at-titudes of Christian devotion.

Auden uses ritual allusions and effects in a variety of ways, but always as a means of invoking and releasing hidden elements in man and nature: the suffering, power, or knowledge of his persona or his protagonist, the inner drive or the inner faith. In his early poems he uses ritual mainly to disclose desires and conflicts and to call upon the healing powers of nature; in the later ones it reveals and celebrates the infinite in the finite, the spiritual essence of ordinary reality. Some of his fairly recent statements on the role of rite in the creative process are extremely illuminating in relation to his own poetry:

> The impulse to create a work of art is felt when, in certain persons, the passive awe provoked by sacred beings or events is transformed into a desire to express that awe in a rite of worship or homage, and to be fit homage, this rite must be beautiful. This rite has no magical or idolatrous intention; nothing is expected in return. Nor is it, in a Christian sense, an act of devotion. If it praises the Creator, it does so indirectly by praising His creatures—among which may be human notions of the Divine Nature. With God as Redeemer, it has, so far as I can see, little if anything to do.

[43] "Matthew Arnold," *The Use of Poetry and the Use of Criticism*, p. 116.
[44] "Conclusion," *The Use of Poetry and the Use of Criticism*, p. 145.

He goes on to say: "In poetry the rite is verbal; it pays homage by naming."[45]

It is, of course, necessary to understand Auden's concept of the "sacred," which he regards as the source of the ritual effects in poetry. In defining the concept, Auden borrows from Coleridge the terms Primary and Secondary Imagination, adapting them to his own purposes. "The concern of the Primary Imagination, its only concern," he says, "is with sacred beings and sacred events." Clearly, for Auden, the sacred is not necessarily derived from or related to orthodox religious experience. "The sacred," he says, "is that to which [the Primary Imagination] is obliged to respond; the profane is that to which it cannot respond and therefore does not know." As a "being," the sacred includes persons and natural phenomena—such as the "Moon, for example, Fire, Snakes and those four important beings which can only be defined in terms of nonbeing: Darkness, Silence, Nothing, Death"—all of which inspire "awe." One experiences the sacred as "an encounter," and it is "from the sacred encounters of his imagination that a poet's impulse to write a poem arises." Perhaps the most direct and revealing remark Auden makes on this subject is: "A poem is a rite; hence its formal and ritualistic character."[46]

In accordance with this definition taken from a lecture given in 1956, Auden's poetry has always been ritualistic; even in his earliest poems, in which he hardly uses traditional myth, when he writes of love, war, sickness, and death, he is the communicant of a "sacred encounter" with such phenomena and with the persons, seasons, and landscapes which enact or reflect the conflict and drama inherent in them. Through this encounter he has become aware of the secret meaning of such experience, and his persona is often that of an initiate who would draw the reader into a hidden society of symbolic revolutionaries, spies, and informants. Thus, in the first of *Poems* (1930 and 1933), which is entitled "The Questioner Who Sits So Sly" in *Collected Poetry*, Auden addresses the reader in cryptic lan-

[45] "Making, Knowing, and Judging," An Inaugural Lecture delivered before the University of Oxford on 11 June 1956, *The Dyer's Hand* (New York, 1962), p. 57. Published in London in 1963.
[46] *ibid.*, pp. 54-59.

guage—like that of a code—and confronts him with a series of questions and instructions. There is no overt action; there are no "bombs of conspiracy." The listener, like an initiate in a secret society, is challenged to engage in an inner and symbolic revolution: the maintenance of his values and his integrity in a degenerate time. No rewards are offered for such a victory: no "gift," "income," "bounty," or "promised country." There is only the possibility of avoiding a "neutralizing peace," and thus maintaining a "sacred" contact with reality, which, in this case, consists of an intense and unflinching awareness of the sickness of society, war, and death.

This sense of deep and secret communication with experience, awesome because of the intensity of fear or pain or the recognition of danger, is present throughout the poems of this volume. Though there are few explicit references to ritual objects or acts, Auden's prophetic and admonitory tone in these poems imbues daily experience with the anticipatory tension of ritual, in which the participant, despite all the evidence to the contrary, strives to control reality by symbolic action. In the second poem, "Which of you waking early and watching daybreak" (replaced in 1933 by "Doom is dark and deeper than any sea-dingle"), the poet, predicting the coming of a new social order, compares each dawn to "the first day . . . when truth divided / Light from the original and incoherent darkness. . . ." As each day reflects the sacred quality of the first day, so each human being participating in ordinary daily experience carries within him the spirit of "earth the mother of all life."[47] Observing daybreak, going to work, being caught in a storm—all these real actions are viewed symbolically as enactments of a prophetic rite of destruction of the present social and economic order and the birth of a new society.

The prophetic voice is dominant in *Poems*: in III it is a goddess, Dame Kind (or Venus in *Collected Poetry*), whose utterance signifies the coming annihilation of evil forces in society; in other poems it is an unspecified seer who perceives in the trivial acts and words of the soldier, the "summer visitors," and the "financier" signs of their inevitable death and replacement. The final poem, a prayer ("Petition" in *Collected Poetry*), might be described as a

[47] *Poems* (1930), p. 39.

245

secular rite. Though God, addressed as "Sir," is consulted as a doctor or psychologist, and is not asked to perform obvious miracles, the very nature of the speaker's request—that this deity "Send . . . power and light" to cure the psychological and moral flaws of society—suggests that something of the miraculous is needed to control and change reality. The speaker is concerned with psychological health and rational behavior, but his language reflects the attitudes and emotions of a participant in ritual, for his wish to disclose the lies and heal the sickness of mankind emerges as a prayer for superhuman power and action: if not he then his projected healer must provide "a sovereign touch"; he must "Harrow the house of the dead. . . ."

Such ritual effects, secularized and generally unconnected with traditional myth, also occur throughout *The Orators*. Auden uses the language of liturgy ironically in this volume, and again concludes with a form of prayer. In the last of the six odes of Book III, addressing God as "Father," he prays for "Our necessary defeat." The poem is an obvious parody of traditional hymns, but it is at the same time a serious plea for the "defeat" of the values and attitudes expressed in the pretentious language of many sacred songs, values which distort and vulgarize man's need for "light" and security. Implicit in the prayer is a conflict—the imagery is that of war—between man's tendency to avoid truth, to bask in the vulgar obscurities of the language and thus the emotional contents of traditional hymns, which Auden parodies, and the effort to break through such obscurity, which he expresses in a few precise phrases as the speaker demands the "direct light" that will "Illumine, and not kill" ("Songs and Other Musical Pieces," *Collected Poetry*).

The deity addressed in the prayers and hymns of these early poems is a force of nature, a power inherent in man himself, which the poet attempts to reach through serious or ironic poetic rites. In the "Prologue" to *On This Island*, a prayer invoking love, Auden adopts the tone and language of entreaty traditionally used to reach an unknown deity, in order to stir the force of love within man himself. This prayer is intended to reach and affect man's unconscious mind, to release "into actual history" a dream, "long coiled in the ammonite's slumber," of England's heroism and compassion. Like all ritual utterance, this is a petition for power: "Here too on our little reef display your power," says the speaker, projecting on "Love" his own grand fantasy:

> And make us as *Newton* was who, in his garden watching
> The apple falling towards *England*, became aware
> Between himself and her of an eternal tie.

As love, or the mythical entity Eros, becomes a major theme of Auden's poetry, he employs allusions to ritual and ritual effects to convey the ambiguity of its nature and to trace the devious courses it takes when denied or misused. In "Casino," the compulsive and ritualistic act of gambling is described as a perversion of love:

> Only the hands are living; to the wheel attracted,
> Are moved as deer trek desperately towards a creek
>   Through the dust and scrub of the desert, or gently
>   As sunflowers turn to the light.

> And, as the night takes up the cries of feverish children,
> The cravings of lions in dens, the loves of dons,
>   Gathers them all and remains the night, the
>   Great room is full of their prayers.

The psychological profundity of the first line is revealed and developed in the next three. Eros, the very drive of life which moves the deer to water and flowers to the sun, is arrested and distorted in man, permitted expression only through his grasping hands. The perverse routes the instinctual drive can take are revealed in the rites performed in this casino, in which sterility and narcissism are continually enacted. Furthermore, the intensity of feeling wasted on the sterile games in the casino is suggested in the "prayers" of the participants, another oblique expression of the inner drive which they surrender to the control of fortune or a deity. But all these rites succeed only in disclosing the loneliness and sadness of the players:

> To the last feast of isolation self-invited
> They flock, and in the rite of disbelief are joined;
>   From numbers all their stars are recreated,
>   The enchanted, the world, the sad.

247

Prayer, feast, and rite are all pathetic enactments of a need to direct feelings twisted into a compulsion, to recreate "the world" to suit their own sad fortune.

In Auden's poetry, ritual not only discloses a general unconscious struggle with the ambiguous powers of Eros; it is also a vehicle of self-revelation through which the poet publicly tests the drive of his own talent against the destructive forces within himself and external nature. Straining against yet including the conventions of traditional elegy in his poem "In Memory of W. B. Yeats," Auden seems to challenge the very poet he celebrates as, in the first two sections, he emphasizes the mortal limitations of the poet and the inability of poetry to influence the affairs of men:

> For poetry makes nothing happen: it survives
> In the valley of its saying where executives
> Would never want to tamper; it flows south
> From ranches of isolation and the busy griefs,
> Raw towns that we believe and die in; it survives,
> A way of happening, a mouth.

It is interesting that even as he insists that "poetry makes nothing happen," Auden repeats, "it survives," and it is perhaps in its assertion of the poem's capacity to survive, to extend life beyond that of the poet and experience beyond the range of man's immediate perception, that the real challenge of this elegy lies. It is met in the third section, in which the ritualistic tone and language indicate the solemnity of the occasion: in honoring the memory of Yeats, who here becomes symbolic of all poets, Auden conducts a ceremonial exorcism of death:

> Follow, poet, follow right
> To the bottom of the night,
> With your unconstraining voice
> Still persuade us to rejoice;
>
> With the farming of a verse
> Make a vineyard of the curse,
> Sing of human unsuccess
> In a rapture of distress;

> In the deserts of the heart
> Let the healing fountain start,
> In the prison of his days
> Teach the free man how to praise.

The allusion to "farming" to create a "vineyard," the traditional symbol of productivity, relates the writing of poetry to ancient rituals for renewal of the earth. The "curse" of death is removed from nature by the poet who, like the priest, invigorates the earth and man. If poetry "makes nothing happen," it is nonetheless "a way of happening," transforming existence through the poet's capacity to "persuade," to "praise," and to "survive." This poetic rite of renewal tells as much about the participant, who is also its creator, as it does about the dead poet for whom it was written. Indeed, it prophesies one of the most important of Auden's future roles and voices in poetry.

In the late 1930s and early 1940s, however, Auden was still struggling with the question of the poet's function in a world consumed by war and political and social injustice. In "September 1, 1939," after depicting the "anger and fear" that overwhelm the "darkened lands of the earth," he imagines a communion of "the Just" who "Exchange their messages." Among the offerings is his own prayer acknowledging the union of "Eros and of dust" within him and, in the face of "Negation and despair," seeking faith in the "affirming flame" of his own talent.

"New Year Letter," dated only a few months later, January 1, 1940, reveals the same kind of self-questioning, but it concludes with a more elaborate prayer directed toward a deity rather than to the inner resources of the poet himself. The title of the poem indicates both its ceremonial and personal nature: it is written on the occasion of the New Year, which even modern secular and mechanized societies celebrate as a time of regeneration, and it is a "Letter" addressed to a friend with whom the poet shares his reflections on the year that has passed, viewing it in relation to man's history since the Renaissance. Part of this history, moreover, is the writer's own struggle to define his identity and function in a chaotic time. While he concedes, as he does in several poems of this period, that the poet cannot influence political action or mitigate suffering, Auden suggests that the poet's function is more important than it may seem. Gently, "like love and sleep," truth, which he here equates with poetry, emerges into the world and affects its conduct. In helping to release it, the poet is like the ancient oracle; the rite he performs may seem unrelated to war, poverty, and death, and his words may seem a mere riddle:

> And often when the searcher stood
> Before the Oracle, it would
> Ignore his grown-up earnestness
> But not the child of his distress,
> For through the Janus of a joke
> The candid psychopompos spoke.
> May such heart and intelligence
> As huddle now in conference
> Whenever an impasse occurs
> Use the good offices of verse.... (pp. 273-74)

Yet, ignoring the "grown-up earnestness" of the politician or the general, the poet speaks to the "child of his distress," reaching into hidden sources of love, narcissism, and aggression, the unconscious motives that the world's leaders do not see. The poem thus serves the function of the ancient oracular rite, revealing

> How hard it is to set aside
> Terror, concupiscence and pride,
> Learn who and where and how we are.... (p. 275)

The poet's aim is to break through "certain patterns in our lives," which control us without our knowledge, obstructing perception and love of anyone but ourselves. Recognizing that the productivity of Eros is hindered and distorted by egotism:

> O what can love's intention do
> If all his agents are untrue? (p. 306)

he expresses in ritual form his craving for a concept of love purer and less ambiguous than the instinctual drive that has always created such havoc in man's personal and social life. In the concluding prayer the poet repeatedly calls on a power more beneficent than human love, as if through this invocation he can perform what he imagines —the transformation of Eros into a purer form of itself, what he is to describe a year later as "a conversion" to Agape.[48] The power he envisions as free from man's limitations is a deity in many forms reflecting the need for wisdom and order in nature and society: "O Unicorn among the cedars . . . O Dove of science and of light . . . O Icthus playful in the deep . . . O sudden Wind that blows unbidden . . . O Voice / Within the labyrinth of choice . . . O Clock and Keeper of the years, / O Source of equity and rest"—yet all of them suggest love of and pleasure in man and the external world. Auden does not turn away from either the personal suffering or the social injustice and waste caused by man's inability to understand and come to terms with the instinctual demands of Eros; rather, he exposes the depth of his knowledge of such frailty to a power he prays may exist in nature, as surely as Eros does, but that it may be untainted by the selfishness and violence of man:

> Convict our pride of its offence
> In all things, even penitence,
> Instruct us in the civil art
> Of making from the muddled heart
> A desert and a city where
> The thoughts that have to labour there
> May find locality and peace,
> And pent-up feelings their release,
> Send strength sufficient for our day,
> And point our knowledge on its way,
> *O da quod jubes, Domine.*   (p. 315)

In this prayer for psychological and civic well-being, Auden asks for instruction and release from repression; it is a New Year's rite derived from the lesson of history, which has taught the poet that human power alone is insufficient to realize his vision of a just city inhabited by free men.

The quest motif, suggested in many of Auden's early poems and

[48] "Eros and Agape," *The Nation*, CLII (June 28, 1941), 757.

throughout "New Year's Letter," is developed through allusions to ritual in the sonnet sequence "The Quest," first published in *The New Republic* (November 25, 1940) and later along with "New Year Letter" in the volume *The Double Man* (1941), and in *The Collected Poetry* of 1945. Auden's note to the sequence in *The New Republic* indicates that he had in mind various traditional ritual quests: "the Golden Fleece and The Holy Grail" as well as those generally found in "fairy tales, legends," and in "boys' adventure stories and detective novels." Throughout this sequence the aim of the protagonist is to reach unconscious feelings and instincts, a dangerous quest because it may become merely a bizarre adventure, an end in itself rather than a "way" to self-knowledge or understanding of man functioning in society. Allusions to ritual throughout these sonnets reveal the poet wavering between psychological and religious insight in this period. The search for knowledge of the unconscious provides neither inner serenity nor religious conviction; instead it leads to the Kierkegaardian conception of truth, "a Way to be followed, an inclination of the heart, a spirit in which all actions are done."[49]

The title of the first sonnet, "The Door," symbolizes the difficulty of the quest, for the entranceway to the unconscious self is also its barrier. Those who set forth to reach and explore it in the subsequent sonnets are never entirely prepared for either its dangers or its revelations. No matter how carefully they follow the prescribed rituals, the self continually eludes them even as it determines their conduct:

> In theory they were sound on Expectation
> Had there been situations to be in;
> Unluckily they were their situation. . . .   ("The Preparations")

In several of the sonnets Auden uses the conventional symbols of the ritual quest to depict both the compulsion and the frustration of the seeker, caught between a psychological need to explore the unknown in himself and the universe and the hope of serenity

[49] *The Living Thoughts of Kierkegaard*, presented by W. H. Auden (Bloomington, Indiana, 1966), p. 17.

through a religious answer. The quest in "The Traveler" (retitled "The Pilgrim" in *Collected Poetry*) only leads back home:

> Nor all his weeping ways through weary wastes have found
> The castle where his Greater Hallows are interned;
> For broken bridges halt him, and dark thickets round
> Some ruin where an evil heritage was burned.

The "evil heritage" is, of course, his own; he has never given up or fulfilled his childhood wishes and concerns; he is the victim of his own unconscious needs, and his quest only partially disguises a life-long compulsion to return to "his father's house and speak his mother tongue."

In "The Way," Auden's mockery of the ritual quest suggests that its conventions and prohibitions merely enact a rejection of one's desires and pleasures; thus it is an avoidance of rather than a search for truth:

> Now everyone knows the hero must choose the old horse,
> Abstain from liquor and sexual intercourse,
>
> And look out for a stranded fish to be kind to:
> Now everyone thinks he could find, had he a mind to,
>
> The way through the waste to the chapel in the rock
> For a vision of the Triple Rainbow or the Astral Clock.

The magic symbols of *The Waste Land* are exposed as the stock vocabulary of escapism, the average man's fantasy of himself as a hero undergoing hardship and danger for a glimpse of the eternal. Such a ritual quest expresses no more than a denial of the self; it is a fantasy that truth lies outside ordinary and present reality:

> Forgetting his information comes mostly from married men
> Who liked fishing and a flutter on the horses now and then.
>
> And how reliable can any truth be that is got
> By observing oneself and then just inserting a Not?

The implicit contrast with the Kierkegaardian "knight of faith" increases the mockery of Auden's portrait of the deluded quester. No abstention is required of the true knight: "He takes pleasure in all things, takes part in everything, and everything he does, he does with the perseverance of earthly men whose souls hang fast to what they are doing." He enjoys the prospect of the dinner his wife is preparing, the sights of the city, the "evening twilight." Only by remaining "in the finite" can he know "the blessedness of infinity."[50]

Auden may well have been thinking of this figure in his characterization of the protagonist of "The Hero." The contrast between this sonnet and "The Way" is immediately apparent. The hero engages in no grandiose fantasies of a ritual quest; instead, having achieved faith, he is as self-assured as a fencer: "He parried every question that they hurled," and as unpretentious as a "grocer." Like the Kierkegaardian "knight of faith," he is distinguished only by "his delight in details and routine."

Auden's adaptation of the ritual on which this sonnet sequence is based, the traditional quest for revelation of a deity or an eternal principle inherent in man and nature, expresses his own search for a "way" in this period; he finds psychological insight not only insufficient as a guide to man's feelings and conduct but a threat to consistent spiritual security in the face of violence and death. His realization of the frightening ambiguity of the creative principle Eros has been an "uneasy and tortured training,"[51] and now he seeks to come to terms with this basic element of the "finite." Thus, he exposes the standard conventions of the quest as expressions of psychological conflict and denial of the real feelings and requirements of man. Because they do not know themselves, most of his questers fail; those who succeed do so either because of a special "grace":

> "A nonsense jingle simply came into my head
> And left the intellectual Sphinx dumbfounded;
> I won the Queen because my hair was red;
> The terrible adventure is a little dull."   ("The Lucky")

a personal quality of health that frees them from the compulsion of the ritual, or, even more important, because of a capacity to see

---

[50] ibid., pp. 111-13.   [51] ibid., p. 113.

the infinite in the everyday, to approach the accidental and the ordinary with the wonder and awe traditionally reserved for ritual observance. Like his successful quester, Auden continues to seek infinity in the finite, and most of his later poems celebrate the scenes and details of ordinary experience in rites that reflect the complex nature of his own response.

In the concluding prayer of "Autumn 1940," in which the point of view is clearly Christian, the poet seems to be speaking of his own art as he asks

> That the orgulous spirit may while it can
> Conform to its temporal focus with praise,
>   Acknowledging the attributes of
>   One immortal one infinite Substance,
>
> And the shabby structure of indolent flesh
> Give a resonant echo to the Word which was
>   From the beginning, and the shining
>   Light be comprehended by the darkness.

One of the chief functions of the "temporal focus," as Auden sees it, is "praise" of creation, but the rites he constructs in the poetry written after his conversion reflect no facile optimism; they do express a heightened awareness of the sources of joy in existence, but it is always accompanied by a consciousness of man's biological and psychological limitations. "The knights of infinite resignation," says Kierkegaard, "are dancers and have elevation." They are able to transform "the leap into life into a normal gait."[52] In some respects, Auden's rites are a verbal equivalent of the Kierkegaardian "leap," a stylized gesture of freedom which expresses the conquest of anxiety and despair through faith and pleasure.

"For the Time Being" employs the traditional framework of the Christmas oratorio: the poem is divided into nine sections which enact in ritualistic form the story of the birth of Christ. Yet the poem's very title indicates that the yearly rites commemorating the event sacred to Christians depict the relationship between the in-

[52] *ibid.*, pp. 113-14.

finite and the finite, "the Time Being to redeem / From insignifi-
cance" (p. 466). The Chorus conveys the essential theme of the
poem in a ritual question about the Incarnation:

> How could the Eternal do a temporal act,
> The Infinite become a finite fact? (p. 411)

Throughout the oratorio, ritual questions reveal the limitations of
man's capacity for understanding, the necessity for faith based on a
knowledge that the "Real" is "absurd." Man resists the answers to
the very questions he feels compelled to ask in his loneliness and
anxiety, trapped in a universe without order and meaning: "All answers expire in the clench of his questioning hand . . ." (p. 413). Yet
he continues to question, seeking both "knowledge" and "illusion,"
discovering the limitations of human life in his very desire to defy
them:

> How can his knowledge protect his desire for truth from illusion?
> How can he wait without idols to worship, without
> Their overwhelming persuasion that somewhere, over the high hill,
> Under the roots of the oak, in the depths of the sea,
> Is a womb or a tomb wherein he may halt to express some
> attainment?
> How can he hope and not dream that his solitude
> Shall disclose a vibrating flame at last and entrust him forever
> With its magic secret of how to extemporise life?
>
> (pp. 413-14)

Such questions, and indeed the dramatic structure of the entire poem, finally lead to the incorporation of the "Absurd," the "impossible," into man's personal, social, and political life. Man can choose
to accept the Incarnation as the ultimate meaning of his own existence. Such a choice is based on a consciousness "of Freedom as our
necessity to have faith" (p. 452).

In the section "At the Manger," the ritual of the nativity enacts the
Incarnation as the culmination of man's quest in dream and fantasy
for untainted love. Singing a lullaby, Mary laments the "anxiety"

that her child must endure as he takes on the burdens of men. Her questions disclose the dangers of incarnation, among them human love:

> Sleep. What will the flesh that I gave do for you,
> Or my mother love, but tempt you from His will?

The answer to this threat lies within the human being himself, in his unconscious choice, expressed in dream. She urges the child:

> Dream. In human dreams earth ascends to Heaven
> Where no one need pray nor ever feel alone. (pp. 441-42)

The unconscious, source of the drive of Eros and its strange paths, among them "Our sullen wish to go back to the womb" (p. 444), is also a source of truth, of "Living Love replacing phantasy" (p. 447), love released from narcissism and despair. The acceptance of the Incarnation is hailed: "O Joy of life revealed in Love's creation" (p. 447), for it symbolizes the possibility that man may experience love freed from the biological and psychological taint of death. Such love, says the poet, partakes of the infinite but can exist within the finite; it is the gift of "the time being," celebrated throughout this oratorio in joy.

Though Auden's point of view in the poetry written after his conversion is consistently Christian, only a few of his poems are based on traditional Christian rite. Even in "For the Time Being," the aim of the rite is to increase the value and pleasure of ordinary experience by revealing "How to love" in the "Kingdom of Anxiety." Auden is always conscious of the present:

> the time is noon:
> When the Spirit must practise his scales of rejoicing. . . . (p. 466)

This theme is again developed explicitly in "In Sickness and in Health" where, measuring Eros against a spiritual ideal, Auden presents overwhelming evidence of man's failure to achieve love in any aspect of his life. At the moment when the reader is utterly convinced by the terrible details from myth and history that enact

his egotism and his sense of desolation, the poet shifts from argument to ritual:

> Beloved, we are always in the wrong,
> Handling so clumsily our stupid loves,
> Suffering too little or too long,
> Too careful even in our selfish loves:
> The decorative manias we obey
> Die in grimaces round us every day,
> Yet through their tohu-bohu comes a voice
> Which utters an absurd command—Rejoice.

In the previous chapter the shift from reliance on the poet's own
"voice" to an invocation to the "Voice" of a deity was shown to reflect Auden's quest for security beyond that offered by the limited
capacity of Eros as a natural force. In this poem he calls upon the
"voice" of a spiritual power to confront man's self-destruction and
despair with the "absurd command—Rejoice." The mythical absolute now demands a ritual of praise for creation, which Auden
depicts as a miracle of order and beauty:

> *Rejoice. What talent for the makeshift thought*
> *A living corpse out of odds and ends?*
> *What pedagogic patience taught*
> *Pre-occupied and savage elements*
> *To dance into a segregated charm?*
> *Who showed the whirlwind how to be an arm,*
> *And gardened from the wilderness of space*
> *The sensual properties of one dear face?*

> Rejoice, dear love, in Love's peremptory word;
> All chance, all love, all logic, you and I
> Exist by grace of the Absurd,
> And without conscious artifice we die:
> O, lest we manufacture in our flesh
> The lie of our divinity afresh,
> Describe round our chaotic malice now,
> The arbitrary circle of a vow.

As the rite of praise refutes the arguments of despair, Auden again concludes his poem with a prayer:

> Force our desire, O Essence of creation,
> To seek Thee always in Thy substances. . . .

Like an initiate, the reader is emotionally prepared for the experience of the rite; he need not accept the Christian, or any other, deity to assent to the arguments of despair into which the poet ruthlessly leads him, only to confront him with undeniable evidence for an "absurd" joy in existence, presented in ritual questions, vow, and prayer.

This is a familiar technique of Auden's later "rites"; evidence of man's delusions and history's crimes is rarely absent from the many poems of praise he has written in the last twenty-five years. Though Auden has employed ritual effects throughout his career to depict the poet's "sacred encounter" with experience—his power to elicit the secrets of nature and man and to exert control by exposure and invocation—it is mainly in his latest phase as a conscious composer of rites that he "pays homage by naming." In the lecture quoted at the beginning of this section, in discussing the nature of poetry, Auden describes his own work of the last twenty-five years:

> Whatever its actual content and overt interest, every poem is rooted in imaginative awe. Poetry can do a hundred and one things, delight, sadden, disturb, amuse, instruct—it may express every possible shade of emotion, and describe every conceivable kind of event, but there is only one thing that all poetry must do; it must praise all it can for being and for happening.[53]

Often a single poem of Auden's accomplishes all these ends: praise does not mitigate sadness and disturbance; instead, it illuminates the variety and ambivalence of human emotion, for in the tradition of the ancients, Auden uses mythical and ritual effects to delight and instruct.

"In Praise of Limestone" (*Nones*) celebrates the weakness of man as a source of his inventiveness, his charm, and finally his ability to

[53] *The Dyer's Hand*, p. 60.

conceive of "a faultless love." The limestone surface symbolizes man's inconstancy and vulnerability, but beneath it lies a "secret system of caves and conduits," feeding the landscape and insuring its beauty and productivity. In man's apparent carelessness and love of pleasure Auden perceives the grace and freshness of "underground streams" and a sense of duty to human values which "calls into question / All the Great Powers assume. . . ." In "Precious Five," a mock ceremonial address to his five senses, Auden asks the tongue to praise the "Earthly Muse," whom he describes as "Now fish-wife and now queen." She is to be revered in all her aspects:

> Though freed from that machine,
> Praise Her revolving wheel
> Of appetite and season
> In honor of Another,
> The old self you become
> At any drink or meal. . . .

The "Earthly Muse" is Auden's own invention, a deity who appears in a variety of forms in *The Shield of Achilles, About the House*, and his most recent poetry. She is a composite of several elements: the ancient concept of benign and powerful Mother Earth, the mythical entity Eros, the Muse who inspires and befriends the poet, and finally a spirit of eternal life which informs and blesses the ephemeral. Discussing "Christianity and Art" in *The Dyer's Hand*, Auden says that "every artist who happens also to be a Christian wishes he could be a polytheist" because in "a polytheist society, the artists are its theologians." In the role of poet-preacher which he often assumes in his later poetry, Auden fulfills his own wish. He includes within the realm of the sacred, pagan deities who represent intrinsic human experience:

To the imagination, the sacred is self-evident. It is as meaningless to ask whether one believes or disbelieves in Aphrodite or Ares as to ask whether one believes in a character in a novel; one can only say that one finds them true or untrue to life. To believe in Aphrodite and Ares merely means that one believes that the poetic myths about them do justice to the forces of sex and aggression as human beings experience them in nature and their own lives.[54]

Long after his conversion to Christianity, Auden continues to interpret and use the ancient gods as "mythical entities," expressing psychological drives and conflicts; furthermore, he creates his own additions to the pantheon, and in poetic rites he summons a Muse who symbolizes unconscious creative power united with "faultless love."

In "Winds," the first of the "Bucolics" in the *Shield* volume, Auden invokes the "Goddess of winds and wisdom," a force within himself as well as in nature, to assist him in the act of creation. The only resemblance these "Bucolics" have to traditional pastorals is that in them Auden suggests an intrinsic or sacred relationship between man and nature. The winds reflect the unpredictable in man and the mystery of his creation: the divine and the unconscious forces that created man as a creature who said, "I am loved, therefore I am." It is this love that the poet "Unconsciously invokes" as he struggles to create his "verbal rite."

The spiritual and creative presence of the Muse is conveyed in the "Bucolics," which contain references to the gods in nature whom the poet hears or senses:

> Old sounds re-educate an ear grown coarse,
> As Pan's green father suddenly raps out
> A burst of undecipherable Morse. . . .   ("Woods")

Through his perception of the sacred: "A well-kempt forest begs Our Lady's grace . . ." ("Woods"), he recognizes the original and exalted form of what has become as ordinary and unattractive as a plain:

> It's horrible to think what peaks come down to,
> That pecking rain and squelching glacier defeat
> Tall pomps of stone where goddesses lay sleeping,
> Dreaming of being woken by some chisel's kiss. . . .
>
> > ("Plains")

[54] *ibid.*, pp. 456-57.

His address to water in "Streams," consisting partly of rhetorical questions, partly of statements—all of praise—begins as a mock eulogy and ends as a tribute to the best in nature, which reminds the poet of the lost innocence of man. At first he imitates the tone of the "mocking" streams, dissociating himself from conventional literary praise of nature; then he pays a personal tribute to water by recounting a dream of his own that was inspired by its sound. One of the figures in this dream is the "god of mortal doting," to whom the poet and his associates offer "cheers of homage" and a ritual dance. The playful rite of the dream leads the poet to psychological insight:

> But fortunate seemed that
> Day because of my dream and enlightened,
>
> And dearer, water, than ever your voice, as if
> Glad—though goodness knows why—to run with the human race,
>   Wishing, I thought, the least of men their
>   Figures of splendor, their holy places.

The day is "enlightened" by the dream because its rite of homage expresses the poet's sense of a spiritual presence in nature, but, as always in Auden's poetry, the result of this conviction is a renewed desire "to run with the human race"; the stream illumines both his sleep and his day.

A technique used rather casually and lightly in this poem—the placing of the ritual observance within the dream—discloses an important and serious aim of Auden's poetry in this period: the fusion of psychological and spiritual need through poetic rite. In "Nocturne II," for example, a prayer to the moon, the poet asks that he may meet his friends "in dreams," a deeper reunion than life usually grants. Also, the moon's presence is required when sleep is less peaceful:

> Shine lest tonight any,
> In the dark suddenly,
> Wake alone in a bed
> To hear his own fury
> Wishing his love were dead.

The moon here is a symbol of spiritual illumination which the poet evokes to alleviate psychological conflict and pain.

The *Shield* volume ends with the "Horae Canonicae," Auden's version of the series of prayers prescribed by canon law for recitation at certain hours of the day. It is interesting that Auden changes the traditional order in only one respect: he transfers Lauds from their usual place following Matins to the end, perhaps in order to conclude his volume with a hymn of praise for a second awakening. The awakening in "Prime," the first of Auden's "Horae," though "Holy" in its innocence, is also a return to a consciousness of man's fallen state, his emergence into his "historical share of care / For a lying self-made city. . . ." Thus, waking is itself a religious commitment, a daily rite of penitence for "Paradise / Lost. . . ."

The rites of Auden's "Horae" are private ones, apparently ordinary acts which indirectly reveal the involvement of the participant in the historical reality of the crucifixion. In "Terce," even as "we are left, / Each to his secret cult" of prayer to "an image of his image of himself," it is "our victim" who knows "that, in fact, our prayers are heard. . . ." "Sext" praises the dignity of man's commitment to his "vocation":

> How beautiful it is,
> That eye-on-the-object look.

Dedication to work is itself a choice of ritual observance:

> To ignore the appetitive goddesses,
> to desert the formidable shrines
>
> Of Rhea, Aphrodite, Demeter, Diana,
> to pray instead to St. Phocas,
>
> St. Barbara, San Saturnino,
> or whoever one's patron is,
>
> that one may be worthy of their mystery,
> what a prodigious step to have taken.

Such achievements have released men from their enslavement to "Dame Kind" and have created "the courtesies of the city. . . ." Yet, ironically, all man's efforts to control the natural world reflect his deepest limitations. Auden adapts Freud's view that guilt is the price man pays for civilization to a Christian point of view by concluding each of the poem's three sections with a reference to the crucifixion, a ritual man now ignores in his determined conquest of "Dame Kind."

"Nones" describes the effect of the crucifixion on the lives of those who know it is "our sacrifice" but try to avoid or ignore it. Yet, "its meaning / Waits for our lives" beneath their ordinary pleasures and achievements:

> wherever
> The sun shines, brooks run, books are written,
> There will also be this death.

In "Vespers" the poet and his "Anti-type"—the "Arcadian" and the "Utopian"—opposite in most respects, are one in their guilt. Both "remember our victim . . . on whose immolation (call him Abel, Remus, whom you will, it is one Sin Offering) arcadias, utopias, our dear old bag of a democracy, are alike founded." The ritual death of the crucifixion qualifies all experience, as Auden views it; its meaning is present throughout his rites of praise. The canonical hours for him are occasions of acceptance of the conditions of life, and of satisfaction in the possibilities of humor, irony, insight, pleasure, work, sleep, and love within their tragic limitations. In "Compline," completing the cycle in a return to sleep, he

> cannot remember
> A thing between noon and three.

The sacrifice is temporarily forgotten as he gives himself over to dream, free of responsibility among "its unwashed tribes of wishes. . . ." The second awakening in "Lauds" is announced in a hymn blessing creation—nature, man, and "this green world temporal," with its limited achievements and ambiguous pleasures, which the previous "Horae" have described and illumined.

In his more recent poetry, Auden's emphasis is almost entirely on

the temporal; he pays homage to the "Muse of the unique / Historical fact" in *Homage to Clio*, and in this volume his poetic rites
celebrate the occasional, the apparently unimportant events which
make up the major portion of human history. Contrasted with
Aphrodite and Artemis, the "appetitive" goddesses of nature, Clio is
described in the title poem as silent and matter-of-fact, totally con-
centrated on the real and therefore most difficult to serve:

> We may dream as we wish
> Of phallic pillar or navel-stone
>
> With twelve nymphs twirling about it, but pictures
> Are no help: your silence already is there
> Between us and any magical center
> Where things are taken in hand.

Imperfect, possessing neither magic powers nor extraordinary attributes, Clio is nonetheless a Muse, a deity, "Madonna of silences,"
whose worshipers must endure a harsh initiation.

Though Auden takes Clio's name from traditional myth, her characteristics and her symbolic role are his own invention; moreover,
his unique method of creating and paying homage to a goddess of
the matter-of-fact reveals an extraordinary function of rite in poetry
which celebrates the secular and the ephemeral. Like all deities worshiped in ritual, Clio represents powers desired by the initiate:

> Artemis,
>
> Aphrodite, are Major Powers and all wise
> Castellans will mind their p's and q's,
> But it is you, who never have spoken up,
> Madonna of silences, to whom we turn
>
> When we have lost control, your eyes, Clio, into which
> We look for recognition after
> We have been found out.

In attributing the power of control over the self to Clio, Auden de-
prives rite of its "magical center" and mystical quality; indeed, he im-

plicitly defines its psychological basis. Looking into the eyes of Clio to obtain her sustenance, the worshiper discovers only his limited mortal nature; seeking her image, he finds only a "photo" of her "in the papers, nursing / A baby or mourning a corpse. . . ." Dedication to Clio is difficult because it results only in an honest recognition of the limitations of the self and in a silence in which the sounds of men and events can be heard and studied. It takes the form of a ritual because in seeking the "recognition" of Clio, the poet as initiate must free himself of the familiar and distracting delusions of everyday life in order to perceive its reality; he must reveal his own terror; he must "have been found out," and he can achieve fulfillment only by discovering what is prescribed—in this case, the unique historical fact. Like all participants in ritual, he gains a sense of control over the conditions of life, but in this rite these are symbolized by a Muse who is herself subject to time, accident, and death. The main difference between this and traditional rite is that, in evoking Clio, helplessness is not projected as omnipotence, nor is fear of death allayed through a vision of rebirth; instead, a Muse is shown to symbolize frailty, suffering, and limitation. These are her virtues, making it possible for her to "forgive our noises" and "teach us our recollections." The arts have no "icon" for her, but a "lover's Yes / Has been known to fill" her silence.

In "Dame Kind" Auden celebrates his goddess of fertility with similar realism. In many respects, she is a conventional mother goddess, who was worshiped by the earliest men in acts of ritual murder:

> To Whom—Whom else?—the first innocent blood
> was formally shed
> By a chinned mammal that hard times
> had turned carnivore,

and she is still a power to be recognized:

> Now who put *us*, we should like to know,
> in *Her* manage?

he asks, and the answer the poem provides is a colloquial and humorous rite of praise for the sexuality and fertility inherent in man and nature. Despite the imperfection, vulgarity, and violence of the goddess:

> She mayn't be all She might be but
> She *is* our Mum.

she represents a threat to the prudish and the sterile, and the possibility of love for those who accept her for what she is.

Many of the poems in *About the House* are celebrations of the ordinary; however, in spite of the light tone and the everyday details present throughout this volume, one feels that Auden takes seriously his pledge in the dedicatory poem:

> But here and now
> Our oath to the living word.

The poems of "Thanksgiving for a Habitat," a cycle in praise of the rooms of Auden's home in Vienna, relate the practical business of daily life to the blessings and demands of "Mother Earth," "Mrs. / Nature," or the "Global Mother," some of the many titles by which Auden addresses the reality of daily experience in order to reveal its satisfactions and to commit his poetic art to its service. Yet his house is also a "fortress" built "for keeping Nature at bay," for he is, as ever, aware of her violence and cruelty. The rites of his house include an acceptance of "the Dark Lord and his hungry / animivorous chimeras" ("The Common Life"). This peaceful celebration of the pleasures of daily life contains a warning against what Freud calls "a kind of prosthetic God." Neither machines nor sacred rites, says Auden, provide the ultimate answer to man's craving for omnipotence.

The final rite of this volume, "Whitsunday in Kirchstetten," is a reflection on an actual rite, the Catholic celebration of the Mass in the village of Auden's Austrian home. Characteristically, Auden imposes his own scheme on the traditional ceremony, emphasizing its psychological meaning and its efficacy in the temporal world. The epigraph, "Grace dances. I would pipe. Dance ye all," sets a mood of joy for the service, and the bells summoning the worshipers cry, "Rejoice," as the poet exults in the meaning of the rite. For him it is an exposure of human delusion and a quest for the real.

In some respects, Auden's God is not unlike his Clio, a principle of reality which strips man of his "tribal formulae" and his fantasies of omnipotence. The religious rite in "Whitsunday in Kirchstetten" suggests that all ritual discloses the limits of human knowledge and, at the same time, conveys the "true *magnalia*," the continuity of life despite inexplicable suffering:

> about
> catastrophe or how to behave in one
> I know nothing, except what everyone knows—
> if there when Grace dances, I should dance.

The "dance" is both an acknowledgment of the spiritual presence of the Holy Ghost, whose descent upon the disciples Whitsunday commemorates, and the poet's celebration of the "Grace" apparent in the human and the temporal.

In one of his most recent poems, "Ode to Terminus,"[55] Auden calls upon the ancient Roman deity of boundaries to aid contemporary man who has become the victim of his own "colossal immodesty" and delusions of power:

> The High Priests of telescopes and cyclotrons
> keep making pronouncements about happenings
> on scales too gigantic or dwarfish
> to be noticed by our native senses. . . .

Auden's interpretation of the ancient numen of boundary marks as a symbol of psychological, aesthetic, and moral limits exemplifies a method, common in his latest poetry, of disclosing the motivation for and function of rite as he employs it. In calling upon Terminus to counteract the influence of "Venus and Mars," the Roman equivalents of his familiar contestants, Eros and Thanatos:

> Venus and Mars are powers too natural
> to temper our outlandish extravagance:
> You alone, Terminus the Mentor,
> can teach us how to alter our gestures.

[55] *City Without Walls* (New York, 1969). Also published in London, 1969.

God of walls, doors and reticence, nemesis
overtakes the sacrilegious technocrat,
 but blessed is the City that thanks you
  for giving us games and grammar and meters.

By whose grace, also, every gathering
of two or three in confident amity
 repeats the pentecostal marvel,
  as each in each finds his right translator.

he indicates that worship of any powers that promote "our outland-
ish extravagance" is indulgence of the "natural" or unconscious
drives which find their devious outlets in arrogance that has "plun-
dered and poisoned" the world. Calling upon Terminus to "teach
us," to "save us," Auden creates a verbal rite compelling us to perceive and accept the very limitations that man has always sought to
avoid in his performance of ritual. His invocation to Terminus is
in fact a plea for a direct expression of man's emotional and intellectual limits which, paradoxically, discloses his true powers: his
capacity to create "rhythm, punctuation, metaphor," to establish
"confident amity," and even to explore and control his universe.
For Auden, ritual, like myth, finally leads to the challenge of disenchantment.

V

MYTH AND HISTORY

THE CYCLIC VIEW
Giambattista Vico and Oswald Spengler

The connection between history and myth is an ancient and perhaps indissoluble one. The two are blended not only in Greek and Roman epic but in the writings of historians such as Herodotus and Livy; furthermore, Vico, the first modern historian to invent a method of exploring man's cultural and intellectual history, used myth and legend as clues to the consciousness of remote civilizations. For some historians myth is valuable not only in uncovering the past; it also indicates the direction of history. Vico's cyclical theory and those that follow, especially Oswald Spengler's, are based on a mythical structure. As Lévi-Strauss says, "In spite of worthy, and indeed indispensable, attempts to become different, history, as its clearsighted practitioners are obliged to admit, can never completely divest itself of myth."[1]

Since myth has always had a social function, linking the individual emotionally to the institutions of his society, it can perhaps be said that myth has a proper role in any extensive historical record. Ancient historians vary in their approach to myth. Herodotus not only records myths and rites of the Greeks, the Persians, and the Egyptians, but piously omits details of the mysteries; moreover, he apparently accepts the validity of myth and folktale. Though Thucydides proudly insists that he differentiates between myth and fact, he not only includes reports of oracular pronouncements in his history but also offers suggestions regarding their proper interpretation. Livy, without consciously intending to do so, uses myth to suggest an atmosphere of the past that factual details alone could not recreate. In the preface to his *Ab Urbe Condita*, he says that he neither

[1] *The Raw and the Cooked*, p. 13.

affirms nor denies the validity of the myth of divine intervention in the founding of Rome. He includes such material, though it may be more suitable to poetry than to history, because it seems to him that a divine origin is appropriate to so noble a nation. In recording this mythical symbol of superiority, which he also considers a sign of invulnerability in warfare, as a moral lesson for his contemporaries, Livy indicates a social function of myth in the ancient past and its persistence in his own time.

Livy's inclusion of myth is at least in part a concession to custom; certainly, he does not consciously employ it as a clue to the character of the men and the society he is describing. The first significant use of myth as a scientific historical tool is made by Vico, whose genetic method of approaching human society depends heavily on mythical material as a primary source. Vico, who "virtually invented comparative anthropology and philology and inaugurated the new approach to history and the social sciences that this entailed,"[2] reveals remarkable insight into the psychological and sociological origins of myth. Attempting to discover and analyze the "mental vocabulary of human social institutions" (355),[3] he studies the gods and heroes of ancient societies as expressions of human nature and behavior (220-21):

> Whatever appertains to men but is doubtful or obscure, they naturally interpret according to their own natures and the passions and customs springing from them.
>
> This axiom is a great canon of our mythology. According to it, the fables originating among the first savages and crude men were very severe, as suited the founding of nations emerging

[2] Isaiah Berlin, "One of the Boldest Innovators in the History of Human Thought," *The New York Times Magazine*, November 23, 1969, p. 77. See also Isaiah Berlin's "A Note on Vico's Concept of Knowledge," *Giambattista Vico, An International Symposium*, ed. Giorgio Tagliacozzo and Hayden V. White (Baltimore, 1969), 371-77; and David Bidney, "Vico's New Science of Myth," 259-77 in the same volume.

[3] *The New Science of Giambattista Vico, Revised Translation of the Third Edition* (1744), trans. and ed. Thomas Goddard Bergin and Max Harold Fisch (Ithaca, New York, 1968). All quotations from Vico, which are referred to in the text by paragraph number, are from this edition.

from a fierce bestial freedom. Then, with the long passage of years and change of customs, they lost their original meanings and were altered and obscured in the dissolute and corrupt times [beginning] even before Homer. Because religion was important to them, the men of Greece, lest the gods should oppose their desires as well as their customs, imputed these customs to the gods, and gave ugly, and obscene meanings to the fables.

Vico's interpretation of myth as a reflection of human emotion and concern, his theory that man creates gods out of fear and projects his own troublesome desires on the gods, foreshadows Freud's view that "in the legend, a human desire is transformed into a divine privilege."[4] Vico's emphasis, however, is always on the social customs and institutions which develop out of the human beliefs and desires that myth discloses. The aim of his "historical mythology" (223) is to discover the true nature of organized society through an understanding of its origins.

From Vico's point of view, the conception of a religion is fundamental to the birth of a nation. He shows how the development of a society can be traced through its use of myths as symbols of political strength and economic and social values: "the serpents of Medusa's head and Mercury's staff signified the dominion of the lands" (541); the "golden apples which Hercules was the first to bring back (or harvest) from Hesperia" not only reflect a metaphorical transfer of one of the "fruits of nature," the "idea of the apples," to another, "the ears of grain," but also suggest that in the earliest stages of civilization "grain must have been the only gold in the world" (539-46). Though myths and fables are stories invented by men, they are at the same time "true narrations" (408) of the feelings and conduct of early civilizations, and thus they are the basis for Vico's new science, which is a "history of the ideas, the customs, and the deeds of mankind" (368). It is "an ideal eternal history traversed in time by the history of every nation in its rise, development, maturity, decline, and fall" (349).

[4] See above, p. 48.

According to Vico's cyclical theory of history, there are three main stages of society through which all nations must pass, inevitably returning to the barbarism in which they began. These phases of history are enactments of the development of the human mind; thus man's psychological, political, and social history are really one in the "successive ages of gods, heroes, and men" (915). The first age emerges from barbarism to a religion characterized by man's invention of gods to whom he ascribes his own fears, desires, and qualities. This is followed by a heroic age, in which human nobility is attributed to a divine origin, and heroic virtue becomes a standard of excellence against which the barbarism of the past is measured and condemned. The third age, the human, bases its customs, laws, and values on reason. The popular governments and the social equality of this phase inevitably degenerate into license, impiety, and excessive indulgence in luxury; in this condition a society either is conquered in war, is temporarily forced by a strong leader to return to earlier values, or regresses to its earliest stage, only to begin a new cycle.

Vico's entire system is based on his belief in "a divine legislative mind" (133) which is ultimately responsible even for man's invention of the gods, who express and define his nature, and for the cyclic development of society. But the cyclic theory of history is by no means restricted to an orthodox religious framework; Spengler's cyclic system grows out of his conception of "Destiny," which he defines as "the *logic of time*, . . . a fact of the deepest inward certainty, a fact which suffuses the whole of mythological religions and artistic thought and constitutes the essence and kernel of all history (in contradistinction to nature) but is unapproachable through the cognition-forms which the 'Critique of Pure Reason' investigates." Spengler interprets the ancient Greek and Roman mythical view of history—their "mythically-fashioned background for the particular momentary present"—as an avoidance or a negation of time: "For Herodotus and Sophocles, as for Themistocles or a Roman consul, the past is subtilized instantly into an impression that is timeless and changeless, *polar and not periodic* in structure—in the last analysis, of such stuff as myths are made of—"[5] whereas modern western man, who has acquired a historical sense, sees history in relation to time and cyclic progression.

Spengler defines "world-history" as "an ordered presentation of the past, an inner postulate, the expression of a capacity for feeling form." The effort to arrive at the organic form or structure of world history is actually an attempt to reach the psychological essence of man (I, 15-16):

> But a feeling for form, however definite, is not the same as form itself. No doubt we feel world-history, experience it, and believe that it is to be read just as a map is read. But, even today, it is only forms of it that we know and not *the* form of it, which is the mirror-image of *our own* inner life.

The difficulty of reaching and defining this form results from the nature of culture itself, which, from Spengler's point of view, exists only as a result of "an inner passionate struggle to maintain the Idea against the powers of Chaos without and the unconscious mutterings deep-down within." Culture, to him, seems to contain its own aim or destiny: it struggles to come into being, and it is destined for destruction: "Every Culture stands in a deeply-symbolical, almost in a mystical relation to the Extended, the space, in which and through which it strives to actualize itself" (I, 106). The historian is thus a discoverer of the intrinsic nature of a culture and the architect of its symbolic or cyclic structure.

In *The Decline of the West*, Spengler proposes his view of "Destiny" as a mythical structure which can replace the ancient myth of timelessness; his concept of "the decline of the West" is itself a means of revealing and imposing order on "inward necessity." He views "Civilization" as the "destiny" of a culture and decline as inevitable for civilization (I, 31):

> Civilizations are the most external and artificial states of which a species of developed humanity is capable. They are a conclu-

[5] Oswald Spengler, *The Decline of the West* (London, 1926-28), I, 7-9. All quotations from Spengler are from this edition.

sion, the thing-become succeeding the thing-becoming, death following life, rigidity following expansion, intellectual age and the stone-built, petrifying world-city following mother-earth and the spiritual childhood of Doric and Gothic. They are an end, irrevocable, yet by inward necessity reached again and again.

Cultures, like human beings, pass through certain phases from childhood to old age. Like Vico, Spengler seeks in myth evidence of man's nature and his growing "consciousness" of himself and external reality. He speaks of a "mythic consciousness" struggling against "all the dark and daemonic in itself and in Nature." He attempts, moreover, to follow the development of culture as an inner process, to describe the emergence of its "full consciousness of creative power" (I, 107). Spengler's effort to explore and define the "destiny" of man as a cyclic development with inevitable decline is based on the evidence of both mythical and historical materials, and is itself a mythical conception of history: for Spengler culture exists in a mystical relationship with chaos, history is an ordered narrative reflecting an inner consciousness and direction, and fate controls human affairs. He concludes *The Decline of the West* with a prophecy which, for all its despair, is nonetheless an assertion of control, since the prophet understands and expresses the workings of fate (II, 507):

> For us, however, whom a Destiny has placed in this Culture and at this moment of its development—the moment when money is celebrating its last victories, and the Caesarism that is to succeed approaches with quiet, firm step—our direction, willed and obligatory at once, is set for us within the narrow limits, and on any other terms life is not worth the living. We have not the freedom to reach to this or to that, but the freedom to do the necessary or to do nothing. And a task that historic necessity has set *will* be accomplished with the individual or against him.
>
> *Ducunt Fata volentem, nolentem trahunt.*

The revival of interest in Vico and the enormous influence of Spengler in the nineteen twenties and thirties were due, at least in part, to their emphasis on historical "consciousness," their conviction that they could reveal the inner direction and form of apparently chaotic events. Certainly, writers like Joyce and Yeats were attracted by Vico's cyclic system, which presented an ordered historical pattern derived from "poetic" or mythic wisdom, and by his concern with "the rhythm of the elemental forms of the mind."[6] For Yeats, "Vico was the first modern philosopher to discover in his own mind, and in the European past, all human destiny. 'We can know nothing,' he said, 'that we have not made.'"[7] Yeats also remarked on his affinity with Spengler, who, he says, "has followed Vico without essential change," and with others who adopted a cyclic view of history, for they "have already deepened our sense of tragedy." The cyclical pattern is a reflection of man's psychological make-up and spiritual yearnings. Yeats continues: "I suggest to the Cellars and Garrets that though history is too short to change the idea of progress or that of the eternal circuit into scientific fact, that of the eternal circuit may best suit our preoccupation with the soul's salvation, our individualism, our solitude."[8]

Spengler's prophecy of the decline of Western civilization reflected the mood of a period emerging from the first World War and faced with economic and political conditions that would inevitably lead to the second. His cyclic structure, based on the assumption that "real history is heavy with fate but free of laws" (I, 118), emerges from the sense of impotence and despair that motivated poets of the period to regard history through the framework of myth and to create structures that would interpret the consciousness of man operating within society and the meaning of his chaotic and tragic public life.

[6] W. B. Yeats, *The Words Upon the Window Pane*, p. 14.

[7] *On the Boiler*, p. 22.

[8] *The Words Upon the Window Pane*, pp. 14-15. See also *A Vision* (1937), p. 261.

W. B. YEATS
History as Symbol

Yeats was drawn to the visionary persona and the symbolic technique of Spengler's work. In *A Vision* (1937), he comments on the remarkable resemblance between his own ideas and Spengler's, noting that *The Decline of the West* appeared only a few weeks after the 1925 edition of *A Vision*. Yeats says that he is aware of "no common source, no link between him and me, unless through

> The elemental things that go
> About my table to and fro.   (pp. 18-19)

hinting at supernatural forces, which, as Seiden suggests, may actually have been his wife's revelations of details from the original German edition of *The Decline*,[9] which had appeared in 1918. In any case, Spengler's concept of "the Destiny-idea" as experienced in "a vision" does elucidate Yeats's symbolic approach to history. In one of his many attempts to define "Destiny," Spengler says (I, 118):

> In the Destiny-idea the soul reveals its world-longing, its desire to rise into the light, to accomplish and actualize its vocation. To no man is it entirely alien, and not before one has become the unanchored "late" man of the megalopolis is original vision quite overpowered by matter-of-fact feeling and mechanized thought. Even then, in some intense hour, the lost vision comes back to one with terrible clearness, shattering in a moment all the causality of the world's surface.

The "vision" is, of course, of man's "Destiny," what Spengler calls "an *all-embracing symbolism*" (I, 163) of man's cyclic role in time. In *A Vision*, Yeats seems to fulfill this "desire" of the soul that Spengler describes; he constructs a symbolic depiction of the cyclic movement of human history, a scheme emerging from the vast unconscious of the human race, which unites the opposing forces in the universe. For him history contains and reflects the patterns of all "the involuntary acts and facts of life" (p. 237) and of all man's

---

[9] *William Butler Yeats, The Poet as A Mythmaker*, p. 113.

apparently chaotic strivings and conflicts. Speaking of the symbolic structure of *A Vision*, Yeats says (pp. 213-14):

> I have now described many symbols which seem mechanical because united in a single structure, and of which the greater number, precisely because they tell always the same story, may seem unnecessary. Yet every symbol, except where it lies in vast periods of time and so beyond our experience, has evoked for me some form of human destiny, and that form, once evoked, has appeared everywhere, as if there were but one destiny, as my own form might appear in a room full of mirrors. When one discovers, . . . at a certain moment between life and death, what ancient legends have called the Shape-Changers, one illustrates a moment of European history, of every mind that passes from premise to judgment, of every love that runs its whole course.

Thomas Whitaker, in his *Swan and Shadow*, deals with Yeats's belief that "a symbolic vision of history . . . should embody and so reveal the desires and conflicts of the poet's entire 'being,' both conscious and unconscious; and it should therefore bring into the light of understanding hitherto unknown areas in the reader's 'being.'" Indicating parallels between Yeats's and Jung's concept of the "anti-self," Whitaker convincingly develops the thesis that Yeats's "visionary and paradoxical dialogue" with history disclosed elements of his own unconscious mind and led him to "a judgment of the dominant qualities of his time."[10] Whitaker emphasizes Yeats's preoccupation with the opposition between "self and shadows—whether antiselves or projections of the self,"[11] which is manifested in historical forces and conflicts. Equally, and perhaps more, important in relation to Yeats's approach to history is his central unconscious conflict (which I have discussed at length in Chapter III) between the desire to avoid and the concomitant impulse to experience the deepest possible awareness of mortality. Yeats, at least for a time, resolved this personal conflict by seeking an immortal principle in the human

[10] Thomas R. Whitaker, *Swan and Shadow, Yeats's Dialogue With History* (Chapel Hill, 1964), pp. 4-20.
[11] *ibid.*, p. 171.

psyche, a principle that he sought to impose on history through a cyclic system which would reveal that history, like man himself, possessed collective memory, soul, and purpose. Yeats's symbolic depiction of historical destiny reveals the conflicting drives behind man's premises and judgments; furthermore, these, arrived at with so much anxiety and effort, like "every love that runs its whole course," are involved in the great "battle of all things with shadowy decay,"[12] which is the essential material of Yeats's construction of history.

In Yeats's view history is inextricably connected with myth and legend, for he is less concerned with the actual events and achievements of man's past and present than with their symbolic expression of inner conflict and resolution. Certainly, in A Vision, history is regarded as an orderly arrangement of events which includes the mythical, the legendary, and the factual. History is based on the Platonic Great Year, which is divided into twelve cycles of about two thousand years each. The first of these covers the period from 2000 B.C. to A.D. 1, and is itself divided into two lesser cycles, each lasting one thousand years and passing through twenty-eight phases of the moon. In considering the significant events of the lesser and major cycles, Yeats makes no distinction between myth and history. In fact, he describes the "Great Year" as beginning with a mythical and ritual act, the rape of Leda by the Swan, which for him is the first "annunciation" (p. 268).

In Book V of A Vision, "Dove or Swan," Yeats begins with this annunciation and then goes on to interpret the history of western civilization in terms of his cyclic view.[13] The expanding and unwinding cones, as in some great dance of the spheres, reduce history to perennial and predictable cyclic movement. As Yeats reminds us, ". . . one must consider not the movement only from the beginning to the end of the ascending cone, but the gyres that touch its sides, the horizontal dance" (p. 270). All of history is encompassed in this

---

[12] W. B. Yeats, The Wind Among the Reeds (London, 1899), p. 101

[13] See Thomas R. Whitaker, "The Early Yeats and the Pattern of History," PMLA, LXXV (June 1960), 320-28; "Yeats's 'Dove or Swan,'" PMLA, LXXVI (March 1961), 121-32; and Swan and Shadow, especially Chapter V.

ritual of turning and widening, winding and unwinding, disintegration and rebirth.

Yeats's mythical view of history imposes his need for order and control on the events of the past, creating a universal scheme into which the incoherent present may be fitted and thus given meaning, and it also evokes the human and personal struggle usually absent in the abstract terminology and factual data of written history. He says (p. 268):

> A civilization is a struggle to keep self-control, and in this it is like some great tragic person, some Niobe who must display an almost superhuman will or the cry will not touch our sympathy. The loss of control over thought comes towards the end; first a sinking in upon the moral being, then the last surrender, the irrational cry, revelation—the scream of Juno's peacock.

History for Yeats is personal, tragic, and heroic: he himself imposes upon it "an almost superhuman will" in order to exert that control through myth which makes even "the last surrender" intelligible.

The euhemerist approach to myth which he found in Fraser also influenced Yeats's view of history. To him mythical heroes represent a stage of development in a civilization and are also its product. In *A Vision*, discussing the "universal law" of the union of "*antithetical* and *primary*" within races, he says that all ancient civilizations, "having attained some Achilles in the first blossoming, find pious Aeneas in their second" (pp. 205-206). The mythical figure characterizes the inner quality of his age.

Yeats's quest for the soul or essence of a historical era led him to value the most remote past he could imagine, for there, he felt, man expressed his nature most freely. In *A Vision*, he opposes his own view to that of the conventional historian (pp. 206-207):

> The historian thinks of Greece as an advance on Persia, of Rome as in something or other an advance of Greece, and thinks it impossible that any man could prefer the hunter's age to the agricultural. I, upon the other hand, must think all civilizations equal at their best; every phase returns, therefore in some sense

every civilization. I think of the hunter's age and that which followed immediately as a time when man's waking consciousness had not reached its present complexity and stability. There was little fear of death, sometimes men lay down and died at will, the world of the gods could be explored easily whether through some orgiastic ceremony or in the trance of the ascetic. Apparitions came and went, bringing comfort in the midst of tragedy.

Though his cyclic view of history prohibits Yeats from preferring one phase to another, he describes this early stage of civilization as a kind of idealized past; most significantly, it is a time when man's "waking consciousness" does not interfere with his expression of a desire for union with the supernatural through myth and ritual. Man in this period is more aware of his unconscious and intuitive needs and feelings, which are expressed in "orgiastic ceremony" and "trance." Yeats attempts to define the unconscious forces that dominate an era: "Nations, cultures, schools of thought may have their *Daimons*" (p. 209), and these are part of nature and history, moving through the Great Year, affecting both individual and collective life.

The heroic and tragic qualities of a past era may be transmitted through a daimon to an individual whose body it inhabits. Such qualities, which challenge and test the present, disclosing its limitations, are conveyed through myth in Yeats's poetry. Thus, Maud Gonne is depicted as a contemporary Helen, not only because of her surpassing beauty but also because she exemplifies the splendor of the age in which the mythical Helen flourished and the courage of the nations she brought to heroic and destructive warfare.

"No Second Troy" is a love poem for both a woman and for the lost civilization she seems to resurrect within her person. Both are tragically unsuited to the present, yet their very presence exalts it. The poet's personal loss becomes one with the loss of history—lover and history mourn together for the tragic "beauty like a tightened bow" which "is not natural in an age like this." The whole poem, which is a series of rhetorical questions, places the personal point of view, the lover's, in perspective against the historical background, which reaches tragic intensity in the final mythical image. The speaker is reconciled to the "misery" of his unfulfilled love by his recognition that a figure of unusual beauty and nobility, a Helen of Troy living among "ignorant men" in an unheroic age, must create havoc. Recognized only by the poet who cannot claim her, she conveys the vitality of an earlier cycle of human history, its energy and nobility unwelcome but alive in the present.

Helen represents both an era and the qualities of personality reborn repeatedly in the human soul. In "The Phases of the Moon," Yeats employs the figures of Achilles and a mythicized Nietzsche, who appear in the twelfth phase of the moon, to suggest that heroic historical periods also represent phases of human character through which all men pass within a lifetime. History is part of the Great Memory, of which all human beings partake.

If the past provides insight into the characters and events of the present, it also offers a vision of the future. This is often dark, a nightmare vision, as in "The Second Coming," in which Yeats sees "anarchy . . . loosed upon the world." Like Spengler, he regards his own period as nearing the end of an era: "the last surrender" approaches, and, before the predicted return of past ages, the established order will "fall apart." This anarchy is prophesied in a "vast image out of *Spiritus Mundi*"; it is known to the ancient Sphinx. A myth in the mind of man, history past and future "Troubles [his] sight." More powerful than the Christian myth of the second coming of Christ, his image of the future mocks such optimism; before any rebirth must come destruction.

The same mood pervades "Nineteen Hundred and Nineteen" and "Meditations in Time of Civil War," both of which deal with the chaos and terror produced by civil war in Ireland. In these poems Yeats sets up images of permanence with which he contrasts the destruction and violent change he perceives in the world around him. Even the myth or "dream" of rebirth and restoration of harmony is challenged by warfare and death. In "Nineteen Hundred and Nineteen," Yeats evokes the "Platonic Year" for reassurance, in the face of chaos, that "the old" way of life, even with its "wrong," will be restored. Actually, all that seemed permanent in the past is threatened in this poem; the myth itself and the ritual dance that enacts it are fragile remnants of a past which is mocked and then destroyed in the present. The poet's "secret meditation" reveals another mythical image—the "labyrinth," which he has himself constructed:

> A man in his own secret meditation
> Is lost amid the labyrinth that he has made
> In art or politics. . . .

The inner "labyrinth" of confusion and despair is externalized in "art or politics." The signs of present chaos and future destruction reach a climax in a "tumult of images" which seem to emerge from nature itself: "Their purpose in the labyrinth of the wind." In this poem images of horror and confusion from myth and legend link the violence of civil war to the poet's inner knowledge of inevitable cyclic decay.

In "Meditations in Time of Civil War," which consists of seven sections tracing the poet's efforts to cling to symbols of permanence in a period of bloodshed and violence, ancestral homes, his own tower, his sword, and his descendants all seem to assure him that old values will persist. But then he cannot avoid facing

> A barricade of stone or of wood;
> Some fourteen days of civil war;
> Last night they trundled down the road
> That dead young soldier in his blood. . . .

In the last section, entitled "I See Phantoms of Hatred and of the Heart's Fullness and of the Coming Emptiness," Yeats contrasts an image of destruction with a myth of permanence. In his "mind's eye" he sees

> In cloud-pale rags, or in lace,
> The rage-driven, rage-tormented, and rage-hungry troop,
> Trooper belabouring trooper, biting at arm or at face,
> Plunges towards nothing, arms and fingers spreading wide
> For the embrace of nothing. . . .

Unnerved by this image, the poet is drawn to those driven by rage, but he is restrained by another vision, the myth of the unicorn, symbolizing the past and the recurrent:

> Their legs long, delicate and slender, aquamarine their eyes,
> Magical unicorns bear ladies on their backs.

The escape to a mythical past and the plunge into violence and terror become one experience as Yeats applies the double adjective "cloud-pale," with which he has described the rags of the troops, to the unicorns:

> The cloud-pale unicorns, the eyes of aquamarine,
> The quivering half-closed eyelids, the rags of cloud or of lace,
> Or eyes that rage has brightened, arms it has made lean,
> Give place to an indifferent multitude, give place
> To brazen hawks.

In the fusion of the two fantasies, the myth of the return and the image of annihilation are revealed as similar in that both are extremes of hope or of violent anger in the mind of the poet; they are, as the title suggests, "phantoms" emerging from the "heart" before he admits that he foresees only a "Coming Emptiness."

Thomas Whitaker suggests that "this poem of dramatic experience" reveals the "complex interior dialogue through which suffering moves toward illumination, as the daemonic is incorporated into the precarious equilibrium of personality—and so transformed." Of course, Yeats does express both his abhorrence of the violence of civil war and his awareness of his own attraction to the very anger he deplores:

> and I, my wits astray
> Because of all that senseless tumult, all but cried
> For vengeance on the murderers of Jacques Molay.[14]

[14] Yeats's note on the stanza in which these lines occur explains his historical symbol and expresses his rational judgment on his own identification with the hatred surrounding him: "In the second stanza of the seventh poem occur the words, 'Vengeance upon the murderers, vengeance for Jacques Molay.' A cry for vengeance because of the murder of the Grand Master of the Templars seems to me fit symbol for those who labour from hatred, and

What Whitaker calls "a partial yielding to the daemonic voice" is, however, actually a conscious effort on the poet's part to apprehend the present brutality and violence through mythical images emerging not only from his unique inner experience but from history itself: "Monstrous familiar images swim to the mind's eye," compelling the poet to perceive the recurrence of hatred as an historical force, the "grip of claw" extending from the ancient past into his own time and his own house. The "daemonic images" must be regarded as conveying far more than "the burden of self-knowledge"[15]; they challenge Yeats's conviction of the existence of an immortal principle determining historical change and rebirth, which he calls "The Primum Mobile" in this poem, and they increase the urgency of his quest for historical permanence outside history itself—in vision and art.

In the third section of the poem, describing the "changeless sword" of Sato as a symbol of permanence, Yeats declares:

> only an aching heart
> Conceives a changeless work of art.

If current political and social crises expose the "daemonic rage" at the heart of traditional myth, and even of the mythical principle of recurrence which he seeks to impose on the present, history can still be molded into a design of permanence and order. The "aching heart" of the contemporary man looks back to a past civilization so perfectly harmonious that in its case history itself is myth, and can be used as the basis for a "changeless work of art." Early Byzantium seems to Yeats the perfect civilization unified by a common love for spiritual beauty. The Byzantium that Yeats describes in *A Vision* is, of course, an idealization, a mythical city created by the poet's imposition of his own design on the facts of history. It is "holy" in his poem "Sailing to Byzantium" not for its position as the center of Eastern Christianity but for its symbolic quality, its

---

so for sterility in various kinds. It is said to have been incorporated in the ritual of certain Masonic societies of the eighteenth century, and to have fed class hatred" (*Collected Poems*, p. 455).

[15] *Swan and Shadow*, pp. 184-85.

capacity to suggest the transcendence of art over the ephemera of life. Jon Stallworthy's interpretation of the word "holy" as also implying that "in the life after death one is in the presence of God" elucidates Yeats's use of history in both this poem and "Byzantium." Referring to Yeats's statement in *A Vision* of 1925 that during the fifth century "Byzantium became Byzantine and substituted for formal Roman magnificence, with its glorification of physical power, an architecture that suggests the Sacred City in the Apocalypse of St. John" (p. 190), Stallworthy says that Yeats may have been thinking of "Roman magnificence with its glorification of physical power" in contrasting "monuments of its own magnificence" with "monuments of unageing intellect."[16] In the "holy" city, the historical, the religious, and the aesthetic become one, as the poet envisions eternity within a period of historical time. The perfection of Byzantium's monuments reflects the cyclic change in the aesthetic impulse, which frees itself from the influence of temporal vanity and achievement, and becomes a devotion to the manifestation of a divine presence. Thus, temple, palace, and mosaic represent "life after death," the eternal existence of the soul "out of nature." In *A Vision* and the two Byzantium poems, Yeats restores the ancient city and imbues it with a new magnificence; the mythical realm created in poetry reanimates vanished history. For Yeats, history uninspired by vision, unformed by art, "plunges towards nothing." Having employed the material of history to establish an eternal city, Yeats, like a mythical hero, has assured his own immortality.

In "Blood and the Moon," he imposes his personal symbolism on the actual history of his own country. The poem was occasioned by the assassination of his friend Kevin O'Higgins, a member of the Irish Senate, whom Yeats admired and whom he mourned in "Death." "Blood and the Moon" depicts the present violence as absorbed into Ireland's long history of revolution, "A bloody, arrogant power," which Yeats opposes with his own symbolic history:

> Blessed be this place
> More blessed still this tower. . . .

[16] *Between the Lines, Yeats's Poetry in the Making* (London, 1963), p. 109.

His medieval home at Thoor Ballylee and his tower represent the continuous tradition of intellectual and artistic achievement which is now threatened and broken by bloodshed; both present society and his tower are "Half dead at the top." Nonetheless, he announces:

> I declare this tower is my symbol; I declare
> This winding, gyring, spiring treadmill of a stair is my ancestral
>   stair;
> That Goldsmith and the Dean, Berkeley and Burke have travelled
>   there.
>
> Swift beating on his breast in sibylline frenzy blind
> Because the heart in his blood-sodden breast had dragged him
>   down into mankind,
> Goldsmith deliberately sipping at the honey-pot of his mind. . . .

Yeats's insistence on extending his personal symbol of resistance to the violence of his time to Goldsmith, Swift, Berkeley, and Burke is a declaration that the individual myth of order supersedes the chaos of actual events. He is making history when he declares that these men inhabited his tower and that the spirit of their presences enhances its symbolic value.

Into this mythical construction Yeats introduces the "purity of the unclouded moon." Though it has witnessed "Seven centuries" of bloodshed, it remains unstained, a symbol of the perfection that human life can never achieve. It provides the ultimate contrast, not only with history's bloodshed, but with the poet's symbolic home and tower:

> Odour of blood on the ancestral stair!
> And we that have shed none must gather there
> And clamour in drunken frenzy for the moon.

The tower, "Half dead at the top," stained with blood, stands midway between the perfection of the moon and the "pragmatical, preposterous pig of a world." The moon's perfect beauty and the wisdom it suggests are beyond the reach of the poet, for whom the tower symbolizes the heroism and creativity that struggle to exist in history. The tower, however, though broken by revolution and violence, can still catch and reflect the perfect light of the moon. In this poem, past history is shaped to a personal, if limited, symbol of nobility, courage, and intellectual power, which absorbs but does not bend to violence and bloodshed.

Contemporary history, as we have seen, is less malleable. Nonetheless, in "Easter 1916," "Sixteen Dead Men," "The Rose Tree," and especially in "Parnell's Funeral," Yeats uses mythical associations to exalt those who died for Irish independence. Out of their sacrifice "A terrible beauty is born" ("Easter 1916"). These dead are beyond the limited logic of the living; they "converse bone to bone" ("Sixteen Dead Men"). In "The Rose Tree," their martyred blood revitalizes the tree in a parched land, a common mythical enactment of rebirth.

The figure of the slain mythical hero is developed more fully in "Parnell's Funeral." The poem begins with a description of a primitive rite of death and rebirth in which "a frenzied crowd" observes a child slain and his heart cut out by "the Great Mother." In his comparison of Parnell's death with this ritual murder, Yeats simultaneously evokes two conflicting feelings: awe at the identification of the current hero with a sacred person and irony at the contrast between past ceremony and present chaos. Parnell, he says, was destroyed by "popular rage"; moreover, this was no stylized drama such as those played out for Emmet, Fitzgerald, and Tone, who were murdered by foreigners:

> An age is the reversal of an age:
> When strangers murdered Emmet, Fitzgerald, Tone,
> We lived like men that watch a painted stage.
> What matter for the scene, the scene once gone:
> It had not touched our lives. But popular rage,
> *Hysterica passio* dragged this quarry down.
> None shared our guilt; nor did we play a part
> Upon a painted stage when we devoured his heart.

The ritual of devouring the heart has lost its efficacy; it is now only an image of parasitical selfishness. For a moment, however, the poet allows himself to imagine that Ireland might have been saved by some attempt to preserve the spirit of Parnell, some effort to restore the meaning of the ancient rite of consumption in order to attain the mana of the sacred person. "Had de Valéra eaten Parnell's heart . . . Had Cosgrave eaten Parnell's heart, . . . Had even O'Duffy—" he suggests, but he realizes that no myth of permanence, no image of continuity, could invest these lesser men with the hero's nobility.

All too often contemporary events, determined by violent and foolish men, seem to escape the control of myth, or perhaps they illustrate all too intensely the last phase of a cycle in history, "the irrational cry" of anarchy before the rebirth of order. In "The Gyres," Yeats expresses an attitude toward contemporary history characteristic of his last poems; he himself describes it as one of "tragic joy":

> The gyres! the gyres! Old Rocky Face, look forth;
> Things thought too long can be no longer thought,
> For beauty dies of beauty, worth of worth,
> And ancient lineaments are blotted out.
> Irrational streams of blood are staining earth;
> Empedocles has thrown all things about;
> Hector is dead and there's a light in Troy;
> We that look on but laugh in tragic joy.
>
> What matter though numb nightmare ride on top,
> And blood and mire the sensitive body stain?
> What matter? Heave no sigh, let no tear drop,
> A greater, a more gracious time has gone;
> For painted forms or boxes of make-up
> In ancient tombs I sighed, but not again;
> What matter? Out of cavern comes a voice,
> And all it knows is that one word "Rejoice!"
>
> Conduct and work grow coarse, and coarse the soul,
> What matter? Those that Rocky Face holds dear,
> Lovers of horses and of women, shall,
> From marble of a broken sepulchre,
> Or dark betwixt the polecat and the owl,
> Or any rich, dark nothing disinter
> The workman, noble and saint, and all things run
> On that unfashionable gyre again.

Ellmann's identification of "Old Rocky Face," which has been interpreted in various ways, as the Delphic oracle seems entirely acceptable.[17] Certainly, it is in keeping with Yeats's ironic approach
to myth in this period of his career. As in "News for the Delphic
Oracle," Yeats instructs this all too innocent prophet—actually a
part of his own inner being—disclosing a darkness and violence
shocking to one who has known and clung to "a more gracious
time." In addressing "Old Rocky Face," he is insisting on his own
total acceptance of the fact that the mythical design must encompass
blood, nightmare, and death. Yeats heaps up the evidence of disaster,
ugliness, and irrationality, repeating his ritual question, "What matter?" The answer of the oracle incorporates the wisdom of a view
focused not on the present "nightmare" but on eternal recurrence:
"Rejoice!" Of course, in accordance with Yeats's doctrine, one must
rejoice in the knowledge that in the next cycle of history anarchy
will be followed by order, destruction by the return of traditional
values. More significantly, the voice from the cavern, instructed in
the movement of the gyres, speaks about the acceptance of life with
all its horror and all its possibility of change: "beauty dies," but it is
reborn. One must not sigh for the past, seeking comfort in "ancient
tombs," but know that from "any rich, dark nothing" can emerge
the "workman, noble and saint." The poem outruns the gyres in
its delight in the possibilities of life. As a mythical design revealed
for Yeats his personal conflicts and terrors, it enabled him to examine
the tragedy of current history and to rejoice in the realization that
even violence and terror cannot destroy the hope of artistic survival
and historical rebirth: "Yet we must hold to what we have that the

[17] *The Identity of Yeats*, p. 154. Curtis Bradford points out that "in Mrs.
Yeats's annotated copy of *Last Poems* Rocky Face is glossed as 'Delphic Ora-
cle'" (*Yeats at Work* [Carbondale and Edwardsville, Illinois, 1965], p. 148).
The most significant argument for another point of view is presented by A.
Norman Jeffares, who suggests that Old Rocky Face refers to "Shelley's
Ahasuerus, the cavern-dwelling Jew in Hellas" (*A Commentary on the Col-
lected Poems of W. B. Yeats*, pp. 435-38). Despite Jeffares' evidence of Yeats's
interest in this figure, however, there seems no specific indication in "The
Gyres" itself that Yeats is referring to him.

next civilization may be born, not from a virgin's womb, nor a tomb without a body, not from a void, but of our own rich experience."[18]

In "The Man and the Echo," the oracular response is more explicitly a part of the self from which the speaker attempts to elicit answers to questions which leave him sleepless and despairing. The "Rocky Voice" is depicted as emerging from "a cleft that's christened Alt," which Jeffares describes as "a rocky fissure on Ben Bulben, perhaps chosen because of its rocky nature, as an Irish equivalent to Delphi."[19] The "Man" in this poem is clearly the poet in his old age, formulating his "secret" regrets and conflicts as questions to the oracle, who responds as "Echo."

Yeats lists these tormenting questions in what may seem to be a curious order:

> Did that play of mine send out
> Certain men the English shot?
> Did words of mine put too much strain
> On that woman's reeling brain?
> Could my spoken words have checked
> That whereby a house lay wrecked?

The first and third questions deal specifically with his responsibility for political disasters of his time, but the considerations of whether his play *Cathleen ni Houlihan* inspired rebellion and led to the deaths of Irish leaders, and whether he could possibly have saved Coole Park and other great houses, grow out of his lifelong conflict over the question of control over violence and death in the universe and society. Thus, his concern with his responsibility for intensifying the emotional disturbance of Margot Ruddock[20] is directly related to the other questions in its suggestion of both individual impotence in the face of irrational forces and the implicit desire to

[18] *On the Boiler*, p. 27.
[19] *A Commentary on the Collected Poems of W. B. Yeats*, p. 511.
[20] For further details on Yeats's references to contemporary figures and events in this poem, see Jeffares, *A Commentary on the Collected Poems of W. B. Yeats*, pp. 444, 512.

control which is here expressed in guilt. There seems no response to these questions except despair:

> And all seems evil until I
> Sleepless would lie down and die.

which Echo reiterates: "Lie down and die."

The speaker cannot accept this inner echo of his conscious unresolved conflicts. He insists on the "spiritual intellect's" capacity to control personal and social history:

> That were to shirk
> The spiritual intellect's great work,
> And shirk it in vain. There is no release
> In a bodkin or disease. . . .

Release can come only from the mind's pursuit of the very human failings and social forces which have so disturbed the speaker, for only an understanding of these can lead to the conviction "That all's arranged in one clear view." When this "work" is done, man "sinks at last into the night." In reply to the echo of this acceptance of death, the speaker demands:

> O Rocky Voice,
> Shall we in that great night rejoice?

The voice from the cavern does not respond to this question, and the answer to it in this poem is not as direct as it is in "The Gyres." The "Man" stops listening for the mythical voice of consolation or despair, for he is distracted by an actual sound of violence and death in nature:

> Up there some hawk or owl has struck,
> Dropping out of sky or rock,
> A stricken rabbit is crying out,
> And its cry distracts my thought.

Though this cry is the ultimate background of all personal and social history, it is not a negative answer to the poet's question. Its sound of pain and protest draws us into "that great night" which is a condition of rejoicing in cyclic renewal. The cry of the "stricken rabbit" is related to the death of the Irish heroes, the destruction of great houses, to violence and decay as historical forces in the universe; these are incorporated into the poet's "clear view," his system, and his own history.

EZRA POUND
The Messianic Vision

Like Yeats, Pound does not hesitate to combine history with myth and legend, but his purpose in doing so and the effect of his synthesis are very different. In attempting to create a modern epic in *The Cantos*, Pound is more self-consciously the historian of his society. Furthermore, unlike Yeats, he approaches social and especially economic history with pretensions to scholarly or at least technical knowledge. Yeats is less concerned with the facts and details of history than with fitting legendary and historical events into the mythical framework of his wheels and gyres; Pound, obsessed with facts and figures, employs them as evidence of the validity of a mythical view he too seeks to impose upon history. Both men invent mythical structures to interpret the apparently haphazard events of the past and to gain prescience into and thus control of the future. There are, however, vast differences in their mythical conceptions of history; Yeats's is essentially heroic and tragic, Pound's violent and moralistic.

Early in his career Pound attributes some of the basic flaws of civilization to disrespect for and distortion of myth, a point of view that he is to develop into a significant theme of *The Cantos*. In *Pavannes and Divisions*, which appeared in 1918, he says:

It was only when men began to mistrust the myths and to tell nasty lies about the Gods for a moral purpose that these matters became hopelessly confused. Then some unpleasing Semite or Parsee or Syrian began to use myths for social propaganda, when the myth was degraded into an allegory or a fable, and that was the beginning of the end. Gods no longer walked in men's gardens. The first myths arose when a man walked sheer into "nonsense," that is to say, when some very vivid and undeniable adventure befell him, and he told someone else who called him a liar. Thereupon, after bitter experience, perceiving that no one could understand what he meant when he said that he "turned into a tree," he made a myth—a work of art that is—an impersonal or objective story woven out of his own emotion, as the nearest equation that he was capable of putting into words. The story, perhaps, then gave rise to a weaker copy of his emotion in others, until there arose a cult, a company of people who could understand each other's nonsense about the gods.

Pound then goes on to explain how myths, which were "once a species of truth," became only "lies and propaganda" when they were "incorporated for the condemnable 'good of the State.'" These lies were told "to the ignorant populace in order to preserve the empire," a stage of society in which "religion came to an end and civic science began to be studied." Artists were then regarded as dangerous: "Plato said that artists ought to be kept out of the ideal republic, and the artists swore by their gods that nothing would drag them into it. That is the history of 'civilization,' or philology, or Kultur."[21] In this essay as well as in "Psychology and Troubadours," which is quoted above,[22] Pound expresses the view that myth originates as a personal imaginative or "psychic experience." Attempting to communicate this inner reality, an individual exposes himself to "persecution" or other "bitter experience." Pound's construction of the events that follow society's reaction to individual discovery of myth elucidates his conception of the basic role of myth in artistic creation and in man's social and religious history. In his view, the first artist was the first maker of myth, who did so to shield himself from a society hostile to his personal emotions and imagination. Neither this artistic construction nor the cults which shared similar creations were left free of the influence of official authorities. Thus, according to Pound, very early in its history the state "degraded" myth, inevitably damaging man and his art, since an authentic be-

[21] "Arnold Dolmetsch," *Pavannes and Divisions* (New York, 1918), pp. 143-44.
[22] See above, pp. 91-92.

lief in myth is essential for man and society. "Without gods," he says, "no culture. Without gods, something is lacking."[23]

In *The Cantos*, Pound constructs his own mythical conception of ancient and modern, eastern and western history. In so doing, he imitates the original creator as he imagines him, transforming myth into art, personal into objective experience. Pound deliberately distorts historical material; he sees historical figures as either heroes or villains, and he involves them with gods and creatures of hell. His narrator is omnipotent and his perspective messianic, for he attempts to create the great historical myth of which western society has been deprived by vulgar and unethical leaders.

Yeats regards history as part of the Great Memory, shared by all mankind; Pound reconstructs history as the memory of his persona in *The Cantos*, who moves through legendary, historical, and contemporary events aided by gods, viewing the past, and creating his own myth of metamorphosis and renewal. Pound's avoidance of "chronological sequence," to which he strongly objects,[24] increases the sense that history is memory. The "ideogrammic method" he uses as his means "of presenting one facet and then another until at some point one gets off the dead and desensitized surface of the reader's mind, onto a part that will register"[25] is an intensely personal one; it is, like the myth of the descent, a means by which Pound reaches beneath the "dead and desensitized" area of his own mind to feelings and attitudes which he projects on historical personages and events, using his personal myth to create an "objective story." By this method, which is associative, pictorial, and allusive, Pound calls forth, as if from some inner record, various historical figures and events which are connected chiefly by the didactic point of view of the persona. It is this point of view inherent in the structure of the ideogram, controlling and ordering the apparently chaotic allusions—juxtaposing historical fact with mythical image, biographical detail with divine attribute, recorded event with timeless ritual—which converts history to myth.

Pound's chief historical sources of ideogrammic material are the Italian Renaissance, the early American Republic, and China from

[23] *Guide to Kulchur*, p. 126.   [24] *ibid.*, p. 60.
[25] *ibid.*, p. 51.

its beginnings to the end of the eighteenth century. Though there are groups of cantos devoted to each of these nations and periods, e.g., the Malatesta (VIII-XI) and other Italian Renaissance cantos in *A Draft of XXX Cantos*, the American (XXXI-XXXIV; XXXVII; LXII-LXXI), and the Chinese (LII-LXI), Pound interweaves elements of all these civilizations and cultures to establish the basic unity of his vision of history. The visionary atmosphere is intensified throughout the historical cantos by ideogrammic allusions to myth, suggesting time and space beyond history and the necessity of eternal values.

The Odysseus persona emerges from Hades into history in the second canto, where the battlefield of Troy and the court of Eleanor of Aquitaine become one. In Canto V, as the ancient world blends into the Italian Renaissance, its myths remain as a lesson and warning:

> And the vine stocks lie untended
> And many things are set abroad and brought to mind
> Of thee, Atthis, unfruitful. (p. 18)

Canto VI begins with a direct address to Odysseus, relating his experience to the history of twelfth-century France, which he now recalls:

> What you have done, Odysseus,
> We know what you have done . . .
> And that Guillaume sold out his ground rents
> (Seventh of Poitiers, Ninth of Aquitain). (p. 21)

In this canto Pound returns to Eleanor of Aquitaine, whom he identifies with Helen of Troy in Canto II and again in Canto VII. As he describes her in Homeric terms, he enlarges her power and influence; as a mythical figure she reaches back in time to Homer and forward into the mind of the narrator. Furthermore, Pound's association of her with the destructive enchantress Helen mythicizes her court, the Crusades, and her entire historical period. In the mind and memory of the persona, Eleanor, like Helen celebrated in song, is a historical ideogram of the mythical principle of destruction, metamorphosis, and rebirth.

Mythical values and ideals are also revitalized in the dominant figures of the Italian Renaissance who represent Pound's conception of the period. Clark Emery has pointed out the "parallel between Odysseus and [Sigismundo] Malatesta," in their careers as warriors and leaders, their success as individuals in accomplishing their goals, and their failures—Odysseus in losing his ships and men, Malatesta in "the type of government which he exemplifies."[26] These resemblances, though actual, are less significant than one which Pound himself suggests in his description of Malatesta in *Guide to Kulchur*. There he speaks of the Tempio Malatestiano, which Malatesta built, as "perhaps the apex of what one man has embodied in the last 1000 years of the occident." Like Odysseus, Malatesta attempted to impose his individual imagination and vision on the world around him: "He registered a state of mind, of sensibility, of all-roundness and awareness." Malatesta becomes one of Pound's main Renaissance heroes because as "a single man," he "managed *against* the current of power."[27]

As Pound reconstructs him, Malatesta is both practical man and legendary hero:

> And he, Sigismundo, was Capitan for the Venetians.
> And he had sold off small castles
>   and built the great Rocca to his plan,
> And he fought like ten devils at Monteluro
>   and got nothing but the victory.... (IX, p. 34)

Builder, fighter, lover, he strains against the restrictions of ordinary humanity. Pound uses Latin to describe his accomplishments, suggesting through the substantial phrases the monumental achievements of Malatesta:

> He, Sigismundo, *templum aedificavit*
> In Romagna, teeming with cattle thieves.... (VIII, p. 32)

Even Malatesta's crimes, Pound indicates, are not to be judged by ordinary standards. His terse summary of Malatesta's rape and mur-

[26] *Ideas into Action, A Study of Pound's Cantos*, University of Miami Publications in English and American Literature (Coral Gables, Florida, 1958), p. 103.

[27] *Guide to Kulchur*, p. 159.

der of a Burgundian woman in 1450, the year of the Roman Jubilee, clearly reveals his abdication of ethical for mythical values:

> And there was the row about the German-Burgundian female
> And it was his messianic year, Poliorcetes,
>   but he was being a bit too POLUMETIS
> And the Venetians wouldn't give him six months vacation.

(IX, p. 36)

The very use of the term "row" to describe the reaction to Malatesta's savage and murderous acts indicates Pound's approach to Malatesta as godlike—beyond ordinary law. In the next line the phrase "his messianic year" strongly suggests Pound's identification of Malatesta with his personal vision of history. The ideogram "Poliorcetes," moreover, which suddenly emerges from the historical consciousness of the poet, reinforces the mythical, messianic view. Malatesta is now identified with the Macedonian king Demetrios (336-283 B.C.) who was known under the title Poliorcetes (Πολιορκητής), "taker of cities," and was deified as "the Savior-God." In this capacity he was given honors usually reserved only for Demeter and Dionysus.[28] Time is suspended as Malatesta renews the role of savior established by a historical predecessor. Furthermore, the name Poliorcetes, taker of cities, recalls the epithet ἑλέπτολις, "destroyer of cities," which Pound uses repeatedly for his mythicized Eleanor / Helen. Thus, in Pound's view, when Malatesta commits rape, it is a god demanding his due; when he besieges and destroys cities, it is as a savior of his people.

The only hint of criticism is essentially exalting: Pound's comment "but he was being a bit too POLUMETIS" now shifts the association to Odysseus. The term πολύμητις, a frequent epithet for Odysseus, describes his sagacity and resourcefulness. The new identification of Malatesta with Odysseus through the traditional epithet also suggests his association with the main persona of The Cantos. In Canto XVI, the poet speaking in the first person and ascending, like Odysseus, from hell to earth, which is described as "quiet" and "light,"

---

[28] Plutarch, Lives, IX, Demetrius, trans. Bernadotte Perrin, Loeb Classical Library (New York, 1920).

peaceful as paradise, encounters "the heroes," the Malatesta brothers (p. 69). Through the associative, ideogrammic technique, Pound thus creates a line of mythicized heroes and heroines whose historical roles reflect the Messianic vision of the historian-poet.

More explicitly identified with Odysseus in the next canto, the persona moves through an ancient mythical realm permeated with the spirit of Dionysus and the sea-nymphs and inhabited by Sigismundo Malatesta and other heroes of the Italian Renaissance, those "men of craft" (p. 78) who reflect the productivity of the mythical past with which they are merged in the mind of the poet. This fertility, however, cannot withstand the destructive effects of usury. As Pound sees it, even the Renaissance heroes were infected with this disease of civilization:

> And "with his credit emptied Venice of money"—
> That was Cosimo—. . . .   (XXI, p. 96)

The era which promised to fulfill a timeless mythical principle of fertility and renewal ends in decadence. But the vision that informed its leaders remains in history. Clark Emery points out that the abrupt shift in *The Cantos* from the Italian Renaissance to the early American republic expresses Pound's conviction that "it was in the American Revolution that the ideas of the Italian Renaissance had their next chance of realization."[29] It need hardly be added that, though Pound depends heavily on historical documents, especially diaries and letters, his interpretation of both the aspirations of the early republic and the causes of its failure to fulfill them is unique; it is, moreover, a direct outgrowth of his mythical view of history.

Typically, Pound presents the history of the early American republic mainly through its major figures. The personalities of Thomas Jefferson, Alexander Hamilton, James Madison, Martin Van Buren, and John Adams, which represent the chief attributes of the state, suggest national characteristics of good and evil, and are used to exemplify the principles of recurrence and destruction which determine the nature of government. Since his American figures are presented principally through quotations or adaptations of their own

---

[29] *Ideas into Action*, p. 33.

words, they emerge as less obviously mythicized than those of the Italian Renaissance. It is not the nature of his American ideograms but the use to which Pound puts them that indicates his effort to convert history to myth.

The figure of Jefferson which dominates Cantos XXXI-XXXIII is presented largely through selections from his letters, which Pound employs in an attempt to depict Jefferson as still another Odysseus figure. Pound describes him as *"polumetis,* many-sided" in *Jefferson and/or Mussolini,*[30] a strange volume, the aim of which is to prove that the principles of Jefferson were reborn under the dictatorship of Mussolini in Italy. In both *Jefferson and/or Mussolini* and the American history cantos, Pound uses the person of Jefferson to represent what he considers perennial qualities of good government embodied in the figure of a "many-minded" statesman. Attempting to illustrate the similarities between Jefferson and Mussolini, Pound deduces "three common denominators or possibly four: agriculture, sense of the 'root and branch,' readiness to scrap the lesser thing for the thing of major importance, indifference to mechanism as weighed against the main purpose, fitting of the means to that purpose without regard to abstract ideas, even if the idea was proclaimed the week before last."[31] It is easy to see that these criteria, general and adaptable as they are, can readily be applied to whatever figure Pound selects as an ideogram for the productive leader. In *The Cantos,* Pound tries to create a portrait of Jefferson as a historical manifestation of the ever-recurring principle of productivity, inherent in Odysseus, reborn in Kung, Malatesta, and Mussolini, and ultimately contained in the mind of the poet, whose province is all myth and history, past and present.

In an essay significantly entitled "The Jefferson-Adams Letters As A Shrine and A Monument," written in 1937, Pound divides American life into four periods: the only years of real "civilization" were from 1760 to 1830; from then on follow periods of "thinning" and "despair"; finally there are "possibilities of revival" based on "a valorization of our cultural heritage." A prime source of national

---

[30] *Jefferson and/or Mussolini* (New York, 1935), p. 89.
[31] *ibid.,* p. 64.

renewal is the Jefferson-Adams correspondence, which Pound calls "a still workable dynamo."[32] Yet Pound's attempt to use this correspondence to establish an exalted legend or a revitalizing national myth in *The Cantos* ultimately fails. In Cantos XXXI-XXXIII, Jefferson's resourcefulness and intellectual energy are indicated in brief passages from his letters, but the portrait is too sketchy and the quotations and adaptations too haphazard to support the grand image that is promised.

The opening statement of Canto XXXI;

> Tempus loquendi,
> Tempus tacendi.
> Said Mr Jefferson . . .   (p. 3)

suggests the sage. This is immediately followed by a quotation from a letter of Jefferson to Washington revealing his judgment about the proper costume for a statue and his information on "water communication between ours and the western country" (p. 3). He is knowledgable about the arts, politics, war, and slavery; but none of the factual or theoretical comments contained in these references justifies the lofty role in which Pound casts him as he repeatedly condemns the Europeans: "Cannibals of Europe are eating one another again. . . ." (p. 9).

Between the two groups of American history cantos Pound deals with European decadence, the destructive effects of usury, the voyage of the Odysseus persona to Hades, his involvement in rites of fertility, and his ascent to earth; finally there is a series of cantos devoted to Chinese history. American history is thus seen as existing in relation to all of the past and present contained within the mind of the voyager-persona, where the principles of good government remain continuous and unchanged, whether exemplified by mythical Greece or Chinese or American history. The Chinese history cantos, which immediately precede the second group of American history cantos, serve to associate the American tradition with an older heritage based on firmly established ritual. Commenting on the Chinese

---

[32] *Impact, Essays on Ignorance and the Decline of American Civilization,* ed. Noel Stock (Chicago, 1960), p. 166.

history cantos, Achilles Fang includes among the "pseudo-Confucian writers . . . John Adams, Thomas Jefferson, Martin Van Buren, J. Q. Adams, and even Homer, considering the way Pound interprets the *Odyssey*."[33] Certainly, the Chinese history cantos express the essential values which Pound feels must exist in any productive society.

In the first of the Chinese group, Canto LII, Pound combines European, American, and Chinese allusions, and history with ritual. It begins:

> And I have told you how things were under Duke
> Leopold in Siena
> And of the true base of credit, that is
> the abundance of nature
> with the whole folk behind it. (p. 3)

Having stated his thesis, that credit must emerge not from usury but from "the abundance of nature," Pound goes on to develop it with a translation of a long didactic passage from the *Li Ki* describing the proper seasonal rites and indicating the myths attached to them. This passage, which has been discussed above in connection with ritual,[34] sets the tone of the entire Chinese history section. History, myth, and rite merge in these cantos, as Pound creates a model for ethics and conduct by summarizing the mythical and actual history of China. Achilles Fang suggests that Pound relied heavily on De Mailla's *Histoire générale de la Chine*: "the Confucians were extolled to high heavens in De Mailla, and they are in the *Cantos*."[35] Kung and Eleusis are equated as sources of perennial fertility and power.

Criticism of Pound's inaccuracy and distortion in his treatment of Chinese history[36] seems a bit naive since it is clear that Pound's purpose is hardly to give an objective or factual account of personages

[33] "Notes on China and the Cantos," *The Pound Newsletter* 9 (January 1956), 3.
[34] See above, pp. 208-209.
[35] "Notes on China and the Cantos," p. 3.
[36] Noel Stock, *Reading the Cantos*, pp. 66-67.

and events. Chinese myth and history are all part of the grand archetypal realm which the poet sets before the contemporary world as a "dynamo" that will regenerate the productive principle of the universe. Thus, Chinese history becomes a series of exempla of proper rites and means for achieving a productive economy which will counteract the evil effects usury has had on western civilization. The heroes control their society by prayer, ritual, and useful labor:

> Tching prayed on the mountain and
> > wrote MAKE IT NEW
> on his bath tub
> > Day by day make it new
> cut underbrush,
> pile the logs
> keep it growing.   (LIII, pp. 10-11)

Pound continually refers to ritual restraints and observances: the prohibition against breaking a twig from a tree that gave shade to a good leader (LIII, p. 15), rituals to avoid famine (LIII, p. 17), the recording of rites (LIV, p. 23), the rite of the silkworms (LIV, p. 29), money for rites (LVI, p. 54), and various other occasions and contents of rituals. History is recorded in these cantos as a series of events determined by proper respect for the principles of productivity and order known to a few wise men who exert control by edict and ritual.

In Canto LIX, writing of the first Manchu ruler, Chun Tchi, Pound is mainly concerned with his acceptance of Confucius:

> De libro CHI-King sic censeo
> > wrote the young MANCHU, CHUN TCHI,
> > less a work of the mind than of affects
> > brought forth from the inner nature
> here sung in these odes.
> Urbanity in externals, virtu in internals
> > some in a high style for the rites
> some in humble. . . .

Both "for Emperors" and "for the people," the Confucian *Chi-King* indicates the precise means by which to "learn" and "attain . . . integrity." Pound reiterates this point in English and Latin: "this book" will "keep us in due bounds of office"; it is "the norm" for inner experience and the occasion for "action":

> CHI KING ostendit incitatque. Vir autem rectus
> et libidinis expers ita domine servat
> with faith, never tricky, obsequatur parentis
> nunquam deflectat
> all order comes into such norm
> igitur meis encomiis, therefor this preface
>   CHUN TCHI anno undecesimo
>   (a.d. 1655) . . . .
>   (p. 70)

It is thus the "affects" which emerge from "the inner nature" of great men that should determine national life. Clearly Pound believes that "the norm" or model of integrity for the individual and the state, which existed within the consciousness of Confucius, is a perennial guide to nations. He uses Latin to suggest the universal and continuous nature of this concept and perhaps to indicate that it emerges as a rite from his own "inner nature" as well. The desire to resurrect Confucian reason and wisdom as a historical rite is expressed throughout *The Cantos* "to keep us in due bounds of office" and to lead ultimately to Pound's own vision of a reversal of time and history, in which the "affects / brought forth from the inner nature" of Confucius merge with those of Odysseus, Malatesta, Jefferson, Adams, and Pound's other heroes to create universal order: "all order comes into such norm."

Pound moves easily from the Chinese cantos back to American history; in the next group of cantos (LXII-LXXI), John Adams is portrayed as a successor to the ideals and goals of Confucius. As is well known, Pound obtained most of his material for this section from *The Works of John Adams*, edited by Charles Francis Adams (Boston, 1852-65), and a good deal of it consists of references, sometimes rather cryptic, to events of Adams' life and items from his correspondence, diary, and political writings contained in these volumes. Pound's point of view is expressed through his portrait of Adams as the "pater patriae," the archetypal fatherly ruler who "saved us" from the destructive influence of the betrayers of the revolution symbolized by Alexander Hamilton, "the Prime snot in ALL American history" (LXII, p. 96).

The image of the "pater patriae" is maintained by references to Adams' achievements, which are related to his essential character:

> His relations with bankers in Amsterdam
> in October a treaty of commerce, by no arts or disguises
> no flatteries, no corruptions. . . .   (LXII, p. 92)

He is portrayed as a direct, realistic man, who dislikes ostentation, yet, if only ironically, can see himself in mythical terms:

> I hate to live in Philadelphy in the summer
>   hate speeches messages addresses levees and
>   drawingrooms
>   been 30 years among these rocks whistling
>   (Amphion) and none wd / ever move without money.
>   (LXII, pp. 94-95)

He comforts himself in the loneliness of his struggle for political liberty and economic stability by identifying himself with Aeneas:

> After generous contest for liberty, Americans forgot
>   what it consists of
> after 20 years of the struggle *meminisse juvebit.* . . .
>   (LXX, p. 158)

Like "pius Aeneas" he is aware of the limitations of his own virtues:

> "My situation almost the only one in the world
>   where firmness and patience are useless" . . .
>   (LXX, p. 155)

and in the final cantos of this section Pound indicates that, despite all Adams' achievements, he is troubled by the lack of cooperation and the opposition of his countrymen:

> aim of my life has been to be useful, how small in
> any nation the number who comprehend ANY
> system of constitution or administration
> and those few do not unite.
> Americans more rapidly disposed to corruption in elections
> than I thought in '74
> fraudulent use of words monarchy and republic. . . .
>
> (LXX, p. 158)

Adams sometimes speaks like Confucius, more often like Pound:

> Every bank of discount is downright corruption
> taxing the public for private individuals' gain.
> and if I say this in my will
> The American people wd / pronounce I died crazy.
>
> (LXXI, p. 162)

and occasionally like a lonely American statesman struggling to establish an effective type of government in a difficult time. This variety of tones is not disturbing, however, for Adams is not significant as an individual or even as a statesman in *The Cantos*; he can be viewed only in relation to Pound's use of history throughout the poem. Here Adams is both the inheritor and progenitor of essential principles of government and law, and in Pound's view these originate in Zeus. In *Jefferson and/or Mussolini* he recalls an episode that occurred in Italy which is related to his historical and political position:

> An old nun in hospital had a good deal of trouble in digesting the fact that I wasn't Christian, no I wasn't; thank God, I wasn't a Protestant, but I wasn't a Catholic either, and I wasn't a Jew, I believed in a more ancient and classical system with a place for Zeus and Apollo. To which with infinite gentleness, "Z'è tutta una religione." "Oh well it's all a religion."[37]

---

[37] *Jefferson and/or Mussolini*, p. 31.

The Adams cantos end with a Hymn of Cleanthes to Zeus, which Pound describes in his Table to Cantos LII-LXXI as "part of Adams' *paideuma.*" Pound's translation of the hymn is as follows: "Glorious, deathless of many names, Zeus aye ruling all things, founder of the inborn qualities of nature, by laws piloting all things."

The laws that Pound envisions in history are not derived from the empirical evidence provided by the Italian Renaissance, China, or the American Republic, but are mythical laws of "inborn qualities of nature" which can be traced not only to ancient concepts of reality but to Pound's own messianic view of order and control. Like Zeus or Odysseus, the poet himself "pilots" all of history to conform to his own construction of an ideal past, which is more myth than history, more eccentric than universal. In *Guide to Kulchur*, Pound writes of his idea of "dynamic form," which is intrinsically related to his belief in the "dynamo" that the past must provide for the present:

> The *forma*, the immortal *concetto*, the concept, the dynamic form which is like the rose pattern driven into the dead iron-filings by the magnet, not by material contact with the magnet itself, but separate from the magnet. Cut off by the layer of glass, the dust and filings rise and spring into order. Thus the *forma*, the concept rises from death.[38]

Pound's myth of recurrence and permanence in history rises from death, for its purpose is ultimately to involve the reader in a ritual of abhorrence of the present and reversion to an idealized inner vision of the past. If his "history" contains some vital persons and events of earlier societies, these are often used to support the hatred and contempt which seem to inspire Pound's visionary pattern. History in *The Cantos* is finally Pound's own creation.

T. S. ELIOT
". . . a pattern of timeless moments"

History for the poet is almost always the visible evidence of time, his enemy and his challenge. Like Yeats and Pound, Eliot is con-

[38] *Guide to Kulchur*, p. 152.

307

cerned with history as a manifestation of temporal existence, a challenge in his conquest of time, but, despite the fact that his approach to history incorporates myth, he builds no structure to control events, and when he recreates the past, he does not idealize it. Eliot's interpretation of history is consistently conservative and orthodox. In as early an essay as "Tradition and the Individual Talent," he writes of "the historical sense" as "nearly indispensable to anyone who would continue to be a poet beyond his twenty-fifth year"; the historical sense, moreover, "is what makes a writer traditional." Eliot is here concerned with literary history, but his conception of the historical sense as a means of overcoming the ordinary limitations of time—"a sense of . . . the timeless and of the temporal together"[39] foreshadows his later poetic use of history in defining the "timeless moment."

Throughout his poetry Eliot, in alluding to history, uses myth to expose its "vanities" and to suggest that temporal experience has a goal beyond their limited satisfaction. The old man in "Gerontion" is a mythicized figure who himself represents history, in both its sterile failure and its vision of heroic glory:

> Here I am, an old man in a dry month,
> Being read to by a boy, waiting for rain.
> I was neither at the hot gates
> Nor fought in the warm rain
> Nor knee deep in the salt marsh, heaving a cutlass,
> Bitten by flies, fought.

Gerontion combines the quality of an ancient mythical figure yearning for release from dryness and impotence with the historical role of those who could only envy the courage and fame of the heroes of Thermopylae. As he sits in his "decayed house," the scene of history's failures, he waits for a sign of rebirth. Though it comes, in the form of a Christian myth, "Christ the tiger,"[40] the old man is

[39] *Selected Essays*, p. 4.

[40] See Williamson's reference to Eliot's essay on Lancelot Andrewes, which further elucidates this passage, *A Reader's Guide to T. S. Eliot*, pp. 108-109.

distracted from it by scenes of temporal vanity—names and occupa-
tions that fill but do not form history. The very sacrament of the
Lord's Supper becomes a participation in over-refined barbarism;
"Christ the tiger" will be "eaten, . . . divided, . . . drunk," consumed
"Among whispers" in "depraved May," the traditional season of rebirth, by sensualists and adventurers: Silvero, "caressing" his porce-
lain, and Hakagawa, "bowing among the Titians," Madame de
Tornquist and Fräulein von Kulp, preoccupied with magic; their
exotic names and their involvement with the products and secrets
of the past suggesting facets of history that may be precious, beautiful, and mysterious, but ultimately without pattern or meaning. Gerontion denies any insight he may have received: "I have no ghosts."
But even as history ignores its knowledge of the Christian myth,
its guilt emerges:

> After such knowledge, what forgiveness? Think now
> History has many cunning passages, contrived corridors
> And issues, deceives with whispering ambitions,
> Guides us by vanities.

The complicated and devious events and issues of history oppose
its most significant influence.

History becomes both an area of intrigue, containing "passages"
and "corridors" constructed for deceit and crime, and a malevolent
force personified as "She." Grover Smith suggests that " 'She' is not
history alone," and goes on to say: "Whatever the reference, it is
covered by the lament that passion comes too late, when not believed in, and that there is given

> . . . too soon
> Into weak hands, what's thought can be dispensed with
> Till the refusal propagates a fear.

The ambiguity, referring as much to belief as to potency or love,
tends to be puzzling when one reads the next section, in which, after
the mention of the tiger, there is no longer any visible connection

with the idea of secularism."[41] Actually, "She" is more than history because, at this point, Eliot constructs a grand image of a general historical memory that seems to emerge from the poignancy of a personal one; all the promise and disappointment, the aspiration and the failure of man's role in history are conveyed through his relationship with a controlling mythical figure—a mother or a beloved, recklessly giving and withholding, without thought to the desires of the "weak" recipient. "She gives" only when we are "distracted" from the central truth; she "gives with such supple confusions" that we are famished by her generosity. The remembrance of individual helplessness and despair interpreted as responses to this malevolent goddess becomes part of history. In fact, Eliot revaluates our accepted concepts of "fear," "courage," and "heroism," viewing them as reactions to the contrivances of this personification of nourishment and deprivation. History feeds our "ambitions" and "vanities," but our "Virtues" are necessitated only by "our impudent crimes." Returning to the image of "the tiger," Eliot suggests that any hope for the salvation of man's spirit that enters history is scorned and denied within its "cunning passages." But, like history, the tiger has a mythical force. The antagonist of the erratic goddess, the tiger, offers no consolation in "heroism" or virtue; it "devours" the disbeliever.

Gerontion has been described as "the protesting, apologetic voice of individual man in the grip of the historical process."[42] As such, he is a victim of history, a dry and sterile scapegoat. Finally, left to "Stiffen in a rented house," he is a symbol of passionless destruction and failure. At the same time, Gerontion is a prophet; lacking "sight, smell, hearing, taste, and touch," he foresees not only his own and his civilization's death, but the victory of "Christ the tiger." Denied or at least reduced to an object to be consumed by the decadent in "depraved May," the "tiger springs in the new year." Gerontion is both his victim and his spokesman.

The opposition in this poem between two myths—that of the an-

---

[41] *T. S. Eliot's Poetry and Plays*, p. 64.

[42] Harvey Gross, "*Gerontion* and the Meaning of History," *PMLA*, LXXIII (June, 1958), 301.

cient scapegoat, futilely awaiting sacrifice and renewal, and the Christian drama of resurrection—is repeated and developed in relation to history in *The Waste Land*. Here Eliot again deals with man's history as ultimately fruitless; all of his past is symbolized in the figure of the maimed Fisher King, waiting for a healer. Specific references to ancient and modern history are directly related to the overall mythical structure of sterility. The victory of the Romans over the Carthaginians at Mylae in the first Punic War is identified with World War I in the meeting of the protagonist with Stetson. As the speaker questions his former comrade in battle about the "corpse you planted last year in your garden," not only the destruction of war is disclosed, but also the futile longing for meaning and renewal in this echo of an ancient fertility rite. Such needs, unacknowledged and unfulfilled in the events of history, are expressed through the symbolism of the Grail legend, which originates in ancient rituals of physical and spiritual renewal and grows into a Christian romance dealing with the cup and lance of the Last Supper and the crucifixion. The historical development of the Grail legend itself contains the theme implicit in *The Waste Land*: the yearning for immortality evident in the historical records of ritual murder and festivals of regeneration can be fulfilled only in the identification of the Hanged God with Christ.

The modern city, "unreal" because of its abnegation of spiritual reality, reflects its heritage of ancient corruption:

> Who are those hooded hordes swarming
> Over endless plains, stumbling in cracked earth
> Ringed by the flat horizon only
> What is the city over the mountains
> Cracks and reforms and bursts in the violet air
> Falling towers
> Jerusalem Athens Alexandria
> Vienna London
> Unreal. . . .

The barbarism and decay of Europe in the present are part of the cycle of destruction and decadence which began in the ancient world.

"London Bridge is falling down . . ."; man's history is "the arid plain" from which the protagonist turns as he waits in the role of the Fisher King for release from its vanities.

In *The Waste Land*, man's narcissism and moral blindness determine the tragedy of his history; both the inner conflict between secular or personal desires and yearning for permanent order and existence beyond time, and the growing conviction that its resolution lies in orthodox Christianity are projected on history in Eliot's later poetry.[43] In *Coriolan*, he uses the legendary hero Coriolanus to symbolize the struggle between self-indulgence and self-sacrifice, between time and timelessness, which he is now convinced is the true material and provides the real data of history.

The role of Coriolanus as a hero who perceives truth beyond his place and time is foreshadowed in *The Waste Land*, where

> Only at nightfall, aethereal rumours
> Revive for a moment a broken Coriolanus. . . .

Imprisoned by his own limitations of character and by the conditions of the world he inhabits, Coriolanus dreams of escaping these bonds. The opening lines of "Triumphal March," the first section of *Coriolan*, remind the reader of Shakespeare's depiction of the victory of Gaius Marcius over the Volsces, when he was crowned with a garland of oakleaves and received the title Coriolanus. Eliot's lines suggest not only the tragic outcome of this victory but also the sad returns of all triumphal marches in man's history. The crowd observing the "oakleaves" and the "flags" and hearing the "trumpets" is limited by the perception of its "Ego," its total involvement in its own needs and satisfactions and therefore its capacity to perceive only the surface of reality.[44] As ancient and modern warfare and

---

[43] For a discussion of Eliot's approach to history from a Christian point of view, see Genesius Jones, O.F.M., *Approach to the Purpose*, especially the chapter "The Perspective of History."

[44] For a commentary on Eliot's use of Edmund Husserl's discussion of the nature of consciousness in this passage, see Grover Smith, *T. S. Eliot's Poetry and Plays*, p. 162.

history are fused in the enumeration of weapons and the conversation of the crowd, the hero appears:

> Look
>
> There he is now, look:
> There is no interrogation in his eyes
> Or in the hands, quiet over the horse's neck,
> And the eyes watchful, waiting, perceiving, indifferent.
> O hidden under the dove's wing, hidden in the turtle's breast,
> Under the palmtree at noon, under the running water
> At the still point of the turning world. O hidden.

The hero's indifference to the facile admiration of the crowd is that of the legendary Coriolanus; as he watches and waits, "perceiving" a reality beyond that of the self, the ancient figure's reserve and dignity are given a Christian dimension. He cannot rejoice in this ephemeral triumph since he is aware that "hidden" within nature is time beyond history: "the still point of the turning world." One would expect a continuation of this mood in the procession to the temple, which follows, but there the crowd sets the tone, and it can see only

> Dust
> Dust
> Dust of dust, and now
> Stone, bronze, stone, steel, stone, oakleaves, horses' heels
> Over the paving.
>
> That is all we could see. But how many eagles! and how many
>   trumpets!

In the second section, "Difficulties of a Statesman," the repeated ritual question, "Cry what shall I cry?" echoing Isaiah (40:6) is answered in a variety of ways, which encompass the conflicting pressures within history that interfere with perception of "the still point." The first answer is that of the prophet, "All flesh is grass," but it is immediately followed by a list of various orders of honor. The next time the ritual question is asked, the reply is a decision to form committees. The perception of his mortality drives man away from eternal to temporal values. Finally, the question elicits a real consideration of its meaning. The answer beginning, "Mother, mother," echoes Shakespeare's Coriolanus responding to his mother's demand that he sacrifice his personal feelings and his pride for the sake of Rome, but in *Coriolan* the hero pleads for a different kind of release from the limitations of history:

> O hidden under the . . . Hidden under the . . . Where the dove's
>   foot rested and locked for a moment,
> A still moment, repose of noon, set under the upper branches of
>   noon's widest tree
> Under the breast feather stirred by the small wind after noon
> There the cyclamen spreads its wings, there the clematis droops
>   over the lintel
> O mother (not among these busts, all correctly inscribed)
> I a tired head among these heads
> Necks strong to bear them
> Noses strong to break the wind
> Mother
> May we not be some time, almost now, together,
> If the mactations, immolations, oblations, impetrations,
> Are now observed
> May we not be
> O hidden
> Hidden in the stillness of noon, in the silent croaking night.

Tainted by indecision, conflicting loyalties, and pride, he nonetheless imagines the possibility of transcending history—"(not among these busts)"—in order to merge with the hidden stillness, which he perceives in nature. The legendary Coriolanus' sacrifice of his reputation and his life here becomes a "self-sacrifice," a surrender of personal satisfaction, even of one's place in temporal history, for a perception of the immortal principle that exists in time. When once again the ritual question, "What shall I cry?" is heard and the demand is made for a committee, the last reply is the repeated plea:

"RESIGN RESIGN RESIGN." This is a resignation from the triumphal march of history for the "stillness of noon," the "still point of the turning world."

The quest for the immortal element, the stillness within time or history, is fulfilled in *Four Quartets*, which is based on the Christian dogmas of incarnation and resurrection. As the divine appeared in human form, the timeless is present in time; history is the path to eternity. Eliot imitates Dante, who "had the benefit of a mythology and a theology which had undergone a more complete absorption into life than those of Lucretius,"[45] viewing history as a pattern in which all time is absorbed in the myth of redemption and the ritual of resurrection:

> The dove descending breaks the air
> With flames of incandescent terror
> Of which the tongues declare
> The one discharge from sin and error.
> The only hope, or else despair
>   Lies in the choice of pyre or pyre—
>   To be redeemed from fire by fire.
> Who then devised the torment? Love.
> Love is the unfamiliar Name
> Behind the hands that wove
> The intolerable shirt of flame
> Which human power cannot remove.
>   We only live, only suspire
>   Consumed by either fire or fire.
>   ("Little Gidding," IV)

In this Christian version of the myth of the torment and death of Heracles consumed by the poisoned robe of Nessus, Eliot emphasizes the limitations of "human power" in history. Love, as he sees it, is "unfamiliar" because it is superhuman, appearing in suffering and offering redemption through sacrifice. Deianira offered Heracles the robe smeared with the blood of the centaur Nessus as a love charm, but it was the cause of his torment and death. Yet

---

[45] "Dante," *The Sacred Wood*, p. 163.

Heracles' end was a triumphant one; he is the one mortal in Greek myth who, through his own labors and sufferings, was raised to the level of the gods. Many elements of the Heracles story are compressed in Eliot's image of the "intolerable shirt of flame": the blindness of Deianira's "human" love, the agony of the deceived and poisoned hero, his final consumption in the funeral pyre, which he himself commanded to be lighted, and the implication that, as Heracles' suffering was caused by a superhuman agent, so "human power" could not "remove it." Thus, if "Love" is offered to man as an "intolerable shirt of flame," its very form is a means to resurrection; it is the "fire" which Eliot uses consistently as a symbol of destruction and permanence, change and everlasting vitality. Though the pain of the struggle between mortal impurity and the refining power of divine love is inevitable, man can recognize and choose the redeeming elements in history and the consuming fire of his own release from its limitations.

Pound ranges outside the confines of ordinary reality, defying the boundaries of time and space to create the eternal laws of history; Eliot seeks the eternal in the local and the visible. In "Burnt Norton" in a manor in Gloucestershire, in "East Coker" at the site of his family's origins, in the rocks and river of "The Dry Salvages," and in the historical associations of the Anglican community in "Little Gidding," he sees evidence of regeneration in destruction: "Time the destroyer is time the preserver." If history in *Four Quartets* is viewed as the pattern of dance, eternity is the stillness within movement; the permanent exists within change.

When Eliot says:

> A people without history
> Is not redeemed from time, for history is a pattern
> Of timeless moments.   ("Little Gidding," V)

he is describing the conditions of his "exploration" of man and events. The discovery in history of the "timeless moments" mapped out by a mythical framework is the fulfillment of his life long struggle against the limitations of the self.

316

W. H. AUDEN
Unconscious Forces in History

Like Yeats, Pound, and Eliot, Auden delves beneath the surface of events for the obscure forces that control history, and, like them, he reveals the intrinsic connection between man's inner nature and his historical role through mythical allusions and symbols. But Auden's approach is neither cyclical, messianic, nor explicitly religious; in his poetry myth, and especially the concept of Eros, is one of the chief instruments he employs in his effort to discover the scientific laws that determine man's historical development and his social existence.

Auden's poetry has consistently reflected his concern with the political and social events of his time. In the thirties, as we have seen, he takes the role of healer, viewing both psychology and art as efficacious in freeing man to create his own history:

> The task of psychology, or art for that matter, is not to tell people how to behave, but by drawing their attention to what the impersonal unconscious is trying to tell them, and by increasing their knowledge of good and evil, to render them better able to choose, to become increasingly morally responsible for their destiny.

Auden regards "destiny" as neither mystical nor determined; his approach to history is based on an acceptance of the concepts of conflict and necessity developed in the writings of Marx and Freud: "Marx sees the direction of the relations between outer and inner world from without inwards, Freud vice versa." To Auden both positions have validity; since "hunger and love" are "instinctive needs," man's personal, economic, and social problems are always related and of equal importance.[46] Moreover, he had learned from Freud that Eros and aggression motivate man's conduct whether he seeks love, political authority, or economic power; the operation of these instinctual drives is apparent in public affairs as surely as in the individual psyche.

[46] "Psychology and Art," *The Arts Today*, pp. 18-19.

In his prose and poetry of the thirties Auden reveals his commitment to an analysis of man's history through a fusion of psychoanalytic, economic, anthropological, and philosophical concepts in unifying myths, which are essentially scientific instruments. "Jacob and the Angel," ostensibly a review of Walter de la Mare's *Behold This Dreamer*, published in 1937, is actually a brilliant essay on a general question Auden raises, which he says "is of much wider importance than questions of literary taste," for it deals with the roots of the political and social chaos of the period: "What attitude should we adopt to that half of life which dominates the night, to the Unconscious, the Instinctive and extra-personal, the Determined, the Daemonic?" Auden's answer begins with a description of an attitude prevalent in the thirties that seems not only valid historically but prophetic when viewed from the vantage point of the present:

> . . . both in art and life, above all in social and political life, we are today confronted by the spectacle, not of a Utilitarian rationalism that dismisses all that cannot be expressed in prose and statistics as silly childish stuff, but rather by an ecstatic and morbid abdication of the free-willing and individual before the collective and the daemonic. We have become obscene night worshipers who, having discovered that we cannot live exactly as we will, deny the possibility of willing anything and are content masochistically *to be lived*, a denial that betrays not only us but our daemon itself.

He then goes on to suggest that the only possibility of "escape" from the nightmare of a society in which "reason . . . more and more leads an underground 'imaginative' life, while politics becomes more and more 'surrealist,'" is authentic commitment to the eternal combat between the unconscious forces that shape man's essential nature and the rational ego, which derives impetus from the very night-world it struggles to understand, control, and use for its own vital powers.

For guidance in this struggle, Auden says we should turn to Darwin, Hegel, and Jung, in addition to Marx and Freud, modifying their ideas, as we must, but seeking their understanding of the nature of man in society. One of the most striking features of Auden's intellectual development is his capacity to assimilate diverse and even contradictory ideas which he synthesizes in a myth that symbolizes their "common and fundamental truth." In this review, Auden denies the validity of a deterministic and mystical conception of Destiny, such as Spengler's, through his interpretation of the contest between Jacob and the Angel as symbolic of the struggle between society's "daemon" and its rational will. Only when such a contest is accepted as inevitable can "the day . . . be reconciled with the night, Freedom with Destiny." The biblical story reveals both the limitations and powers man has in creating his own history:

> The daemon creates Jacob the prudent Ego, not for the latter to lead, in self-isolation and contempt, a frozen attic life of its own, but to be a loving and reverent antagonist; for it is only through that wrestling bout of which the sex act and the mystical union are the typical symbols that the future is born, that Jacob acquires the power and the will to live, and the demon is transformed into an angel.[47]

In Auden's view both "the sex act" and "the mystical union" express man's desire to direct his unconscious energy and aggression toward a deliberate and productive goal.

Auden's concern with the unconscious forces that influence the nature of human society and are always an essential factor in its history is undiminished by his conversion to Christianity; nor is his approach to the problem of controlling and directing these forces essentially changed by religious conviction. Characteristically, he adapts his basic position regarding such unconscious elements to his new acceptance of a spiritual presence in the universe. In a review of Reinhold Niebuhr's *Christianity and Power Politics*, he explains the necessity for "a sense of the Unconditional" on the basis of unconscious feelings:

> Recent history is showing, I think, and Dr. Niebuhr suggests here and there that he would agree with me, that man cannot

[47] *The New Republic*, 101, No. 26 (December 27, 1937), 292-93.

live without a sense of the Unconditional: if he does not consciously walk in fear of the Lord, then his unconscious sees to it
that he has something else, airplanes or secret police, to walk in
fear of.[48]

For Auden "walking consciously in fear of the Lord" has become a
means of diverting instinctual cravings and anxieties into conscious
belief, but his acceptance of the "Unconditional" does not restrain
his persistent effort to understand and come to terms with man functioning as a biological and psychological entity. He continues, moreover, to view Freud's method of approaching the unconscious as a
guide to history as well as to the individual psyche. In a review published in 1954, Auden says that Freud "made a real knowledge of
the psyche possible by regarding mental events, not as natural events,
but as historical events to be approached by the methods of the historian."[49]

In a recent review article, Auden's discussion of man as "a biological organism, . . . subject like all living creatures to the impersonal
drives like hunger and sex" is reminiscent of his early fusion of
Marxist and Freudian thought. Auden's scientific attitude toward
man's role in history is constant throughout his career; he may waver
and change in his interpretation of Eros, and certainly the addition of
a Christian deity to his world view is significant, but more so is his
consistent emphasis on man as at once "a social political individual"
and as "a unique person who can say *I* in response to the *thou's* of
other persons," who "transcends his time and his place, can choose to
think and act for himself, accept personal responsibility for the consequences, and is capable alike of heroism or baseness, sanctity or
corruption."[50]

Throughout his poetry Auden is concerned with the "biological,
the social, and the personal" aspects of man, which are "seldom in
complete accord,"[51] and in many of his poems myth discloses the

[48] "Tract for the Times," *The Nation*, 152, No. 1 (January 4, 1941), 25.
[49] "The Freud-Fliess Letters," *The Griffin*, June 1954, 8.
[50] "Byron: The Making of a Comic Poet," *The New York Review of Books*,
August 18, 1966, 17.
[51] *ibid.*

conflicting demands of these sides of man's nature in his history and indicates the possibilities of choice and change within its patterns. In much of his early poetry (*Poems*, 1930 and 1933, and *The Orators*), his persona combines the roles of antagonist and physician, struggling against the sickness of contemporary society, a heritage of the past, which provides material to be probed and tested by the poet. The obscurity of these poems results, at least in part, from Auden's use of a unique analytic and symbolic code to expose the disease of his society and to effect an inner transformation. Thus, in these poems, the figures are often vague and dreamlike revolutionaries and spies, symbolizing the need for violent change yet performing little overt action; they are "secret agents" who probe and analyze the corruption within the consciousness of society. Herbert Greenberg's view of nature as the dominant element in Auden's early work, "as the force behind history, as norm and natural law,"[52] is certainly valid, but it is important to observe that, if nature and history sometimes opposed, they are more often treated as common elements of observation, from which the poet extracts symbols of destruction, revolution, growth, and change. In the poems of this period, Auden uses both nature and contemporary history to develop a technique which later becomes a familiar one in his poetry: though he does not yet employ traditional myth to any significant extent, he mythicizes characters, scenes, and landscapes in order to reveal their hidden and essential features.

In "Doom is dark and deeper than any sea-dingle" (II, *Poems*, 1933; "Something is Bound to Happen" in *Collected Poetry*), Auden's echoes of the Anglo-Saxon poem "The Wanderer" suggest the long history of man alienated from his society; this is, moreover, no particular man, but a generalized figure, like a mythical hero, aware of "doom" and in quest of peace. Nature is also mythicized: the protagonist leaves home in the spring, the time of renewal when the "day-wishing flowers" contain volition and hope for one seeking regeneration. His way is difficult, and he meets the traditional hazards; though he misses the familiar and comfortable past, there is

---

[52] *Quest for the Necessary*, p. 33.

little doubt in the poem that his symbolic quest will be fulfilled. In
the last stanza, in lines that suggest both a charm and a prayer, the
narrator asks that the quester be saved "from hostile capture, / From
sudden tiger's spring at corner." Auden's hero is clearly man facing
the terrors of growth and change as he discovers a new phase of himself in history. Only by breaking with his past can he be renewed.
His wanderer

> waking sees
> Bird-flocks nameless to him, through doorway voices
> Of new men making another love.

It is unnecessary to interpret this poem in relation to Auden's political position in the thirties, but there is little doubt that through
the mythical framework of the lonely and fated quest he explores
the historical necessity of man's alienation from the familiar and his
discovery of what is still "nameless" and "new" in nature and himself.

In other poems of these volumes there are more specific references
to the necessity of rejecting the organized and inhibitory assumptions
of the past which persist in contemporary society: "It is time for
the destruction of error," a line from "It was Easter as I walked in
the public gardens," explicitly states a major theme of *Poems*. In the
passage that follows Auden develops this theme in symbolic and
analytic terms:

> The chairs are being brought in from the garden,
> The summer talk stopped on that savage coast
> Before the storms, after the guests and birds:
> In sanatoriums they laugh less and less,
> Less certain of cure; and the loud madman
> Sinks now into a more terrible calm.
>
> The falling leaves know it, the children,
> At play on the fuming alkali-tip
> Or by the flooded football ground, know it—
> This is the dragon's day, the devourer's:
> Orders are given to the enemy for a time

With underground proliferation of mould,
With constant whisper and the casual question,
To haunt the poisoned in his shunned house,
To destroy the efflorescence of the flesh,
The intricate play of the mind, to enforce
Conformity with the orthodox bone,
With organized fear, the articulated skeleton.

The most ordinary details of life are invested with a sense of fore-boding of the coming destruction. The horror increases with the "calm" of the "madman" and in the movement of "the falling leaves," and it reaches a crescendo in the mythical expression of in-evitable death and destruction: "This is the dragon's day, the de-vourer's." Auden extracts from the talk and laughter of man, from his physical and emotional illness, and from the annual decay in nature, a prophetic message: the inevitable destruction of the estab-lished social order and political institutions. The "dragon" then ap-pears as a mythical projection of all that the guests and the birds, the leaves and the children unconsciously "know": that death must be accepted as part of their nature and their role in history. The poem ends with an acknowledgement that love "Needs death, death of the grain, our death, / Death of the old gang. . . ."

Nature is mythicized in "Since you are going to begin today" through her prophetic address to the decadent ruling class of the present, but her speech is an analytic one, explaining the process of evolution in history, relating the fate of the twentieth-century bour-geoisie to that of the ancient Romans, and warning those foolish enough to attempt escape: "Before you reach the frontier you are caught." In "Consider this and in our time" (XXIX, *Poems*, 1930 and 1933; "Consider" in *Collected Poetry*), the inevitable destruction inherent in natural law is given mythical form as the "supreme Antagonist." As such, its power over nature and man is revealed in its dramatic inevitability and pathos. It is

More powerful than the great northern whale
Ancient and sorry at life's limiting defect,

and the speaker himself, accepting its dominance in his own society, urges it on:

> Summon
> Those handsome and diseased youngsters, those women
> Your solitary agents in the country parishes;
> And mobilize the powerful forces latent
> In soils that make the farmer brutal
> In the infected sinus, and the eyes of stoats.

The poet has listened to this force of nature

> By silted harbours, derelict works,
> In strangled orchards, and the silent comb
> Where dogs have worried or a bird was shot.

and he now assumes its prophetic voice as he observes those who still clutch their symbols of power in a dying social and economic order. Addressing the "Financier," he tells him: "The game is up for you and for the others," and he warns, "You cannot be away"; there is no escape from history, which is more truly revealed by the "supreme Antagonist" than by the financier in his "little room / Where the money is made but not spent" or in the "College Quad or Cathedral Close."[53]

In *The Orators*, the analytic code is often so private that the poet seems to be creating a personal myth out of his own and his friends' experience and their response to the demands of their families and their society. In the "Prologue" ("Adolescence" in *Collected Poetry*), the young hero, who is portrayed as a rather mild Zeus, "a swan" to "earth's unwise daughters," receives only vilification from his country and family. Returning, apparently from war or some mission on behalf of his society, he

> Receives odd welcome from the country he so defended:
> The band roars "Coward, Coward," in his human fever,
> The giantess shuffles nearer, cries "Deceiver."

[53] *Poems* (New York, 1934), pp. 53-54. The address to the Financier is omitted from the poem in the version printed in *Collected Poetry*.

The "giantess" is the archetypal mother as a force in society, confronting her offspring with her awareness of his hidden self; he is not what he seems—a proper young man who has defended his country—but one of a band of young rebels with a code of behavior and a language of their own, like those described in Section II, "Argument": "Walking in the mountains we were persons unknown to our parents, awarded them little, had a word of our own for our better shadow."[54] Like the "airman" of Book II, he is opposed to all the inhibitions which the "giantess" symbolizes.

In Book I, 1, "Address for a Prize-Day," Auden confronts the reader even more directly with an analytic myth: "Imagine to yourselves a picked body of angels, all qualified experts on the human heart, a Divine Commission, arriving suddenly one day at Dover. After some weeks in London, they separate," each going to a different area of England. Then, "when every inch of the ground has been carefully gone over, every house inspected, they return to the Capital again to compare notes, to collaborate in a complete report, which made, they depart as quietly as they came. Beauty of the scenery apart, would you not feel some anxiety as to the contents of that report?" The speaker continues, making his point in a series of intense rhetorical questions:

> Do you consider their statistics as to the average number of lost persons to the acre would be a cause for self-congratulation? Take a look round this hall, for instance. What do you think? What do you think about England, this country of ours where nobody is well?[55]

In *The Orators*, the airman and his colleagues take the role of these angels. They analyze the sickness of the "enemy" of their society, pointing out both symptoms and serious diseases. Furthermore, like the orator of the Prize-Day Address, they are both perceptive and slightly comic in their frenzy and their arrogant certainty. The poet has invented a band of limited "angels," themselves infected by the disease of the society they explore and condemn; his myth thus exposes the ambivalent nature of its own heroes, their naivete and

---

[54] "The Orators," *ibid.*, p. 99.   [55] *ibid.*, p. 93.

egotism as well as their courage and intelligence in seeking physical and psychological health as social values.

In *On This Island*, Auden emphasizes the ambivalence inherent in mythical islands—their beauty and their desolation, their connotations of peacefulness, mystery, and narcissistic alienation—to develop his view of England's isolation in contemporary history. The island motif is also related to his conception of love or Eros as a historical and political force. In many of the poems of this volume, the island is both England, existing as a nation in a world threatened by war, and its inner realm of dream, fantasy, illusion, and potential unconscious strength and beauty, where its destiny is formed. In "The Prologue," Auden indicates that the desolation of the island is evident in daily life:

> In bar, in netted chicken-farm, in lighthouse,
> Standing on these impoverished constricted acres,
> The ladies and gentlemen apart, too much alone. . . .

Yet hope lies within the island itself, in the capacity of its inhabitants to respond to the restorative powers of love, which is addressed in a type of prayer for aid to England in a period of danger. In this poem Auden uses two dreams, the first a romantic dream from the past which "Is already retreating into her maternal shadow," and the second a dream of the future:

> Some possible dream, long coiled in the ammonite's slumber
> Is uncurling, prepared to lay on our talk and reflection
> Its military silence, its surgeon's idea of pain;

> And out of the future into actual history,
> As when *Merlin*, tamer of horses, and his lords to whom
> *Stonehenge* was still a thought, the *Pillars* passed

> And into the undared ocean swung north their prow,
> Drives through the night and star-concealing dawn
> For the virgin roadsteads of our hearts an unwavering keel.

It is possible that the word "ammonite" has a double meaning here, the obvious one being a curved fossil shell, and the second one, from which this derives (*cornu Ammonis*), a reference to Ammon, the oracular Egyptian god, whom the Greeks identified with Zeus. Through the image Auden seems to unite the mythical with the physical past. This dream, emerging from man's archaic and mythical heritage, rooted in his geological and psychic history, is a prophecy of ultimate courage, like that of Merlin, which love must restore in this time of crisis. The dream issuing from fossil and myth dismisses "talk and reflection"; its method is harsh, but its demands are more realistic, for it aims beyond the surface, at "the virgin roadsteads of our hearts."

Auden is aware, however, of the ambiguous nature of love, and in other poems of this volume he tracks its devious course in man's long history. In III, "Our hunting fathers" ("In Father's Footsteps" in *Collected Poetry*), he tells of early man's recognition of a form of "Love" in "the lion's intolerant look / Behind the quarry's dying glare. . . ." The next lines describe the ancient hunters' conversion of this instinctual drive into the idealized form of the mythical Eros:

> Love raging for the personal glory
>   That reason's gift would add,
> The liberal appetite and power,
>   The rightness of a god.

But this conception of love, which incorporates man's appetites, his desire for power, and his reason reflects an early stage of man's history; the dangerous and painful qualities of Eros are recognized only later, as society develops:

> Who, nurtured in that fine tradition
>   Predicted the result,
> Guessed Love by nature suited to
>   The intricate ways of guilt. . . .

Though Auden does not use the term Eros in *On This Island*, the word "love" in this volume often connotes the Freudian Eros; certainly in its historical role it symbolizes the ambivalence of man's instinct for survival, tainted as it is with aggression and death. It is the only hope of his "island" and, at the same time, it is infected with narcissism and despair.

The contrasting views of the "island" in V, "Look, stranger, at this island now" (in "Songs and Other Musical Pieces," *Collected Poetry*), and VII, "Hearing of harvests rotting in the valleys" ("Paysage Moralisé" in *Collected Poetry*), express Auden's idea that history is a product of the fantasies, dreams, and ambivalent longings that make up man's inner life. The imagery and musical effects of "Look, stranger . . ." suggest that the island is as much an inner vision as it is an actual place. Its enchantment lingers in "the channels of the ear," and its scenes "move in memory. . . ." In "Paysage Moralisé," however, the danger of this idealized vision is revealed. It is an expression of man's narcissism and isolation from his fellows, and its promise of escape from the reality of the "harvests rotting in the valleys" is deceptive:

> Knowing them shipwrecked who were launched for islands,
> We honour founders of these starving cities
> Whose honour is the image of our sorrow. . . .

Because the cities contain so much evidence of man's failure in history, he continues to console himself with a dream of escape:

> Each in his little bed conceived of islands
> Where every day was dancing in the valleys
> And all the green trees blossomed on the mountains
> Where love was innocent, being far from cities.

The promise of the "gods" who "visit us from islands" is a projection of man's yearning for omnipotence as he confronts the barrenness and hopelessness of his society. The speaker's tone expresses compassion for those victimized as much by their illusory islands as by the "unhappy cities," and the concluding line of the poem: "And we rebuild our cities, not dream of islands" is both a personal appeal and a demand that man take an active role in forming his history.

In XVII, "Here on the cropped grass," Auden is more specific about the frightening and depressing condition of Europe. He speaks of "Gross Hunger" as an active and consuming force:

> Erecting here and everywhere his vast
> Unnecessary workshops . . .

of financial failure and war. These are seen in the light of past history: "The hopes of time" defeated by the violence, the attraction to death, inherent in "the laws of love." Nature itself accepts this union. The "thunder mutters" its knowledge of society's and history's involvement with death, and its message is confirmed by the speech of the "bones of war," revealing man's choice of "hatred" over "disciplined love," which can result only from the kind of inner combat that Auden describes in "Jacob and the Angel."

Throughout *On This Island*, the many direct allusions to dictatorship and war:

> Ten million of the desperate marching by,
> Five feet, six feet, seven feet high,
> Hitler and Mussolini in their wooing poses . . .
>
>   ("A Bride in the 30's")

to poverty, fear, selfishness, and isolation suggest that "the daemonic" within man is achieving mastery in this contest. Still Auden does not relinquish the possibility that the productive capacities of man can be channeled into social expression. Love or Eros, an unconscious, amoral force, can be directed, despite its limitations, by man's will and reason:

> But love except at our proposal
> Will do no trick at his disposal,
> Without opinions of his own performs
> The programme that we think of merit,
> And through our private stuff must work
>   His public spirit.   ("A Bride in the 30's")

Auden's poetry of the late thirties and early forties records his effort to discover an inner "law of love" which, despite its revelations of conflict and failure, could offer a means of controlling "the dangerous flood / Of history." Thus, he symbolizes many of the complex and elusive forces which create history, "that never sleeps or dies, / And, held one moment, burns the hand" (*On This Island*, XXX), in the operations of Eros. It is his chief instrument for probing and elucidating contemporary history in such works as "Spain 1937,"

"September 1, 1939," "New Year Letter," and "For the Time Being." In these poems Auden is as much the explorer as he is the commentator; he is searching beneath the surface of the devastating events of his time for a principle of compromise between the "daemonic" or determined and the rational, disciplined, and willed.

In "Spain 1937,"[56] the country itself involved in civil war becomes a symbol of these contesting forces in history. The poor, victimized by war, ask:

> "O show us
> History the operator, the
> Organizer, Time the refreshing river."

demanding some principle of order to account for the present destruction. The poet hears a similar cry from the great powers:

> And the nations combine each cry, invoking the life
> That shapes the individual belly and orders
> The private nocturnal terror:
> "Did you not found once the city state of the sponge,
>
> "Raise the vast military empires of the shark
> And the tiger, establish the robin's plucky canton?
> Intervene. O descend as a dove or
> A furious papa or a mild engineer: but descend."

In contemporary political allegiances and military action, Auden sees the oblique expression of a plea to Eros, "the life," idealized and evoked as a powerful father or a rational and peaceful god. To expose such delusions Auden creates a mythical composite of ambivalence, deviousness, and endless adaptability in the voice of "the life" that answers this plea, "if it answers at all." It

> replies from the heart
> And the eyes and the lungs, from the shops and squares of
> the city:
> "O no, I am not the Mover,
> Not today, not to you. To you I'm the

---

[56] *Spain* (London, 1937); reprinted as "Spain 1937" with changes in *Another Time* and in *Collected Poetry*.

"Yes-man, the bar-companion, the easily-duped:
I am whatever you do; I am your vow to be
          Good, your humorous story;
I am your business voice; I am your marriage.

"What's your proposal? To build the Just City? I will.
I agree. Or is it the suicide pact, the romantic
          Death? Very well, I accept, for
I am your choice, your decision: yes, I am Spain."

Man's productivity and aggressiveness, his capacity for love and his attachment to death are manifested in his images of society and the actual world he constructs. The "life" which speaks is Eros as a biological and psychological drive, subject to man's rational will, toward which it reaches as it emerges in conscious expression. Auden's optimism about man's capacity to control and direct his instinctual drives is qualified by the apparently casual statement, "if it answers at all," which indicates the elusive and unpredictable quality of the unconscious. Even as the mythical voice asserts the necessity of acknowledging unconscious forces in history, it suggests the difficulty of recognizing them and of controlling them by "choice" and "decision."

Yet, for Auden in this period, the imposition of conscious will on acknowledged instinct, however frightening and demanding, is the only means by which man can create his history, and Spain is the symbol of this possibility. As the unconscious Eros insists that it can become subject to man's decision, it becomes Spain and history itself. The poem ends with an uncompromising statement of the implications of such a position, and a warning, which is actually prophetic:

The stars are dead; the animals will not look;
We are left alone with our day, and the time is short and
          History to the defeated
May say Alas but cannot help or pardon.

The idea that history is ultimately determined by each man's lonely struggle with his own daimon or angel is also a challenge, which Auden faces continually in this period; both Eros and history become his contestants in the poems of the late thirties and early forties, as he gradually turns to a power outside man that he believes can both "help" and "pardon."

"September 1, 1939," in which Auden speaks in the first person, reveals his deeply personal involvement with history. "Uncertain and afraid," he sees the "anger and fear" of the decade "Obsessing our private lives. . . ." He interprets the violence of past and present history in psychoanalytic terms—as resulting from sickness, obsession, and delusion. The struggle against the psychopathology of the age is also personal. The poet's hope is fragmented by his experience of the limitations of Eros, the sole productive element in history, which too often operates in both individual and social life as a narcissistic and deceptive influence.

In his poetry of the early forties, Auden's growing conviction that individual knowledge and will cannot control the unconscious aggression responsible for "the crimes of history" is expressed in his depiction of Eros as a primarily destructive social and political force. Though in "New Year Letter" he continues to probe for potential regenerative functions of Eros, the evidence of history can only convince him that "Love's vigour shrinks to less and less" (p. 280).

Actually, in "New Year Letter," the poet is in quest of a historical principle more efficacious than Eros in promoting the "universal love," which in "September 1, 1939" he regards as the sole source of health and which, in creating the "Just City," he increasingly envisions as established on a framework of religious faith. Characteristically, Auden attempts to analyze the "situation of our time": in "New Year Letter," he is both a detective investigating "a baffling crime" (pp. 271-72) and an oracle, seeking hidden motives and guilts. Probing the soul of man, he finds Eros misused by "agents" who are "untrue" to its productive powers and who are guided by an "Ego" removed from the reality of man's nature. Considering its responsibility for "our potential distress," he describes the Ego, in language similar to that of "Jacob and the Angel," as leading "An attic life all on her own" (pp. 306-307), but he has lost faith in the contest he depicted so convincingly in that essay. To Auden, man's history since the Renaissance indicates that freedom and will can exist as agents in history only if they operate in relation to a principle or law more dependable than the protean instinctual drives and the "Self-known, self-praising, self-attached" ego of man.

The religious position Auden takes in the poetry he has written since the forties is consistently related to his view of the Incarnation as a climactic historical event. It is presented in this way in "For the Time Being," and it is assumed as the essential background of Clio, the goddess of historical fact whom he evokes in his later poetry. The historical setting of the Incarnation is established at the beginning of "For the Time Being" in the muttering of the crowds, who say, "Love is not what she used to be," and the answering yawn of Caesar. The failure of classical humanism and the decadence of ancient society are expressed in the Semi-Chorus' description of the "lost" and aimless Hercules and in the Chorus' remarks on the absence of faith and purpose:

> The prophet's lantern is out
> And gone the boundary stone. . . .

The "civil garden" of love is overwhelmed by "a wild passion / To destroy and be destroyed" (pp. 407-408).

The Narrator's summary of the "political situation" suggests that any society in which the "occupation of space is the real and final fact" (p. 409) is incapable of determining its own history. Therefore, its members experience no sense of self, no identity as citizens or even as private persons, but merely a frightening "Void" (pp. 410-11) which can be filled only by faith. Auden considers belief in the Incarnation a matter of choice—for those who were present at the event and for future generations. It is this choice, he says, that ultimately provides man's freedom in temporal history. Since a belief in the Incarnation is based on an acceptance of the "Absurd," faith is essentially personal, an inner knowledge of a spiritual presence in the finite, which provides the ultimate meaning of history.

Auden seeks to replace the "collective and political myth of Eros" with the Christian myth of Incarnation and redemption as historical "Law," guiding man "so that his Eros may have the courage to

333

take decisions." What he calls "self-actualization"[57] can occur in human society only when love, its essential productive element, functions as a spiritual power of more stability, unity, and selflessness than the human Eros can achieve, and as one to which instinctual drives are continually directed.

The concept of the "Just City," which first appears in Auden's poetry of the thirties, becomes a pervading image in the poems written after his conversion, an ideal against which the historical ancient and modern city, corrupted by the rule of "Caesars" and "managers," is measured. In "The Fall of Rome," as in many other poems of *Nones*, Auden uses ancient Rome as a dominant image; the city, like a realm of the unconscious, is a mythicized past which constantly makes its demands on the present. The lofty image intensifies the failures of reality: the "Ancient Disciplines" do not impress mutinous Marines; as Caesar enjoys his "double-bed," a clerk pathetically reveals his discontent. But there is another realm which sets in perspective both the ancient fallen city and those who inherit its myth:

> Altogether elsewhere, vast
> Herds of reindeer move across
> Miles and miles of golden moss,
> Silently and very fast.

These reindeer create a third dimension, neither glorified but tainted past nor urgent present, but eternal and recurring nature, whose commentary is implicit in its presence.

The title of "Memorial for the City" contains the dominant image of the poem: the city as a symbol of man's collective aspirations and limitations, and his yearning for the "City of God," a phrase from the epigraph, a quotation from Juliana of Norwich. The poem begins with a distinction between the Homeric conception of reality and the Christian one, which Auden calls "ours." Homer's view of the world is that perceived by the "eyes of the crow and the eye of the camera"; it is the limited world of naturalistic perception:

[57] "Eros and Agape," p. 757.

> First and last
> They magnify earth, the abiding
> Mother of gods and men; if they notice either
> It is only in passing: gods behave, men die,
> Both feel in their own small way, but She
> Does nothing and does not care,
> She alone is seriously there.

It is a world dominated by Mother Earth, the mythical expression of man's awareness of his ephemeral life in nature, which is continuous and unconcerned with its limited offshoot, man. This secular view is stark but curiously satisfying compared with those of the societies which follow and, inheriting this conception, cannot maintain it without grief. The cities that follow in history are ones in which the crow is to be seen in the "crematorium chimney" and the camera is found "roving the battle. . . ."

The vision of both crow and camera, according to Auden, is deceptive. As he earlier rejected the naturalistic view expressed in the stark and ambiguous symbol of Eros, he now turns from the Homeric acceptance of man's lot, always determined by his mortality:

> The steady eyes of the crow and the camera's candid eye
> See as honestly as they know how, but they lie.

He cannot accept "time" as the "crime of life." Even "Among the ruins of the Post-Vergilian City," in chaos and pain, we must realize "Our grief is not Greek," for he finds, beyond the despair of man's violence and destructiveness and his fear of time, the hope of redemption.

In the second section of the poem Auden traces the history of the city in Christian society. The "Sane City" of the medieval world degenerated into the "Sinful City," whose "obscene" machinery for absolution through payment "Luther denounced." Neither the city of the Renaissance, which worshiped art, nor the "Rational City" of the Enlightenment fulfilled man's quest for a social realm to which he could attach his craving for permanence and order. His distorted images of these values appear in the "Glittering City" and the "Conscious City" which he has built in modern times, and these, as Auden indicates in the third section, have become the scene of barbarism and destruction—the "abolished City" of dictatorship and war.

No city which man has created has withstood his corrupt values and his compulsion to self-deception, but ironically hope lies in man's weakness. As in "The Managers," this weakness, which is man's real power, because it is an acknowledgment of dissatisfaction with merely material achievement and fruitless goals, is expressed in myth. Auden mingles Christian and pagan myth with legend and folktale to suggest the variety and extent of man's yearning to overcome his mortality and the limitations of his spirit. Thus, psychological and spiritual need become one in the rejection of the corruption and falsehood of organized society in which man has acted out his history. In the fourth section, called *"Let Our Weakness speak,"* man reveals his true nature as he tells of intimate involvements with Adam, Prometheus, Adonis, Orpheus, Narcissus, Psyche, Hector, Oedipus, Diotima, Tristan and Isolda, Galahad, Faustus and Helen, Hamlet, Don Quixote, and others. It is as if with these mythical and legendary persons he can be himself—sometimes foolish and shortsighted, but at least honest enough to renounce the city for the deeper realm of his own heart. In the end he rejects the city, certain that he "shall rise again to hear her judged."

The "abolished City" of the contemporary world is treated more extensively in "The Shield of Achilles," the title poem of Auden's next volume. Nowhere else does Auden use myth more effectively to arouse intense emotion through allusion and ironic contrast. The reader's response to the poem depends not only on his knowledge of the description of the "Shield" in *Iliad* XVIII, 480-617, but on the way in which Auden evokes and twists his memory of the Homeric passage through ironic allusions. In recalling the idealized city of Homer's shield, Auden seems to be exposing unconscious assumptions about man in history to the violations of the contemporary mechanized and military state.

The shield of Homer's Achilles depicts the whole universe. Earth,

sky, ocean, and vineyard are the background for various activities
of man: feast, rite, song, dance, work, and war. Thus, man's bel-
ligerence is seen in perspective against the sweeping depiction of his
life in all its possible grace, productivity, and pleasure. The wrath
of Achilles and the Trojan War are only a portion of man's concern
—disorder within essential order. Auden refers to "vines and olive
trees," to "ritual pieties, / White flower-garlanded heifers," to "altar"
and "dancing-floor" only to emphasize their absence. The modern
city or state has become totally absorbed in mechanized warfare;
the soldier himself is anonymous, his feelings deadened:

> A million eyes, a million boots in line,
> Without expression, waiting for a sign.

and his attitudes are based entirely on commands and statistics. He-
phaestos, the artist of the gods, has become the "thin-lipped armorer,"
the imitation of the Homeric double epithet intensifying the horror
of his role. And Achilles, who is mentioned only at the end of the
poem, is described as:

> Iron-hearted man-slaying Achilles
> Who would not live long.

This last ironic allusion to the mythical Achilles' choice of a short
heroic life over a long but unfulfilled one is a commentary on the
failure of the humanistic conception of heroism, its belief that immortality could be gained by courage and dedication to an ideal—
the *virtutis opus*, which is the basis of the heroic code. The long
history of this ideal has ended in the figure of an Achilles in whom
the passion for victory appears in its most elemental and brutal form
as a compulsion to slaughter and whose yearning for immortality
through valor is revealed as a dedication to death.

In his poetry of the 1950s and 60s, Auden increasingly uses myth to
unite the "primary world" of history and the "secondary world" of
imagination and the arts. In his recent essay, "The World of the
Sagas," he says: "The Historian cannot function without some assistance from the Poet, nor the Poet without some assistance from

the Historian but, as in any marriage, the question who is to command and who to obey, is the source of constant quarrels." Since the primary world—"the objective world outside ourselves"—is limited by factual reality, only the secondary world can express man's feeling that "certain beings and events" are "sacred, enchanting, valuable in themselves." It is, moreover, only through the products of the secondary world that man can portray his fantasies of omnipotence and omniscience and can recreate "evil and suffering . . . in a simplified more comprehensible form." But "awe, wonder, enchantment," and all the yearnings of the human spirit can exist only in relation to knowledge of and activity in the primary world. Thus, difficult as the union between these two realms may be, historian and poet, says Auden, must be aware of and even include both.[58] In his effort to analyze and interpret the unconscious forces in history through traditional myths, Auden has always struggled to unite these two realms of experience, but in his later work, especially in *Homage to Clio* and *City Without Walls*, there is a new element in his use of myth: though he still probes for the unseen and unacknowledged sickness of man in society, he now evokes goddesses and other mythical presences and allusions in order to suggest the mystery and dignity inherent in the "unique historical fact." In both these volumes there seems to be a conscious effort to employ myth in the service of the "primary world" of limited, objective reality.

Certainly in "Homage to Clio" Auden evokes a being of the secondary world—who, despite her traditional name, is actually his own creation—in announcing his allegiance to the primary one. The goddess, who symbolizes the silence and patience needed to perceive history in the episodes of daily life, reveals the individual human contribution and response to historical events. She represents, moreover, the element in ordinary presences and limited experience that elicits "sacred awe."

In "Makers of History" (*Homage to Clio*), Auden opposes those celebrated in traditional myths to those whom "Clio loves," the men involved in the daily problems and tasks which create history. Tradi-

---

[58] *Secondary Worlds* (New York, 1968), pp. 49-52.

tional myths and legends of the "Composite demigod" performing
superhuman feats reflect

> the phobia, the perversion,
> Such curiosa as tease humanistic
> Unpolitical palates.

The poet as disciple of Clio turns our attention and our misplaced
admiration from the heroes of those tales that reveal only wishes
and fantasies, to the enchantment of the real:

> Clio loves those who bred them better horses,
> Found answers to their questions, made their things,
> Even those fulsome
> Bards they boarded. . . .

The primary and secondary worlds become one, unified in the figure
of Clio, who establishes a new legendary stature for the active men
who "made their things" and for the "Bards" who approach her
province with awe.

The subject of the poet's relation and obligation to history is developed in several poems of *Homage to Clio*. "Secondary Epic," a
half-serious unfavorable review of Vergil's treatment of history in
his description of the shield of Aeneas (*Aeneid* VIII, 626-728), is also
a commentary on the poet as historian. Auden criticizes Vergil's
method of recounting history through the prophetic scenes of the
shield, since his summary, which serves his own "political turn," ends
with Augustus' triumph over Anthony in 31 B.C. Yet Vergil does
not entirely fail:

> As rhetoric your device was too clever:
> It lets us imagine a continuation
> To your Eighth Book, an interpolation,
> Scrawled at the side of a tattered text. . . .

Auden, assuming the role of the "down-at-heels refugee rhetorician"
who provides this "continuation," describes the successful invasion
of the Goths and praises Alaric, the conqueror of Rome. What Auden
objects to is obviously not Vergil's inability to foresee the details of

history beyond his own time, but the fact that his exalted account of past history in the form of prophecy—"Hindsight as foresight"— implies a similar future of conquest and power, ordained by fate. But a prophet, says Auden, should surely be aware of the inevitable outcome of Rome's actual history—"war after war"; there is indeed a "Providence" for Rome, implied in its past but unknown to the ancient poet:

> (Surely, no prophet could afford to miss
> No man of destiny fail to enjoy
> So clear a proof of Providence as this)
> The names predestined for the Catholic boy
> Whom Arian Odovacer will depose.

Those names, Romulus Augustus, recall the superhuman power attributed to Rome's legendary founder and the exalted self-image of its long line of emperors; the "continuation" of such delusion, Auden implies, must inevitably be defeat and destruction.

In "The Epigoni," he expresses sympathy for the poets of Rome's Silver Age, whom he considers the victims of history. Living in a decadent society, threatened by "guttural tribes," they could expect only death or slavery. Yet they avoided "dramatizing their doom. . . ." Auden sees a kind of nobility in their "preposterous mechanical tricks," which reflect their awareness that "the language they loved was coming to grief. . . ." Their curious indirect rebellion against the barbarity of their times

> Can safely be spanked in a scholar's footnote,
> Called shallow by a mechanized generation to whom
> Haphazard oracular grunts are profound wisdom.

But Auden sees it as an honorable retreat from as well as a comment on a phase of history.

In the title poem of his most recent volume, *City Without Walls*, Auden uses myth to intensify the ever-present threat of annihilation that infects contemporary society. Myth, which contains the history of man's past and present delusion and arrogance, projects a vision of a hideous future that is a reenactment of prehistoric barbarism.

In "City Without Walls," the thoughts of the poet "at three A.M.," emerge in bizarre but accurate images of the present city and in fearful predictions of its future. The poem begins with the frightening statement that the mythical forms in Byzantine painting that

> Were a shorthand for the Unbounded
> beyond the Pale, unpoliced spaces
> where dragons dwelt and demons roamed . . .

are now part of everyday life. Man has learned to live with horror in his daily environment. Monstrous myths

> are visual facts in the foreground now,
> real structures of steel and glass. . . .

The houses of the city are jails, its streets "Asphalt Lands." Woman, as in Auden's early poetry, retains something of Eve in her quest for food, and man of Adam as he "hunts an easy dollar," but they "eat their bread in boredom of spirit." They are the victims of history, for computers may soon "expel from the world / all but the top intelligent few. . . ."

Imagining such a world as another beginning, Auden returns to Freud's "scientific myth" of the primal horde. But in the realm of the new barbarism even instinctual drives are machine-made:

> Against Whom
> shall the Sons band to rebel there,
> where Troll-Father, Tusked Mother
> are dream-monsters like dinosaurs
> with a built-in obsolescence?

Aggression has been channeled into worship of "*General Mo*"; the fables of elves and dwarves, "cunning in craft," now tell of

> the treasure-hoards of tin-cans . . .
> they flatten out for hut roofs. . . .

The old myths have new endings, programmed by machines for the "human remnant" of the future. The poet's reverie is broken by his own ironic comment on his role as "Jeremiah-cum-Juvenal," but the voices of reason which interrupt his musings sound too familiar, too much like those heard daily in the "Megalopolis," to offer much comfort.

Withdrawal from the meaning of history has never offered Auden comfort for long; he has sought the silence of Clio in an effort to comprehend "History's criminal noise" ("the Common Life"), and in a recent poem he evokes the mythical moon to gain perspective on man's successful moon landing. He begins the poem "Moon Landing"[59] with a comment on the psychological motivation for the feat:

> It's natural the Boys should whoop it up for
> so huge a phallic triumph, an adventure
> it would not have occurred to women
> to think worthwhile. . . .

Though the motives were "somewhat less than *menschlich*," the landing, he admits, was a "grand gesture." Nonetheless, it was no more than was to be expected "from the moment / the first flint was flaked. . . ." The landing on the moon was inevitable in the history of a creature "adroiter / with objects than lives. . . ." Auden does not entirely disparage man's ingenuity and skill, but he places them in perspective against other qualities—the beauty, dignity, and decorum retained for him in the traditional image of the "Moon," which the successful landing could neither reach nor destroy. He does not deny that the moon was "Worth *going* to see," but "*seeing*" it hardly seems worthwhile; he finds no charm in a desert. "Seeing" for Auden means perceiving the delights and values of life, and these he symbolizes in the traditional image of the garden:

> give me a watered
> lively garden, remote from blatherers
>
> about the New, the von Brauns and their ilk, where
> on August mornings I can count the morning
> glories, where to die has a meaning,
> and no engine can shift my perspective.

[59] *The New Yorker*, September 6, 1969, p. 38.

The garden and his mythical Moon which "still queens the Heavens" are Auden's defense against "the usual squalid mess called History. . . ." Like Yeats in "Blood and the Moon," Auden here conveys the opposition between the values transmitted in myths of the moon and those of the men who make history. For Yeats, however, the moon remains outside history, "unclouded" and perfect in its mythical "purity." For the contemporary poet such a position is no longer possible. Yet if Auden admits that the moon has undeniably become part of scientific and political history, this new role does not diminish its mythical value for him. In this poem, as throughout his poetry, he suggests that myths contain "old warnings" against "Hybris" and "Irreverence," and that these are a force in history.

VI

EVOLVING MYTHOLOGIES COMPARED

IN the work of the poets discussed in the preceding three chapters, myth discloses experiences as deep and as complex as those it conveys in ancient poetry and drama. An evolving form, myth adapts to the inner voice of the poet, revealing many levels of feeling and perception at once. It adapts to his environment also, incorporating its changing approaches to reality, its assumptions about nature and man. Most important, myth expresses a continual interaction between the chaotic unconscious and the controlling conscious mind straining together and finally united in a stylized yet flexible symbolic structure.

Though there are vast differences in the themes and techniques of Yeats, Pound, Eliot, and Auden, myth functions in the work of all these poets to convey the complex and ambiguous experiences of love and aggression and the consciousness of death. In fact, it can be said that in their poetry classical myth discloses the operation of instinctual drives as a perennial force within history, society, and the individual psyche. All these poets, intuitively or deliberately, rely on the characteristics of myth that insure such revelation: the conflict, either overt or implicit in its narrative, between human frailty and superhuman longings; and thus, the continual recurrence of struggle and at least partial resolution, the drive toward conquest or metamorphosis, destruction and renewal; and the ever-present tension between denial and disclosure through a distorted portrayal of nature as purposeful, prescriptive, and ritualistic, qualities which indicate the devious psychic routes of instinctual drives.

Yeats's whole mythical system is built upon conflict: in the beginning "the struggle of the dream with the world"; later "the con-

344

flict of opposites," the being "struggling with the Body of Fate"; and throughout, the contest with decay and mortality. Love in his poetry is sometimes identified with a mythical conception of perfection; as such it is portrayed as a symbolic conquest of death, a force that emerges from the unconscious mind in the form of a dancing girl of perfect beauty, like Helen of Troy. Untainted by mortality, however, she is also inhuman. In later and more profound mythical symbols, love is depicted as struggling in an uneasy union with death. In "Her Vision in the Wood," for example, the speaker, like Yeats himself, employs traditional myth as the basis of her "vision," an exalted narrative of stylized grief and ritual worship, which finally reveals the very reality it would deny: the violence and suffering inherent in human love and the conquest of love by death. Yeats's *A Vision* is a myth apparently created to control time and history; actually, it accomplished what its creator intended: "I wished for a system of thought that would leave my imagination free to create as it chose and yet make all that it created, or could create, part of one history, and that the soul's."[1]

The psychological revelations contained in Yeats's visionary writings seem to have had little effect on Auden. Commenting on Yeats's *Mythologies* in 1959, he is concerned mainly with Yeats's confusion of the mythical and the religious. Perhaps because such a distinction is important to his own development as a poet and thinker, Auden does not see beneath the surface of Yeats's adaptations of myth. Though he recognizes the important role of myth in Yeats's poetry, he finds "most of Yeats's later writings about his beliefs hard to take." The "visionary system" of *Anima Mundi* merely elicits a "yawn" because Auden "cannot attach any meaning true or false to the words."[2]

For Auden myth, especially the mythical concepts Eros and Thanatos, conveys psychological truth, but ultimately this is insufficient. Yet, as we have seen, Auden never entirely relinquishes myth as a clue to the unconscious; though he insists on the distinction between

[1] *A Vision* (1925), p. xi.
[2] "The Private Life of a Public Man," *The Mid-Century*, No. 4 (October 1959), 8-11.

myth and belief, the psychological revelations of myth, particularly as symbolized in the Freudian Eros, are essential elements in his concept of Agape. In describing what he regards as the "dialectical relation" between Eros and Agape, Auden says Eros is "the basic will to self-actualization without which no creature can exist and Agape is that Eros mutated by Grace, a conversion, not an addition, the Law fulfilled, not the Law destroyed."[3] Auden uses the mythical concept Eros most effectively in the poetry written after his acceptance of Christianity; in these poems it discloses the very qualities of human and external nature which mythical thinking distorts and represses: the narcissistic and destructive aspects of human love expressed in the idealized forms of Cupid and Venus, and the chaos and destruction inherent in the society organized for material production, in which unconscious drives, "like a god or a disease," demand release, no matter how firm the barriers. Unlike Pound and Eliot, Auden does not seek to avoid the unconscious conflict to which myth provides access; if Agape offers him a measure of consolation, a "Law" that fulfills his need for order and purpose, which, he must admit, Eros does not contain, he never relinquishes his mythical quest for greater insight into man.

As we have seen, the quest of *The Waste Land* ends in a passive ritual in which the maimed protagonist, having turned away from man and society, waits for spiritual renewal. Eliot, of course, did not approach myth with the background in psychology or the scientific interest in the human unconscious that is so apparent in all of Auden's poetry. Yet in some of Eliot's major poetry, as in Pound's, we are struck by the many levels of conflict which myth suggests, by the drive of the myth to express inner experience through an objective symbol or persona. In the first edition of *A Vision*, Yeats describes Eliot and Pound as men of Phase 23, "absorbed in some technical research to the entire exclusion of the personal dream." The poets and sculptors of this phase are contrasted with Rodin, "creating his powerful art out of the fragments of those Gates of Hell that he had found himself unable to hold together—images out

[3] "Eros and Agape," p. 757.

of a personal dream, 'the hell of Baudelaire not of Dante,' he had said to Symons." Yeats's sympathies clearly are with those who pursue and depict "the personal dream"; Pound, Eliot, Joyce, and Pirandello, who "eliminate from metaphor the poet's phantasy," seem to him dehumanized.[4]

For both Eliot and Pound the symbol of hell adapted from Dante is, as Yeats indicates, essentially an impersonal one. In Eliot's allusions to Dante's *Inferno*, the tortures of the human soul are viewed in a Christian framework; in Pound's, in a social and economic one. Nonetheless, in Eliot's poetry the hell of Dante and other mythical symbols sometimes reveal more about the "abyss" within man than perhaps Eliot realized. For Pound the myth of the underworld— more often and more significantly Homer's than Dante's—provides his most flamboyant disguise, and for the reader it is a key to the voice beneath it.

In Eliot's "Prufrock" and *The Waste Land*, myth discloses the personal terror and the feelings of impotence and despair which the protagonist objectifies in relation to society and history. Like Yeats and Auden, Eliot is ever aware of the seeds of death within the experience of love, but for Eliot there is no contest between the two; in *The Waste Land*, love retreats before its enemy as the protagonist takes on the role of the passive and maimed mythical king. Perhaps the most significant disclosure of unconscious feelings lies not in the actual myths Eliot uses in *The Waste Land*, but in the way mythical figures merge into each other. Like creatures in a dream, they depict the conflict and suffering of the protagonist and his distaste for the self which is finally defined by all of them. No doubt Yeats was correct in placing Eliot among those who attempted to exclude "the personal dream" from their work; certainly Eliot avoided the deepest psychological revelations of the very myths he employed. The conflicts and terrors that dream reveals, however, and indeed its very methods of condensation and merging, of disguising the self in a variety of forms, are present in his use of myth.

Myth strains against depersonalization even more subtly and force-

[4] *A Vision* (1925), p. 211.

fully in Pound's poetry. I have discussed the way in which the persona of Odysseus expresses Pound's identification with both the dehumanized emotional state and the superhuman power of those who inhabit the mythical realm of the dead. Furthermore, his use of the myths of Eros and other gods of love throughout *The Cantos* discloses the essential hollowness of Pound's (and his commentators) avowals that love is "the permanent element in [his] universe."[5] In much of Pound's poetry love is not only involved with death; it is ultimately infected and destroyed by its influence. In *Hugh Selwyn Mauberley*, the "anaesthesis" of feeling is treated directly, as the creative principle Eros dies within the soul of the protagonist. Throughout *The Cantos*, death is an active force that is inherent in the beautiful but destructive women and goddesses with whom the persona associates and in the entire atmosphere of Hades which he bears with him as he wanders through time. It is in opposition to the "chaos" represented by the female, the "biological process" which ultimately ends life, that the protagonist creates what he believes is a lasting concept of man and history.

In his frequent evocations of Aphrodite, moreover, Pound is as aware of her capacity for destruction—"δεινὰ εἶ, Κύθηρα / terrible in resistance" (Canto LXXIX)—as he is of her creative powers, and his persona identifies with both. In Pound the ambiguous productive drive symbolized by Aphrodite and other gods of love apparently produces little inner conflict. His superhuman persona takes on the energy and inventiveness of these gods along with their capacity to destroy; as they support his fantasies of his own omnipotence, they encourage the rage he vents on man and history. The mere appearance of Aphrodite in *The Cantos* is hardly evidence of "an outflowing of love."[6] One of the few remnants of conflict between love and death evident within the persona of *The Cantos* is expressed in his plaintive appeal to the Sibyl for release from Erebus, "from the dulled edge beyond pain." In Pound's poetry Thanatos won an early victory over Eros; in Eliot's the conflict is allayed through a religious

[5] George Dekker, *The Cantos of Ezra Pound*, p. 77. See also Guy Davenport, "Persephone's Ezra," pp. 187-88.

[6] George Dekker, *The Cantos of Ezra Pound*, p. 77.

solution; in Yeats's and in Auden's the continual war is intrinsic to the vision and the creation.

Employing myth to express profound and even unconscious levels of thought and feeling, the poet extends the boundaries of his own and his reader's inner experience. His communication with the reader through allusion to or depiction of the stylized, the extraordinary, and the supernatural suggests the ancient origins of art in magic.[7] This is especially true when poets use myth in conjunction with ritual effects. The incantations, prophecies, prayers, invocations, and other adaptations of ritual by the poets considered in this book all indicate an attempt to extend the boundaries of poetry itself. The essential components of rite—symbolic action, such as ritual dance, murder and replacement, the descent into the underworld, the quest; prescribed forms, such as ritual questions, chants, stylized appeals to a deity; identification of the participant with symbols of super-human power, such as sacred objects, natural phenomena, or gods—are used by all these poets to suggest that in the role of magician, hero, initiate, disciple, or preacher, each of them involves the reader in an emotional and spiritual drama. Reacting to the religious skepticism that was perhaps the most significant intellectual result of the technological revolution of the early twentieth century, to political conflict, wars, economic disasters, and vast cultural and social change, and all too aware that "poetry makes nothing happen," these poets use rite either as a symbolic expression of their unique power or as a means of transcending the experience they cannot influence.

Both Yeats and Eliot use dance as a symbolic enactment of a yearning for immortality. Yeats emphasizes movement, which enacts the "complexities" of the dancer's feelings; his awareness of time and his vision of immortality are expressed in the sound and rhythm of intense and rapid motion. For Eliot, dance movement is significant principally because it exposes the "still point," the motionless silence that foreshadows eternity. In movement and stillness these poets suggest the possibility of transcendence: in a depiction of ritual movement Yeats resolves the unendurable conflict between the pressure of

---

[7] See Freud's *Totem and Taboo*, SE xiii, 90.

time and the longing for immortality; Eliot himself becomes an initiate in a rite of "self-sacrifice" and a vision of the infinite. In many poems, Yeats uses ritual effects as an assertion and an illustration of the power of art to unify disparate experiences and ambivalent feelings and to arrest the destruction of time. For Eliot, ritual provides an aesthetic means of expressing a religious vision; in his poetry, adaptations of both pagan and Christian rites enact the persona's quest for meaning and permanence in the universe; his doubt and suffering are depicted as penitential and sacrificial acts in the drama of achieving faith.

Yeats's vision of permanence is often fulfilled through the poem itself; in Eliot's poetry, rite asserts the power of faith to transcend the limits of art, time, and history; in *The Cantos* of Pound, rite creates the superhuman power and knowledge of the persona, who is initiate, priest, hero, and god. Engaged in a perpetual conflict with the contemporary world, the persona of *The Cantos* asserts control over time and events through invocation of superhuman mythical figures and identification with their attributes and experiences. He conducts and participates in rites of renewal, and he assumes the role of a deity in a universe that he establishes and rules. It is from the perspective of a superhuman being formed in continual rites of death and resurrection that he judges the errors and crimes of history.

Auden's ritual effects are also related to his concern with the limitations of man as they are reflected in past and present history, but while he employs rite to uncover the "sacred" in man and nature, he also exposes dangerous fantasies of omnipotence as unacknowledged instinctual drives conveyed in ritual form. In his early poetry, skeptical of orthodox religion, he nonetheless uses prophecy and prayer in an effort to discover some principle of order in a world consumed by war, hunger, and dictatorship. Many of Auden's early poems end in secular prayers which seem to demand some power in the universe—within man or nature—that can judge and order human events more justly than man has done in the past. Only after his conversion to Christianity do Auden's rites concentrate on the limitations of man, exposing a basis of rite itself as a craving for powers of control which contradict the nature of mortality. Aware that rite, like myth, reveals unconscious desires and needs, in his rites of homage, Auden opens the way to a heightened perception of the hidden beauty and power that exist within the limits of the finite. Eliot uses rite to convey the stillness of the infinite, Auden to create an intense silence in which the reader can listen to the sounds of history. In many of Yeats's later poems, ritual effects intensify the contrast between an ideal of permanence and actual decay, between the traditional "hero" and the current "demagogue"; both his and Auden's "verbal rites" probe the nature of the human soul that demands an idealized image of itself and creation.

Though history seems an inhospitable area for myth, both historians and poets have used mythical allusions and structures in describing, analyzing, and interpreting historical data and events. Paradoxically, the very distortions of myth often disclose motivations and attitudes unapparent in the factual details of man's social and political life, and poets use myth as a means of asserting control over the mass of "real" occurrences which appear formless and often inexplicable. Yeats, Pound, Eliot, and Auden all use myth as explorers in history; they repeatedly set out to discover causes, patterns, or laws that exist in human society and determine its conduct. Through the myths they choose and construct, and through their adaptations of the distortions of myth to the realities of history, they sometimes enlarge the area of history itself, indicating the operation of both conscious and instinctual human drives within its boundaries. Furthermore, they always disclose the nature of their own response to the "primary world" and its inevitable connection with the "secondary world" of their own art.

Both Yeats and Pound impose a mythical pattern on past and present events. Yeats views civilization as a tragic protagonist in a symbolic drama, and history as the cyclic expression of the "antinomies" of the universe and man's nature. In *A Vision*, he constructs a scheme which accounts for the perennial operation of conflict in history and explains it as a law of existence: history for Yeats includes reality and illusion, objectivity and subjectivity; within its framework of determined events there is, however, the possibility of individual freedom, for "our inner world of desire and imagination" (p. 73) constantly interacts with the objective, external world.

Yeats's mythical and symbolic view focuses intensely on the cultural details that characterize a nation and on the signs of change and decay that mark the end of an era, but it also emphasizes his rather narrow, anachronistic approach to history, especially to the political upheaval and social changes of his own period. In *A Vision*, particularly in the section "Dove or Swan," his analysis of western history from 2000 B.C. to the present can hardly be considered a balanced factual account of historical events, but as he traces various phases of Greek, Roman, and Byzantine history in relation to his moving wheels and gyres, he does illuminate the art, religion, and philosophical concepts of the ancient world. His concentration on the details that illustrate his thesis, "Each age unwinds the thread another age had wound" (p. 270), results in an extraordinarily sensitive interpretation of the way in which classical, Alexandrian, and early Christian philosophy, sculpture, and painting convey the inner life of the civilizations in which they were created.

However, Yeats's personal aesthetic conception of historical events sometimes emphasizes his aristocratic bias and his abhorrence of all that he regarded as Philistine, obscuring his view of what he calls the "rich experience" of history. In "Nineteen Hundred and Nineteen," for example, his contempt for "the multitude," whom he caricatures as "the mockers" of all that is noble and heroic, is supported by his cyclic notion of inevitable decadence before rebirth. Much later, in *On the Boiler*, he becomes so involved in the drama of the disintegration of civilization that he dismisses many of its protagonists as "the mere multitude" which "is everywhere with its empty photographic eyes."[8] Yet in "Nineteen Hundred and Nineteen," as well as in "Meditations in Time of Civil War" and other poems dealing with Ireland, the descriptions of destruction and terror, which also reflect his mythical system, reveal historical details of human involvement, conflict, and suffering. The "widening gyre" of "The Second Coming" vividly expresses the historical reality of an age fearful of its own impulse to effect violent and anarchic change.

[8] *On the Boiler*, p. 24.

Yeats's symbolic structure of figures, motives, and events depicts a personal adaptation to what he regards as the tragedy of history, in which inner response is always present in external reality; it is this construction of experience that Yeats considers a heritage for the civilizations he foresees as continually reborn.

Pound's approach to history is also a personal one, but, unlike Yeats, he assumes an objective stance. The highly idiosyncratic view he takes of history is revealed, almost in spite of himself, through his fusion of traditional myth and the data of history to establish a mythical realm as a moral example. He is determined to create gods and dogma for the culture he considers non-existent without them. Though the "vast design" of Yeats's *A Vision* is admittedly his own creation, it does provide the reader with recognizable "geometrical diagrams" (p. 73) for the poet's speculations on history. The wheels and gyres, the primary and antithetical cones, like the form of a drama or a poem, establish the framework and limits of the poet's vision. Pound's "ideograms," however, allow for an unlimited scope and arrangement of historical and mythical events. Though he describes the ideogrammic method as a "scientific one,"[9] Pound uses it to create a personal mythical structure through which he juxtaposes his own examples of good and evil, productivity and destruction, past and present.

Pound uses Greek myth in conjunction with Italian Renaissance, English, Chinese, and American history to construct a pseudo-historical framework for a personal vision of society, which is essentially a primitive one. Though he considers ancient culture—western and Chinese—indispensable, as Cleanthes' "Hymn to Zeus" was "part of Adams' paideuma," he does not believe that man living in the present world can absorb the heritage of classical history and myth. Instead, this "paideuma" provides what Pound would call the "forma" for his own vision of a society controlled by ritual and dogma, and guided by the economic principles and political wisdom of an Odysseus, a Kung, or Pound's version of a modern equivalent.

Eliot and Auden approach history through more traditional mythical patterns. Though both these poets finally rely on a Christian view

[9] *ABC of Reading* (Norfolk, Connecticut, n.d.), pp. 20-21.

of temporal reality, their interpretations of Christian myth in relation to history express very different attitudes toward man and society. There is, however, one important similarity: Eliot and Auden both elucidate Christianity as a historical phenomenon. They depict its appearance in history—in time, and in a particular era of man's existence, filling his psychological and spiritual need.

In Eliot's poetry, classical myth and legend reveal the continuous and fruitless violence of man's history: its "Triumphal March" leads nowhere. Like Yeats, Eliot regards secular history as cyclic, but for him observation of the recurrence of seasons and lives provides neither insight nor control. Only the "timeless moments" within the cycle of time illuminate historical reality. The "Choruses from 'The Rock'" contain his most explicit description of the cyclic movement of temporal history, barren except for the essential stillness of eternity and the presence of "Love," which is "itself unmoving." In "Choruses from 'The Rock,'" he places the Incarnation within history itself, or "what we call history," and shows how men "struggled in torment towards GOD" until the "predetermined moment . . . not out of time, but in time, . . . transecting, bisecting the world of time," gave "meaning" to time and history.

Auden is even more specific and detailed in his depiction of the Incarnation and crucifixion as climactic events in history, occurring as challenge and hope within material creation. Perhaps because Auden's religious convictions reflect his long struggle to discover a psychological basis of social regeneration, his allusions to Christian myth and dogma are more deeply rooted in secular history than are Eliot's. If for Auden the "Real" is "Absurd," it can be discovered and experienced only in the world of the temporal. In the silence created by his goddess of history, he does not expect affirmation of the eternal; he tries to catch the "decisive sound" of men and events, their unique and "sacred" quality.

Throughout Auden's poetry one can trace his concern with "the Myth and the Law"[10] of personal and social history, which for him are always related. In the thirties and early forties, he adopted the Freudian Eros as the myth that could define social and economic law

[10] "Eros and Agape," p. 757.

operating in contemporary history. His poetry of this period reveals remarkable insight into its economic and political struggles and into the personal—sometimes unconscious—attitudes and conflicts he has illuminated as forces in and products of history. Even his quest for spiritual fulfillment of psychological law in the ideal principle Agape is depicted in his poetry as determined by historical necessity. Christian myth, like scientific myth, has served Auden as a clue to the role of the unique occurrence within the pattern or law of history. The Muse of his later poetry, Clio, is described from her "photo," which the poet has seen "in the papers." It is to her "eyes" that the poet looks for "recognition." Yeats's mythical scheme could reveal only "empty photographic eyes" in the "multitude"; Auden demands and creates from the same source a goddess who discloses the unique fact and the particular quality of current history.

IN the work of Yeats, Pound, Eliot, and Auden, myth unites individual with general experience, connecting the apparently incidental to characteristic forms or patterns of human feeling and conduct. Thus, personal and historical conflict are related as they are conveyed in mythical allusions or structures; individual loneliness and fantasy are exposed in ritual observance of the supernatural and the infinite. Though each of these poets uses myth to express his unique experience and to create his own voice and tone, it can be said that in many respects their work illustrates general functions of myth in twentieth-century poetry. Certainly, in a great deal of this poetry myth depicts the inner conflict or despair resulting from the loss of traditional values, and relates such experience to the objective reality of past and contemporary history. Furthermore, mythical figures such as Demeter (or some version of a fertility goddess), Odysseus, Leda, Helen, Narcissus, Aphrodite, and Eros, and places such as legendary Troy, the Cretan labyrinth, and the regions of the underworld, which are employed so frequently as image and symbol in the poetry of this century, provide a degree of recognition and association for the most idiosyncratic and even bizarre revelations. A brief survey, which must

355

omit far more examples than it can include, will indicate that classical myth functions as a major aesthetic device in the work of many twentieth-century poets besides those already discussed; poets as different as Robert Graves, Edwin Muir, George Barker, Conrad Aiken, John Crowe Ransom, Allen Tate, Robert Penn Warren, Robert Lowell, and W. S. Merwin use myth as a common language which adapts to each writer's unique consciousness of suffering, conflict, love, and death. In their poetry, myth sometimes discloses feelings of isolation in and revulsion from twentieth-century society, but it also relates the individual response to the history of man's inner experience.

Like Auden, Robert Graves in his early work reveals his involvement in psychoanalytic theory and makes a conscious effort to use "emotional conflict"[11] and dreams as the material of poetry, but Graves's approach to what he calls "poetic psychology"[12] in his early writings is at once more clinical and more personal than Auden's. In his subtitle for *On English Poetry*, his first critical work, published in 1922, he describes it as "an Irregular Approach to the Psychology of This Art, From Evidence Mainly Subjective," and in *Poetic Unreason and Other Studies*, which appeared three years later, he says that poetry enables the poet "to be rid of the conflicts between his sub-personalities," and for the reader it acts "as a physician of his mental disorders."[13] Whereas Auden is concerned with the social function of psychology and art, in his early poetry assuming the role of physician who merges these two disciplines to cure the sickness of society, Graves sees them primarily as personal therapeutic instruments for the emotional problems of the poet and his reader.

Writing about this period many years later in *The Common Asphodel*, Graves describes himself as a "neurasthetic . . . interested in the newly expounded Freudian theory," but he could accept this theory, which he obviously oversimplified, only "when presented with English reserve and common sense by W.H.R. Rivers, who did not regard sex as the sole impulse in dream-making or assume that

[11] Robert Graves, *On English Poetry* (London, 1922), p. 18.
[12] "Author's Note," *Poetic Unreason and Other Studies* (London, 1925).
[13] *ibid.*, p. 2.

dream-symbols are constant."[14] For Graves the application of Rivers' psychoanalytic method to the creation of poetry resulted in an effort to imitate "rhythmic dream utterance,"[15] expressing in symbolic and mythical form his own unconscious conflicts.

Such poems as "The Bedpost," "Outlaws," "Rocky Acres," and "The Pier-Glass," the last three of which Graves has retained in as late a volume as the *Collected Poems* of 1966, deal with unconscious fear, sexual conflict, aggression, and violence, hidden beneath the surface of daily life. In "Outlaws,"[16] as in many poems of this period, Graves, like Auden, uses "gods" and "ghosts" as generalized mythical figures which suggest the unconscious motives that lurk beneath man's decisions and acts. The poem, first published in *Country Sentiment* (1920), is both a warning to the poet and his reader against the dark forces within man and the universe and a prophecy of Graves's later worship of such forces symbolized in the many ancient and primitive deities merged in the figure of the White Goddess. The "outlaws" are

> Old gods, tamed to silence, there
> In the wet woods they lurk,
> Greedy of human stuff to snare
> In nets of murk.

Graves warns himself and the reader, "Look up, else your eye will drown / In a moving sea of black"; and again,

> Look up, else your feet will stray
> Into that ambuscade
> Where spider-like they trap their prey
> With webs of shade.

Yet his very admonition conveys his fascination with and awe of the dark powers, and he seems to lament modern man's avoidance of

---

[14] *The Common Asphodel, Collected Essays on Poetry, 1922-1949* (London, 1949), p. vii.

[15] *On English Poetry,* p. 20.

[16] Unless otherwise noted, all quotations from Graves's poetry are taken from *Collected Poems 1966* (New York, 1966).

the ancient gods, which is a denial of an intrinsic part of his own humanity:

> For though creeds whirl away in dust,
> Faith dies and men forget,
> These agèd gods of power and lust
> Cling to life yet—.

These "Proud gods" may now live with "ghosts and ghouls," but, though they are "humbled, sunk so low," the "power and lust" which they symbolize are perennial threats to man. In this poem Graves moves from fear to worship, from the admonition, "Look up" to the nostalgic remembrance of a time when ancient gods "spoke with thunder once at noon / To prostrate kings. . . ."

Even in this early stage of his career, when he regards poetry as primarily therapeutic, his image of the poet is that of a "highly developed witch doctor" and he is concerned with preserving the magical origins of poetry,[17] a theme of much of his later writings. Though the fear of hidden lust and violence and the awe of projected deities who symbolize them expressed in "Outlaws" recur in other early poems of Graves, he does not explore the psychological connection between such ambivalent feelings. He is content to record dream and nightmare, to narrate what the conscious mind regards as "taboo."[18] Throughout the 1920s and 1930s, Graves uses both general and specific mythical figures and narratives to express the suffering and desolation caused by unconscious drives. In such poems as "The Succubus," "Leda," and "Ulysses," he conveys his horror at his own feelings of lust through myths of bizarre and violent sexual experience. "The Succubus" is almost a clinical description of a nightmare, but the last line: "Yet is the fancy grosser than your lusts were gross?" expresses the poet's shame and despair at this revelation of his own desires. If Graves, in writing his "Leda," was aware of Yeats's "Leda and the Swan," he was certainly not influenced by that poem's depiction of a ritual union of violence and tenderness, its celebration of creation from antithetical elements in the universe. Graves's "Leda" describes the "beastliest" qualities of sexual union

[17] *On English Poetry*, pp. 19-20.   [18] *ibid.*, p. 20.

and the resultant pregnancy "Of bawdry, murder and deceit." For him the mythical and ritual rape of Leda suggests neither knowledge nor fruitful creation. Instead, it enacts the "horror" of sexual compulsion; both Leda and the "god" are victims of their own desires. Graves's "Ulysses" is also a victim. The hero's mythical adventures and conquests are all interpreted as encounters with his own lust: the "much-tossed Ulysses" for Graves is essentially the "love-tossed" male, compelled to enact experience he cannot control.

It was not until 1944 that Graves's preoccupation with his own drives and conflicts and his projection of these on the "old gods" who rule the natural and instinctual realm were unified in a religious system. In mid-career he created a mythical structure centered around worship of the White Goddess, based on Greek, Celtic, and Welsh myths which record the power of ancient female deities, and in poem after poem he continues to celebrate a concept which for him at least unites fear and awe, love and hate, destruction and permanence. Like Yeats in *A Vision*, Graves in *The White Goddess* imposed his own conception on traditional myth and ritual gathered from a multitude of sources, and constructed a mythical framework for some of his most important poems. Both *A Vision* and *The White Goddess* present history through a pattern which provides for antithesis, regeneration, and transcendence, and both describe a deity who symbolizes inner or psychic experience. Both Yeats and Graves, seeking to understand temporal reality in relation to recurrent experience, rely on "trance" and vision,[19] and the suspension of ordinary time in dream (*The White Goddess*, p. 377). Though Graves writes scornfully of Yeats's use of myth,[20] he seems to be imitating Yeats's attempt to control both external events and inner experience through the imposition of a mythical system which is the basis of much of his poetry.

[19] See *The White Goddess*, rev. ed. (New York, 1958), p. 385ff. All quotations from *The White Goddess* are from this edition.

[20] "These Be Your Gods, O Israel!" *The Crowning Privilege, Collected Essays on Poetry* (New York, 1956), pp. 123-24. In the same essay, with incredible insensitivity to their aims, methods, and even their real limitations, Graves also denounces Eliot, Pound, and Auden; though he is hardly enthusiastic about Dylan Thomas, he is more restrained in his judgment of him.

It is unnecessary to dwell on the obvious differences between *A Vision* and *The White Goddess*: Yeats's concentration on the cyclic history of the world and Graves's on the history of a group of myths and rituals which he interprets as expressing a single theme, or Yeats's effort to analyze and describe human psychological types and Graves's "obsession" (a word he himself uses[21]) with divinity. The most important difference, though less obvious, provides an essential clue to the ways in which both men's mythical systems function in their poetry. Yeats, as we have seen, concludes *A Vision* by questioning the entire structure; the unconscious knowledge released through its mythical order freed him to accept the chaos of contemporary history and the limitations of mortal life. Graves insists that his goddess is to be worshiped, not questioned or analyzed;[22] he bitterly attacks not only the sympathetic critic who attempts to explain *The White Goddess* in rational terms but the psychoanalytic theory on which this analysis is based.

Randall Jarrell convincingly demonstrates that in *The White Goddess* "Graves' world-picture is a projection upon the universe of his own unconscious, of the compulsively repeated situation in which, alone, it is able to find satisfaction"; furthermore, he says, "this world-picture is one familiar, in structure and in much detail, in the fantasies of children and neurotics, in dreams, in fairy-tales and, of course, in the myths and symbols of savages and of earlier cultures." Jarrell suggests that "details of case-histories, much of Freud's theoretical analysis are . . . specifically illuminating about Graves' myth," and that Jung's discussion of "the *persona* and *anima*, and what happens when a man projects this *anima* upon the world and

[21] "The White Goddess," *A Lecture for the Y.M.H.A. Center, New York,* February 9, 1957, 5 *Pens in Hand* (New York, 1958), p. 54.

[22] For a comparison of *A Vision* and *The White Goddess* from a somewhat different point of view, see Daniel Hoffman, *Barbarous Knowledge*, pp. 14-15, 221. Hoffman suggests that Yeats and Graves "each had to make for himself the usable tradition that his culture had failed fully to provide" (p. 15). Though Hoffman deals only briefly with *A Vision*, he discusses *The White Goddess* at some length, concluding that "the great value of this mythic pattern to Graves is that it elevates to divine, eternal, and archetypal significance the experience of love as it may be known to the individual sensibility" (p. 211).

identifies himself with it" describes the nature of Graves's conception and method. The main point of Jarrell's analysis is that the White Goddess is an idealized mother figure—"Mother-Mistress-Muse"—and, since she is a projection of the unconscious fears and wishes of the poet, she is finally Graves himself: *"There is only one Goddess, and Graves is her prophet—and isn't the prophet of the White Goddess the nearest thing to the White Goddess?"*[23]

It would seem difficult to deny the accuracy of Jarrell's analysis of the essential motivation for the creation of *The White Goddess* and of the personal and idiosyncratic quality that dominates it, and most critics of Graves's work have accepted and drawn upon his conclusions. Graves himself, however, in a lecture on the White Goddess objected strongly to Jarrell's comments and launched an attack on psychoanalysis itself,[24] a position that at first seems surprising in a poet who for many years claimed that he was adapting the theory and method of psychoanalysis to poetry. Yet, in the light of his early need to modify Freudian theory with "English reserve" and his unwillingness or inability to apprehend the connection between his fear of unconscious desires and his awe of the primitive deities he himself evoked, such a reaction is not unexpected. Graves's insistence that his "world picture" in *The White Goddess* "is not a psychological one"[25] must be taken seriously, for his "grammar of poetic myth" does not aim at psychological revelation; its purpose is to promote religious devotion.

The thesis of *The White Goddess* is "that the language of poetic myth anciently current in the Mediterranean and Northern Europe was a magical language bound up with popular religious ceremonies in honour of the Moon-goddess, or Muse, . . . and that this remains the language of true poetry" (p. vi). Graves is convinced, moreover, that the "function of poetry is religious invocation of the Muse" (p. x). Although, in *The White Goddess*, Graves uses historical evidence chiefly to argue that the creation of "true" poetry requires religious

[23] "Graves and the White Goddess," Part II, *The Yale Review*, XLV, No. 3 (March 1956), 474-77.
[24] "The White Goddess," *5 Pens in Hand*, pp. 61-62, 69.
[25] *ibid.*, p. 62.

dedication, in defending that work, he traces the history of matriarchal religions as a background for speculation on the possibility
that "the present technological civilization," which he deplores, will
either collapse or reach "the stage of perfect nuclear automation";
in any case, he says, the changes that take place "will obviously be
reflected in religious dogma. The new Heaven may house two gods
and a goddess," or, from Graves's point of view a preferable arrangement, "two goddesses, one of intuition, one of fertility, aided by a
technological male god of the Vulcan type."[26]

In both his prose and poetry related to *The White Goddess*,
Graves attempts to restore to myth functions it has long since outgrown. He has described himself as an initiate in a private cult of
worship, and he justifies his conversion of fear into awe on the basis
of ancient mythical narrative and ritual practice. Furthermore, like all
cultists, he judges others—in this case poets—on the basis of their
willingness to accept the emotional satisfactions and taboos of the
initiate. As is typical of the participant in ritual worship, he seeks to
control his inner fears and desires, and the precarious conditions of
all mortal life, by creating a deity who encompasses the cruelty and
rage he cannot accept in himself and the superhuman gentleness
and strength he has vainly sought in others.

The actual experience of the poet or reader invoking the goddess
involves fear and awe (*The White Goddess*, p. 12):

> The test of a poet's vision, one might say, is the accuracy of his
> portrayal of the White Goddess and of the island over which she
> rules. The reason why the hairs stand on end, the eyes water,
> the throat is constricted, the skin crawls and a shiver runs down
> the spine when one writes or reads a true poem is that a true
> poem is necessarily an invocation of the White Goddess or Muse,
> the Mother of All Living, the ancient power of fright and lust—
> the female spider or the queen-bee whose embrace is death.

The "island" of the White Goddess, like Auden's mythical island,
suggests isolation within the ambivalence of the unconscious mind,

[26] *ibid.*, pp. 64-66.

but Auden's admonition, "And we rebuild our cities, not dream of islands," would be lost on Graves; from his point of view, man's narcissism—his terror of his own limitations and his fantasies of magical powers—is to be neither revealed nor conquered, only projected in the form of worship. The fearful "spider-like" gods of "Outlaws" are now revered in the form of a goddess characterized as "the female spider or the queen-bee." Moreover, she is at the same time the embodiment of all that is secret, beautiful, and productive in the female; thus she is the Muse, the source of creativity, which conquers the principle of death, which she also contains.

Graves believes that for the poet who worships the White Goddess the "main theme of poetry is, properly, the relations of man and woman" (*The White Goddess*, p. 501), and much of the poetry Graves has written since his preoccupation with matriarchal myth deals with this subject. Yet his love poetry has a curious coldness. No woman he writes of can measure up to his goddess, and the poet is always aware of the disparity between his ideal and the actual female. Graves has spoken directly of this distinction, one that is implicit in much of his love poetry. In fact, the poem "In Her Praise" can be described as a poetic restatement of a point he makes in the lecture on the White Goddess mentioned above, in which he speaks of her influence over actual women:

> But the real, perpetually obsessed Muse-poet makes a distinction between the Goddess as revealed in the supreme power, glory, wisdom and love of woman, and the individual woman in whom the Goddess may take up residence for a month, a year, seven years, or even longer. The Goddess abides; and it may be that he will again have knowledge of her through his experience of another woman.[27]

The poet of "In Her Praise" thinks of "each new lovely woman" as merely a temporary receptacle for his fantasies of "majesty." She can never retain her exalted role for long, and he speaks of her with some condescension since eventually she must reveal her true nature,

[27] *ibid.*, p. 69.

"groping back to humankind." The value of women, as Graves sees it, is to inspire the poet to visions of his own immortal powers of insight and creation:

> Nevertheless they call you to live on
> To parley with the pure, oracular dead,
> To hear the wild pack whimpering overhead,
> To watch the moon tugging at her cold tides.
> Woman is mortal woman. She abides.

The goddess contains and exceeds all women, and for Graves the beloved woman is at best a symbol of the goddess' power to exalt and destroy.

Graves's "Goddess" poems are most effective when he imitates and adapts the "narrative shorthand of ritual mime"—his definition of "true myth" in his "Introduction" to *The Greek Myths*[28]—in order to evoke her as a creative power. In such poems as "The White Goddess," "Return of the Goddess," "The Sirens' Welcome to Cronos," "Darien," and "To Juan at the Winter Solstice," Graves uses mythical allusion and narrative, ritual questions, and incantatory effects to convey the atmosphere of a mysterious, self-contained realm in which the poet participates in extraordinary power and experience.

In "Return of the Goddess," first printed in order to "placate her" in *The White Goddess* (p. 540) and retained in his volumes of *Collected Poems*, he describes her as "A gaunt red-leggèd crane," one of the many forms in which she appears, investing the natural order with her magic powers. "Darien" deals directly with the poet's relation to the goddess as his beloved:

> It is a poet's privilege and fate
> To fall enamoured of the one Muse
> Who variously haunts this island earth.

The whole earth is here the island of the unconscious mind, and the poet's total dedication is to the power and productivity symbolized in the goddess' role as Aphrodite, who controls the cycle of love, creation, death, and replacement.

---

[28] *The Greek Myths*, 2 vols., Penguin Books (Baltimore, 1955), I, 10.

This theme is developed more fully in "To Juan at the Winter Solstice," in which Graves states explicitly:

> There is one story and one story only
> That will prove worth your telling,

instructing his son in the traditional lore to prepare him for a mythical role, like that of the "learned bard" or the "gifted child" of the *Mabinogion*. In either form he will tell of the goddess' magical influence on nature and man: he is to be a discoverer of her secrets, and as such he will write in praise and worship. Like a priest addressing an initiate, the poet poses a series of ritual questions, the implied positive answers to which are an acceptance of transcendent knowledge and control:

> Is it of trees you tell, their months and virtues,
> Of strange beasts that beset you,
> Of birds that croak at you the Triple will?
> Or of the Zodiac and how slow it turns
> Below the Boreal Crown,
> Prison of all true kings that ever reigned?

> [* * *]

> Or is it of the Virgin's silver beauty,
> All fish below the thighs?
> She in her left hand bears a leafy quince;
> When with her right she crooks a finger, smiling,
> How may the King hold back?
> Royally then he barters life for love.

> Or of the undying snake from chaos hatched,
> Whose coils contain the ocean,
> Into whose chops with naked sword he springs,
> Then in black water, tangled by the reeds,
> Battles three days and nights,
> To be spewed up beside her scalloped shore?

This series of questions suggests that the poet as disciple must identify emotionally with "each new victim" of the goddess—the succession of solar heroes who are both loved and destroyed by her, as they appear in various forms, such as Osiris, Gilgamesh, or Jason. Once the initiate has accepted the complex and difficult nature of his role, he is given his final instructions:

> Dwell on her graciousness, dwell on her smiling,
> Do not forget what flowers
> The great boar trampled down in ivy time.
> Her brow was creamy as the crested wave,
> Her sea-grey eyes were wild
> But nothing promised that is not performed.

In accepting the goddess totally—even the inevitable destruction he must face at her hands—the initiate transcends death, for he achieves the immortality of the gods and heroes who merge with and absorb her power. His identity is enlarged to include his successor; "the God of the Waning Year" and the "God of the Waxing Year" (*The White Goddess*, p. 11) are finally one.

Effective as such poems as "Darien" and "To Juan at the Winter Solstice" are in creating an atmosphere of ritual worship, which the poet restores out of fragments of the archaic past and charges with his own associations, the reader is rarely involved in the experience. Instead he is made to feel that he is an observer of a private transport in which the object of worship is the creative powers of the worshiper. Perhaps the best illustration of the essentially narcissistic quality of Graves's rites is the poem he called "In Dedication" in *The White Goddess*, which has been reprinted under the title "The White Goddess" in his volumes of *Collected Poems* ever since. In the first stanza Graves separates himself from "all sober men" as he declares his allegiance to the goddess:

> All saints revile her, and all sober men
> Ruled by the God Apollo's golden mean—
> In scorn of which we sailed to find her
> In distant regions likeliest to hold her
> Whom we desired above all things to know,
> Sister of the mirage and echo.

Setting out on his mythical journey, the poet indicates its inward direction in the last two lines of this stanza; his entire pilgrimage is centered around a deity who is related to "the mirage and echo." The poet's idealized fantasy and the "echo" of his own inner voice become the objects of a lifelong quest, which leads him deep into the "distant regions" of his own mind. In depicting his journey in the next stanza, Graves says that he sought the goddess "Beyond the cavern of the seven sleepers," referring to the same legend that Yeats does in "On a Picture of a Black Centaur by Edmund Dulac." In this poem Yeats uses the image of the ancient martyrs of Ephesus whose sleep symbolizes their unchanging faith to indicate that the treasures —the "full-flavoured wine"—which he brings forth from his unconscious mind are equally valid and lasting. But, as we have seen, Yeats suggests, not only in this poem but throughout his work, that such rewards come only after terror and conflict, and, most important, with a knowledge of the limits of human life achieved in the "mad abstract dark" of his own soul. For Graves the "cavern of the seven sleepers" is but a stage in his journey; he goes beyond it, seeking a vision of the goddess who is both hideous and splendid, and discovers her not only in the "Green sap of Spring" but "even in November / Rawest of seasons. . . ." Overcome by "her nakedly worn magnificence," he says:

> We forget cruelty and past betrayal,
> Heedless of where the next bright bolt may fall.

The fantasy of immortal presence and beauty obliterates the memory of real "cruelty and past betrayal"; suffering is merged with all experience as the province of the goddess, and is thus given meaning within her divine scheme. What Graves calls his "headstrong and heroic way" is essentially a celebration of his discovery that matriarchal myth can be interpreted as a history and an echo of his own inner experience.

All of Graves's efforts to describe the mysterious presence and the magical influence of his White Goddess cannot disguise the fact that, whatever her remote origins, she is essentially an example of a fairly

common twentieth-century poetic phenomenon: a mythical construction which reflects its creator's application of contemporary anthropological or psychological theory—and sometimes both—to ancient
myth and ritual. The preceding chapters have indicated that other
poets use such mythical constructions to disclose and come to terms
with unconscious drives and fears, or to worship the myths they
themselves recreate. Edwin Muir, who, like Graves and Auden, began by consciously applying psychoanalytic theory to myth and
dream, wavers between a desire for self-knowledge and a yearning
for religious faith, feelings which are revealed and in some respects
unified in his lifelong construction of his "fable" in poetry. Muir's
An Autobiography, like Yeats's *A Vision* and Graves's *The White
Goddess*, is a work of prose which incorporates and explicates the
mythical and legendary background of much of his poetry. He implies as much in the title of his first version of this autobiography,
The Story and the Fable (1940), which he later revised and included
in the extended account of his life published under the title *An Autobiography* in 1954. Muir's discussion of the nature of his autobiography, moreover, indicates a deliberate effort to construct a "fable"
that brings to the surface unconscious elements of his own personality
that are characteristic of all men.

In attempting "to understand human life not as a life of routine
and machinery, but as a fable extending far beyond the experience
given to us by our senses, and our practical reason,"[29] Muir applied
the insights gained from his own psychoanalysis to dream and myth.
Though he says that if he were writing an autobiographical novel, he
would feel more free to reveal "correspondences" between dream and
reality, and could "show how our first intuition of the world expands
into vaster and vaster images, creating a myth which we act almost
without knowing it,"[30] a good portion of *An Autobiography* does in
fact deal with dreams which Muir often interprets in mythical terms.
He goes on to say that "no autobiography can confine itself to conscious life . . . ; sleep, in which we pass a third of our existence, is a

[29] Edwin Muir, *The Story and the Fable* (London, 1940), p. 236.
[30] Edwin Muir, *An Autobiography* (London, 1954), p. 48. All further references to this work are to this edition.

mode of experience, and our dreams a part of reality" (p. 49). Dreams are a primary component of the fable, which Muir regards as the essence of his and all autobiography (p. 49):

> In themselves our conscious lives may not be particularly interesting. But what we are not and can never be, our fable, seems to me inconceivably interesting. I should like to write that fable, but I cannot even live it; and all I could do if I related the outward course of my life would be to show how I have deviated from it; though even that is impossible, since I do not know the fable or anybody who knows it.

The fable is clearly the pattern of man's inner life, which emerges in dream, fantasy, and myth. Muir says he can discern "One or two stages in it," which he identifies as "the age of innocence and the Fall and all the dramatic consequences which issue from the Fall" (p. 49); in his poetry he explores not only these stages but others, unknown to him at this point.

Both in his autobiography—especially in recordings of dream and fantasy—and in his poetry, Muir is preoccupied with the question of how a man can know himself.[31] "Religion," he says, "once supplied that knowledge, but our life is no longer ruled by religion." Nonetheless, just as he conceives certain stages of the fable in religious terms, he regards the possibilities of self-knowledge as based on a concept of immortality: "Yet we know what we are only if we accept some of the hypotheses of religion. Human spirits are understandable only as immortal spirits" (*An Autobiography*, p. 51).

Influenced by Jungian psychology, Muir seeks evidence of immortality in the unconscious mind. Like Yeats and Graves, he employs "trances and visions" (*An Autobiography*, p. 159) in his quest for a knowledge of himself and other men deeper than any that ordinary experience can provide. He records dreams in which, assuming the form of a mythical animal or a hero contesting "fabulous" creatures, he experiences a sensation of immortality or rebirth (pp. 159-67). Though he is aware that these dreams can be interpreted as revealing "naive spiritual vanity," he insists that such a view can be taken

[31] See especially *An Autobiography*, pp. 49-51.

only if one regards the dream as invented by the dreamer: "if it was really invented by me and did not 'come' to me, as I felt at the time it did, and as I still feel: it was not 'I' who dreamt it, but something else which the psychologists call the racial unconscious, and for which there are other names" (p. 164). It is through his conception of this "racial unconscious"—which he regarded as the continuous unconscious experience of man communicated in myth and dream—that Muir finally fulfilled his yearnings for immortal existence. "I realized," he says, "that immortality is not an idea or a belief, but a state of being in which man keeps alive in himself his perception of that boundless union and freedom, which he can faintly apprehend in time, though its consummation lies beyond time." It is a "realization that human life is not fulfilled in our world, but reaches through all eternity" (p. 170). The timeless realm of the unconscious mind —its "freedom" to join past with present experience, fantasies of the supernatural with real figures and occurrences, and to convey a sense of eternal recurrence and "union" in the imagined merging of human personalities, despite their separate existence—is the subject of much of Muir's poetry.

No poet has employed myth with more awareness of its capacity to convey unconscious experience. In fact, many of Muir's poems in which myth figures prominently can be traced directly to the dreams, memories, and fantasies he records in *An Autobiography*. One of his earliest poems based upon myth, "Ballad of Hector in Hades,"[32] is also one of his most effective in transmitting an episode of childhood apparently forgotten but retained in the unconscious and recovered in adulthood, not only as part of his personal past but as an archetypal experience of mankind. In *An Autobiography*, Muir says that this poem "was really a resuscitation of the afternoon when I ran away, in real terror, from another boy as I returned from school." In associating his own experience with Hector's, he interprets it as an enactment of an unconscious feeling released by the actual chase but reflecting a deeper and more general fear, which appears repeatedly in man's dreams. Muir also recalls that his unconscious response to his childhood home on the island of Wyre in Orkney was expressed

[32] *Collected Poems* (New York, 1965). All quotations from Muir's poetry are from this edition.

in a universal fantasy: "The bare landscape of the little island became, without my knowing it, a universal landscape over which Abraham and Moses and Achilles and Ulysses and Tristram and all sorts of pilgrims passed; and Troy was associated with the Castle, a mere green mound, near my father's house" (p. 206).

Like Muir, Hector in the poem recalls the episode of his flight from his enemy from a distance in time and place; in Hades—a common symbol of the unconscious mind—the memory occurs with both the vividness and the elusiveness of "a deadly dream." Muir no doubt was influenced by Homer's comment on the episode: "as in a dream it is of no avail for a man to pursue one who flees from him; the one cannot escape and the other cannot overtake him" (*Iliad*, XXII, 199-201), which itself suggests that the encounter between Hector and Achilles acts out a rage and terror that all men recognize in themselves. Certainly, the Hector of Muir's poem recounts the traditional pursuit as a tale of man's continuous endurance of his own unconscious feelings. Achilles in "Ballad of Hector in Hades" is finally not an actual person but the "shadow" of Hector's own wrath:

> Two shadows racing on the grass,
>> Silent and so near,
> Until his shadow falls on mine.
>> And I am rid of fear.

Muir depicts Achilles' defeat of Hector as a union of pursuer and pursued, which releases Hector from his rage and terror. "The race is ended," he says. Now

> Far away
> I hang and do not care,
> While round bright Troy Achilles whirls
> A corpse with streaming hair.

His own conflicting emotions enacted, he is at peace, while Achilles, who symbolizes the deepest wrath a man can endure, continues to pursue the inevitable course of unconscious hostility and violence. At the end of the poem, Hector is like a man who has awakened and recalls the narrative of an ever-recurring dream; he is no longer involved, only aware that Achilles continually "whirls" in his rage around Troy.

Troy appears frequently in Muir's poetry as the "universal landscape" of man's inevitable fall from a happy and secure state. The protagonist of "Troy" and the speaker of "A Trojan Slave" are not unlike the questioner of "the Fall" in that all look back to an earlier period of legendary happiness. In "The Fall," it is Eden that is the interior landscape; in "Troy" and "A Trojan Slave," the historical city has become a myth in man's memory. A "brave, mad old man" in "Troy" who remains "among the sewers" after the fall of the city lives with his fantasies of the heroic past until he is killed by robbers "seeking treasure / Under Troy's riven roots." The "treasure" that his attackers demand until he dies is clearly the mythical ideal of splendor which the fallen city symbolizes, buried in its roots, but haunting the imagination of both the mad old man, who dreams of restoring it, and those who hope to snatch it from him. In "A Trojan Slave," the speaker, who was taken captive by a Greek, tells of Troy and its heroes "before the fall." He reveals his resentment against the Trojan leaders who did not trust their slaves to fight against the Greeks, and wonders why even now, when he is "an old man," he should still be shaken by "that one regret." The answer, which is contained in his entire speech, is his love of and loyalty to Troy, which even now "Remains, as if in spite, a happy memory." Troy, like Eden, is a stage in the fable of man's inner life; both are ideals from which he has fallen, but they remain in his memory and define his nature.

In Muir's poetry, ancient sites, gods, and other mythical figures seem to be natural components of man's inner life; Muir's equanimity in the face of the most painful, bizarre, or violent stages of his fable is reflected in his mythical reconstructions which, even when they depict sorrow and conflict, express a basic serenity. His poem "The Old Gods" suggests none of the dread or horror of Graves's response to such mythical figures; Muir, imagining a

> Goddess of caverned breast and channelled brow
> And cheeks slow hollowed by millenial tears,

feels only admiration for "thoughts so bountiful and wise" and comfort in the "vast compassion curving like the skies." For him, the ancient past buried in man's soul offers a continuous heritage of beauty and wisdom as well as a record of conflict and suffering.

Even the labyrinth—a frequent image not only in the poems of *The Labyrinth* but throughout Muir's work—while it conveys the devious and frightening ways of the unconscious mind, is depicted as a recurring stage in a symbolic quest for freedom. Like Auden, Muir uses the myth of Theseus' tortuous route through the labyrinth as a symbol of man's continual struggle against the binding terrors of the unconscious mind, which sometimes appear in the most common features of his daily life. "The Labyrinth" is Muir's most detailed treatment of this symbolic contest; the speaker is Theseus who, having emerged from the labyrinth, carries the memory of its terrors with him into the "lovely world." He recalls himself in the labyrinth as like a soul in Hades. Time and motion were suspended as he roamed its passages in the twilight, fearing to meet himself or his ghost at every turn. Now, even in the external world, he sometimes seems to be imprisoned in the maze, and the whole earth seems "a part / Of the great labyrinth." He is caught between conflicting feelings: a conviction of choice—"All roads lie free before you," and a fear that he is forever trapped—

> "No, do not hurry.
> No need to hurry. Haste and delay are equal
> In this one world, for there's no exit, none,
> No place to come to, and you'll end where you are,
> Deep in the centre of the endless maze."

Declaring that he "could not live if this were not illusion," the poet nonetheless accepts the labyrinth as a part of life: "It is a world, perhaps; but there's another." The resolution, like the conflict, emerges from the unconscious mind:

> For once in a dream or trance I saw the gods
> Each sitting on the top of his mountain-isle. . . .

These gods look down upon the world, and find "all permissible, all acceptable," while they exist in eternal peace:

> But they, the gods, as large and bright as clouds,
> Conversed across the sounds in tranquil voices
> High in the sky above the untroubled sea,
> And their eternal dialogue was peace
> Where all these things were woven, and this our life
> Was as a chord deep in that dialogue,
> As easy utterance of harmonious words,
> Spontaneous syllables bodying forth a world.

Within man's unconscious mind, in "dream or trance," there is an image that can free him from the compulsive and violent quest in the labyrinth; the old gods speak of a concept of continual growth and harmony of which man knows only "a chord." Though he accepts the contents of this "eternal dialogue" as "the real world," the speaker has not entirely escaped the maze; he now knows, however, that it is only a part of his being:

> Oh these deceits are strong almost as life.
> Last night I dreamt I was in the labyrinth,
> And woke far on. I did not know the place.

Both Auden and Muir suggest that man can free himself of the imprisonment of the labyrinth only when he identifies with a principle more consistent and more reliable than any individual human life can exemplify. For Auden this is the Christian deity; in his view, man's labyrinth becomes one "of choice" only when he accepts a power beyond that of his own mind. Muir is more ambivalent; the gods in "The Labyrinth" are as much a part of the unconscious as is the labyrinth itself. In poem after poem he returns to this image— the "sweet and terrible labyrinth of longing" ("The Return"), "The haunted labyrinths of the heart" ("The Island")—seeking to overcome the compulsions and terrors of the unconscious by his conviction that man can glimpse a harmony beyond the maze. This harmony is projected on the gods, secure in their vision of recurrent productivity, the continuous life of the universe which exists despite individual conflict and death. Immortality is interpreted as "a state of being" in which the poet identifies his individual life with the history of man as it is recorded in both pagan and Christian myth.

Even in the poems of *One Foot in Eden*, in which the themes and images are mainly Christian, Muir does not take an orthodox religious position. In "Adam's Dream," the fall of man is described as a dream after his "daydream in the Garden." Both the perfection of the first stage of life and the terror and sorrow experienced after the fall are treated in psychological rather than religious terms; in fact, the whole universe transformed by the fall is described as the product of a dream.

"The Killing," a depiction of the violence of the crucifixion, is essentially a commentary on the psychological experience of the observers. Muir describes them as emerging from a labyrinth:

> Zion was bare, her children from their maze
> Sucked by the demon curiosity
> Clean through the gates.

He tries to understand their feelings:

> Yet all grew stale at last,
> Spite, curiosity, envy, hate itself.

and then he explores his own:

> I was a stranger, could not read these people
> Or this outlandish deity. Did a God
> Indeed in dying cross my life that day
> By chance, he on his road and I on mine?

The question with which the poem ends is that of the poet constructing his fable of man's life, which "reaches through all eternity." For him, Christian and pagan myth alike record intense love, loyalty, hate, conflict, fear, and, most important of all, the continuous existence of man, who inherits all the inner experience of the past; but there is no doubt that in Muir's fable classical myth has a much more significant role than any other. He identifies emotionally far more readily with a fallen Trojan than with the fallen Christ.

Like Odysseus, whom he depicts "on the long / And winding road of the world" ("The Return of Odysseus") or on the "treadmill of the turning road" ("Telemachos Remembers"), Muir wanders through the mythical realm of antiquity, curiously at home in the most remote places and at ease in the most bizarre encounters. Both in *An Autobiography* and in his poetry he is explicit on this subject:

> Into thirty centuries born,
> At home in them all but the very last,
> We meet ourselves at every turn
> In the long country of the past.
>
> ("Into Thirty Centuries Born")

It is this long historical and mythical view of experience that convinces Muir that "Time shall cancel time's deceits," and that man's unconscious need for continuity will overcome the destructiveness of the present, the only century in which he cannot feel "at home."

In one of his most powerful poems, "The Horses," Muir imagines the world enduring the effects of "The seven days war," his depiction of atomic destruction as an inversion of the myth of creation. He begins in the language of myth:

> Barely a twelvemonth after
> The seven days war that put the world to sleep
> Late in the evening the strange horses came.

These horses enter a world of death and silence. To those who have survived the war, the horses seem like "fabulous steeds set on an ancient shield." Yet they also serve as animals who "have pulled our ploughs and borne our loads." Patiently, these half-mythical creatures restore for man the natural world he had destroyed and abandoned, for they are a remnant of his "long-lost archaic companionship," a symbol of human values and the continuity of human life. Both Auden in "City Without Walls" and Muir in "The Horses" use myth in constructing an image of a future society created by the barbarism of the atomic age. Auden's myths are hideous ironies, transformed by the mechanized world in which they survive; Muir's remain constant, transforming the destroyed earth and providing "their own Eden." Yet both poets employ ancient myth to reveal the indignity to human life of the values and products of the atomic age; the two poems are not as different as they seem.

In his last poem, "I Have Been Taught," Muir seems to be saying that his fable is complete:

> I have been taught by dreams and fantasies
> Learned from the friendly and the darker phantoms
> And got great knowledge and courtesy from the dead. . . .

He accepts the "phantoms" of the unconscious mind for the wisdom they offer him, but he distinguishes between "that unspending good" of traditional lore and the "sultry labyrinth" which even at the end threatens terror and destruction. Essentially, Muir's fable is completed by his conviction that he has

> drawn at last from time which takes away
> And taking leaves all things in their right place
> An image of forever
> One and whole.

The sense that his own inner life is part of the mythical experience of thirty centuries is for Muir a conquest of time and mortality.

Yeats's "Vision," Pound's Odyssey between earth and Hades, Graves's White Goddess, and Muir's Fable, though vastly different in content, and in the degree of historical or factual reality and the range of experience they encompass, nonetheless serve a similar function in establishing a continual and fairly consistent symbolic framework for the body of their poetry. The concept of Eros operates in the same way in many of Auden's poems, accommodating both acceptance and skepticism, and finally a new interpretation of itself. For many other twentieth-century poets who do not employ a single mythical structure as a pervasive frame of reference, classical myth—often the very mythical persons and narratives which appear in the structures already discussed—is also an essential aesthetic device for exploring and recreating their individual experience and apprehending contemporary man's response to the central questions of his time.

George Barker, for example, like Auden, uses the mythical figures Venus, Eros, and Thanatos, clearly alluding to Freud's "entities," yet they function in his poetry as a highly individual, even personal, mode of expression. Directly related to another mythical character —Narcissus—Eros and Thanatos emerge as the deepest antagonistic forces that together create the tormented priest or prophet who is the speaker of many of Barker's poems. The very titles of some of these poems—"Triumphal Ode Mcmxxxix," "Holy Poems," "O Who will speak from a Womb or a Cloud?" "Secular Elegies," "Sacred Elegies," "The Mnemonic Demigod"[33]—suggest a sacerdotal tone and theme. In these poems and others, the central problem that Barker wrestles with is a common one in twentieth-century poetry and is most fully explored by Auden: the ambiguous nature of love, which is a condition of man's personal and political survival and yet is subject to his narcissism and violence. Barker's approach to this theme is characterized by his continual merging of various realms of experience, personal, sexual, religious, and social, and his constant preoccupation with conflict; unlike Auden, he rarely seems to seek and only occasionally achieves any resolution. Throughout Barker's poetry, the fulfillment of a need for union with a divine and a human presence is threatened by his alienation from both, by his compulsion to struggle against the beloved woman or brother or God, even as he seeks their nurture. In depicting the perennial contest, Barker often combines the role of prophet inspired by a vision of potential salvation and his adversary, ever tempted by self-love, the will to destruction, and death itself.

The adversary appears sometimes as Narcissus: in the poem of that name, absorbing the poet in a compulsive quest for his own image, or in the first of "Holy Poems," speaking, murmuring, and whispering to him of death, or in the sixth of "Cycle of Six Lyrics"—

[33] *Collected Poems 1930 to 1965* (New York, 1965). Unless otherwise indicated, all quotations from Barker's poetry are from this edition.

"Narcissus and the Star"—equated with the devil, "a demon" within the "hot pit." In I of "Holy Poems," Narcissus is a manifestation of the principle of death in the universe, in the guise of self-love:

> Narcissus, embalmed in glass and rivers,
> Speaks to me with the lisp of the tides;
> Murmurs to me late in the summer evenings
> When he goes down with the last fish, whispers:
> "The kiss of doom is death. So deep a kiss,
> No love knows as the hermaphrodite worm:
> With it I lie always at the sex of bliss,
> And this is loss."

Opposed to this self-destruction is "Venus, naked against the face of the day," or even more effective the "gaze of God," which is both externalized as a force of love in the universe and represented as an inner quality, the "God I in me. . . ." In "Holy Poems," as in much of his poetry, Barker imposes the psychological implications of the myth of Narcissus and the Freudian conception of Eros and Thanatos on the traditional Christian contest of the "Siamese monster of Christ and the Devil," viewing his personal conflicts within the context of "the mad tides of the time," and himself tied to the "Andromeda world, fixed to God's rock . . ." (I).

Barker uses classical myth in his poetry to suggest that the infection of love by violence and death, the hell implicit in the promise of eternity, and the conflict ever present in the world around him spring ultimately from the same warring powers in the universe. These exist within God himself, who is described as part of the poet's own nature, or as a beneficent yet threatening figure with whom he merges—Zeus nourishing him as his son Dionysus, whom he will also "smother":

> O God will smother me like a father
> Mothering the son still hanging in his thigh.
> ("Holy Poems" III)

or as "Love," which is involved with yet defies death: *"Who is a god to haunt the tomb but Love?"* ("O Who will speak from a Womb or a Cloud?").

In his "Elegy on Spain," Barker, like Auden, mythicizes the nation, discovering within it the principle of love surviving in the current destruction and slaughter. The poem, though on a political subject, is an intensely personal one. Speaking "to the photograph of a child killed in an air-raid on Barcelona," to whom the poem is dedicated, Barker describes the war in language and imagery that indicate a personal identification with the contending forces of love and death:

> And if I feel your gaze upon me ever,
> I'll wear the robe of blood that love illumines.

Spain itself is depicted as a mythical female figure, involved in a struggle to survive an eternal contest: she is a "sleeping beauty" who "finds her kiss" in "the lips" of the "wounds" of her defenders; she is compared with Venus:

> . . . but Spain shall not drown,
> For grown to a giantess overnight arises,
> Blazes like morning Venus on a bleeding sea,
> She, he, shall stretch her limbs in liberty.

Repeatedly myths of regeneration—"Sirius shall spring up from the kill," "my phoenix who leaves ashes / Flashing on the Guernica tree and the Guadalajara range"—suggest the continuity and the magnitude of the antagonistic forces manifested in the present struggle.

As the prophet who uncovers love and death as the roots of all personal and general experience, and of political conflict and achievement, Barker is most effective in his "Secular Elegies" and "Sacred Elegies." In the "Secular Elegies," death is the dominant principle: it replies to "all future questions" of "history" itself; it exists within the "instinct of the bird" and "governs its acts of war" (I), and it lies within the "islands" of man's pride and narcissism (III). Man dies "of pride" (II) and even "God has just died" (III). All human

activity and exploration seem unconsciously aimed at the discovery of
the principle of death:

> Everything that we touch, sooner or later,—
> The uprooted arbutus hung at the head of the bed,
> The untouchable trophies in the arcanum of nature,
> The dizzy stars, the testes, and the sacred
> Dove—everything that we dissect for data
> Dies as we finger for the heart of the matter.   (IV)

Love as the sexual and reproductive principle exists in the "Secular
Elegies" mainly as the victim of "My mother Nature," the "Gay
corpse, bright skeleton" (V) who determines the death of generations.

In the "Sacred Elegies," the poet, as prophet, rather than merely
enduring the contest, enters it, as an adversary struggling to control
instinctual forces through his voice and language. The instincts become "sacred" entities, expressed in mythical terms: lovers are like
"twin stars," and love itself is a "dominant Venus" (I). Though
death is ever present:

> But who at the kiss, who has not seen, over
> The waterfalling hair at the shoulder of Life
> Death from his own face staring out of a glass?   (IV)

and the poet seeks to expose its existence in "that closet of / The
coffined I" (IV), his confrontation is also at least a partial conquest.
Identifying death and love as Freud's mythical entities:

> Thanatos, thanatos! The labourer, dropping his lever,
> Hides a black letter close to his heart and goes,
> Thanatos, thanatos, home for the day and for ever.
> Crying, from the conch of Venus the emergent Eros
> Breaks free, bursts from the heart of the lover,
> And, at last liberated from the individual,
> The solitary confinement of an evil lease,
> Returns to the perfect. Azrael, Azrael,
> Enters with papers of pardon releasing
> The idiot poet from a biological cell.   (IV)

Barker envisions Eros as separable from "the heart of the lover," and therefore from Thanatos, only when it is freed from individual man's narcissism, possibly only by death itself. Ironically, Eros and the poet it inspires can be released "from a biological cell" by the powers of the poet's insight and voice only when he admits the "errors" or delusions involved in the quest for love. Both God and love reveal their nature "in absence" (V). In the fifth of the "Sacred Elegies," Barker equates Eros with God's love:

> O all things, therefore, in shapes or in senses,
> Know that they exist in the kiss of his Love.

but his image of God is essentially a portrayal of the powers of creation and destruction in the universe. It is this capacity for objectivity that frees the poet to express both his need for a perfect deity and the impossibility of its fulfillment:

> Wheresoever Thou art our agony will find Thee
> Enthroned on the darkest altar of our heartbreak
> Perfect. Beast, brute, bastard. O dog my God!

His image of God is itself a recognition of the operation of Eros and Thanatos within and beyond his own nature and his own existence.

In "Goodman Jacksin and the Angel," the angel demands the same kind of objectivity of Jacksin, ordering him to

> leave the two-headed self
> To peep both ways with a knowing leer;
> The world is still your better half,
> And it's not somewhere else—it's here.

As Jacksin and the angel—which is, of course, his own deepest awareness of life—speak about the dilemma of man, who perpetually wrestles with error, evil, and death, Jacksin seems increasingly to absorb the spiritual courage and knowledge he at first resisted. When the angel describes the brutality inherent in human love, Jacksin responds:

O Minotaur! A maze! A maze!
We only know what we have done
And through what hecatombs have been
When, there before us, we come upon
Bleeding our crying footprints run
Across, ahead. And we have seen
The lost tracks, like a fugitive son,
Of some long forgotten cause.

Like Auden and Muir, Barker uses the image of the labyrinth to portray the confusion and terror implicit in man's unconscious motives and his consequent suffering. These feelings are inevitably expressed in "the antinomy of love," and it is the discovery of the "law" of love which is both the purpose and the outcome of the dialogue. In the angel's conclusion:

Thus Love and Death together got
Under a dark constellation,
And in their fever they forgot
That even Love and Death are not
Exempt from generation.
Then from their open-eyed embrace
Rose the first god that ever was,
With doom in his face.

love and death are united in a mythical principle, a god who symbolizes the nature not of divinity but of man. At the end Jacksin, speaking for the poet and the angel, accepts both the mystery of his existence—the "maze"—and the law which defines but cannot explain or control it.

Barker may interpret Eros and Thanatos as biological or instinctual entities, but he also views them as warring ethical concepts, existing, like good and evil, within a Christian framework. Much of his poetry deals with man's struggle against his "monstrous" and ephemeral role; in *The True Confessions of George Barker*[34] he describes this

[34] *The True Confessions of George Barker* (Denver, 1950).

as not unlike that of the "amoeba" which

> sinks down into the cold slime
> Of Eden as Ego. (p. 32)

Man, as Barker suggests in this and many other poems, lives in fear of "the Abyss," protected only by "self-delusion" (pp. 32-33); the poet sometimes uses his own loneliness and suffering as offerings, negative evidence of God's existence or at least of the human need for a divine presence. Barker's poetry records a personal struggle to forge an image of the self as man and poet out of the very elements that seem to threaten its existence and to deny its efficacy: the inner conflicts which remind him that he is a product of a long history of instinctual warfare, and which alienate him from the divine and human love he seeks.

A more complicated and more interesting depiction of the struggle to define the self as both the product of and the consciousness within a mechanistic universe is established in the poetry of Conrad Aiken, who in 1965, in the "Préface" to *Preludes*, a new printing of *Preludes for Memnon* and *Time in the Rock*,[35] describes these works as "an exploration of the fragmented ego."

Looking back to the period when the poems of these volumes were written,[36] Aiken summarizes what he calls the "psychological predicament" of the twentieth-century poet:

> ... the preludes were planned to be an all-out effort at a probing of the self-in-relation-to-the-world, the formulation of a new *Weltanschauung*. For where was one to go, or what stand upon, now that Freud, on the one hand, and Einstein on the other, with the shadows of Darwin and Nietzsche behind them, had suddenly turned our neat little religious or philosophic systems into something that looked rather alarmingly like pure mathe-

---

[35] *Preludes* (New York, 1966).

[36] *Preludes for Memnon* first appeared in 1931, and *Time in the Rock* in 1936.

matics? Where was poetry to go, and the word of which it was made, and the beliefs that sustained it? And where too was ethics to go and all that had depended on those vanished credos?

The poems of *Preludes for Memnon* and *Time in the Rock*—"separate poems, but constituting a kind of mathematical series"—were intended as both a "statement" of this predicament and a means of overcoming it through definition; these poems indicate the way to *"acceptance"* of the "relationship between being and speaking: of the world and the word." Aiken's resolution of the dilemma of twentieth-century man seeking to replace "the many mythical wonders" he has lost is entirely secular and aesthetic. There is, moreover, no separation for him between the poet's consciousness of his own response to reality and the language in which he expresses his psychological and philosophical attitudes. Finally, his poems are more than an "exploration" and an *"acceptance"* of "the fragmented ego"; they are "a celebration of it and of the extraordinary world in which it *finds* itself, as well."[37]

There is no doubt that *Preludes for Memnon* and *Time in the Rock,* which for Aiken "constitute one unit,"[38] are "the very center of his work, its core, emotionally and intellectually."[39] In the poems of these volumes he comes to grips with the central psychological and aesthetic problems of his time; furthermore, he performs what elsewhere he says is the poet's function: "he succeeds in making real for himself the profound myth of personal existence and experience."[40] The key to *Preludes for Memnon* and *Time in the Rock* lies in Aiken's exploration, use, and creation of myth. Though it would be profitable to trace his use of classical myth throughout his long career, the limits of this survey preclude such a study. Moreover, the two volumes of *Preludes* mark a climax not only in Aiken's poetic development, but also in his adaptation of traditional myth to

[37] "Preface" to the 1966 edition of *Preludes*, pp. v-vi.
[38] *ibid.*, p. v.
[39] Jay Martin, *Conrad Aiken, A Life of His Art* (Princeton, 1962), p. 120.
[40] *Poetry and the Mind of Modern Man*, a radio broadcast for the Voice of America.

his explorations of physical and psychological reality. Thus, I have restricted my discussion to these two major works.

The very title *Preludes for Memnon* indicates the central myth of the series: Memnon is addressed as both the Ethiopian king, who was the son of Tithonus and Eos, and as the Colossus near ancient Thebes in Egypt, which was partially destroyed by an earthquake in 27 B.C. and whose stones thereafter were reported to sing at dawn in honor of Memnon's mother. Memnon is thus the son of ever-recurring Dawn who cannot be rescued from his mortality even by the prayers of his mother, and the ruined Colossus, symbolizing both man's grand aspirations yielding to time and nature and the miracle of song which emerges from the very fissures caused by these destructive forces. In *Preludes for Memnon* Aiken explores man's "consciousness"—one of his most frequent and most important terms—of his vulnerability to the forces of destruction within himself and the universe, and his effort to apprehend these forces in a form which expresses and defines his nature.

In explaining the titles of *Preludes for Memnon* and *Time in the Rock*, Aiken says that he "had intended to call the first volume *Preludes to Attitude*, to indicate its psychological intent," but was dissuaded by his publisher. *Time in the Rock* was to have been entitled *Preludes to Definition*; both these original titles remain as subtitles of some importance. The word *Preludes*, especially in connection with "attitude," suggests not only the "psychological" basis of the poems but their origin in the unconscious mind. These poems reveal the unconscious drives and conflicts which are the "preludes" to the formation of an "attitude" toward reality and a "definition" of man's role in "the new order."[41] Aiken's lifelong interest in psychoanalytic theory, especially the work of Freud, is reflected not only in his desire to discover the unconscious elements that are the prelude to all conceptions of and attitudes toward the human role in the universe, but also in his use of myth to depict various levels of human perception and consciousness.

[41] "Preface" to the 1966 edition of *Preludes*, pp. v-vi.

Preludes for Memnon begins with an exploration of "the abyss of the mind," which continues throughout the series of poems of this volume and of *Time in the Rock*. Here are heard

> The wings angelic and demonic, the sound of the abyss
> Dedicated to death. And this is you.   (I)[42]

This abyss includes all that man experiences in feeling and thought. Dream and memory are extremely important. At first, the speaker resists the very revelation he seeks, dreading the implications of knowledge:

> Dream: and between the close-locked lids of dream
> The terrible infinite intrudes its blue:
> Ice: silence: death: the abyss of Nothing.   (III)

He calls out to God:

> O God, O God, let the sore soul have peace.
> Deliver it from this bondage of harsh dreams.
> Release this shadow from its object, this object
> From its shadow. Let the fleet soul go nimbly,—
> Down,—down,—from step to step of dark,—
> From dark to deeper dark, from dark to rest.
> And let no Theseus-thread of memory
> Shine in that labyrinth, or on those stairs,
> To guide her back; nor bring her, where she lies,
> Remembrance of a torn world well forgot.   (III)

Like many of the poets discussed in this book, Aiken employs the myth of the Cretan labyrinth to symbolize the terrors of the unconscious. Here he begs for release from the thread that guides the wanderer back to a world that must be altered by his consciousness of his own dark and tortuous route. The myth of the labyrinth recurs in *Preludes for Memnon*, expressing the speaker's increasing willingness to confront the destruction inherent in a purposeless nature

[42] *Collected Poetry* (New York, 1953). All quotations from Aiken's poetry are from this edition.

and the chaos of his own mind. The image of god—often in the lower case—is even more significant throughout both volumes of *Preludes*, for the poet continually summons it as he depicts the inner drama of his recognition of the deepest feelings and the most complex attitudes which the concept of deity has symbolized in the history of the human soul.

In a passage of *Preludes for Memnon* reminiscent of the opening pages of *Ushant*,[43] Aiken's autobiography of memories and associations, the poet asks:

> And how begin, when there is no beginning?
> How end, when there's no ending?   (XIII)

In the light of such awareness of the absence of direction and purpose in nature, the most ordinary assumptions and perceptions of daily life take on a quality of the monstrous, threatening man with extinction:

> They will perish:
> The drop of blood, the windflower, and the world;
> Sound will be silence; meaning will have no meaning.
> The blade of grass, in such a light, will grow
> Monstrous as Minotaur; the tick of the clock,—
> Should it be taken as the clock's dark secret,—
> Is chaos and catastrophe; the heart
> Cries like a portent in a world of portents,
> All meaningless and mad.   (XIII)

The labyrinth exists within nature itself, for implicit in the apparent innocence of "a blade of grass" are the monstrous, consuming qualities of the Minotaur. At this point, however, the poet does not ask for release from such revelations; he accepts the "portents" both of his "heart" and the "world." In XXXIV, he declares to his beloved that he leaves the scene of the present and the familiar to descend into the labyrinths of his own soul:

[43] *Ushant, An Essay* (New York, 1952), pp. 3-4.

> Woman, and I am lost to you, I go
> Downward and inward to such coils of light,
> Such speed, such fierceness, and such glooms of filth,
> Such labyrinths of change, such laboratories
> Of obscene shape incessant in the mind,
> As never woman knew.

In describing the deepest levels of the unconscious mind, Aiken combines the myth of the descent into Hades and that of the labyrinth. The journey "downward" to "glooms of filth" reveals the organic nature of the soul:

> There, like the worm,
> Coiling amidst the coils, I make my home;
> Eat of the filth, am blessed; digest my name;
> Spawn; am spawned; exult; and am spewed forth. . . .

The "coils" of the labyrinth are also the winding paths of Hades and the "coils" of the intestines. Mind and body, man and worm, life and inevitable decay are revealed as organically intertwined in this descent.

Another familiar myth—the story of Narcissus—is also employed by Aiken as an effective device for self-exploration and revelation in both *Preludes for Memnon* and *Time in the Rock*. Furthermore, he uses the mythical figure as an analytic instrument to disclose the function of God in man's psychic history.[44] Narcissus first appears admiring his own image in a mirror and evoking "God's pity on us

---

[44] Aiken had dealt with this subject earlier, for example, in "Changing Mind" (1925; *Collected Poetry*, p. 277) the speaker declares:

> "You! Narcissus!" I said!
> And softly, under the four-voiced dialogue,
> In the bright ether, in the golden river
> Of cabbalistic sound, I am plunged, I found
> The silver rind of peace, the hollow round
> Carved out of nothing; curled there like a god.

but it is in *Preludes* that he explores the deepest implications of his own equation of narcissism with the quest for a god.

all!" because "we must die." His regret is entirely for the loss of youth and beauty:

> To think that so great beauty should be lost!
> This gold, and scarlet, and flushed ivory,
> Be made a sport for worms!

Suddenly, however, the full meaning of his mortality intrudes upon his total self-absorption, and even his appeal to God no longer offers comfort:

> The mirror spoke the truth. A shape he saw
> Unknown before,—obscene, disastrous, huge,—
> Huge as the world, and formless ... Was this he?
> This dumb, tumultuous, all-including horror?
> This Caliban of rocks? This steaming pit
> Of foisting hells,—circle on darker circle,—
> With worlds in rings to right and left, and other
> Starbearing hells within them, other heavens
> Arched over chaos? ...
>   He pondered the vast vision:
> Saw the mad order, the inhuman god;
> And his poor pity, with the mirror dropped,
> Wore a new face: such brightness and such darkness,
> Pitiless, as a moonblanched desert wears.   (XVII)

The mirror now reflects his unconscious knowledge of the chaos of the universe and the fear and horror within his own soul. The God he so glibly asked for pity now becomes "the inhuman god," an externalization of "the mad order," the mythical embodiment of man's inability to control and order the chaos within and surrounding him.

    Throughout *Preludes for Memnon* Aiken insists that man himself is God:

> Search the dark kingdom. It is to self you come,—
> And that is God.   (XIV)

> No gods abandon us, for we are gods ...   (XLVII)

Jesus is not the spokesman of the Lord:
Confucius neither, nor Nietzsche, no, nor Blake;
But you yourself. (XLIX)

but it is in *Time in the Rock* that the concept of God as a projection of the many facets of the self is most fully developed. Here Aiken is even more explicit than in *Preludes for Memnon* in demanding that man give up what he regards as the delusions and false comforts of fantasy and live with a continual awareness of the beauty and power of the ephemeral in nature and man; he asks, moreover, that man recognize the symbolic nature of the "angels" and "churches" that have for so long served to distract him from the reality of chaos and death, and he demands a way of life that reflects man's consciousness of his own symbolic constructions:

… let the churches be our houses
defiled daily, loud with discord,—
where the dead gods that were our selves may hang,
our outgrown gods on every wall;
Christ on the mantelpiece, with downcast eyes;
Buddha above the stove;
the Holy Ghost by the hatrack, and God himself
staring like Narcissus from the mirror,
clad in a raincoat, and with hat and gloves.
(*Time in the Rock*, XI)

The painful recognition that Narcissus and God are one opens the way to a new awareness of a "flower" or "the hand that reaches for the flower" (XI), the whole of creation which man can apprehend only if he can discard the projections of his own unconscious desire for omnipotence. There is, however, no end to this struggle; in LXXXV, Narcissus reappears—as man, as god, as evidence that "once more, / eternity makes heartbreak peace with time."

Unlike Eliot, Auden, or Barker, Aiken expresses neither despair nor anger at this revelation of essential human narcissism; in fact, he seems to exult in his increasing awareness of the unconscious feelings expressed in traditional myths and to expose their nature and meaning with a kind of ruthless love for man, his "mad order," and the very symbols he uses to disguise its terrors. In *Time in the Rock*, even more strongly than in *Preludes for Memnon*, he insists that human beings perceive and take satisfaction in the violence and indifference of physical reality:

> turn again
> to the cold violet that braves the snow,
> the murder in the tiger's eye, the pure
> indifference in the star.

To be able to partake fully of such experience is to be a god:

> Why, we are come
> at last to that bright verge where god himself
> dares for the first time, with unfaltering foot.
> And can we falter, who ourselves are god?   (II)

This direct statement that the term god is an expression of our unconscious knowledge of limitation and death is also a demand that man live with full consciousness of his true powers. Awareness that we are "brought to birth / between one zero and another" (II) affords the only possibility of achieving the dignity and power that man formerly projected on gods.

Recognizing that it is fundamentally man's "hunger" for security and grandeur that "shapes itself as gods and rainbows" (*Time in the Rock*, XXVIII), Aiken creates a new mythical concept: God is finally the symbolic expression of man's capacity for full consciousness of the anxieties, conflicts, and longings, the terror of his own limitations, and especially of death, which he has for so long repressed or acknowledged only in distorted and misleading forms; God is at the same time man's consciousness of all that he can achieve and enjoy in the face of the monstrous within himself and nature. The god in man functions in the poet when he employs the chaos of the unconscious mind as the material of creation, imposing order and beauty on its apparent formlessness. In his creation of "Lord Zero" who, he says, is "our dream," Aiken forms a deity out of his consciousness of the lack of purpose and order in the universe;

"Lord Zero," in whose honor the poet offers his rites of "devotion" (*Time in the Rock*, LXIX), himself represents the imposition of reason on chaos, and is a creation out of void.

In *Ushant*, Aiken speaks of his realization that "now at last the road was being opened for the only religion that was any longer tenable or viable, a poetic comprehension of man's position in the universe, and of his potentialities as a poietic shaper of his own destiny, through self-knowledge and love. The final phase of evolution of man's mind itself to ever more inclusive consciousness: in that, and that alone, would he find the solvent of all things."[45] In shaping "his own destiny" by rational and aesthetic means, Aiken accepts the loneliness and terror that his own myth of consciousness discloses, and celebrates his "poetic comprehension" that there is none to replace it.

In Aiken's poetry, as in Yeats's, Auden's, Barker's and Muir's, myth continually discloses the complex interaction of the self and the world; these poets use myth primarily to convey the individual conflict as representative of the general "fragmented ego" which is an essential, if often unconscious, factor in determining the course of man's history. The three major Southern poets of this century, John Crowe Ransom, Allen Tate, and Robert Penn Warren, approach history from a different perspective, emphasizing moral rather than psychological elements within it. For Ransom and Tate, myth is seldom a vehicle for disclosing unconscious drives or personal conflict; instead, it functions mainly as a means of depicting the traditional and evolving historical conditions—which include religious, social, and political elements—that these poets consider a vital background for individual experience. Warren, who is also concerned with historical ideals and concepts, sees history as "the big myth we live,"[46] a magnified image of the struggle between the longing for innocence and the disposition to evil within man.

In *God Without Thunder*, an early work in which Ransom deals

[45] *Ushant*, p. 220.
[46] Robert Penn Warren, "Foreword," *Brother to Dragons* (New York, 1953), p. xii.

with "the function of the myths in human civilization,"[47] one of his major points is that society benefits from religious orthodoxy based on belief in a *"virile and concrete God."*[48] He believes that the significant myths are religious ones, which become dogmas and function within a social framework:

> The Gods who have been legislated into official existence by the will of the whole society are defined in myths which tell what they are like; how they have performed in the physical universe and in human history; what sort of conduct they require from their subjects, the members of the community.

The powers of such deities represent "the social will that lies behind them." Ransom sees no separation between myth, law, and revelation: "Under the picturesque terms of the myth this ancient body of legislation comes down to us translated into Divine Revelation, and this old and continuing will of society becomes Divine Authority. These are the mythical sanctions of the myth."[49]

Although Ransom's later writings indicate a more flexible attitude toward the role of organized religion in society, his conception of myth has not essentially changed. Certainly, in his poetry one finds consistent evidence of his continuing belief that the "psychology of myth-persistence is the psychology of religion."[50] Furthermore, his analysis of the nature of myth in *God Without Thunder* elucidates the myths and legends that are frequently implied beneath the surface of the episodes in some of his poems. In defining the mythical quality within experience, Ransom says:

> The myth of an object is its proper name, private, unique, untranslatable, overflowing, of a demonic energy that cannot be reduced to the poverty of the class-concept. The myth of an event is a story, which invests the natural with a supernatural background, and with a more-than-historical history.[51]

In his poetry Ransom suggests the "more-than-historical" nature of apparently ordinary incidents by indicating that it is their mythi-

[47] *God Without Thunder* (New York, 1930), p. x.
[48] *ibid.*, p. 328.   [49] *ibid.*, p. 84.   [50] *ibid.*, p. 85.   [51] *ibid.*, p. 65.

cal or legendary background which determines the action of the participants.

Although references to traditional Greek myths occur in Ransom's poetry, his most interesting uses of myth are less directly allusive. In "Prometheus in Straits" and "Philomela,"[52] the ancient myths function mainly to imply perennial standards which expose present pretentiousness and inadequacy. Both myths are treated historically: Prometheus is an alien presence in the modern political and cultural milieu, Philomela in the literary one. The mythical figure in "Prometheus in Straits" is himself transformed into a type of historical personage who feels rather superior to the "Windy gentlemen," with their political jargon, and "the radiant band," with their aesthetic palaver, whom he encounters in the modern world. His conception of the enlightenment he has offered mankind, which he describes as "my pious offices," makes him sound more like Cicero than like the magnanimous hero of Aeschylus' *Prometheus Bound*, and his decision to return to his rock:

> I will go somewhere by a streamside abounding with granite
> And but little human history and dereliction;
> To the Man Unknown I will raise an altar upon it
> And practise my knees with brusies of genuflection.

is clearly intended as the commentary of a pious spirit on human history, but it conveys neither the compassion nor the grandeur of the mythical Prometheus.

"Philomela" traces the literary history of the classical myth with its associations of "liquid" sound and "classic numbers," and ironically laments its inability to "run democratic." The speaker's tone is the most interesting characteristic of the poem; it communicates the modern poet's "despair" at the loss of Philomela's "fabulous provinces" and his honest appraisal of the language and mode of his own time.

Most of Ransom's mythical references are less direct; submerged Southern legends and Biblical myths occur in his poems implying

[52] *Selected Poems* (New York, 1969). All quotations from Ransom's poetry are from this edition.

a "demonic" influence in history which is experienced in feelings as commonplace and personal as love, loneliness, or despair. "Emily Hardcastle, Spinster" is one of many women in Ransom's poetry whose lives enact the dark side of the legend of Southern aristocracy. Her very name suggests her lonely and compulsive adherence to a lost world and, since she rejects the "merchants" whom current history supplies as suitors and whom her sisters chose, "being unbelievers both," she must find "her grizzled Baron" when she becomes a "Bride and Princess" in death. The "Stranger" in "his castle in the gloom" is as much dead history casting its influence over the present as he is a lonely woman's final tragic fantasy.

In "Old Mansion," the speaker identifies himself as a "historian" who wishes to examine an old "Southern Manor" and is sent away by the servant of the "old mistress" who is ill. The poem deals with all the evidence of decay and death in the house and gardens; the legend is in ruins, yet it is powerful enough to make the intruder feel his "courage shaken" since, excluded from it, he must "dip, alas, into some unseemlier world."

Ransom has himself explicated the submerged myth in "Prelude to an Evening" in a commentary that is extremely significant not only in relation to this poem but to his poetry in general. Discussing his revised version of the poem, Ransom describes its subject as the soliloquy of a man so obsessed by the "world's evils" that he speaks of himself as "pursued by Furies."[53] Ransom has, moreover, come to think of the man "as Adam" and "the woman whom he apostrophizes as Eve; these are the names they must bear in our Great Myth." In explaining his decision to discuss his poem in mythical terms, Ransom says:

> In a true poem it is as if the religious dogma or the moral maxim had been dropped into the pot as soon as the act of composition began; sinking down out of sight and consciousness, it is as if it became a fluid and was transfused into the

[53] All quotations from Ransom's "Comment" on this poem are from pp. 151-59 of his *Selected Poems* (1969).

bloodstream of the poet now, and would be communicated to the bloodstream of his auditors eventually. The significance of the poem is received by feeling; or, more technically, by immediate unconscious intuition. So let the man of my poem be Adam, let the woman and mother of his children be Eve; if the poem did not name them, let the commentary do it. At once we are moving over an old and familiar terrain; bearing these names the figures will be invested for everybody with their moral and religious properties.

These comments, which appear in both the *Selected Poems* of 1964 and of 1969, indicate that Ransom's present approach to the function of myth is very similar to the one he took in *God Without Thunder*, which was first published in 1930. It is interesting that Ransom, like many of the poets of this century, believes that myth functions on an unconscious level; his conception of this level of experience, however, is very different from Yeats's, Auden's, Muir's or Aiken's, since for Ransom the significant unconscious communication that myth establishes is essentially religious and dogmatic. Beneath the "commonplace" situation of "Prelude to an Evening" Ransom sees the pattern of the "great Familial Configuration which had been ordained in our creation"; thus, from his point of view, the man returning to his household at evening enacts "a crucial and habit-forming moment in his history," which symbolizes the continuous religious history of mankind.

Allen Tate also uses myth to suggest a historical and religious frame of reference, but for Tate history, as it is contained in myth and legend, is essentially a heroic ideal. In much of his poetry the ancient Roman concept of *pietas*—which connotes not only reverence for the gods but loyalty to familial and ancestral values—haunts the memory of modern man as a challenge and a burden. The figure of Aeneas is Tate's most obvious mythical symbol of such *pietas*, but the concept is also implied in allusions to the *Iliad* and to ancient history as well. In Tate's poetry, myth is internalized as the historical ideal of his speaker or protagonist, whose character reveals the effects of historical loss and change on individual man.

The Vergilian Aeneas dominates "The Mediterranean" and "Aeneas at Washington";[54] in both these poems Aeneas' wanderings and his commitment to heroic accomplishment exist within the consciousness of modern man as ever-present remainders of his own yearning for a nation that embodies ethical and spiritual ideals which can involve his deepest feelings. The "we" of "The Mediterranean" includes the reader in the quest for such fulfillment, which is internalized in a metaphorical rite of consuming "dish and bowl to take that sweet land in," as the Trojans' arrival in the destined land was recognized in their eating of the "mensas," the cakes that served as "tables" for their food (*Aeneid* VII, 116-27). The quest expresses both modern man's yearning for "earth's paradise" and his awareness that his fantasy cannot be realized. With no outlet or site for his *labor*, no means to "locate" his ideals and beliefs within a nation he has established, he turns inward, continually aware of his *dolor*, his aimlessness and suffering.[55]

In "Aeneas at Washington," the modern speaker at first identifies totally with the mythical hero, but soon recognizes his own ambivalent relationship to the tradition that Aeneas represents—the ideals of conduct that he can neither renounce nor fulfill. The first four lines of the poem are a literal translation of Aeneas' account of the fall of Troy in *Aeneid* II, 499-502. The speaker then goes on to describe his "Disinterested and honourable" commitment to rescuing his people and establishing them in the destined land. As he continues his narrative, gradually the voice becomes that of a modern man in the political center of his nation, facing its inadequacies and failures. The mythical ideal within him is now seen in relation to the actual world he inhabits, and the record of commitment and

[54] *Poems* (New York, 1960). All quotations from Tate's poetry are from this edition.

[55] For a commentary on the change Tate makes from *labor* to *dolor* in the line he quotes from Vergil in his epigraph to "The Mediterranean" and a more extended discussion of Tate's use of ancient poetry, see Lillian Feder, "Allen Tate's Use of Classical Literature," *The Centennial Review*, IV, No. 1 (Winter 1960), 89-114.

accomplishment, of suffering and endurance cannot save him from the solipsism of the present:

> I see all things apart, the towers that men
> Contrive I too contrived long, long ago.
> Now I demand little.

but the ideal image of fallen Troy, reborn in Latium and in men's minds ever since, continues to torment him: "I thought of Troy, what we had built her for."

Though the appearance of Tate's Aeneas, like Ransom's Prometheus, in the modern world only points up the decay of traditional values in society, the two figures actually represent very different uses of myth in relation to history. The "pious offices" of Ransom's Prometheus are not shown to emerge from the deep inner conviction manifested in the *pietas* of Aeneas. Furthermore, Prometheus, as Ransom interprets him, stands apart from modern man, judging him unfit for his influence. The Aeneas of Tate's poem is part of the psychic make-up of the speaker; myth and history haunt the imagination of modern man with a concept of "unity of being" which he feels he cannot achieve in the contemporary world.

Tate attributes this failure to a form of narcissism—the quality of man regarded so often in modern poetry as the root of his personal suffering and his inability to achieve a "just city" or a peaceful society. Tate's analysis and depiction of narcissism differ markedly from those of Auden, Barker, and Aiken, all of whom deal with it as a manifestation of unconscious psychological drives. The emphasis in Tate's approach is philosophical rather than psychological, general rather than individual; in his prose and poetry, and especially in his essay "Narcissus as Narcissus," he develops the view that "solipsism," which he defines as "a philosophical doctrine which says that we create the world in the act of perceiving it," explains modern man's inability to achieve a dignified and productive way of life. Solipsism, which "denotes the failure of the human personality to function objectively in nature and society," is essentially a modern social manifestation: "Society (and 'nature' as modern society constructs it) appears to offer limited fields for the exercise of the

whole man, who wastes his energy piecemeal over separate functions that ought to come under a unity of being."[56] Elsewhere he
says that only a "traditional society" can "pass to the next generation, under a definite conception of human nature, a code of conduct; and this code of conduct, apart from its utility, is a symbol
of the excess of attention and love which is art and religion—a proof
that men have mastered not only a productive process but themselves as well."[57] Tate's position is that man's character—Aeneas'
capacity to remain "Disinterested and honourable" in the face of
danger, to maintain "a code of conduct" dedicated to an ideal beyond his personal gratification, and modern man's sense of alienation and purposelessness—is formed by historical and social forces.

The image of a "traditional society," not only in "The Mediterranean" and "Aeneas at Washington" but in "Ode to the Con-
federate Dead" and other poems as well, is that of the ancient
classical world recorded in myth and history. In "Ode to the Con-
federate Dead," the theme of "solipsism"[58] is developed in contrast
to the Homeric concept of the heroic code and its implicit loyalty
to traditional values. Furthermore, the leaf image, which is an extremely important one in Tate's "Ode," echoes the well-known
passage in *Iliad* VI, 145-51 in which Glaucus' comparison of "the
generations of leaves" with those of men qualifies his exchange of
information on his noble lineage with Diomedes and the heroic
code itself. Within the framework of the Homeric heroic code and
the answering strain of the leaf image, which appears in the first
and last strophes and in the refrain as a constant reminder of the
"rumors of mortality," Tate introduces the "jaguar" which discloses
the destructive and self-devouring elements of the Narcissus figure.
The "jaguar," who "leaps / For his own image in a jungle pool,
his victim," expresses the poem's final definition of solipsism.

[56] "Narcissus as Narcissus," *On the Limits of Poetry* (New York, 1948),
pp. 250-51.

[57] "Liberalism and Tradition," *Reason in Madness* (New York, 1941), pp.
209-10.

[58] See Tate's "Narcissus as Narcissus" for a discussion of solipsism in relation to this poem.

In "Sonnets of the Blood," VIII, mythical symbols both portray the evils of modern society: "Call it the house of Atreus where we live—" and convey the poet's demand for an honest reckoning:

> Which one of us the Greek perplexed with crime
> Questions the future: bring that lucid sieve
> To strain the appointed particles of time!
> Whether by Corinth or by Thebes we go
> The way is brief, but the fixed doom, not so.

In recalling the courage and insight of Oedipus, Tate asks, "Which one of us" dares to face the future with the self-knowledge and the historical wisdom that the past provides. Such insight is frightening, for it contains the record of moral blindness and irrational evil to which man is prone, but it is the only weapon he has in coming to terms with "the fixed doom."

Sonnet IX warns the "Captains of industry" of the dangers of their abuse of power. References to ancient history symbolize the inner war between the lust for power and the capacity for reason. The poet speaks directly to a representative of the rulers of modern industrial society:

> Let you, brother, captaining your hour
> Be zealous that your numbers are all prime,
> Lest false division with sly mathematic
> Plunder the inner mansion of the blood,
> The Thracian, swollen with pride, besiege the Attic—
> Invader foraging the sacred wood. . . .

Ancient history, myth, and rite are part of the "inner mansion" of modern man; they are his perspective, his means of evaluating the "aimless power" promoted by his own social and economic structure, which, from Tate's point of view, can lead only to solipsism and despair.

The moral insight and the consequent challenge that history affords is a major theme of Robert Penn Warren's *Brother to Dragons*, his most ambitious historical poem. It is mainly this quality that is suggested in his description of history in his "Foreword" as "the big myth we live, and in our living, constantly remake." *Brother to Dragons* is almost a literal enactment of that statement, since Warren, as "R.P.W." in the poem, lives in both past and present history, which he remakes as he creates a legend.

Warren uses the techniques of legend—the conversation of the living with the dead, the suspension of natural time and place (the dialogue occurs "No place" and at "Any time"), the addition of new characters involved with actual figures of the past, and the development of motivation and incident through allusions to mythical narrative—in order to disclose what he regards as the basic moral forces in history. These, reduced to their simplest terms, are good and evil, but the inextricable connection of these forces in the lives of the characters and the drama of their manifestation in the events of American history are complicated and interesting in Warren's legend.

The theme of evil in history is introduced before the main incident which portrays it—the murder of a Negro slave by the nephews of Thomas Jefferson—is mentioned. It is Jefferson, speaking to "R.P.W.," who first expresses an awareness of the monstrous and the foul in all existence, and he does so in an extended allusion to the Cretan labyrinth. This myth, so familiar in modern poetry as a symbol of the devious way to the instincts of man, is a dominant one in *Brother to Dragons*, where the labyrinth is used as a type of hell that man must acknowledge exists both in himself and his history. Warren's effort to reveal the motivations for a brutal murder by members of Jefferson's family and to indicate the effects of this episode on Jefferson himself, and the other characters involved, has been analyzed from a psychological point of view,[59] but such an approach seems inappropriate to Warren's attitude and intention in the poem. The psychological insights hinted at in Warren's adaptation of the myth of the labyrinth seem primitive when compared with those of Auden, Muir, or Aiken; moreover, both in such allu-

[59] Frederick P. W. McDowell, "Psychology and Theme in *Brother to Dragons*," *PMLA*, LXX (September 1955), 565-86.

sions and in other efforts to explore the darkness of man's soul, Warren's emphasis is always moral.

The first reference to the labyrinth occurs near the beginning of the poem, as Jefferson is revaluating the great events of his life, which have become American history. Speaking of the delegates to the Continental Congress at Philadelphia, Jefferson now sees them as ordinary men:

> But what I had meant to say, we were only ourselves,
> Packed with our own lusts and languors, lost. . . .

They are "lost" because they are caught in the mystery of themselves and of time:

> Each man lost, in some blind lobby, hall, enclave,
> Crank cul-de-sac, couloir, or corridor of Time.
> Of Time. Or self: and in that dark no thread,
> Airy as breath by Ariadne's fingers forged.
> No thread, and beyond some groped-at corner, hulked
> In the blind dark, hock-deep in ordure, its beard
> And shag foul-scabbed, and when the hoof heaves—
> Listen! the foulness sucks like mire.   (p. 7)

The external world in which man makes his history, time, the unknown entity which history records but cannot control, and the inner self, whose ideals and unacknowledged "lusts and languors" determine the decisions and events of history, are all merged in the image of the labyrinth. The absence of Ariadne's thread is, of course, the absence of the clarity of vision love can offer to overcome the darkness of the self and time.

Warren develops the image of the labyrinth further as Jefferson goes on to speak of Pasiphaë's strange union with the bull—the bizarre episode which led to the construction of the Cretan labyrinth:

> The beast waits. He is the infamy of Crete.
> He is the midnight's enormity. He is
> Our brother, our darling brother. And Pasiphaë—
> Pasiphaë, huddled and hutched in the cow's hide,

Laced, latched, thonged up, and humped for joy,
What was the silence then before the stroke?
And then your scream.
And through the pain then, like a curtain rent,
In your mind you saw some meadow green, or some grove,
Some childhood haven, water and birdsong, and you a child.
The bull plunged. You screamed like a girl, and strove.
But the infatuate machine of your invention held.
Later, they lifted you out and wiped your lips in
                          the dark palace.
We have not loved you less, poor Pasiphaë.   (pp. 7-8)

Like Yeats's Leda, Warren's Pasiphaë engages in a ritual act as she both accepts and struggles against the beast whose union with her characterizes an era of history. The beast, "the midnight's enormity," is also "our darling brother," for he is a symbol of the fertility and power human beings desire and the lust and violence they fear. In this poem, the scream of Pasiphaë as she receives the embrace of the beast is a prophecy of the violence inherent in the love of Jefferson's nephew Lilburn for his wife Laetitia; the same violence is later expressed in his murder of a slave, an episode which incorporates the evil inherent in the very structure of Southern society.

Jefferson admits his late and reluctant acknowledgement of the "foulness" evident in man and society, which he had earlier idealized. Commenting on his adaptation of the mythical narrative, he says:

I had not meant to speak thus. Language betrays.
What I mean is, words are always the truth, and always the lie,
For what I say of Philadelphia *now*
Is true, but true now only, not true *then*.   (p. 8)

When, however, he recalls his total dedication to a vision of man's perfectibility, he realizes that even that stage of his life, with its unlimited intellectual and spiritual aspirations, reflects the darkness and horror of the labyrinth. Immediately following his recollection of his "joy" in the "brightness" of his image of "Man," he says:

And thus my minotaur. There at the blind
Blank labyrinthine turn of my personal time,
I met the beast. And the time I met it was—
At least, it seems so now—that first moment
When the alacrity of blood stumbles and all natural joy
Sees Nature but as mirror for its fear,
And therefore, to be joy, must deny Nature
And leap beyond man's natural bourne and constriction
To find some justification for the natural.
Yes, then I met the beast. Well, better, indeed,
Had it been the manifest beast and the circumstantial
Avatar of destruction. But no beast then: the towering
Definition, angelic, arrogant, abstract,
Greaved in glory, thewed with light, the bright
Brow tall as dawn. I could not see the eyes.   (p. 9)

Jefferson's recognition that his "towering / Definition" of man was actually the other face of the "minotaur," the "beast" within his personal labyrinth, his "personal time," is a central theme of the poem. In this passage, through the voice of a historical figure, Warren suggests that all man's visions of perfection are derived from his desire to "deny Nature" or natural limitation, to avoid "the manifest beast" which symbolizes not only destructiveness and evil, but time itself. The personal or national impulse to "leap beyond man's natural bourne and constriction" leads inevitably to an "arrogant, abstract" conception of life, and finally to disaster.

Only after this revelation of the intrinsic connection between man's "angelic" and his "arrogant" conceptions, between what Warren regards as the good or noble impulses and the evil and monstrous ones, does Jefferson begin to discuss the story of Lilburn and Isham Lewis' murder of the slave George. Throughout the dialogue about the unhappy relationship of Lilburn and his wife Laetitia, Lilburn's obsessive attachment to his mother, the details of the murder itself, and the betrayal by Aunt Cat, the scream of Pasiphaë and the lurking minotaur in the labyrinth recur to indicate that the particular events of the poem are representative of man's contest with irrational evil. "R.P.W." speaks of "that beast" with his "murderous devotion" who "can wait" until man will recognize him and discover not only the nature of evil but of "virtue," which demands an awareness of "anguish" (p. 30).

The central character of the poem, Jefferson, is developed mainly in relation to the myth of the labyrinth and the actual murder, which makes the presence of the bestial in his family and his society all too specific and evident. First he speaks of his disillusionment and despair:

> The death of that black boy was the death
> Of all my hope and— (p. 132)

but gradually he begins to respond to other qualities inherent in his family and himself—the compassion and reason manifested in Lucy's acceptance of the "cost of the human redemption" (p. 193). In his dialogue with the murdered slave George, Jefferson concludes that "the possibility / Of reason" can emerge only from "the circumstances of our most evil despair." He returns to the "coiling darkness" of the labyrinth in the hope that in its very "midst" he can create the "incandescence of the heart's great flare" (p. 195); the knowledge of violence and evil he has acquired has also revealed his own pride and self-delusion and has thus opened the way to a more realistic conception of reason than his early idealization of man could allow. Jefferson's descent into the dark corridors of time, family, and history ends with his joyous call to a ritual dance:

> Dance back the buffalo, the shining land!
> Our grander Ghost Dance now, and shake the feather.
> Dance back the morning and the eagle's cry.
> Dance back the Shining Mountains, let them shine!
> Dance into morning and the lifted eye.
> Dance into morning past the morning star,
> And dance the heart by which we have lived and died.
> My Louisiana, I would dance you, though afar! (p. 195)

This is a celebration of redemption through knowledge of the pain as well as the dignity of man's history. It is a rite that recalls what man in his violence has destroyed, and it acknowledges his limitations as well as his aspirations for himself and his land. Warren's Jefferson emerges as a more valid legendary figure than Pound's "many-minded" sage, because in *Brother to Dragons* Jefferson incorporates both the ideals and the failures of American history. More important, he suggests in his own person the gradual and difficult process of comprehending "the heart by which we have lived and died" as a force in history. Like many of his contemporaries, Warren adapts some of his most effective techniques for recreating history from legend and myth, and there is little doubt that *Brother to Dragons* is his conscious effort to produce a legend for his own time.

Although the poets discussed throughout this book all reached artistic maturity in the first half of this century, it should not be assumed that myth is any less important in the poetry of the fifties, the sixties, and the present. Certainly during these years Pound, Auden, Graves, Muir, and other established poets continued to employ myth extensively, and some of them developed original concepts of mythical expression and new techniques in adapting mythical symbols to their own changing themes and attitudes. Furthermore, some of the younger poets who emerged in the fifties and sixties have employed classical myth in modes such as confessional and Beat poetry that, on the surface, seem unsuited to its traditional associations.

The career of Robert Lowell, whose first book of poems, *Land of Unlikeness* (1944), reflects the influence of Eliot, and whose more recent confessional poetry in *Life Studies* (1959) has itself had a significant effect on the work of younger poets, bridges the years between the first half of the century and the present. Lowell's interpretation of the myth of Persephone, which is discussed in the opening chapter of this book, indicates how basic the psychological, ritual, and historical implications of myth are to the theme and structure of one of his major poems, "The Mills of the Kavanaughs" (1951). His original and mature adaptation of traditional myth in this poem marks a climactic stage in his career. In earlier poems, such as "Between the Porch and the Altar," "The Death of the Sheriff," and "The First Sunday in Lent,"[60] Lowell uses the myth of the fall of Troy to intensify his protagonists' suffering and to generalize the emotional conflict in the episodes in which they are involved. "Falling Asleep Over the Aeneid"[61] relates a dream based on the account of the funeral rites for the hero Pallas in *Aeneid* XI, 22-99, which revives the submerged perceptions and feelings of an old man's childhood, and makes death almost unbearably real and present. But skillful as Lowell is in transforming myth into metaphor and symbolic dream in these poems, myth does not convey the intensity of inner experience or the drama of self-revelation that it does in "The Mills of the Kavanaughs," in which the unconscious conflict in the human mind, compounded of instinctual need, familial and historical obsessions and guilts, and the yearning for spiritual security, emerges through the figure of Anne Kavanaugh as Persephone.

In *Life Studies*, which marked the beginning of what has been called confessional poetry, Lowell's techniques of self-discovery exclude myth; he concentrates on the personal and intimate episode, and his language is direct and sometimes colloquial. Important as this volume is as an expression of Lowell's new voice and his growing power to elicit from the absurd remark or the pathetic incident a link to the deepest levels of human suffering, and vital as it was in influencing younger poets, such as Sylvia Plath and Anne Sexton, it represents only one phase of his development as a poet. Lowell has gone on in later works to combine the mythical method of his early poetry with the direct and sometimes shocking psychological revelations of *Life Studies* and, in so doing, has reached beyond the compulsive inner probings of that book for a deep and intimate knowledge of human feelings as they are manifested in the larger realm of natural, social, or political life.

The identification of ambivalent unconscious human drives with the uncontrollable attractive and destructive forces of nature in "Near the Ocean"[62] is itself a mythical construct. The poem begins at the conclusion of a performance of an ancient Greek tragedy, in-

[60] *Lord Weary's Castle* (New York, 1946).
[61] *The Mills of the Kavanaughs* (New York, 1951).
[62] *Near the Ocean* (New York, 1967).

tentionally generalized as in a dream. The movement is backward in time as two scenes of Aeschylus' *Choephoroi* seem to emerge: first the death of Clytemnestra and then an earlier scene in which she is confronted by her children, Orestes and Electra. These are followed by a mythical image of Orestes' guilt:

> His treadmill heart will never rest—
> his wet mouth pressed to some slack breast,
> or shifting over on his back . . .
> The severed radiance filters back,
> athirst for nightlife—gorgon head,
> fished up from the Aegean dead,
> with all its stranded snakes uncoiled,
> here beheaded and despoiled.

The next line, "We hear the ocean," suggests that the terror and guilt of past crimes lurk in that sound. But the ocean also seems to offer release from the past:

> Older seas
> and deserts give asylum, peace
> to each abortion and mistake.
> Lost in the Near Eastern dreck,
> the tyrant and tyrannicide
> lie like the bridegroom and the bride;
> the battering ram, abandoned, prone,
> beside the apeman's phallic stone.

Finally, the scene is local and present; on the New England coast a modern man demands the peace of sleep and forgetfulness:

> Sleep, sleep. The ocean, grinding stones,
> can only speak the present tense;
> nothing will age, nothing will last,
> or take corruption from the past.
> A hand, your hand then! I'm afraid
> to touch the crisp hair on your head—
> Monster loved for what you are,
> till time, that buries us, lay bare.

Both the mythical drama with which the poem begins and the last lines expressing the ambivalence of love deny the speaker's insistence on his separation from the experience of the past. The ocean unifies his awareness of his tie to the suffering and guilt the dreamlike myth recalls and his desperate wish to be free of such burdens, for the ocean in this poem, like the unconscious mind, contains all of the past hidden beneath the surface of "the present tense."

In later poems, which he calls "Five Dreams,"[63] Lowell continues to associate the mythical with immediate and intimate experience. In the first, "The Old Order," the vision of "a bull's head, Cretan black-bronze" appears, followed by one of Pasiphaë: "a girl's Bacchanalia with a wicker cow's-head." The next line abruptly thrusts the dreamer into the contemporary world: "she died of sleeping pills," but the experience retains a remnant of the ancient and continuous past:

> but there's a tongue
> of silverfoil still sticks in the wicker mouth. . . .

In this and other "Dreams," Lowell juxtaposes the mythical with the actual; in "Agamemnon" and "The House in Argos," associations from the *Oresteia* are mingled with details of modern family life. The speaker in "Onion Skin" tells of his almost human relationship with "the fancy functional things" that are part of his daily experience. In a piece of typing paper he feels the presence of the goddess "Fortuna," bleeding as if she "felt the bloody gash that brought my life." Myth in these poems and others—such as "The River God," "Clytemnestra," and "Wind"—in *Notebook 1967-68*, assumes an informal yet deeply intimate quality; it suggests to the reader that a colloquial phrase or a witty remark with which it is blended comes from a deeper source than the poet's understatement would indicate.

A study of myth in the poetry of the generation following Lowell's would reveal some remarkable adaptations of traditional mythical

[63] *Notebook 1967-68* (New York, 1969).

narratives and figures to accommodate the responses of new poets to the disorder and brutality that have increased in immeasurable proportions in the social and political life of the last two decades, and have deeply affected the poet's concept of his art. Here it is possible only to mention a few of the ways in which myth continues to evolve to the emotional and aesthetic requirements of the poets who employ it and to reflect the atmosphere of their society and their time. It is significant, for example, that, as the key to the poetry of Conrad Aiken, faced with a world without acceptable credos or visible order, is the myth of total consciousness, the mythical construct of importance in the poetry of Sylvia Plath is its opposite, the dark god of unconsciousness. Whether she takes the role and voice of Phaedra, Medea, or Medusa, she is concerned with controlling only one realm —death, which in her poetry is an imaginary pure and peaceful underworld of the unconscious. Speaking to its god, her construct, she says:

> And I, stepping from this skin
> Of old bandages, boredoms, old faces
>
> Step to you from the black car of Lethe,
> Pure as a baby.[64]

This controlling and consuming myth is a clue to both the mind that conceived it and the age that fostered it.

The Beat poets Allen Ginsberg and Gregory Corso also use myth to convey their effort to exceed the limits of rational consciousness of reality. In their poetry, myth depicts an expansion of consciousness into the realm of dream and vision, in which ordinary events and places take on a magic and mystical quality; as Ginsberg puts it in "Kaddish":[65] "We're all alive at once then—even me & Gene & Naomi in one mythological Cousinesque room—screaming at each other in the Forever—" Both classical and Christian myth express the many roles in which the poet defines his own conscious-

[64] "Getting There," *Ariel* (New York, 1966).
[65] *Kaddish and Other Poems, 1958-1960*, 4th ed. (San Francisco, 1965).

411

ness: in "The Reply,"[66] he sees himself as "Old One-Eye of dreams in which I do not wake but die—" and in "Lysergic Acid,"[67] he can imagine himself as divine:

> I allen Ginsberg a separate consciousness
> I who want to be God
> I who want to hear the infinite minutest vibration of eternal
>   harmony. . . .

Both Ginsberg and Corso interpret myth as a comment on accepted standards of rational perception. In a moving poem on Polyphemus called "Mortal Infliction,"[68] Corso insists that "Polyphemus bellowing his lowly woe," after being blinded by Ulysses, continues to exist: "he will remain like that," but "Ulysses is dead." Corso questions the proverbial wisdom of the resourceful and rational Ulysses; for him the "fumbling hands" and the cry of the savage and lonely Cyclops, "a thing of immortality," more truly represent the recurrent experience of man.

Other contemporary poets are closer in their conception and use of myth to their predecessors of the first half of the century. Sometimes a mythical allusion or image in the poetry of Robert Duncan, Radcliffe Squires, or W. S. Merwin will recall the work of Pound, Eliot, Auden, Graves, or Aiken, but such echoes indicate continuity rather than imitation, the natural evolution of mythical symbols. The poetry of Merwin is especially interesting in this respect, for myth is his most important and powerful vehicle in defining the role of the poet in the present.[69]

Like Aiken, Merwin attempts to achieve the deepest consciousness of both the external world of nature and society and the elusive inner self; the communication of this consciousness through myth

---

[66] *ibid.*

[67] *ibid.*

[68] *Selected Poems* (London, 1962).

[69] For an interesting discussion of Merwin's use of myth, see Alice N. Benston, "Myth in the Poetry of W. S. Merwin," *Poets in Progress*, ed. Edward Hungerford (Evanston, Illinois, 1962), 179-204.

is, he feels, the poet's imposition of order, form, and love on chaos. In many of his poems classical myths and mythical figures—Odysseus, Dido, Aphrodite, Proteus, Medusa—symbolize the endless layers of human knowledge and experience, overlapping in space and time. Merwin also employs both traditional mythical figures and his own conceptions of the gods to portray the struggle to reach the hidden pain and the reserves of the self, which are the ultimate source not only of myth but of creation as well. In his interpretation of the myth of seizing the elusive Proteus as a quest for the gifts of wisdom and prophecy, which man projects on the gods, Merwin describes the struggle to hold the ever-changing, powerful, and violent seer, and the greater agony of realizing that "The head he turned toward me wore a face of mine." The poem ends with a dramatic confrontation of the speaker and his mythical projection, which expresses the pain of self-discovery but also the integrity of the spirit compelled to fulfill the quest:

> Here was no wisdom but my own silence
> Echoed as from a mirror; no marine
> Oracular stare but my own eyes
> Blinded and drowned in their reflections;
> No voice came but a voice we shared, saying,
> "You prevail always, but, deathly, I am with you
> Always." I am he, by grace of no wisdom,
> Who, to no end battles the foolish shapes
> Of his own death by the insatiate sea.[70]

Merwin's starkest portrayals of the recognition of human limitation convey a degree of satisfaction—even exaltation—in the depth of insight which is both the price and the reward of the mythical contest.

There is a curious similarity in Merwin's and Graves's approach to the Odysseus figure,[71] which is interesting mainly because it

---

[70] "Proteus," *The Dancing Bear* (New Haven, 1954).

[71] W. S. Merwin, "Odysseus," *The Drunk in the Furnace* (New York, 1960), and Robert Graves's "Ulysses."

points up a more important difference in their interpretations of his mythical adventures. Both poets dwell on the hero's many love affairs, and both suggest that sometimes the qualities of his women or goddesses merge in his mind, so that to Graves's Ulysses "Penelope and Circe seemed as one," and Merwin's Odyssus "sometimes . . . could not remember" which of his women "wished on his departure / Perils" that would destroy him, and which, "improbable, remote, and true," was the ideal figure "he kept sailing home to." But in Graves's "Ulysseus" this confusion of "wife" and "whore" indicates only that "flesh had made him blind," whereas the adventures of Merwin's Odysseus reflect his growing self-knowledge.

Without the drama of disgust or guilt, Merwin's Odysseus accepts the "knowledge of all that he betrayed" until "it was the same whether he stayed / Or went." He has, of course, betrayed more than a wife or a vision of "home"; he has betrayed the ideal image of Odysseus—the myth itself. He does not encounter bizarre adventures and varied experiences but only the fact that "Always the setting forth was the same." The "sea," the "danger," love itself, have a sameness, a limitation, which neither his name nor his story promised. His betrayal of the fantasy is a form of knowledge of the boundaries of the world and the self, and of his impulse both to define and extend them: "Therefore he went."

In his more recent poetry, Merwin uses classical myth only occasionally, but in the volumes *The Lice*[72] and *The Carrier of Ladders*[73] myth itself is as important a poetic device as it is in his earlier work. In *The Lice*, Merwin develops his method of probing within the structure of myth for the unconscious forces that motivate its creation through an exploration of the nature of generalized "gods" or "divinities" rather than through allusions to particular ancient mythical figures or narratives. The gods of his poem "Divinities," for example, explain their extraordinary power as images; man can "*simply exist*," but divinities, though "they cannot inhabit" the air,

---

[72] *The Lice* (New York, 1967).
[73] *The Carrier of Ladders* (New York, 1970).

"are never absent" from it, for it is "their memory." They permeate the atmosphere of life, for they are the energy man expends in his yearnings and errors, and the symbols of his ultimate failure: "the dead sing them an unending hymn."

Another poem, "The Gods," expresses this idea explicitly:

> The gods are what has failed to become of us
> Now it is over we do not speak. . . .

These gods convey man's barely conscious awareness that he is trapped, blind, and inarticulate as he struggles to come to terms with his own nature. In this poem, the speaker makes an effort to describe "darkness" for his "blind neighbor," but no sooner does he "begin" than he is interrupted by the sounds of "centuries" of violence and grief. The gods, laconic, barely present, continually seem to ask: "What is man that he should be infinite. . . ." Merwin's method of suggesting both the presence of these gods and their tantalizingly amorphous nature, their impulse to speak to or from man, and their perennial alienation from him, creates the shadowy realm of unconscious conflict, fantasy, and yearning which man acknowledges only indirectly. The peasant, addressing his "thousand gods," confesses his shame at recognizing that they did not "make" him, but he insists: "I am bringing up my children to be you" ("Peasant").

Gods also hover over the lives of the speakers in Merwin's latest book of poems, *The Carrier of Ladders*: naked and abstract in "Plane," tainted by a history of loss and violence in "Psalm: Our Fathers," and reduced to the most essential form or equation of myth and ritual in "Words From a Totem Animal," in which the sacrificial beast and the participant in rite become one in their relation to the silent, cold, unreachable self which these gods so clearly represent. In this volume Merwin also returns to a traditional classical motif; in "The Judgment of Paris," he tells the story of Paris' choice among the three goddesses, but his emphasis, as always, is on the limitations implicit in apparent freedom. Athene's offer of wisdom and power is qualified: *"you will forget anyway,"* as Hera's

415

of pride and glory also is: *"you will suffer anyway,"* but the most terrible limitation lies in Paris' actual choice: *"Take / her,"* the words of Aphrodite imply, *"you will lose her anyway."* Helen, introduced as a feeling that fills the "mind" of Paris, emerges for him as "one girl gathering / yellow flowers," an evocation of her ancient association with Persephone. The myth of Paris' choice in this poem lies deep within the structure of men's lives; it exists in the intuitive feelings of the mason "working above the gates of Troy," who "thought he felt the stone / shiver," in "the head / of the arrow for Achilles' heel," which "smiled in its sleep," and in the inevitable association of love and death in the minds of the chief protagonists.

Merwin's poetic analyses of the symbolic nature of the very myths he employs is not a new technique in modern poetry; we have seen such an approach to myth in Yeats's later poems, and in the work of Auden, Aiken, and other poets for whom myth is as much a self-revealing instrument as it is a traditional and continuing language. The "ultimate end" of myth, says Susanne Langer, "is not wishful distortion of the world, but serious envisagement of its fundamental truths; moral orientation, not escape."[74] The poet's consciousness of this "ultimate end" or effect is an important subject of modern poetry, in which myth functions as a symbolic language that mediates between the inner experience of the unconscious mind and the conscious awareness of daily reality and of society and history. Its distortions reflect the perennial delusions of man as well as the present errors and crimes of a mechanized and dehumanized society, yet through those very distortions, either deliberately or without conscious awareness, the poet often discloses the roots of personal and general arrogance, narcissism, and despair.

Myth continues to flourish in modern poetry because it contains and enacts man's long conflict between his yearning for omnipotence within his own being or in a god he worships and his desire to accept his aloneness in a chaotic, uncontrolled universe; it also expresses his need to comprehend his own history and to discover some meaning and order in its record of violence and failure. If myth reflects modern man's compulsive hold on past values and attitudes,

[74] *Philosophy in a New Key,* p. 176.

it also depicts his lonely and courageous questioning of traditional beliefs and solaces. "To see the gods dispelled in mid-air and dissolve like clouds," says Wallace Stevens, "is one of the great human experiences."[75] This is an experience the ancient gods and heroes themselves, revealed in all their projected glory and suffering, provide in many modern poems. Twentieth-century poets do not only employ myth as a mode of symbolic expression; they continually elucidate its rich and complex nature, and produce new varieties of the species.

[75] "Two or Three Ideas," *Opus Postumus*, ed. Samuel French Morse (New York, 1957), p. 206.

INDEX

419